Storm Over Morocco

Finding God in the Midst of Fanatics

by

Frank Romano

ISBN 978-1-934209-43-1

10-digit ISBN 1-934209-43-0

$17.99

Published by World Audience, Inc.
25 Sickles Street, Suite 6E, New York, NY 10040

World Audience Publishers (www.worldaudience.org) is a global consortium of artists and writers, producing the literary journal *audience* and *The audience Review*. Our periodicals and books are edited by M. Stefan Strozier and assistant editors. Please submit your stories, poems, paintings, photography, or other artwork to: submissions@worldaudience.org;   inquiries   about   being   a   reviewer: theatre@worldaudience.org. Thank you.

Storm Over Morocco

by

Frank Romano

A World Audience Book
(www.worldaudience.org)

January, 2007

New York

To my Mother

Table of Contents

---

[1] Her real name was Marie-Laure. Peggy was her nickname.

Introduction

This book chronicles my search for truth, life and for love—I dedicate it to you. I initially wrote my story so I would never forget what happened or what I had learned—my purpose wasn't to share my voyage with others. However, so profoundly did I live the events related in this book, that every time I read the manuscript over the ensuing twenty-five years, I shook with uncontrollable emotion and cried many tears upon reaching the end. I eventually decided that if what I had experienced in Maghreb, the "land of the setting sun," had so impacted me, perhaps others would be moved and learn something of value.

My voyage began when I realized that my life was and would remain empty until I found answers to such questions as "To whom did I owe my existence, if to anyone?" I felt that my very essence, even my continued existence in the sane world, could only be nourished and maintained by answers.

One day, I found myself on a train from Paris to Morocco, with $50 and a one-way ticket in my pocket. My journey lead me to an Islamic mosque, where I lived with a sect of militant followers of Muhammad and the Qur'an. It is true that my life became a hellish descent into darkness and the fear of possible death. But even in the midst of fanatic followers, I received answers to some of my questions.

The words that you will read could be misconstrued by some as a criticism of Islam—this would not be true. Please do not misunderstand my intent, as some have distorted and misinterpreted sacred truths, to the detriment of universal understanding and peace.

What you are about to read is the story of one man's spiritual search. . .his quest for a life of passionate purpose, spiritual meaning and palpable solutions in a world largely unsupportive of individual truth and expression.

There are many ways to conduct a spiritual search—I do not pretend to have the only roadmap. Everyone walks their own unique path to the conscious embodiment of universal love. I think, however, you will find my search extraordinary, exceptionally risky but ultimately profoundly revealing.

But don't take my word for it—read on!

So welcome to a part of my life's story. And remember, my dear friend: this one's for you.

Frank Romano
Paris, January 18th, 2007

Acknowledgements

Special thanks go to Ethel and Frank Romano Sr., my parents, who have always supported me with their unconditional love, who believed in me and even in my dreams.

I thank my sister, Lorna Romano, who carefully proofread and edited the last version of the book. Our spiritual conspiracy has nurtured me over the last few years.

I'm grateful to Concetta Miano, for encouraging me to draft a third and final version. Her loving support has been a safe harbor on the edge of turbulent seas.

I'm indebted to many others for their support. To my children, Frankie, Victoria, Juliana and Regina and for Sylvia Romano for their perseverance and patience throughout the years during my work and meditations that sometimes took me far away from them; to Craig Paul, a longtime friend, for his patient advice and support which transcend the meaning of friendship; to Tom Romano and Chris Taylor, artists "extraordinaires".

And finally, I thank Mike Strozier, my editor, for his dedication to the publication of this work. His encouragement and tireless work ethic have been welcome gifts.

Prologue

As the mist began to rise above the dusty paths of the outskirts of the "Ancienne Medina" of Casablanca, I was dreaming of the impassioned sermon made by the Imam last Friday. His gray-black beard spilled over his pearl white djellabah and beads of perspiration streamed down his face as his hypnotic voice told the story of his rebirth as a Moslem soldier, having been a mercenary in the trenches in Southeast Asia. I assumed the "julus" position, half-sitting, half-kneeling in the back row, my eyes following his every gesture. I was afraid to blink, not wanting to miss the intense emotion of the moment. I leaned forward, intent on absorbing every detail, my hands clutching the sides of my striped djellabah.

The dream was shattered, the memory of its intensity sent to the archives of my mind, by the jolting realization that I was a prisoner here. A pat on the shoulder by a fellow Islamic monk chased the dream away forever, alerting me that the dawn mass would soon begin. The master and the omnipotent Imam expected everyone below in the prayer room at 5:30 am sharp.

I was snuggled warmly in my sleeping bag, laid out alongside other monks in the loft of the stone mosque, from which rose a sleek white minaret. I had called the mosque home for the last two weeks.

I gathered up my drooping body, emerging from the dark-blue cocoon. Half asleep, my body cringed as I gently pulled the djellabah over me, my bearded face, shaved head popping through in the shadows of the early morning light. I stood up, slipped on my pointed Arabian shoes and shuffled to the door, behind which a spiral wooden staircase awaited me.

My body swayed like the trunk of an aged elephant as I ambled down the staircase. As I reached the bottom of the stairs, voices emanating from the minarets next to the white, stone mosques broke the silence, entreating, inviting and cajoling the sleepy inhabitants to rise and walk to the mosque for prayer.

I entered the washroom where cans of water were waiting for the worshippers, next to the toilets. I started my ablutions, trying to remember in which order I was supposed to wash my body—my mind was still fuzzy from the restless tossing and turning in my sleeping bag the past night. The cold water splashed on my arms elicited masses of tiny goose bumps, but at least I was more awake.

I sat on a wooden pedestal so that I could wash my feet, commencing with the left. A brother monk entered, his gray eyes closely watching me, desperately trying to follow the order of ablutions. I quickly dropped the left foot and grabbed the right one. He smiled and proceeded to cleanse his body.

After washing my left foot, under the close surveillance of the monk who had stopped washing his arms to behold my awkward movements, I stood up to leave.

"You begin by washing the right foot, Muhammad," he said, his gray eyes fixed on me. I nodded and passed through the double doors on my way to the main prayer room.

My footsteps echoed in the deserted hallway, as I padded along the cold floors in my pointed, tan-colored shoes, hastily purchased in the "souk" of the Ancienne Medina before becoming a monk at the mosque. It was called the "Masjid Nord" (North Mosque), for reasons I would never know, and reputed to be very politically active.

A green curtain separated the hallway from the prayer room; I placed my hand to the right side of the curtains and opened them wide enough to slide my body through. In front of me was a line of worshippers preparing for the dawn prayer session. I joined them, taking a half-sitting, half-kneeling position: the inside of my left foot was under me, my right foot was in a vertical position and my toes were pressed against the mat made from lake reeds.

I had taken my usual position in front of the door, through which I could see the main door separating me from this world and a freedom I once knew. Its gray, ominous sides rose up to over twelve feet, like the door to a vault—the thick, reinforced bulk seemed to dare anyone to penetrate it.

As I stood up and pronounced "Allahu Akbar," my eyes met those of the turbaned guard standing in front of the closed main door; his beady, bright eyes pierced mine as I recited the "Fatiha." I bent over, placing my hands on my knees, and repeated "Sobhana rabbiya al Al-ala." ("Glory be to God almighty") Looking up, it appeared as if the same guard saw through me: my body felt like a prism, sending my thoughts in different colors to him who, I imagined as a cold shock electrified my entire body, could someday become my executioner.

My body shivered at the thought of the guard reading my inner thoughts—that I was a prisoner, not a guest, that I desperately, silently needed to escape before it was too late, before my life had been assimilated into a new culture, before I became a certified member of the nodding masses, agreeing with every word of the Imam, standing in the corner of the mosque.

Even though we numbered fifty, it seemed as though the intense, dark eyes of the Imam, the master, were staring into mine, as well as those of the others, at the same time. My eyes strayed to the mat ahead of me in fear that the all-intelligent, omnipresent Imam would also divine my thoughts.

As I prostrated myself, placing my forehead on the woven mat, reciting "Sobhana rabbiya al adhime," ("Praise be to thee my Lord, the most high") I thought to myself that even though the will to escape burned inside me, it was more and more compromised by the slow, daily, ebbing away of my strength.

I rose again and before reciting the "Fatiha," I looked out the door again and the guard was not in his usual position before the gate. I was convinced that somehow he had read my mind and now was disclosing to the spiritual leader of the mosque my intentions to escape, that I was not a believer but an infidel, and that I should be punished.

As I bowed my head, clasping my knees with my hands, I waited for the sentence to be cast against me. No new movement was made against me. As I stood, repeating "Allahu Akbar," I noticed the guard had resumed his position before the door, his mirthless smile curled into his dense, black beard.

After prostrating myself again, I sat on the mat as the words "Allahu Akbar" echoed in whispers throughout the room. I thought to myself, avoiding the eyes of the overly attentive guard, that in proportion to the ebbing of physical strength, my resistance grew weaker; I became resigned to the possibility I might never leave that prison, that I would forever be mentally and physically held captive to the doctrines reverberating within the walls of the mosque, which towered over the dusty suburbs like a desert tomb. . .

10

Chapter I

The Womb of All Quarters

The magical beauty of Paris had been hidden from me until the day I arrived on a train from Brussels, Belgium. That day, December 31st, 1976, was to mark my soul forever with indelible ink. There I had spent the last three months studying economics at the Université Libre de Bruxelles, which was linked to European Union (formerly the European Community). As I descended the train, the waves of an impassioned madness carried me into the turbulent city of love.

From the vast avenues lined with majestic apartment buildings bulging with wrought iron balconies, to the charming petites rues—streets that could individually fill volumes of history books—I wandered through this culturally explosive human and supernatural dream city. A myriad of small, quaint streets flowed in and out of large avenues, like creeks into a river. They ebbed and flowed with the tide of thousands of years and people, dressed in anything from knickers to tight jeans. By chance, I would run into a charming old café inhabited by ancient wooden tables, surrounded by walls with rococo designs, embellished by olive leaves and shells carved in wood.

Strangely calm, eye-of-the–storm air engulfed the city as I strolled along the Seine that evening. The light from the street lamps reflected on the shining undulations of a perturbed Seine, perhaps to remind me of the turbulent times embedded in its history (as depicted in the lives of the characters in Victor Hugo's *Les Miserables*). The magic of this night sent me to the shores of times past, into a sort of hypnotic trance, in which I entered the tempest of times and wars long ago waged and spent. I didn't know and didn't care if the sun rose or set tomorrow.

I returned my gaze to the reflections on the Seine. Small, angry waves lashed the sides of the ancient stone braces, supporting bridges crossed by Napoleon's soldiers, or perhaps a knight in quest of a maiden. These same bridges joined the Ile de la Cité with the rest of Paris. The Seine, my Seine now...I felt I was part of it as it gushed down the channel with the turbulent history of the western and eastern world riding on its waves— thousands of years of cultural revolutions, wars, love and romance, the Plague, death and rebirth. And yet the Mother Seine continued to flow.

The Sorbonne, deep within the secure embrace of the Latin Quarter, radiated beautiful knowledge; its hallowed walls were adorned by ancient paintings and deities etched in wood which had withstood the revolutions that had rattled the very roots of the Parisian underground. Sometimes ripped from its historical shelters, catapulted into the violent thrashing of the birth of a new world, it was forever an institution cradled by the cafes and bohemian hang-outs surrounding it.

As a first-year student of philosophy, I, as well as the other "green" philosophy students, was mesmerized by the lectures opening up a new and intellectually stimulating world to us; nothing was immune from analysis and eventual criticism. Mysterious words that somehow found their way into my mind and heart beckoned me to the world of the unknown. They dared me to question all the secure "comfort zones" that I had relied upon heretofore, especially during troubled times. My inner secrets were exposed, my soul revealed. I felt as vulnerable as a child on the very first day of school. But somehow I knew I was going through some kind of a cultural, mental, even spiritual rebirth; the latter would eventually dominate my thoughts, leading me through Spain to Morocco, where I would risk even my life searching for the Supreme Truth.

The philosophy professors spoke French, the sound of which reverberated with a deep resonance against the old wood-paneled walls of the ancient amphitheaters, monuments of a world-renowned intellectual aristocracy.

The marble staircase of the Sorbonne was flanked by golden banisters leading to an intellectual palace, reaching all the way to the heavens; it seemed to my modest, defenseless self. Even the library was a masterpiece. Its ceiling and walls were adorned with sumptuous rococo designs, golden rocks interwoven with shells, scrolls and branches full of leaves. Ancient books were neatly placed in rows surrounding one central study area. I thought the quiet and deep serenity of the place, in the presence of the ancient volumes, would inspire thought. Instead, I found myself dreaming of a beautiful, golden place. My eyes drifted from rock to shell to scroll engraved in the ceiling. I couldn't even open a book.

During the day, the Latin Quarter, surrounding and attending to the Sorbonne like a court to its Queen, exploded with energetic waves of artists, actors, students, writers, workers and professionals, whisking through the Luxembourg Gardens. After arriving at their favorite café, they would sit, sipping their "café crème," espresso or cappuccino, while discussing Plato's *Republic*, Kant's *Criticism of Pure Reason*, Nietzsche's *Beyond Good and Evil*, or the latest art gallery opening. People strolled, ran, skipped by my outdoor table, laughing, crying, moaning on the way to school, to their jobs, to the art shows, to the Sorbonne, to their professors waiting for them with wrinkled brows, who would scold them for their lateness. Sometimes on pedestals, the professors would entreat the students with gyrating gestures and then caress them with soothing, flowing French, definitely worthy of literary world deity.

Inspired by the intense intellectual realm in which I was thrust, I attacked volumes of Plato, Kant, Nietzsche, Sartre, Hegel, Descartes and Rousseau like a starved beast, having hungrily roamed the wild mountains of Oregon—where I was born—for many years. I struggled to understand, due to my limited French, the dialect of the philosophers, from whom I hoped to obtain more than mere peripheral knowledge of the secrets of life, of the universe. They inspired me to delve into my very identity, which often tottered on the edge of perdition. I questioned my own consciousness, the existence of existence, of God, life, hope, good and bad. Sometimes my searching turned into a confused collage of principles leading to others, without the faintest bit of clarity. I was often lost but struggling to understand. After all the years of taking it for granted, my life became one big "question mark."

I wandered down many an obscure Parisian street late at night, in order to discover my inner relationship with the architecture and people. I explored how the different shapes and sizes of the buildings affected me. Strangers walked by, not even shifting a wandering eye towards me, like nameless shadows floating in the night. I felt an ecstatic loneliness, a feeling never before felt, but yet very pronounced—a mixture of emptiness and adventure. I spent infinite hours in little cafés "perdus" (lost cafes) beating my brow in search of a meaning to life, of my "raison d'être." It almost seemed to be the trite search of the "young

12

and the restless" that I had so often seen depicted in movies, with the main character engaged in some type of clichéd soul searching, often ending in the "boy meets girl" happy ending.

I chided myself at the thought that I was viewing my life as some cheap, third-rate movie. I needed life, for once, to be real; I needed to be real, alive, and I needed to be me. I sometimes wondered, however, if this lonely search would lead me down the dismal, empty path of eventual insanity. Or, would I finally bridle this wild, searching beast inside me and somehow turn out better for it?

The heavy, pensive Parisian air made me go so far as to question the very meaning of life. It seemed to weigh on me, forcing an intense introspection. Never before had I done that.

At night, the smoothly gliding current of the Seine often became tormented, relentlessly pounding the stone walls inhibiting its free flow, containing the full force of this mighty river. I likened the pulsating water to a tidal wave of new ideas impeded in its flow into a world desperately in need of change. But I would not be stopped – I would intensify my search for universal truth, knowledge, inner peace...for God, if a higher power existed, crossing over to a culture far removed from the streets of Paris.

Chapter II

American Theatrics

The narrow rustic streets of the Latin Quarter supported many an artist—portfolio under arm, cigarette between lips—and student, attaché case bulging with books, papers, and pens, with the taste of café espresso on his lips and shining, upbeat eyes. The cultural, bohemian melting pot awakened creative hunger in many a culturally deprived Frenchman, foreigner, country dude or city slicker. Paris was the cradle for the "oser faire" philosophy, the "dare to do, think, or express" oneself despite the outcome. I dared to dream of expressing my artistic nature fully without abandoning my raison d'être - to find my way out of the ideological maze and into the truth at the core of my being. I didn't have to wait long for my chance.

I visited the small American liberal arts college in which I was enrolled for the next semester. On reading the bulletin board, on a faded, yellow piece of paper were the words, "Actors wanted" for a school theater production sponsored by the college. I dialed the phone number on the announcement, spoke to the theater group director and made an appointment to see her that afternoon at the school.

At the appointed time, I was directed to a large room with a piano. Seated in the front row was a short-haired French woman in her 30's. She motioned me to sit next to her and introduced herself; then the theatrics began. As tears glistened at the corners of her eyes, she explained that the American student who had initially been given the part, and who had been rehearsing with the group for the last few months, had to leave the country unexpectedly. She went on to say that the opening day of the play was scheduled in two weeks and unless she found another actor to take his place, she would have to cancel the show. I told her I'd do it. The emotion of her embrace was sincere as she thanked me for saving the show.

She told me that the next rehearsal was scheduled for Friday at 5:00 and that I should be there about ten minutes early. "Oh!" she exclaimed as her cheeks flushed with embarrassment, "I forgot to tell you the name of the play; it's 'L'Apollon de Bellac' by French playwright Jean Giraudoux, and you are, by the way, the President. You need to buy a copy of the play, which you will find next to the outdoor market on the Rue Daguerre." She thanked me again, holding my hands in hers before she left the room.

I lingered in the big room next to the piano, wondering if this was all real. I had just arrived in Paris and I was already going to be an actor. "Oh well," I thought, "it's only a bit part." After leaving the building, which sat on the Rue Daguerre, I followed the road until it lead to an outdoor market with fruit stands displaying many rows of fresh apples, oranges, pears, and mangos, all draped with grapes. The radiant decor of the stands was tempered only by the more stoic cheese stands, which emitted the pungent odor of ripe camembert, Brie, Roquefort, goat cheese and hundreds of varieties from the world's cheese capital. About half-way through the fruit stands, off to the right, was a small sign that read "Librairie"

(Bookstore) where I guessed I was supposed to buy the play. I told the salesman the name and author, and after he poked around the stacks of paperbacks, which appeared to be randomly stacked, he found it. I paid him six francs for a copy of the play. Before leaving the store, I leafed through the book and was shocked and delighted to discover that what I had thought was a bit part featured dialogue on almost every page.

As I curled up in bed that night to take the first look at the play, I figured that memorizing it would be possible. Anyway, it would be a great French work-out. At second blush, I panicked a little, wondering if I could memorize the hundreds of lines in only two weeks. The sobering reality of the exploit set in and I resigned myself to sleepless nights and agitated days as I cloistered myself to memorize my lines.

Friday came and my performance was not exemplary. I hadn't had enough time to learn the lines. I hadn't had enough time to even touch the surface of all the lines I had to memorize. One of the directors sat me down and helped me eliminate some lines, without deleting the last line of the monologues, the cue for the actor or actress who was to follow. I read a scene or two while the others recited their parts, without hesitation. The director advised me not to be intimidated since the actors and actresses had been rehearsing their parts all winter.

It was January. I calculated that they had a three- to four-month head start on me. Since they had already spent a great deal of effort on this play, I understood why they wanted the show to go on, but I wondered how I would be ready.

"L'Apollon de Bellac" was a dramatic comedy staring my wife-to-be, Agnes, and...me. Agnes, who was afraid of men, was advised that she would wield great powers over men if she simply appealed to their vain nature. The script revealed that by appealing to my vanity, she proceeded to seduce me and finally won my hand in marriage.

The play was marvelously written and incredibly funny but even that did not make my task easier. Here I was in the City of Love, in all its beauty, only to spend the next two weeks, apart from one final rehearsal, closed off in my bedroom memorizing my lines.

I had rented a room in a home at Porte d'Auteuil and would be living with a French family, who invited me to dinner twice a week. I was also allowed to prepare my breakfast, consisting of bread, jelly and tea, in their kitchen every morning. Apart from that, I had no contact with the outside world. My bedroom was in the loft, from which I could hear the sounds of the pigeons roosting overhead. An occasional pigeon would rise from the lower floors, passing outside my window, until it reached the top where the nest was. The incessant chirping proved that several families had squatted above. It soothed me as the only representative of nature I could find in my self-imposed prison. Every once in a while, a pigeon would fall from the heights, passing my window with rocket speed to the depths below. I imagined that my friend was leaving this world for pigeon paradise.

I lived on apples and peanut butter during the day, bread and tea in the morning. After falling asleep around 3:00 in the morning, without undressing and after memorizing a paragraph, I'd wake up—often in a cold sweat—and memorize a few more lines before dozing off again. This went on twenty-four hours a day for about ten to twelve days, until the final rehearsal.

That proved to be a farce. I still hadn't memorized my lines and only three days remained until opening night. I tried reciting, at first, but since I hadn't mastered all my lines, I was unsure when to stop and go: I hadn't spent time learning my cues. One female student, Judy, a tall, short-haired blond with small, finely-etched lips angrily accused me of sabotaging the production, in the attempt to motivate me to deliver a more polished performance. I told her that her approach was unproductive and would only make it more difficult for me. She would hear nothing of my excuses; and, thereafter, simply reminded me of my commitment to perform, and perform I must.

The other actors and actresses looked at me in silent compassion. The director said that all I could do was my best and that there will be a prompter in the audience helping me with my lines. She encouraged me to try and relax. Agnes—I called her the name she had in the play—a short, golden-haired girl with a kind smile and perfect red lips, like the wax ones girls would wear Halloween night, hugged me and said it would be alright. She also suggested that before the production, I should drink a little wine to help me loosen up. Such was the send-off back to my room.

The day before the play, something started to click. It seemed as though I was starting to understand my role; the words began to flow more easily. I still was far away from being performance perfect, not having memorized all the lines, but perhaps out of boredom and a desire to shake up the routine a bit, I began using gestures more fluidly.

The morning before the play, I realized I would never have time to fully memorize all the words, so I attempted to learn my cues, and extract from them clues as to what I was supposed to say. I mentally eliminated some difficult words and glossed over a few of the run-on sentences and prose in order to simplify my task.

After this intense session, which seemed to last for hours, my watch indicated that two hours remained before curtain time at 8:00 p.m. I calculated that fifty minutes was what I needed to take me to the theater—one of the classrooms at the school—by subway. I also calculated that I should have enough money to buy a bottle of cheap red wine and an omelet at the local brasserie.

I took a quick shower and put on a suit and a tie; after all, I was to be the President that evening. The house was empty so, because it was Friday night, I figured the family had gone out to eat. I left the empty house carrying my book bag which held the bottle of red and the copy of the play, which had barely weathered the last two weeks. The pages were scuffed and bore markings of all kinds, words were underlined and the corners of almost every page were violently creased at the corners. I mused that after the play, I would, for an encore, stage a formal burial of the poor paperback. A silent, perhaps morbid, chuckle resounded from deep within my mind as I gobbled down the omelet, lapping up the juices with a piece of baguette. All that washed down easily with a glass of red wine.

"Well, they told me to drink up!" I laughed at myself. After the first gulp, I finally asked the proverbial question, "What have I gotten myself into this time?" I knew I'd be infinitely relieved when it was over and prayed I wouldn't destroy the play, making a fool of myself in the process.

I took the metro, caressing my book bag without opening the book. I felt I had reached the end; any more memorization and recitation and I would explode into a million words! I needed to meditate, take my thoughts away from everything. As the subway rolled along, I dreamed of running wildly over sand dunes on the beach in northern California, jumping into the crashing waves at full speed.

I arrived at Denfert-Rochereau station somewhat refreshed, having taken my first meaningful break from my lines in twelve days. With renewed energy, I stepped off the subway. Remembering my high school football coach, I tried to "gut up" as he had put it, while he stared out at a mass of helmeted heads, fourth quarter sweat dripping down our serious faces as we huddled...that seemed like a hundred years ago.

The Rue Daguerre took on a new splendor at night, with the lights of the brasseries reflecting off of the metal frames bracing the empty outdoor market.

People stood at the entrance of the schoolroom/ theater, waiting for judgment day. I quickly walked passed them, opened the front door and slipped down the stairs to a room below the main entrance. I opened my book bag and grabbed the bottle of red wine. Popping open the cheap plastic top, I took two big gulps. It was rot gut, but following my cast mate's advice, I knew it would relax me a bit.

Feet pounded above. I looked at my watch: ten minutes remained. I climbed the stairs and was greeted by Agnes and the others. Their faces were pasted with serious panic. Agnes smiled nervously. She cried "I thought you wouldn't make it! I wouldn't blame you, all the pressure others placed on you. Don't worry. But you're here, that's all that matters."

I replied, "How could you even think I would do such a thing?" She smelled my breath, said I smelled like a brewery and that she hoped I felt okay, as she pulled at my book bag. I didn't have time to figure out what she meant by that gesture as the others retreated to the actors' waiting room and motioned us to follow. But a touch of warmth crept up my spine and melted the bits of red wine grapes caked at the corners of my mouth. Her soothing words acted like a magic spell on my anguish.

I told the others I'd be right back as I slipped down the steps again to take a final swig from the bottle, now slippery in my clammy hands. As I ascended the stairs, I felt a gentle flush touch my cheeks. Entering the waiting room, I mumbled something idiotic like "Here goes!" The actors and actresses stared at me, shaking their heads. Agnes looked away. I knew they all thought I was drunk. I almost wished I were but I was frightfully sober. The wine had done little to comfort or relax me. The director asked us to take our seats in the theater. We sat in a row alongside the wall in front of the audience.

The show opened and, all of a sudden, I found myself taken by the current of the play; the web spun by Jean Giraudoux had caught us all. The words flowed like a cold, clear stream of mountain water. There was no hesitation and no cues were missed. It was magic...it was a dream.

I only forgot one word—"bague," or ring—I was to use when I proposed to Agnes. The prompter quickly, and without raising her voice, articulated the word, which I repeated with ease. It was so smooth that the audience was unaware of the exchange. The play ended with thundering, impassioned applause.

Following the diatribes against me, now my cast mates said I had saved the show. Hypocrisy abounded, especially in the form of Judy's hugs—gentle, caressing, enfolding me like a long lost friend—followed by an invitation to a cast party. All I could think about was that I was free again to embrace the Paris that seemed so far away. Although it was on the other side of the theater door, it felt as if it was at the end of the world.

I abruptly grabbed my book bag and left the theater, to plunge back into blissful freedom, to roam aimlessly through Paris. Freedom...I took a deep breath and cried at the top of my lungs as I slammed the theater door behind me. It seemed as though all of Paris yelled with me, the walls echoing their welcome.

Chapter III

Breaking Free

The end of the play marked the renewal of my search for the reasons I was placed on this earth and by whom. I remained a loner in Paris, but I didn't mind. I attended courses at the Sorbonne and at the private school—where my reputation as the Play Saver continued—but nothing more; I came and went. Every now and then, I spied Agnes in the hall of the private school and winked. She winked back, and that was all. Judy cornered me in the hall one day and said she was saving herself for me. I smiled but Paris was a jealous lady who wouldn't share me with anyone else. She would eventually loosen her grip as I abandoned her for an unknown land to find my unknown self and an unknown God.

At night, I continued my strolls along the Seine, heedlessly running its endless course, the eddy swirling the past like a leaf caught in a whirlpool.

I walked near the Conciergerie. "Let them eat cake" echoed off its walls, which had imprisoned Marie Antoinette, as the peasant population vehemently echoed back its reproach. "Vivre sa vie à fond" ("To live life to the fullest") was the Parisian slogan, with or without money. I tried not to let money, the little that I had, interfere with my search for the truth.

In between never-ending conversations with French classmates in cafes and all-night sessions discussing works ranging from Plato's *Republic* to Einstein's Theory of Relativity, my life drifted like the ideas flowing in and out of me; it took me in and out of apartments, bookstores, classrooms, student restaurants, subways and through the streets.

"L'Apollon de Bellac" was now ancient history, a page turned, never to be revisited. I wondered how I could share such an intensely emotional experience with others, yet experience no remorse at the end. The play must go on as it must end. But somehow I loathed losing past feelings that I had cherished. I fought against passiveness, an indifference to time and space. I feared that this would lead to loss of sensitivity to love, to the suffering of others. Would I be another casualty of intellectual bantering, an activity dear to the rich, the bourgeoisie and the bored? Would I become a victim of hypocrisy and the intellectualization of my very emotions, justifying my indifference until the end of my days, while the world despaired and died of starvation? Wasn't that the aloofness attributed to the city slicker and not a country bumpkin like me?

To vary my routine, I would occasionally stroll through a park—Luxembourg Gardens, usually—and even was invited to spend a weekend in the country; Dizy is a small town near Epernay, not far from the rolling hills of Reims, the capital of Champagne country. But then I'd return to the frenzied pace of the city the moment I stepped off the train at Gare de l'Est.

Paris, resounding with mysteries and shadows of love, lies and truths, was far removed from the more familiar life I lead in Northern California, where I grew up among the undulating hills of the wine country. The fresh country air was sweetened by blooming flowers, pine trees and mornings filled with the smell of freshly cut wood and damp earth.

How could I abandon the years of working on farms, waking up to the cock-a-doodle-doos of the rooster and fresh wheat pancakes at 6:00 in the morning, before tilling the fields of grapes dotting the hills surrounding Healdsburg? After all, I was just a country/suburban dude in the city. In spite of its beauty, the Parisian streets jolted my senses with the clamor of city life.

My country-bumpkin eyes bore incredulous witness to the masses of people that seemed to swarm to every corner of the city, consuming the last remnants of country tranquility embedded deep within me. Through country eyes, I admired the elegant façade of the magnificent opera building but it could not transcend the beauty of a vineyard in the rugged Northern Californian wine country or the champagne country surrounding Reims.

In order to improve my French and get back to the elements that had nurtured me all those rustic farm years in California, I volunteered to work as a cashier in a health food store. The clientele was made up of the 7th district well-to-do, able to pay the high prices of organic vegetables, fruits and specially baked organic bread. The organic bakery supplied us with fabulous organic pies, pastries and cookies, baked with carob instead of chocolate.

Our clientele seemed a little overly preoccupied with what was placed in their bodies. I remember one day there was a run on organic salads and at the end of the day, there remained nary a one. A regular customer, a lady with frizzy brown hair and sagging jowls, demonstrated her dependence by attacking my standing as a cashier because of my failure to order enough salads. A fanatic, she sighed in frustration, slamming the door behind her.

After pushing back the curtain at the back of the store, clients walked down a narrow plant-lined corridor until they came to an oasis of plants, light and a kaleidoscope of flowers. This opened into a large alcove which served as an organic restaurant called Le Jardin. There was a skylight overhead, allowing the owner to plant flowers and shrubs in the middle of her restaurant.

This was not just an ordinary garden: it became a meeting place for destiny and me. Ideas, as well as plants, took root and grew faster than time flew. The garden became a secret place where I would go to sip herb tea and listen to the kitchen helpers hum songs from the *Qur'an*.

One night after closing the store, I retreated to the Jardin, where I sipped organic mint tea in the semi-darkened room. One of the kitchen helpers passed through the restaurant carrying a sack of wheat to the storeroom. In spite of my desire to be left alone, I motioned for him to approach my table. He arrived and respectfully bowed. I introduced myself and in his broken French, he told me his name was Fouad and said he was pleased to meet me. Then, he hoisted the heavy sack over his shoulders and made his way to the storeroom on the other side of the restaurant. Fouad had an olive face, chiseled by the winds of the Mediterranean. His short, salt-and-pepper hair framed an oval, slightly chubby face, with a chin that sported a couple of days' growth.

The next day, I had made my evening retreat to sip my tea in the darkened restaurant, when Fouad visited my table again. I could see his smile glistening in the dark, thanks to his gold-plated front teeth. He said he wanted to introduce Muhammad to me. As he pointed to the kitchen, he spoke a strange language, and another kitchen helper appeared in the doorway. Muhammad hesitated; but upon the coaxing of his friend, he came closer to my table. Fouad broke the silence and introduced me to Muhammad, who shook my hand, nodding.

Muhammad hovered over me silently, contemplating my every gesture. His wind-burned, shiny, copper face revealed two beady crystals for eyes. Fouad explained, with his friend looking on, that he and Muhammad were kitchen helpers who spent the day and evening hours cleaning the kitchen, cutting vegetables and baking the vegetarian crepes for the lunches and dinners.

I ran into the two of them often. They began joining me for tea at the table; we drank mint tea in the shadows of the abandoned restaurant sometimes until after midnight. They began to feel comfortable enough to describe their dear mother country, Morocco, where their families lived. Fouad related that he came to France to work and send money back to his wife and kids every month. Muhammad listened; his deeply engraved eyes glistened in the dark, capturing every gesture. I knew he didn't trust me, but I hoped someday he would tell me his story.

Many times I'd drink my tea alone as the two cleaned the kitchen to the rhythm of a strange chanting that often lulled me to sleep. I pictured the songs glancing off the sand dunes of the Sahara as Muhammad rode his camel to the market place. After several evenings of listening in the dark, I felt as if I were being carried off on a magic carpet to a foreign land.

As I sat there listening to the mystical chanting one night, there was a sudden silence. Muhammad peered at me through a crack between the door and the wall; perhaps he had been mysteriously communicating with me through the songs.

One day, as I was silently meditating in the garden, breathing in the air purified by the plants, Fouad approached me. He asked me if I were praying to my God. I told him that I was meditating to a kind of cosmic force that I guessed you could call God.

He said that I seemed to be linked to his God. I asked him what he meant by that and he commented that he saw me attentively listening to him singing songs with Muhammad. I asked him why that meant that somehow I was linked to his God. He responded, "Those are songs from the Qur'an; Allahu Akbar!" (God is Great!). He smiled that gold smile.

"It seems that a lot can be understood about Islam by just listening to songs from that holy book, and I. . ."

"But,", before I could continue, he interrupted, "you don't really need to understand Arabic to understand the songs," he grunted as he walked by with a sack of brown rice on his shoulders. When he arrived at the storage house, he began singing those mysterious songs again.

I had put in a long day; it had started at the Sorbonne where I was taking a course from my favorite instructor, Professor Birault, on Hegel and other German philosophers. We were all in awe of his eloquence and the raw energy he put into his lectures. According to Professor Birault, Hegel taught that it was a long and painful road leading to absolute knowledge and philosophy served to lend us the necessary tools with which to build the path. After the course, I felt drained but deeply motivated by his words, which seemed to stimulate the inner thinking process that had been dormant until then.

After class, I jumped on the subway to take me to work. Fifteen hours later, I was sitting at the usual table in the corner of the Jardin, listening to Fouad sing, my head resting on my open palm.

That night, it felt like my quest was starting to fall into place. There was some logical pattern moving me to follow the chanting, to construct a road that would lead me to truth. I was beginning to tire of pure intellectualizing the form of the path, exacerbated by my plunging into my studies of the works of philosophers and then discussing them with classmates. I was fascinated by studying French, German and Greek philosophers but I was increasingly experiencing the bizarre sensation of being alienated from reality, that I was becoming an intellectual fortress where the size of my head was disproportional to the size of the other parts of my body, including my heart. To build this path, I convinced myself that I needed to act, to move out of the mental dialectic into the life stream flowing from spiritual sources empowered by love and passion.

Fouad returned from the supply room and sat down beside me. He held out his hand and gently took mine in his, saying "You should come to my country, Morocco, where you will be surrounded by God's people chanting the *Qur'an*. As you are seeking Allah, they will embrace you during your journey. You could visit my village in Southeastern Morocco where you can come and go as you please. You will not be forced to follow anyone or to do anything you don't want to do. Come and breathe the fresh desert air blowing in from the Sahara in southern Morocco, which is filled with the love of Allah and hard- working peasants. You will find truth there, Frank, away from the harsh, impersonal Parisian streets."

Fouad's fatherly words repeated in my mind as I walked to my room. The soft tone of his voice reminded me of my father. That night I dreamed of him.

I dreamed of the times I had sat in front of the fire in Ashland, Oregon, and in our Santa Rosa, California, living room, talking about love and war with him. A former 2nd lieutenant with the U.S. army in World War II, he had served mainly on the Japanese front; he had had a ringside seat, witnessing the cruel butchery and ravages of war which turned people from good, loving families into killing machines. It was a living nightmare that my father, at first, chose not to share with me. But, after my relentless prodding, he disclosed portions of the dark caverns into which much of mankind has been thrust in the name of freedom. He shared with me the loss of buddies, the maiming and the blood flowing from the mouths of disbelieving youngsters caught up in something beyond their ability to fathom.

His voice trembled so much, at times, during his eloquent dissertation on human suffering, that I thought he was going to trail off. Then, he would turn the page to describe a new blood-curdling scenario.

In the same breath he had described the killing; he talked about why man was created. According to my father, man was born to love and share; he never forgot living in poverty and the years he had spent in an orphanage as a child. From the Hobbsian approach, that there is no limit to man's cruelty, he turned to Rousseauian observations of the beauty of man's true nature. He spoke especially of the love shared between a man and a woman—about mom and him. Tears filled the corners of my eyes as he, after all those years, showed he was still deeply in love with Ma, and more so every day.

He returned from the killing and suffering convinced that man, to be happy, must seek and find the truth. Classical religions, contemporary conservative fundamentalism and esoteric philosophies would not provide the answers—man needed to seek a universal truth. As he passed under the Golden Gate Bridge in a huge naval vessel after World War II was over, to greet his country and future wife, he held the dream-of a political unity beyond what governments could achieve-within him. As proven in Europe, Asia and beyond, bureaucracies historically nurtured the nationalistic fervor that had created so many of the world's problems.

After the signing of the United Nations Charter in 1945, in his dear San Francisco, it all came together for Dad. I can hear him now: he would say something like "We must embrace all cultures, all races, with a child's curiosity and acceptance, and construct our world on tolerance and love rather than hate and protectionism."

He would sometimes talk to me about religion. Before and during the war, he was a devout catholic. He told me many times that it was his spirituality that gave him strength to overcome poverty and the orphanages, the cold, cruel prisons in which he grew up. And finally, buried in foxholes in the middle of an island rice paddy, he was strengthened through prayer.

After his return from the war, his spiritual fervor accelerated. Although he had respected and deeply appreciated the patriarchal Catholic church, which fathered and nurtured him when hope was only a fleeting afterthought, he began to believe that humankind needed something beyond the classical religions to guide us toward world peace and beyond—to world love. Dad believed that we, the people, were often overly attached to ritual, which could lead to a dependency on it as representing the truth. Its actual purpose was to accompany true faith and the love of God.

He joined the Baha'i movement. Looking towards world peace, he believed that a religion that was an amalgam of the different religious philosophies—in the spirit of the U.N.—would bring together competing national belief systems and create an environment of "entente." He believed that the Baha'i religion would inspire spiritual unity by furthering tolerance and a true understanding of other ideologies, thereby propelling the world toward unity. Such spirituality and political interdependence would lead, as Dad believed, toward peace and progress—as opposed to the hate and destruction—that exist in today's world.

I asked him what the Baha'i faith was. He patiently explained that its followers were originally Moslems living in Iran, and even though Islam was considered by many as a universal religion, the Baha'i believe in bringing together the world religions into one unified faith. He believed that there was one religion and that the disparities between the major religions were due to the vicissitudes of the times rather than their fundamental natures. He lastly emphasized to me the importance the Baha'i religion places on letting people know they are citizens of the world first before they are citizens of one country. This correlated to the importance my father placed on the development of the United Nations.

The concept was vague and bizarre, yet the idea of unifying the world under the auspices of the U.N., guided by the application of universal law, seemed incredibly complex, and to think of doing the same for religions seemed impossible.

And then he planted a seed in my young mind that many years later would inspire me to use the idea of universal political unity to create a hybrid definition of universalism. The dictionary defines universalism as the state of being universal, as including or covering everything without limit or exception. I define universalism as a universal awakening through the search for a common denominator underlying all things, preferences, particular identities, cultures and philosophies. This led me to extend the definition to encompass universal principals such as universal law, i.e. universally applied legal principles such as human rights laws, in particular, those pertaining to genocide and crimes against humanity. I felt that only the search for universalism would allow us to attain true knowledge, leading to a greater degree of tolerance of other races, ethnic origins, other cultures, tempering ignorance, hate and blind nationalism.

This idea of universalism motivated me to seek the universal religion. Maybe it would be Islam; somehow I was convinced that I needed to travel far away to find the path that would lead me to truth and I needed to do the walk as well as the talk.

That night in my room, after reading about the violence in Palestine and in the Middle East, I meditated on world peace. It was 3:00 in the morning. While I floated in a dreamlike, meditative trance, solutions to world confusion, hate, ignorance, blind nationalism and exaggerated protectionism presented themselves. I opened my book on comparative religions and read until the sun's rays filled the roof-top opening of my "chambre de bonne" (servant's quarters) high above the Seine.

I reread passages about Buddhism, the eight-fold path, the four noble truths, and passages from the Bhagavad-Gita. I was especially interested in reading about detachment from material things. It states that it is by the attachment to acts that ignorant people act. The wise must similarly act, but without such attachment, focusing on the integrity of the universe. I had read that passage many times before but that night, new meanings came to me. In Luke, Chapter 18:18-25 and Matthew 6:19-21 of the New Testament, importance is placed on seeking treasure in heaven as opposed to on earth. In the *Qur'an*, those who spend money on God's path are denounced and principles similar to those in the New Testament concerning money and spirituality are espoused. In the Torah, greater value is placed upon Heaven's gifts as opposed to worldly wealth. Buddhist teachings convey the importance that wealth cannot bring happiness, that on the contrary, an intense desire to amass riches brings suffering instead. According to these great books, material things seemed of so little importance, so meaningless.

So, the common denominator of all those religions is the belief that true, pure love expressed to each other is similar to the love one feels for the supreme force which links us all altogether. In order to realize that, I believed we needed to educate each other to overcome society's pressure urging us to seek power, sex and money, all temporal goals.

I was even more convinced that world peace depended on the promotion of a universal faith. My spiritual itinerary would be to cross France and Spain and take a ferry to Morocco. Then I would take a train, bus or hitchhike across Maghreb, Libya and Egypt, ending my journey in the spiritual center of the world–the Holy Land.

Chapter IV

Maghreb Express

As the ideas started flowing, everything happened fast. The next day, I bought my ticket to Tangier and an Arab language study package, complete with cassette and booklet to help me learn the language.

Peggy, my girlfriend, accompanied me the next day to the train station and begged me to either take her or stay in Paris. I gently told her I had to travel alone; I was seeking something but was not yet sure what it was and did not want to drag her into something I knew almost nothing about.

As I settled into my seat, the last thing I saw on the quay was her silky hair wound into a neat bun and her rose-colored face. Her concerned hazel eyes, puffy from crying, peered up toward the window from which I was waving. The train coughed and sputtered, finally settling into a chugging rhythm as we left the station farther and farther behind. My destination: southern Spain. From there, on to Tangier and then Casablanca, Morocco.

As I entered the cabin, even though we had not reserved particular seats, I noticed they were all marked "Reserved." A short, mustachioed man wearing a fez entered before me and without hesitation grabbed all the "Reserved" signs, tossing them out the window. He sat in front of me, and leaning over, his curled, gray mustache moving as he spoke, said the seats were now reserved for us. His gentle, brown eyes blinked and twinkled with amusement.

He leaned toward me again, saying "Welcome to the Maghreb[2] Express." I asked him what that was and he responded, "This is the midnight train of Montparnass, as slow a chugger as you can get, and it's full of Moroccans returning home. My name is Ibrahim. By the way, what are you doing here?"

I explained that I wanted to visit Morocco, learn the language and find out what Islam was all about. While I talked, he looked in disbelief as another man wearing a turban joined us in the far corner of the cabin. The other, who introduced himself as Abdullah, peered back at Ibrahim and with a vacant smile on his face, turned to look me over. He spared no part of me in his penetrating gaze. I wondered if the silent communication between the two meant something. I felt a huge gap between us in the form of a gigantic puzzle—as I perceived my life to be—where many pieces were missing. I was hoping to find them, perhaps in some corner of Casablanca or at the base of a Saharan sand dune, scorched by the daily diet of sun and sweeping winds.

---

[2] Maghreb comes from the word "Al Maghrib," which is a synonym for Morocco. It means "of the setting sun."

My life had seemed so simple on the farm in California. Now everything was so mysterious; adventure lurked on every seat. The wind blowing through the opening above the window felt like a hidden hand trying to rouse me, warning me that it was not too late to turn back. Yet nothing deterred me as I embarked on a voyage from which there might be no return.

"So be it," I thought. I needed to know at all costs why I was on this earth. I needed to know if there was something beyond the superficial nightclubbing, strobe light illuminated world of beer and hot dogs—a world where values were ridiculed or ignored, and human life was sacrificed in the kind of meaningless violence I had sometimes witnessed living in the Ghetto.

Fear of what the future would bring...I realized I really didn't know where I was going and where I truly came from. I needed to risk everything—my health, my life, and even sanity.

My thoughts comforted me as I reflected on other times when I blindly swam in a sea of confusion, not knowing if I were swimming to shore or out to sea. Buffeted by strong currents, I had no idea where they were taking me—like when I moved to the ghetto to understand what life was all about.

Miles and miles of pastures, rivers and small towns blurred before me as I contemplated my life in the African ghetto in Santa Rosa, California. I recalled my father encouraging me to try and understand, not hate, other people, other races. He reminded me of my Italian heritage and that he hoped I was proud to be one. He explained to me that Italians were not initially well received in the states: they were stranded on Ellis Island outside of New York City, herded like cattle on the way to the slaughterhouse, deported to Italy while it was experiencing a famine. Or, perhaps they were fortunate enough to enter "the promised land" after several days of weathering ferocious ocean storms, finally able to eat the land of plenty. My Neapolitan family came to America in pursuit of the American dream.

My dad said Italians were spit upon and treated like dirt. They were forced to live in ghettos and given nothing with which to survive. His father, my grandfather, had been a poor baker who died of a broken heart three years after his wife died giving birth to my dad. His emotions flared as he explained that he was forced to live in a series of orphanages, surrounded by high fences, like those surrounding penitentiaries.

When his sister was old enough to take him in, he was high school age, having spent his childhood behind bars. He shared fond memories of his dear sister, Louise, with me, who did all she could to raise him in spite of their poverty. I had to turn my head away from dad as the tears touched the corners of my eyes; I truly felt for him and the way he had lived his youth. I so loved him.

But Dad wasn't finished telling his story. He said life for Italians was harder than most. He was especially treated badly because of his dark skin, to the extent that he always reminded me that Italians—themselves victims of ethnic discrimination—had no right to be bigoted. Dad believed they should have only compassion for the suffering of those targeted for their race, culture or social standing. He prohibited all jokes about Italians, other ethnic groups and races on the grounds that they were racially motivated. He was probably right about that, and certainly sensitive to racism and intolerance, as reflected in his life experiences.

Growing up in California and Oregon, I did not feel that same way. I did experience it once in awhile, when applying for a job and the employer would look down at me through his spectacles and disdainfully say, "You're Italian, eh?" Sometimes I would correct him and say that no, I was Italian American—and notice the expression of relief. Occasionally, I wouldn't correct the employer and watched his hateful eyes glare down at me as he waved me out the door. Such must have been the way Italians were treated in times past.

As a football player in high school, I met a lot of black and Latino athletes and we quickly became friends. I learned that on the football field, at least, there was no race, no religion. We were one, fighting for the same cause. No matter how hard our heads clashed in battles fought on the five yard line, the taste of unity on the football field was sweet. But a bitter pill was awaiting me in the real world.

I was eager to explore other cultures, in particular that of the African-Americans, Mexican-Americans, and Italian-British-Americans (my heritage). When I dropped out of San Francisco State University after the first year—I had dedicated far more to the anti-Vietnam war movement than my studies—I found a job on the assembly line in a prefabricated home factory near Santa Rosa, California, where my parents lived. I loved them but because I still felt the umbilical cord between us, decided I needed to live away from them; I needed to separate myself from the warm, parental nurturing that had surrounded me all my life.

I worked as a tar and gravel roofer during the hot summer months. The 110 degree weather was exacerbated by what seemed like three hundred degree tar pots. I rented a room in a rooming house full of retired folk. Silence was the unspoken agreement. I was invisible there, but the incognito standing made me feel a glimmer of independence.

As I walked into the room, the patchwork comforter resting on my bed reminded me of the one in my grandmother's house, lovingly hand-stitched by my aunt, with pastel-colored flowers in full bloom, carriages, farmhouses and an occasional bluebird gripping a branch of a dangling willow tree.

I opened the side window next to the bed. Off to the right loomed the tall chimney of my junior high school. Just a few blocks beyond was the home I had shared with my family during my elementary and junior high school years; I remembered them as times of tears, pain and surges of ecstasy. The bright sunny day seemed to grow darker as my thoughts clouded remembrances of the only bright spots in my youth. My awareness returned to my dark, stained overalls, feelings of failure as a University student and struggles to escape the roofer's hot tar pot.

I eventually fought my way out of the scalding tar pot and changed gears after being motivated to return to college. Years later, it seemed as though I was changing gears again. The train's incessant chugging became an ominous rumbling, warning me of stormy times ahead.

I must have been daydreaming for hours. When I noticed the time, it was about 5:00 a.m. The silence gave way to the low moaning of the train as it chugged slowly across the French countryside, stopping at every small town between Paris and the end of the line. I glanced around the cabin and noticed that my two companions were snoozing, wedged inside the seats. "After all," I thought to myself, "This is the Maghreb Express—without couchettes." (Sleeping cars.)

Abdullah quietly stirred from a deep slumber and placed a clean towel on the opposite, unoccupied seat. He sat down on the towel, crossed his legs and began mumbling what seemed to be prayers. His face was almost completely hidden beneath a woolen hood. Once in a while, his face would pop out of the hood as his lips continued to move. The beginnings of a mustache covered his upper lip.

The train rolled on, bending and turning, with sometimes constant thumping noises emanating from somewhere underneath the train. Abdullah stared into the night blurred by the window.

I must have dozed off; I awoke some time later, startled by the screeching of the brakes. The heat of the sun warmed my face, stirring me from the cold depths of sleep.

The train stopped at a village nestled between two hills. A woman and her daughter got on and passed the cabin. The woman glanced inside and quickly yanked her child away as she settled into another seat. Was she afraid of us—we were a motley group—or was she concerned because we looked like we were from Morocco, perhaps not from the same social class as hers? I didn't want to be negative but somehow I felt her hate right between my eyes. It was a strange feeling to be judged by association with others. I felt so protective of my companions that I would have defended them against the attacks of a racist. I looked around; they luckily had simply ignored her. Maybe I should have, too, but I just couldn't. My Dad's words came back to me, warned me.

The train slowly started up again. I was so engrossed in my thoughts of the lady and her daughter; I had not noticed that Abdullah had sat on the usual towel to begin his afternoon prayer session. His eyes seemed to search for something out the window; I could actually see the hills and valleys that we passed reflected in his eyes. There was something mysterious and deep about him. I wondered if he could be a friend. I very much wanted to believe in, trust people. After his prayer session, I tried to start up a conversation, so I complimented him on his faithfulness.

"Faithfulness?" he questioned.

I felt awkward and stammered, "I mean, the fact that you keep up your faith even in the train, when all the rest of us think about is sleeping, sitting around. . ."

He flashed a broad, kind, almost naïve grin. Was there something deceiving in his grin or was I just being too cautious? Maybe, his naiveté was a mask, like a protective smokescreen, designed to prevent me from penetrating his thoughts. Would I dare to? Something from that grin told me not to talk any more about religion. But I felt that the ice was broken, and maybe I could try a different subject.

"By the way, where are you headed?" That sounded trite, as if I were in a bar asking someone what sign they were, or something like that.

He said he was going home, to the hills around Tangier. I asked him what it was like to live there. He corrected me. "I don't live there—I'm just visiting my family."

"Oh, okay." I guess I was being a bore. I looked out the window as I withdrew into my thoughts. I imagined he would have members of his family at the ferry in Tangier, who would hug and kiss him, and whisk him away to a warm, home-cooked dinner in the wild hills. But there would be no one to greet me; no one even knew I was coming. I would be alone.

And then I tried to visualize Peggy, standing on the quay in Paris, desperately waving as the train chugged out of sight.

Chapter V

Marie-Laure[3]

My girlfriend, a petite Parisian, with chestnut-colored hair—my companion over the last few months—helped me pack my knapsack to hold my sleeping bag, food items and cassette player. She was a frail, slender, young lady who I had met at a party for foreign students a few months earlier. We had been living together for the past months, house-sitting for friends in a small studio apartment near the Place de la République. She tried to convince me to take her with me, but I ruled against it due to her frail condition. The voyage would be long and hard and we'd be required to perhaps sleep outdoors in Morocco, due to limited money. That night, we cried in each other's arms, her tender caresses tempting me to take her along.

I'll never forget how I had met her. One gloomy, late Saturday afternoon, I was awakened by the sun's rays dancing through the holes in the flapping curtains and ricocheting off the sides of the chest of drawers next to the open window. I was undecided whether I wanted to go to a dance at a student clubhouse in the Place de la Sorbonne—it was supposed to start at three o'clock.

As I walked along the Seine at 5 p.m., I watched the waves angrily slapping against the sides of the rock columns that held up the Pont St. Michel, as I contemplated another lonely Saturday.

Walking up the Boulevard St. Michel, I felt tormented once again by the hordes of tourists, students, artists and vendors trying to entice people into their dress and jeans shops and stalls with rows and rows of books. I could not look at another book as I had spent the entire week trying to improve my weak French grammar skills. I took a left and came across the Sorbonne—its spiral columns greeted me with the reminder that I was an intellectual infant at the feet of the ageless wisdom of yesteryear.

The student center was situated on the other side of the Place de la Sorbonne, across from my favorite café, L'écritoire. There, I had spent many hours with fellow philosophy students, trying to decide if we existed, and if so, on what basis? The knowledge that had filtered down hundreds of years, from Plato and Aristotle to Rousseau, Nietche and Sartre, served as our parameters. We exchanged thoughts on our identity, as influenced by indoctrination, and how we were to overcome our socialized, programmed thinking in order to become free thinkers.

As I entered the long hallway, billboards on both sides drew my attention away from L'écritoire to the announcements about events, symphonies, dances and art shows at the Sorbonne. I came to a set of double doors, behind which I could hear the rock-n-roll music of an old British band whose name I couldn't remember. The door opened and two girls approached; the blond asked, in guttural French, if I were looking for the foreign student

---

[3] Her real name was Marie-Laure. Peggy was her nickname.

dance. She was a little stout, her lipstick painted on thickly, reminding me of a blooming rose. Her disarming smile, without the sometimes present Parisian ulterior motive, incited my pensive yearnings—in fact uprooted me from thoughts of philosophical bantering at L'écritoire, and yanked me into the "here and the now." She grabbed my right arm and the other girl then felt obliged to reach for my left hand, which I volunteered. I tried to smile but it was an insipid attempt; I felt a little awkward walking into a dance with one girl on each arm, as if I was parading as a modern Don Juan.

The other girl was a slim brunette, her smile compromised by the stern set of her mouth, linear and severe. Her sleek body was clothed in a drab, gray outfit, purposely covering any of the fair graces she perhaps appreciated about herself, in secret. She did not dare look at me as the blond one did, as her shyness overruled this, but her hand timidly held my arm, as though she had never been so close to a man before.

As we entered the dance floor, the blond girl released me first, and with her head bobbing up and down, she wished me a "fun day," in that guttural, Slavic accent. My eyes followed her as she walked to the other side of the room to join a group of people. The other girl looked straight ahead, refusing to let my arm go. I had to subtly cast an eye in her direction, and she, not able to meet my eyes but intuiting that I wondered why she was still holding my hand, gently withdrew her hand from my arm. She remained standing next to me, however.

I was intrigued by this girl, entranced by her timidity, although her touch felt anguished, gloomy—for some reason, profoundly sad. It was so refreshing in that city where many people seemed jaded, full of ulterior motives at the expense of spontaneity.

A band was playing a song and couples were all dancing the "rock français," where the man twirls his partner, as in American swing, except there are no particular steps. Dresses were swirling like windmills, and feet were kicking every which way. The couples danced around and sometimes over each other, culminating in a hug sometimes so subtle that the naked eye failed to detect it. A man and a woman to my left were smiling at each other as the man twirled her. She dizzily returned a half-cocked smile and accidentally stepped on his feet. He tumbled to the floor, emitting a belly laugh that filled the air, while she, embarrassed, pulled him up and the cycle repeated itself.

I danced with a dark-haired Parisian with hair typically cut straight across in front. She barely looked at me as I tried to swing her to the beat of a song I didn't know. I tried American swing moves, but they weren't the same: she had to lead. After several sweaty dances, we walked to the bar and then sat down nursing glasses of Perrier and lemon squeezes.

As we watched the people on the dance floor, couples twisted and turned to the beat. A slender girl with dirty-dishwater blond hair slithered between the couples, dancing, turning, bending her knees as she headed across the floor; a bearded young man, her apparent dancing partner, could hardly keep up with her. Her body spun around as she pirouetted, and then dipped, swayed and pirouetted again. Her last turn coincided with the end of the song, during which she sank down to the floor, clasping her hands as if she were praying. This seductive enchantress had managed to attract the eyes of all at the dance. As she passed me, her shifting eyes fixed on mine, her faced flushed from her exertions.

A voice came over the loudspeaker and announced the last dance. I asked the timid girl still standing to the left of me but my invitation was greeted with a shy refusal. I had anticipated that. Then I glanced across the dance floor and on the other side, the dirty-dishwater blond stood talking to another girl. I moved to a position closer to her. As the song announced was to be one from the latest Earth Wind and Fire album, my courage rose to the occasion. I quickly walked the remaining distance between us until I found myself face to face with her.

I held out my hand and she inclined her head towards me, cocking it to one side as if she were trying to figure out who I was. Her small, blue, painted eyes dared to look into mine. As her small mouth, which reminded me of the girls in Modigliani's paintings, curved in a smile, she folded her small, pale fingers over mine as I gently pulled her in the direction of the dance floor. She slid past me, still maintaining her grip on my hand, desiring to lead me.

As she swung her hips, I guessed that she had probably taken "Hustle" dance lessons as her hips moved to the beat of "That's the Way of the World." A friend of mine in the States had also shown me the steps, so I jumped forward, swiveling my hips as well, which surprised her, as she had surely thought herself the only one in the crowd who could dance like that. She shook her head, a smile spreading across her face.

I was totally drawn into the spirit of the music; the essence of soul and jazz recalled the intense moments I had lived in the ghetto. I remembered Grover Washington's songs, in particular "Mister Magic" and "Wine Light," that I had so cherished when I was a university student in California. My dancing partner's sleek, feminine physique was almost forgotten as the sweet remembrances of my African American friends, all of us dancing and singing together, washed away some of the more unpleasant ghetto memories.

As I twirled around, my back turned to her, I could feel two blue eyes piercing my protective armor; as I turned towards her, they were fixed squarely upon mine. Perhaps it was new for her to meet someone—especially a man—who did not stare at her appealing gyrations while dancing, her head turning from side to side, perhaps expecting every man to follow her as she turned and swayed across the dance floor. But she appeared to be a frustrated seductress, as her dance mate—me—was not giving her the attention she thought she was due.

I began to lead her to her table, which stood in the back of the dance floor. As we approached it, my eyes fixed on the timid, dark-haired girl standing farther away, closer to the wall, where she was talking with an elderly lady. I motioned to her to join us. She hesitated, pointing to herself with a question in her eyes; I nodded. She said goodbye to the lady and slowly sauntered over to us, as if she was on her way to a funeral, glum and sullen. I smiled as she placed her tiny purse on the table, trying to give her confidence and send her a message saying that I wanted to talk with her.

The blond looked on, openly curious. I asked the brunette her name; she responded that it was Sandrine. I was in the middle of introducing the blond to her when I stopped, realizing that I did not know her name either. I asked her and she replied that her name was "Marie Laure," but everybody called her Peggy. They looked at each other, then at me. It was a confusing, but funny moment. Finally, a voice over the loud speaker interrupted our conversation by announcing that the dance was over but all the party goers could meet for cocktails at a Russian bar at the Place Saint Michel in about an hour.

Not knowing what else to say, I suggested to the girls that we meet there in about an hour. We drifted to the door, following the others who were leaving. A couple ahead of us opened the main door and white flakes blew in, settling on our hair and shoulders. The first fallen snow of winter took us all by surprise!

We followed the crowd to the street where everyone was standing around in disbelief. Gathering around, we behold two to three inches of newly fallen snow, all of which had fallen during the past two hours while we were dancing inside. As we stood there, the crisp, snowy wind gusted against the sides of our heads, turning them around almost simultaneously.

Then one by one, two by two, the dance hall patrons began the thirty minute walk to the Place Saint Michel; slipping and sliding, some picked up snow balls and tossed them to others walking behind or to their friends walking beside them. Inspired by the white blanket of snow covering the balconies above and the streets below, I reached out and grabbed the hands of the two standing next to me and without thinking, started running slowly—they followed. As I slid, they slid with me across the street. Coasting into the tires of a parked car, we straightened our legs as our feet bounced off the tires, which catapulted us into the middle of the street into a tangled mess of feet, arms and legs. Laughing uncontrollably, I wondered if the others would think we were mad. I looked up and saw them running, throwing snowballs at each other, not paying the slightest attention to us.

We stood up, brushed the snow from our clothes and headed for the sidewalk. As we climbed over the curb, I picked up a snowball and flung it at Sandrine. It hit her in the back of the head and she turned to face me, coldly scowling at me. I did the same thing to Peggy who turned, her red cheeks burning, but she smiled all the same. For the next thirty minutes, time seemed to stand still. We sang nursery rhymes, childishly skipping over the snow-packed sidewalk. Crossing over into the street, running ahead of cars as the drivers slammed on their brakes, heading back toward the sidewalk, we stumbled and fell across it, sliding a few feet before stopping. I ran ahead of the girls, lobbing snowballs which fell at their feet. Sandrine continued to glare at me, her eyes deep inside her hood. Peggy was the closest to me and playfully smiled every time I tossed a snowball in her direction. Sometimes it found its mark, splattering over her tan hood.

As the distance grew between us and the dance hall, more and more people gave up the walk to the Place St. Michel, entering local "brasseries" to shelter themselves from the biting wind. As we reached a small square, I looked around and could not find any familiar cafes or other places—I was lost. Peggy and Sandrine caught up with me and were equally confused as to our location.

Sandrine pointed to a narrow street off to the right, the Rue Fosses St. Jacques, saying that we were next to the Pantheon and if we followed the street to Rue St. Jacques, it would lead us to the Boulevard Saint Germain. Without turning around, she began briskly walking down the street she had pointed out to us. Peggy and I followed; I did not really care where we were going—I was living for that moment of time, carefree, carrying out childish whims while letting the streets of Paris guide me to whatever corner they desired. Even more intriguing was that I was accompanied by two girls, extremely different in every way.

When we arrived about an hour later at the Russian café, we were soaked to the skin and cold. I opened the door and hot air immediately met my cold cheeks, my body welcoming the heat as we sought a table. Out of about seventy-five people that had been at the dance, only seven people had arrived and were seated at one table. We ended up finding a table completely isolated from the main group, and for the next hour I was subjected to a bizarre competition between Sandrine and Peggy. The latter boasted that she could play classical piano whereas Sandrine timidly responded by recounting her experiences as a member of the church choir.

It was so strange listening to them, contemplating my life in Paris spent alone most of the time; now my solitude was interrupted by this scene. It was implied that eventually I had to make a choice, and so I did, much to my regret later on.

My life, so full of new discoveries and insecurities, seemed to be opening to more of the same. Thus, after that fateful evening, I sought the company of the candidate least likely to make a lifelong companion, most likely to keep me guessing—doubting even my own identity, I chose Peggy. I ran into Sandrine following that evening from time to time at youth group gatherings, but we only exchanged cordial greetings, nothing more. My attention thereafter focused on the seduction of Peggy.

We met a few times in cafés where we would, at first, exchange bits of small talk until we grew comfortable with each other. It turns out that she had not finished high school and was registered at a local private school to learn accounting and secretarial skills.

I invited her to dinner at the Russian café where we had spent that memorable evening with Sandrine a few weeks earlier. I arrived about thirty minutes late. I opened the door of the café and sitting at a table on the opposite side were Peggy and a bearded man. I approached the table as Peggy turned her head in my direction. She triumphantly introduced Antoine as her very close friend, while subtly smiling at him. She then informed me he was an archeology major at the University of Paris. He responded to this attention with a wide grin, promptly sliding his chair closer to her. His black hair was an anarchic jumble, except for a brush above his brow, which curled his hair to keep out of his eyes. His face was rather pudgy, meaty with pale, plump cheeks—"My rival," I thought to myself.

That evening, Peggy played the role of referee and provocateur. Antoine was clearly anti-American and voiced his opposition to uncultivated Americans coming to Paris, with their chocolate-stained shirts and cameras hanging from any available body part. I countered by suggesting that not all Americans were like that; many were, in fact, very cultivated, such as great writers like Hemmingway, Mark Twain, and political figures like Abraham Lincoln and John Kennedy, etc. Peggy intervened by commenting that she had read something by Faulkner.

I had to admit that I knew much more about French literature. Antoine began his interrogation of me in this area, questioning my knowledge of Victor Hugo, Rousseau, Voltaire, Zola, Balzac and others. Realizing that I could hold my own in that area, the subject of the conversation quickly changed to archeology, his specialty. During his monologue about the latest paleontology discoveries, Peggy, who was sitting on a sofa, laid her head to rest on the back of it, her eyes half closed.

She then told us that she did not feel well. I knocked over the wine glass as I reached for her arm, to comfort her. Antoine reached for her with the same result. If someone had been present with a camera and shot a picture at that time, it would have depicted a short-haired, bearded man and a long-haired adolescent both touching the arm of the queen...and a table with two overturned wine glasses and matching red stains on the white tablecloth.

Peggy's face was flushed, with red splotches peeking out from under strands of unrestrained hair falling over her face. She pushed back the sofa and leaned forward, attempting to stand up. Antoine quickly slid his chair over, smiled, and again touched her arm.

"Can I help you?" His voice was such a purposefully loud whisper, that even Peggy cringed a bit.

"No, thank you; I'll be fine." Peggy stood up and wandered through the maze of chairs until she arrived at the foot of the staircase winding upwards. My eyes followed her as she turned her head slightly towards our table and then slowly walked up the stairs.

Silence reigned at the table. Antoine, sitting right across from me, stared at the empty wine glass. I tried to make conversation by asking Antoine how long he had known her.

"Probably a lot longer than you," he replied.

I did not understand the subtle, bitter tone in his voice. I continued, changing the subject.

"I wonder how Peggy is doing." He shrugged his shoulders.

His affected nonchalance motivated me to take some initiative. I excused myself and in a few seconds I had climbed to the top of the stairs. Out of the corner of my eye, I saw Antoine's face was pointed, like that of an Irish setter, in my direction. Peggy was waiting in line outside the women's bathroom. As I approached her, she appeared to be gloomy, her small features set in a slight frown. She leaned against the wall; strands of her dark blond hair shrouded her somber face. I held my hand out and she took it and placed my arm around her neck; then she leaned her head back, resting on my arm.

All of a sudden, she turned her head; her eyelashes began fluttering, her face maintaining its somber expression as she said, "I feel strange, like I want to make love or something."

If I had been closer to the stairway, I may have fallen down. My knees buckled slightly. That was the last thing I would have expected coming from her mouth. I could not respond to such a clear-cut invitation, believing that it was not made to me, personally. Before I could collect my thoughts, an elderly lady opened the bathroom door and exited, holding a tiny, shaggy dog in her left arm. Peggy opened the door and abruptly closed it behind her—the suspense increased minute by minute.

As we strolled back to the stairs, I dared reach for her hand. She did not let it go until we reached the stairs and her eyes met Antoine's, who followed our progress down the stairs to the table.

He said sardonically, "Hope you enjoyed yourselves."

Peggy reached for his hand in order to reassure him that she didn't favor me, but also to make me jealous, especially in light of her earlier statement.

After one last round of red wine, Peggy announced that it was late and if we did not hurry up, we'd miss the last subway. After paying the waiter, we headed for the door and within a few minutes, found ourselves weaving in and out of the labyrinth at the Odeon station.

I told her I would be taking the subway headed toward Porte Orleans; Peggy mumbled that she wasn't sure when Antoine interrupted saying that he would accompany her, then headed to the Clignancourt car, going in the opposite direction. I stood there dumbfounded as Peggy tugged at my hand with hers while her other was being gently pulled by Antoine. As a human chain we headed to the Clignancourt exit.

When we arrived at the latter, I expected to say good-by to both of them when, without warning, Peggy kissed Antoine's cheeks, French style—two times on each cheek—then abruptly, almost coldly, stated, "Antoine, good night. We'll have to leave you here."

Antoine stood there, confused, smiling nervously, following us with his eyes as we turned away toward our subway entrance at the end of the corridor. I felt his presence, even after we had turned the corner and lost him from view.

This was such a strange turn of events that I could not muster up much conversation as we exited the subway a few minutes later. We found ourselves soon standing in front of Saint-Sulpice; at 1:00 in the morning, the mist was settling over the two towers rising above the square, Place Saint-Sulpice. Only a few people were wandering along the sidewalk bordering it. We walked slowly to the rooming house where I was staying, hand in hand, an anxious silence between us. The quiet evening and shadows of Saint-Sulpice contrasted with the pulsing feelings within me, confusion alternating with happiness and sadness. I wanted to know how the evening would go, what was going to happen ahead of time. But for the moment, I cherished the delicious anguish of not knowing if we were to talk the rest of the evening, sharing our most intimate dreams, or make love among the soft pillows piled high on my single bed in the rooming house.

She finally broke the long silence: "I love this place; it is so calm, but so full of history." She explained to me that the two towers of the church, standing directly in front of us, were completely different—one was completed while the other appeared unfinished, its bare sides evidence that the work had stopped for an unknown reason. She explained to me that it was probably due to one of the many wars that had ravaged the city that one tower was left unfinished, thereby providing a monument to the consequences of war. Another Parisian standing nearby informed me that the striking difference was due to the fact that the two towers were not designed by the same architect and that one of the architects, depressed over the results, committed suicide by jumping off one of the towers. To this day, the two towers remain notably different and I am still not sure which story is true.

As we climbed the stairs of the rooming house on our way to the fifth floor, my knees began to slightly buckle with nervous trepidation; I wondered if this was all wrong—I hardly knew her. Why was I already inviting her to my room? Yet, perhaps she was inviting herself; perhaps she was orchestrating all this, and I was going along with it out of intrigue and a desire to be close to her. My intuition told me we were going too fast, yet I wanted to be spontaneous. I chastised myself for fearing the unknown and tried to convince myself that letting go in unbridled sexual expression was "true love." My deeper thoughts, however, kept returning to the truth, giving me an empty feeling as I contemplated both being manipulated into a sexual encounter and my own amorous fantasies...and fears.

Climbing the last flight of stairs, warmth spread through me with the knowledge I would not be alone that night. I fumbled in my pockets for my keys and for an instant, panicked at the thought I might have lost them in the confusion of the night—that our opportunity to share love would be forever postponed. I finally found the keys in my overcoat pocket, where I must have placed them as I hurried down the stairs that morning.

The long, cast-iron key reminded me of the ones I had seen only in the movies. It turned and grated against the old iron interior of the keyhole. The door creaked open, and we entered the room in the dark. I groped for the small lamp on a chest of drawers next to the bed. Peggy sat in the chair next to the bed, since that was the only one in the room. I guessed she did not want to appear too forward by sitting immediately on the bed. I sat there, however, as I had no other place except the floor.

We contemplated each other in the total silence. She leaned back in the chair, in the same position as earlier at the Russian café, her eyes closed slightly. Then she said that she was tired and needed to sleep. She began undressing: her boots first, then pants, blouse, and scarf, without looking at me. She appeared to have no qualms about being naked in front of a man that she did not know. I got up, trying to occupy myself; while washing my face in a wash basin I noticed in the mirror that she had slipped between the covers.

I naively supposed that her fatigue had overcome her modesty, and she desperately needed to sleep. Letting go of thoughts of lovemaking, I decided to sleep in the chair next to the bed and walked to the drawer to pull out a thin, gray cover. I would be cold that night but I was in ecstasy to share my room with somebody rather than be inside four empty walls. Sitting in the chair and pulled the cover over me. Up to that point, her face had been turned toward the wall. She rolled over, her eyes opening slightly.

"Aren't you going to accompany me? I'm cold."

I gallantly took my clothes off to come to the aid of the young lady, thinking that we might rub our bodies together within the cold sheets, but our intimacy would be reserved for another time, upon knowing each other better. As I slipped between the sheets next to her, she turned away from me, but then slid her frame up against my trembling one.

This was so unforeseeable that I withdrew a bit, then realized by doing that, I would not be complying with my chivalrous duty to warm her cold body. She continued to rub her back against my chest, which I interpreted as an advance. She was in total charge as I knew not what to do, without appearing overly eager to join our bodies in warm caresses.

She continued to rub against me. I was overcome with emotion at the prospect of joining our hearts that evening. I then succumbed to her overtures, grasping her with my arms, our bodies intertwining. Outside, Paris hummed with life, enveloping both of us in love's embrace, behind gossamer curtains in the heart of the left bank.

Chapter VI

Romance and Illusions

We lay there until the flickering of the moon's rays through the curtains created a design of light and dark forms dancing on the stone floor.

My head next to hers on the pillow we shared, the warm, rhythmic exhalations on my cheek made it clear that she had fallen into a deep sleep. I quietly tiptoed around the room, collecting articles of clothing strewn about the floor. I could not at first find my sweater, rolled up in a ball under my bed, but it didn't bother me that I could not figure out how it got there. I was in a daze, a moonlit Paris daze, filled with emotions coming from places I never knew existed before. The aged hue of the old city added a profound luster to the smooth, youthful girl lying beneath the covers. My love—an ageless feeling so intense I had even forgotten how I met her, how we got there—the delicious beauty of the moment was all that mattered.

I made my way down the stairs and arrived at the ground floor, the "rez-de-chaussée," where I had two choices: to go out the main door or through a partially opened door which had always been closed. I chose the latter, opening the door wider; it opened into a lobby which I quickly entered. As I walked among the easy chairs and sofas, I noticed a kitchen to the left. There must have been a party there earlier that night as the drain boards were loaded with dirty dishes containing half-eaten pieces of strawberry cake, "baba rhum" and other pastries. I looked in vain for a coffee maker in hopes that I could offer a cup to my guest. Opening a cupboard door containing clean dishes, trays and silverware, I closed it and decided to leave the premises in search of coffee and hot croissants, which I would take to Peggy for breakfast.

I left the building and turning the corner, directly in front of me was the famous Saint-Germain des Près market which had barely opened for business. I easily found a bakery café, the odor of freshly baked butter croissants filling the air with a sweet warmth blanketing me from the harsh cold outside. I bought four oven-fresh croissants and two cups of coffee. The waitress trusted me with coffee in regular coffee cups upon my promise to return them after breakfast. I wondered if anywhere else in the world I could take coffee "to go" in real ceramic coffee cups without knowing the bakery attendant.

I made my way back to the rooming house and entered the lobby, easily finding my way to the kitchen. There I found a clean dish in which I placed the croissants, a sugar bowl with white and brown sugar cubes, and spoons. Placing everything on a tray, I headed upstairs.

I opened the door to the room to find Peggy sitting up, a blue haze shimmering in her eyes as if she were not there, as if she were a million miles from me.

"Bonjour," she said ever so slightly, with little emotion—this from the lips of someone with whom I had been so passionately intertwined, just a couple of hours earlier.

And yet she seemed so distant, sitting in the shadows created by the play of early morning sunlight and the outgoing radiant moon filtering into my room.

"Bonjour," I responded.

As I carried the tray into the room, her barely open eyes, showing the faint remnants of deep slumber, lit up. I set the tray on the bed and our attention shifted to the warm buttered croissants and steaming hot coffee in the small espresso cups.

We sat on the side of the bed, munching on the pastries and sipping the coffee. The sun's rays became more blurred as morning proceeded; as it rose, spreading sunshine everywhere, the last remnants of the stubborn moon vanished. It was almost as if it was trying to hold onto the magic of the night before, as it and our kisses faded into the awakening of day.

After breakfast, Peggy had to leave so that she could be at her parents' apartment in Montmartre before they awoke. I walked to the door with her and accompanied her down the stairs. At the bottom, I wrapped my arms around her and kissed her gently on the cheek. Then she opened the door and was gone before the espresso taste had left my mouth. I slowly mounted the stairs, opened my door and buried myself in the covers and within seconds I was fast asleep.

After that night, witnessed by a sultry Parisian moon, Peggy would visit me during the last hour before I was to close the organic food shop. She would usually make her "grand entrance" about 6 p.m., walk across the main floor while waving to me, and carrying herself proudly, briskly make her way towards the back of the store as I rang up a client on the cash register. She acted as if she were the owner of the place: sitting at a wooden table with two or three wooden chairs, she would watch me, as if she was supervising my work. Then, she would wait for me to count the money in the till and clean the premises.

After bidding goodnight to my Moroccan friends who worked in the kitchen at the end of the corridor, I would invite Peggy to step out the main door which I closed behind us. We then walked to Rue de Verneuil near the Seine, my new place of residence for the past month since moving from the rooming house near Saint-Sulpice. I had a small room called a "chambre de bonne," (maid's room) located on the eighth floor of one of many old, but well-kept bourgeois apartment buildings in the seventh district of the Left Bank. There was no elevator; this was a carry-over from earlier times when well-to-do families living in the large, luxurious apartments in the district each provided maid's quarters on the highest floor of the building. Accommodations usually consisted of a small room big enough for a bed, a small table and a water faucet with cold, running water. The bathroom, located off the hallway outside the room, contained a toilet consisting of a hole in the cement and a lever to flush water through it.

The room was painted blue; hence we christened it the "chambre blue." We reveled in each other, the first few nights in our new location, totally absorbed in our seemingly endless passion.

One night, after supping on organic vegetable crepes and sipping fruit juice, as we lay in bed wrapped snugly in each other's arms, I suggested to her that she move in and we live as common-law husband and wife. She smiled, giggled and in her soft, squeaky voice, said "On verra" (We'll see), rolled over with her back to me and fell fast asleep.

Peggy had a friend who worked in the Ministère de la Culture (Ministry of Culture) who gave her free tickets to the symphony and the opera and was allowed to invite a guest to all performances. We would sometimes sit in the box reserved for dignitaries and watch a famous symphony perform below us. I remember clearly, one night we arrived early and were ushered to the sumptuous box in the center of the symphony hall; it was the best seat in the house. When the usher closed the door of the box, we wrapped our arms around each other in an embrace that seem to last forever. When we separated, I could only dream of the next time we would kiss like that. In an hour the symphony started. It was entitled "The Works of Debussy"; the dream-like music sent me to a faraway fantasy world as I held Peggy's hand tightly in mine.

After the performances, we would walk the streets, talking about life in California, France, and literature. She seemed so intrigued by everything, especially when I described the redwood tree groves of northern California, where I was raised—her voice would resonate with energy and dynamism. I would watch as her chestnut-colored hair, held in a tight bun on top of her head during the performance, gradually became unfastened during the evening and would blow freely as we walked down the Avenue des Champs-Elysées. The gold-tinged waves would flow over her shoulders, arms and face, covering her red cheeks, but barely tempering their radiance.

I was getting used to the luxury of living, working, studying and loving in Paris. However, my idyllic existence was greatly impacted by her occasional absences. After spending an evening together, she would tell me she would return the next day to the organic food store at closing time but Peggy would often fail to arrive as planned. I would close the store even an hour later, in hopes that she would finally arrive, but to no avail. I would slowly trudge to the cold maid's room, high above the skyline of the city of love— without my love.

Three to four days later, she would show up around closing time, as if nothing had happened, sit in the same place at the wooden table, and stare at me until the last customer had left. I would walk slowly over to her, trying not to show my desperation, and sit down next to her, taking her hand. I would usually break the silence by expressing my disappointment that she had not at least phoned me at the store to tell me why she could not come.

She would say that she had forgotten our rendezvous or she had gone on a retreat to some monastery in the south of France for three days, which she needed to do in order to return to her spiritual self. She would ask me to forgive her. By then, my cheeks were inflamed with desire and passion; I would forget her transgressions the moment I was in her arms in the "chambre blue."

But I could neither understand nor accept her unannounced absences, which became more frequent. Each time we parted, I wondered if I would ever see her again. I almost felt that she understood how anxious I was, a feeling which welded me even more fervently to her when we were together again. It felt like her absences were designed to make me even more dependent on her, more jealous and desperate, aggravated daily by the fear of losing her. She must have known this as her absences almost always followed an impassioned evening together in "our" place, overlooking the turbulent waters of the Seine.

One night, after a week during which she had been absent, Peggy arrived just as I was locking the door of the store. I felt a faint tap on my left shoulder and turned around, startled. She was standing directly in front of me, a wide, Cheshire-cat grin on her face and a bouquet of flowers in her hand. I told her I was busy that night, that I wished she had contacted me earlier. I left her standing in the shadows of the closed store and walked down Rue du Bac. As I turned the corner, I spied, out of the corner of my eye, her lean silhouette, the flowers still in her hand, standing in the doorway.

In fact, I had decided that no matter what happened, I would not give in to her charms and that I would return to my room and study that night since I was about three weeks behind in my classes. And besides, I wanted to teach her that she could not show up whenever she liked and sleep with me, whisper how much she loved me and then disappear in the early morning light, not to be heard from for a week.

After slowly opening the door to the room, whose blue walls had faded to a sullen gray, I stepped inside, closed the door behind me and fell limp on the bed. Then with an impulsiveness impassioned by conflicting desires surging within me, I jumped up and stormed out, violently slamming the door behind me. I leaped down the stairs, clearing four to five steps at a time, and ran the five blocks to the front of the food store. From a distance, I thought I saw her slender shadow, even the flowers waiting for my gentle touch; upon arriving close enough, a half a block away, I saw merely the shadow of the mailbox next to the door—Peggy was not there. I ran to the subway stop, tore down the stairs, jumping over three to four steps at a time. I entered the quay of the subway only to find it deserted.

I returned to my room, feeling even more abandoned and lonely. The tears flowed as I flopped on my bed; slamming my fist repeated into the pillow, I finally fell into an exhausted sleep.

I castigated myself the next day for turning into an emotional sop. Looking at myself in the small mirror hanging from a nail over the sink, I saw a red-eyed, naïve boy in love with a girl who was in charge of his soul, disposed to do anything she pleased, whenever she pleased. I decided that I must not see her again or she would make an emotional puppet out of me, and that soon, I'd be worthless to myself and the world.

Vowing not to spend any more time with her, that is how I began my day. After going to class, which I had missed for the past two weeks, I went to the organic food store to begin work at 4 p.m. As I opened the door and walked in, I noticed there were no customers. I walked past the organic vegetable bins and observed Cecile, the woman who I usually replaced to begin the evening shift, sitting at the wooden table. Her short, brown hair hugged the side of her plump, dimpled face. She was talking to a young girl with a pink scarf and naturally bright-red cheeks…Peggy.

I was upset she would just show up and linger where I worked, pretending everything was all right—again. Even though I showed no emotion, Cecile, a sensitive woman, sensed a problem and said, "Frank, come sit down in my chair. If you wish, I can serve the clients while you speak to your fiancé in private."

"My fiancé?" I thought to myself. I nodded as she stood up and quickly made her way behind the cash register as two customers came in through the front door. I sat opposite Peggy; she looked at the painting hanging on the wall, full of rich reds, blues and purples. I gazed at the shiny, hardwood floor, not knowing what to say as emotion surged through me, battling my brain for hegemony.

"Je suis désolé," (I'm sorry) she said, her eyes meeting mine and, finding an emotional receptivity in them, she continued:

"I came early, this time, to avoid missing you." Her small mouth curled down as I fidgeted in the chair, tongue-tied, my cheeks burning. My passion, my love for her, my profound desire to be with her persisted in spite of the vow I had made earlier, which fell into the archives deep within me, buried and forgotten, forever.

Instead of returning to the chambre de blue, we decided to go out that night. But first, she said she had to deliver a document to a friend. We took a series of subways until we arrived at the gateway to the Marais, one of Paris' cultural artistic centers, at the time.

Peggy walked briskly ahead. As we approached a tall apartment building on the other side of the museum of modern art, the Beaubourg, she stopped so abruptly I almost fell over her. She entered a code for what was apparently a telephone intercom system; the door opened. We entered a small, obscure lobby that contained two chairs, a lamp and a table; it was almost as barren as a prison holding cell. The furnishings were minimal since the room was for people awaiting the elevator. The elevator returned and Peggy, before entering, told me she would be five minutes. My gaze shifted up, focusing on a box above the elevator shaft revealing an arrow and the number of each of the floors. It finally stopped and pointed at number 6, the floor where Peggy must have exited.

Several minutes passed and no Peggy. The elevator descended several times to either take passengers to the ground floor or pick up passengers; each time the elevator door opened, I positioned myself in front, but there was no sign of her. Forty-five minutes passed and I was castigating myself for going with her, for entering again into her web of questionable stories and maddening midnight rendezvous, for again being a dupe, soft putty in her hands. When the elevator began its descent one more time, I decided if Peggy was not on it, I would leave.

As the door opened, Peggy entered the lobby. I was sitting in the lone chair next to the window, on the opposite side of the room.

I yelled across the room, letting it all out, all the accumulated frustration: "You said you'd be gone only five minutes; you've been keeping me waiting for over forty-five!"

She responded, "Oh sorry, Frankie. I had to speak to someone."

"I thought you said that you were just going to drop off a document."

She responded, "Yes, but I also wanted to quickly talk to someone. He was my former boyfriend, who had dumped me. I wanted to enjoy the moment when he'd make advances at me and then I would tell him that a young man was waiting for me downstairs. That young man is you. I just wanted to get back at him since he had treated me so badly."

My heart pumped as I responded, "But you did not need to bring me in on it or at least you should have told me about it. I did not need to waste forty-five minutes since I have other, better things to do with my time." She said that she was sorry and that she would not do that again. But that was not the end of it.

A week later, it would be the fourteenth of July, a Friday night. That night, we planned to go to a dance at a local fire station: that was the tradition on Bastille Day, celebrating the storming of the Bastille during the French Revolution. On Wednesday, she arrived a few minutes before closing, as usual, and we went directly to the chambre blue. She wanted to dress up for the occasion on Friday, but she did not have enough money to buy a dress. I gave her 50 francs but it was not enough; she needed another 100. I told her that I did not have it.

Friday came. The plan was that she was to meet me at the chambre blue. I had given her a set of keys so she could arrive before me and make preparations. I arrived a little late. As I turned the iron key in the aged key hole, I heard water running inside. The door opened to reveal Peggy bending over the sink, washing her face; she wore a flowing, bright-red evening gown. She stood up and drops of water rolled down her face and onto the dress. She came to me and hugged me with her wet hands.

"Do you like the dress?" she asked, her brow arched, waiting for my response. She then stepped back a few paces as I closed the door.

"Tu es ravissante!" (You are smashing, beautiful!)

The color of her cheeks matched the deep, blush-red of her dress. I quickly put on my suit and tie. It was 11 p.m., and still not too late. We rushed down the stairs and headed to the fire station. A half a block away, the folksy sound of the accordion tantalized us. At the entrance, there were people of all ages lined up, waiting to get in; we slipped through the crowd, weaving through and around those who were dancing, singing and drinking and the children playing tag. We finally arrived at the main dance area situated in front of the live band, consisting of several accordion players, a drummer and a guitarist. They were wearing shiny hats of red, white and blue, the colors of the French flag. The white teeth of the accordion players flashed under enormous black mustaches as they dipped their shoulders, sometimes swinging their accordions around to the beat of French folk songs.

I led Peggy to a position right in front of the band. She gently held the side of her dress between her index finger and thumb as we danced the "rock Français." She smiled when I spun her around on the tips of her toes as the band increased the tempo; it was like "déjà vu", as I reminisced about the first time I had met her, on the dance floor of the student club at the Place de la Sorbonne.

As the music took us back all the way to the French revolution, when the "Marseillaise" was played by the exuberant musicians, we slid into the mood of old France, the music, the ambiance. Yet I wondered if I knew her better than that first day I had met her at the student club. I brushed those thoughts away as she took my arm and spun me around, nearly into the crowd standing next to us.

The next morning, I awoke to a sun beating down on us at midday. Peggy was already up and washing herself at the basin. After exchanging "Bonjours," she mumbled something about going to see a photographer and if I so desired, I could accompany her.

When we arrived at the studio in the northwest of Paris, she told me to wait outside, that she would only be a few minutes. She pressed a button then entered and closed the door behind her. I moved closer to the building; it was an independent, one-story structure wedged in between two five-story apartment complexes. Through the window, I watched a young, bearded man hug Peggy and lead her into a room with photography equipment, landscape backdrops and tall lamps. He closed the door behind them.

After forty minutes, I began pacing the walkway outside the building. I felt so foolish that I had let her do this to me again. I thought to myself that she must have thought I was an easy touch, that she could drag me around to her boyfriends and suitors and then use me, perhaps to provoke jealousy in the others. *And why is it always a bearded man?* I scowled. I decided to leave this time and started to walk away. After a few yards, I stopped myself, returned and pressed the same button that Peggy had before she entered the studio. After a few minutes, I saw the bearded man open the door, Peggy following him, her hair mussed.

I imagined that I could give in again to her charm and ignore this latest episode. But this time I was determined not to let her behavior slide. As soon as we were alone, I told her that she had made me wait again while she cavorted with a man. Before she could answer I continued:

"I do not trust you anymore and you clearly have no respect for me after what you have done lately. How dare you make me wait while you have relations with someone else! In any case, this will be the last time that you will use me again in that way. I feel like a total fool to have trusted you again. So, leave me now; I am going to walk to my room."

I turned and started walking—I could hear her footsteps behind me. I began walking faster, but she kept up with me. Turning to her, I said, "It's no use following me. You will not, in any way, share the rest of this evening with me."

She responded, the edges of her mouth beginning to quiver slightly: "You are a jealous fool. I only had a quick session with a photographer, who has offered to find me a job as a model. You are so childish!"

I turned to the left and headed for the subway, walking very quickly before entering the subway turnstiles.

Returning to my room, I was not looking forward to sleeping alone. I vowed never to see her again; I had fallen victim to her designs involving other men, who she sought to manipulate as she manipulated me. My simple country upbringing had not provided me with the experience to understand what was happening nor with a way to defend myself from her jaded intrusions into my heart.

Two miserably lonely weeks went by without seeing her. I had her phone number— she stayed with her parents—but I resisted the temptation to call her. As each day passed, I grew more and more anxious to see her. Whenever the door to the shop opened, I would quickly glance over to see if she had finally come.

To fill the void, I spent more and more time reading about Eastern religions, especially Islam. I bought a language cassette course and began studying the Arab language for one hour a day. At the end of the day, I would retreat to the garden where I would continue meeting my Moroccan friends. We drank mint tea while discussing the beauties of Islam and the truths taught by the prophet Muhammad.

One day, as I was arranging the fruit bins, my boss, Mrs. Fontaine, tapped me on the shoulder and motioned that I should join her for lunch. She invited me to partake of a delicious onion pie, sprinkled with comestible yeast. She was a middle-aged vegetarian; her reddish-gray hair hung over her brow as she savored each morsel of her vegetarian "galette". Her large, hazel eyes—radiating intensity and openness— seemed to animate my entire being. Her smile reflected a kindness of spirit and revealed two rows of pearly-white teeth. She was wearing one of her long granny dresses, as usual embroidered with flowers. It gracefully fell over her shoulders and upper arms.

I decided that it was a good time to inform her of my decision to visit Morocco for a month and that I would be leaving in one month. She was not surprised as she had heard me talking to the Moroccan kitchen workers; she told me not to worry that she would have no problem finding someone to replace me during my absence. I thanked her for being so kind and understanding and I got up to go. She reached over to me and pressed her hand on my arm while asking me to sit down.

She said, "By the way, your girlfriend borrowed 100 francs from me to buy a dress for the 14th of July celebration and said she would pay me back in a couple of days. It's been two weeks since I saw her. What's happened to her?"

Emotions whirled inside of me: I could not believe Peggy would have dared to borrow money from my boss and then not pay her back. I pulled out my wallet and took out two 50 franc bills and put them on the table in front of Mrs. Fontaine. She folded the two bills and slid them into her blouse pocket, and smiled. I returned to work.

One day while I was working in the fruit bin section, replacing overly ripe apples with fresh ones, a gentle tap on my shoulder sent a chill from the middle of my back to the ends of my toes. Before I could turn around, a little voice spoke,

"Monsieur, could you please sell me a kilo of butter cookies?"

It was her. My eyes closed as I gritted my teeth to contain my emotions. Then I faced her. Looking into her hazel-blue eyes made me completely forget about the money she had borrowed from my boss.

"Bonjour. Ca va?" (Hello. You ok?) I responded coldly, as distantly as possible. But the twinkle in her eyes showed clearly that she was not fooled. I had not changed—I was still putty in her hands, to shape as she so desired. At her whim, I could be transformed into a happy-go-lucky young man, the passions flowing with first love, or an anguished introvert, trying to hold on to an elusive love. Knowing that she "had my number," she smiled and walked over to the cookie bins to the left of the fruit section.

It seemed unfair. She, acting the part of a customer, had found a captive and faithful audience since she knew, as an employee, I was bound to follow and assist her. The owner was standing behind the counter, inspecting the display of products and different breads; I could not coldly tell Peggy, as I had rehearsed a hundred times, to "Get out of my life—get out and never come back."

That soft, little voice and the silk waves of her chestnut hair still were massaging we with invisible hands as I stood in back of her, describing the ingredients of the "petits fours" (small pastries or cookies) she indicated. She finally made her selection—a kilo of hazelnut cookies. I weighed them under the careful supervision of the owner, who had approached from behind the counter. Pretending to do an inventory of the jelly jars, she carefully observed us out of the corners of her eyes, a puzzled expression on her face.

Peggy followed me to the cash register, where I took a bill of 50 francs from her and gave her 30 francs change. When she reached for the change, she left a small folded piece of paper on the counter in front of her. She nodded to my boss (who was still pretending to be busy, this time arranging the organic breads in back of me), and not saying anything about the money she had borrowed from her, left the store. Closing the door, she looked back briefly. I was still standing at the register, the piece of paper carefully placed beside it.

After Mrs. Fontaine left later on, I tried opening the piece of paper but it fell to the floor; my nervous fingers quickly grabbed it. The note read, "Please call me tonight after 8 p.m. I love you." It was a good thing that the owner had already left, as she would certainly have noticed the brilliant red of my cheeks, the result of a tidal wave of emotions.

That night after closing the shop, I walked to the café at the corner of Rue du Bac and Boulevard Raspail. Sitting next to the window in a room adjoining the bar, sipping my café crême, I waited for the clock on the wall to strike 8 o'clock. The second hand ticked in unison with my heartbeat, which seemed to intensify with each pulse. At the appointed time, I went immediately to the public phone located in the cellar with the bathrooms. They were unclean and the suffocating stench was at first unbearable. But after I dialed her number and I could hear the phone ringing, the intense smell dissipated.

Peggy responded after two rings. I simply informed her that I wanted to talk to her at the café. She replied, "Chéri, il est tard..." (Dear, it is late...)

"Now!" I interrupted.

A long silence followed, a silence in which I could almost feel the pounding of my heart in my ears. My hand trembled as it clamped down on the telephone to hold it against my ear. I was bathed in perspiration—drops formed under my ear and trickled down the sides of my tense neck.

"I'll be there in an hour."

An hour-and-a half later, she arrived, wearing a flowing purple, gold and black dress, her hair with the usual bun carefully wound on top of her head. Her entrance lit up the brasserie. Through the mirror on the wall of the adjoining room, I could see everything that was happening at the bar. Middle-aged men were drinking beer and smoking, their red eyes following her as she walked by. I saw her come in but my elation turned to anguish as I saw the triumphant expression on her face, her small mouth in a broad smile, her blue-gray eyes shining as she came over to me. We kissed each other's cheeks, French style.

She sat facing me awhile, without saying a word. Finally, "Voila, je suis là." (Well, here I am.)

I nodded. After all the days of tormented, imaginary discussions with her, I was speechless. She broke the ice.

"Tu m'as manqué," (I missed you) she said, reaching for my withdrawing hands, grabbing them and holding them in hers. My hands trembled but I kept them in hers, afraid to let go, as if it was for the last time. I told her about my plans to travel to Morocco in a couple of weeks; she thought it was a fantastic idea. It was the first time I had revealed to her my interest in learning Arabic and visiting Maghreb. I told her about the Moroccan kitchen workers who had inspired me to take this trip.

She told me that she knew a couple who would let her use their studio while they were away on vacation, and that I could save money before the voyage if I stayed there with her. Without waiting for a response, she began reminiscing about the fun we had had going to the symphonies and holding hands during the entire productions. Our chairs edged closer as we spoke; we finally ended up touching each other as our lips gently met. We were back!

That night, she stayed with me in the chambre blue. The next day was Saturday and we made plans to move to the new location. I paid my rent for the month and left a note for the landlord on the way out. I did not have many possessions so we could take everything in only one trip.

The studio apartment was located on the fifth floor of an apartment building overlooking a small square, near the Place de la Republic. Walking up the flights of stairs was slow going lugging two suitcases, one in each hand; Peggy carried a long duffle bag loaded with bedding.

When we reached the fifth floor, we were exhausted. Peggy found the two, large wrought iron keys in her purse and opened the big locks, one at a time. As the top key turned, the grating noise did not even bother me as I sat on the brown suitcase, my energy having been drained long ago.

We entered the small studio, consisting of a kitchen with a double-bed mattress, and set the luggage and bedding in the corner. Peggy opened the window wide, the better to embrace the panorama of tall trees surrounding the square outside.

I finally got my dream: we were to live together for two weeks. During that period, Peggy made dinner using organic foods—sometimes an omelet with organic mushrooms— and for desert, she would soak wheat berries and then douse them with honey and a squeeze of lemon, a concoction we would eat while sipping cinnamon herbal tea.

One day as she was preparing tea after dinner, Peggy mentioned that she had gone to the mayor's office to inform herself on certain procedures—marriage procedures. I sat looking out the window, my mind already traveling to Morocco; it was already floating over or skimming the dunes in the Sahara.

"Did you hear me?" she persisted.

"Yes, you said something about marriage documents. Why?"

She dropped the subject. I sat on the mattress with my back up against the wall. After serving the tea, she sat next to me, with her back also against the wall.

"I thought it would be easier for us to get married: that would simplify your immigration problems. After all, I could live with you and make you a good wife."

"We'll see about that after I return." My voice must have sounded distant as she did not respond. Instead, she rolled over and fell fast asleep.

After that, Peggy daily mentioned how nice it would be for us to live together, to even have children together. She was, perhaps, in her own way, trying to convince me to stay and not travel so far away.

The day of my departure approached. Peggy and I were sleeping in, when she turned to me and said in her small voice, "I could go with you. You need someone to take care of you."

I told her that the voyage would be difficult and sometimes I might be forced to sleep outside. She responded that it would not bother her, but I knew that she, having been born and raised in the city, was a true city slicker and unprepared to rough it on the road. As we hugged each other through the night, perhaps for the last time, deep emotions filled my heart. We both cried, trembling in the dark, mourning the impending dissolution of our intense passion; my sadness was somewhat tempered by visions of the path before me, leading to the doorstep of Africa.

Chapter VII

The Spanish Underground

There's such a big difference between traveling alone and leaving a station where someone knows you. I thought about Peggy; her smooth body was soothing to my course frame. I pictured her arms entwined around my neck, covered by my long hair. Her hands pulled at my beard...

"Ouch!" I cried.

I opened my eyes as Abdullah was tugging at my beard. Touching the sleeve of my sweatshirt, he said "You should visit where I was raised, in the hills around Tangier." He smiled.

With eyes half closed, I mumbled words, which seemed to fall on deaf ears as Abdullah cupped his ear with his hand. I made an effort to turn my head in his direction as I asked about the village where his family lived, his brothers and sisters, what the family did on weekends, silly things like that so that I could contemplate his invitation.

In the end, I accepted and told him I would be delighted to visit his family. He repeated his offer, promising to put me up in his parents' house for a few days. We agreed I was to give him French lessons in exchange for lessons in Arabic. I excitedly anticipated heading to the hills and meeting a nice mountain family after debarking the ferry in Tangier. I thought about sharing dinners with the family and eating couscous, a favorite North African dish that I had heard about in Paris.

We talked about the things we had in common, namely that we were both raised outside of a big city and shared a mutual disdain for it, with the tall buildings and the metro winding under the streets like a snake.

He sat back, cushioning himself, while he opened a plastic bag and retrieved a piece of flat bread. He mumbled a few words, then with yellowing teeth bit into the crust. He chewed each morsel until every crumb was gone. Each time he swallowed, he uttered more indistinguishable words. I couldn't help but watch him, how he ate so solemnly, so carefully. He noticed my observation and motioned with his hands to join him. I told him to wait a moment while I dug in my travel bag and found the jar of honey. Opening it, I handed it to him. He looked blankly at the dark, rich substance. I took a piece of flat bread and dunked it into the jar. He smiled and did the same.

Abdullah sat back, savoring the bread and honey, and began to look me over, from head to toe. Not a wrinkle was left out of his regard. I couldn't understand the strange expression upon his oval face; was it disdain or surprise that I had shared my honey with him? I felt fear, feeling apprehensive about what was in store for me across the Mediterranean.

46

The train hummed relentlessly. With every passing second, it seemed I was leaving the modern, bourgeois, intellectual world, traveling farther and farther south, as we rumbled toward the Mediterranean and beyond.

At Biarritz, we changed from a French to a Spanish train that would take us to Madrid. It was easy; we descended the steps and in front of us was the train that would lead us even farther away from civilization.

The only difference between the Maghreb express and this train was the instructions were in Spanish. We all managed to sit together in a cabin all to ourselves, about the same size as the other. The only difference was the yellow-white stuffing pouring out of the holes in the seat. I could already smell the fresh sea air of the Mediterranean as the train rolled on.

It was about 4 p.m. and we were all tired. I hadn't slept but a couple of hours since leaving Paris. I dozed off and the next thing I knew, the shrill horn of the train was blowing. I looked up as Abdullah announced that we were entering Madrid. Abdullah and Ibrahim must have awakened earlier; their possessions were neatly packed beside them. I frantically threw my things on the seat next to me and stuffed them into my backpack. I made sure the lid to the honey was screwed on tightly before putting it in my small travel bag and then dumped it inside my back pack.

As the train crawled through the suburb stations on the way to the central station in Madrid, people began to mass together on the quays. As the train arrived at the station, I looked out the window. Bedlam was more the rule than the exception: people weren't running, they were flying, some of the women with half-naked babies sucking at their bosoms. Baggage was flying, dogs were barking, control agents were screaming.

Ibrahim stood over me yelling, but all the train station commotion drowned him out. He gave up and motioned for me and Abdullah to follow him. He jumped off the train and was lost in the current of human bodies streaming down the quays, a tidal wave of movement fanning out in all directions. Abdullah launched himself after Ibrahim and I followed on his heels, touching the back of his olive green overcoat so as not to lose him. Abdullah seemed to know where he was going; we flew through an exit, a huge intersection of madness. He grabbed my shoulder and pointed to a sign indicating destinations and departures. I headed there and he followed. Abruptly, he pulled at my backpack, motioning me to stop. Leaning towards me, he yelled something in my ear. I vaguely understood that we were to change something. I returned a blank look. He laughed, his yellow teeth flashing a contrast to the gray, metal pillars of the train station.

Grabbing my hand, he pulled me down an adjoining corridor. After a maze of hallways and staircases, we arrived at a ticket office. I was finally able to hear Abdullah say something; he explained we had to buy tickets for the subway which would take us to another station, where we would catch the train to Costa del Sol, Spain, and then to his home. Abdullah pointed out that the tickets indicated our departure was in forty-five minutes and the subway would take thirty minutes to cross Madrid. My heart sank as my eyes followed the line snaking down the corridor to an adjoining waiting room.

He again grabbed my hand, pulled me across the room away from the line, motioning me to follow, and then took off running, luggage and all. I was on his heels, sometimes tripping over his ankles; he frowned as he looked back, without missing a beat. We jumped down a flight of stairs, taking two to three steps at a time, until we arrived at a turnstile—Abdullah climbed over, yanking me with him. I almost crashed through the doors of a subway stalled on the platform.

We fell into two seats in the corner of the subway car, as the doors screeched shut; the subway sped ahead with a clanking unknown to an almost soundless Parisian subway. The car was lined with graffiti in all colors and shapes, far from the clean, white walls of Paris cars. I assumed the hot, steamy air reflected the humid climate of a Madrilenian summer.

Abdullah, whose hands were plastered to the walls, was concentrated on reading the subway map, probably looking for our train station. He sat down beside me and rested his head in his outstretched hands.

I started to sputter a few words which did not get out. I just sat there watching Abdullah read the signs each time the subway stopped. I wanted to ask him which metro stop was the right one, but my voice refused to produce words. I was drained by the running and resigned to letting him inform me when we were to disembark.

Thirty minutes went by before Abdullah yelled at me that our stop was the next one. I put on my knapsack and stood behind him—he was already up and holding on to the lever of the door. The subway stopped and as he pulled the lever, the doors opened to let us out. Only a few minutes were left before departure, and he madly ran down the quay. On the way, he asked people questions and was directed to an exit at the end of the quay.

I don't know how I mustered the energy to do it, but I ran full speed on the heels of Abdullah. After running up and down a labyrinth of stairs, we arrived at the station; the departure sign loomed ahead. Abdullah was in full sprint. I started to falter and I fell on my knapsack; I couldn't go any farther. Perhaps his youth gave him more stamina, or maybe his faith. He turned back and yelled at me that the train was ahead, as a horn blared in the distance. I dragged myself off the filthy floor and chased after him.

The train in front of us was already moving. I began to slow down; it was all over, I sighed—we had missed the train. Before I could lament about being stuck in Madrid, I felt Abdullah lift me up and literally drag me to the back of the train which seemed to move in slow motion. We got abreast of the door which was miraculously not yet closed. Somehow Abdullah got behind me and with one big boost, shoved me through the door and then jumped through, landing on top of me. We laughed in relief as our bodies separated; I stayed scrunched up on the floor and couldn't move.

A train agent, who had been running alongside the train glared at us, blowing a whistle and motioning us off the train. He was in full stride and pounded the sides of the train in disgust as the doors closed. The wail of the whistle was lost in rumbling chugging as we dragged our belongings from cabin to cabin, looking for a couple of seats. The train was overflowing with people.

I looked for Ibrahim as we boarded the train. There was no sign of him. While we were walking down the corridor gasping for breath, in search for seats, I asked Abdullah what had happened to him.

He nonchalantly responded, "I can only guess that Ibrahim's phony passport was discovered by a train inspector who probably took him into custody. He'll be deported tomorrow."

48

His response was totally void of emotion, as if it was a common scenario. In any case, we didn't see him again. We found a cabin, a couple of cars from the one in which we had landed. This time it was full, except for two places in the middle of one seat. We stashed our belongings in the compartments above and sat down at about the same time as the ticket agent passed to ask for our tickets. Across from us sat a young man of about twenty-five years of age. He gave Abdullah the once over, then me. A robust, black-haired lady with bright red cheeks was speaking in Spanish to her daughter; she machine-gunned the words so fast I couldn't make out a single one.

I slouched deep down in the seat, which gave way a little to my weary frame. I fell fast asleep as the sweat rolled down my cheeks, my clothes sticking to my body like a wetsuit.

While dreaming, in a half-awake stupor, incessant thumping stirred me to open an eye. A strange cloud of darkness hovered over the room. I was helpless as I was only half awake and couldn't move my limbs. I wanted to cry out but my mouth would not open. I shook the sleep from my head and gradually awoke, as the cabin grew lighter—then the shadow returned. The silhouette of two people was reflected as they stood outside the door, turned toward the window. I soon realized the train had been traveling through a tunnel and the dark and light must have been the result.

Abdullah and the young man were missing from their seats. The train exited the tunnel and I saw both men had replaced the silhouettes. Abdullah turned his head toward the cabin and saw my eyes looking back at him. He motioned me to join them. I had to coax my reluctant joints into movement, stood up and lumbered out the cabin door.

Abdullah interrupted his conversation and said, "I want you to meet Muhammad."

I shook hands with the young man, the dark, copper skin on his face pulling into a grin displaying teeth as sharp as razors. His eyes danced with the gleam of someone older than his years. "Nice to meet you," I finally blurted out and Muhammad responded in broken English, rolling his 'r', "My pleasure. Are you American?"

I specified, "Yes, but I'm a resident of Paris. How about you?" He told me he was also living in Paris and studying engineering at one of the Universities of Paris. The exact name didn't register. "Abdullah tells me that you want to visit our country, and he will take you to his house. You are lucky—Moroccans are very hospitable people. Why you go there?" His left eyebrow rose above the other, curling like a huge question market, as he studied me. I was beginning to get used to such inspections, with curious brown eyes scanning my entire body, but I feared he would detect my thoughts from my eyes. Maybe experience in other cultures had taught them to be more observant, for fear of underestimating someone, perhaps not detecting a hidden knife.

My head hurt so much for lack of sleep that I excused my self for withdrawing to my seat in the middle of the conversation. Abdullah and Muhammad continued talking with their backs turned to the other cabin occupants.

It was announced over the loudspeaker that we were entering the town of Algeciras, Spain. The train's brakes screeched as the cabin cleared. The quays were clean and white and no masses of people were there to greet us, as in Paris and Madrid. The ocean breeze softly touched my cheeks and the sun's congenial rays warmed us as we hiked about a half-mile to the ferry that was to take us to the shores of Africa.

Chapter VIII

The Door Opens

We saw the massive white hull looming ahead long before we boarded her. As we walked along the paths leading to the ferry, we could already see people in the distance climbing the long ramp, while grasping guardrails, to the top. All noses pointed toward the gigantic ship like those of hunting dogs—it was to carry us to a new world.

As we approached, the masses began to join forces, all heading in the same direction. I glanced around and saw entire families moving toward the ship, the fathers wearing turbans. There were also American tourists, whom you could spot a mile away, sporting chocolate-stained shirts, with cameras dangling from their necks.

The ramp leading to the ship was backed up the from the bottom gates, through which we had just passed, to the top. As I glanced up the ramp about a hundred feet, I saw the cause of the slow-moving line. A row of inspectors and customs agents was seated behind a table, checking each person, his or her papers and luggage. Suitcases were strewn over the deck area as plastic-gloved agents carefully rummaged through their contents.

When we arrived, topside, the Ferry was already quite full; people occupied the corridors as far as the eye could see. Children were throwing balls, bouncing them and running all the way down the corridor, skipping over shoes, chased by dogs. Mothers chased after their urchins, who threw toys on the floor to impede their progress.

Tourists fanned their faces as the stifling summer sun beat down upon them. Some wore chic, white, wide-brimmed travel hats. There were old and young alike, babies in cradles, scheming adolescents—black, white, olive-skinned, I passed a kaleidoscope of people in an array of colors, all headed toward a new-world frontier, to the shores of Africa.

Paralyzing vibrations underneath the floor announced that the fanfare associated with departure was underway. I looked over the rail and noticed the main entrance was locked. The workers below untied the giant ropes that moored the ship and it began to inch its way from the dock.

Abdullah and Muhammad were stationed at the rail opposite the departure activity, their conversation still waging. I was abandoned but didn't care that much for the excitement of leaving was upon me.

As I walked to the head of the ferry, I saw the Rock of Gibraltar jutting out of the Mediterranean like a mountain towering over the flatlands. As we passed, I felt completely assured of leaving the European continent—western living, with all the cities, complexities, and materialism—for a country where I would be able to embrace a return to the basics. An ecstatic smile splashed over my face like sea water on the sides of the ship. My face was wind-swept as I peered through the fog, hoping to catch a glimpse of the North African coastline, hoping I would not be disappointed in my return to nature.

My Arab friends huddled together at the opposite railing, positioned a trifle ahead of me; out of the corner of my eye, I noticed them pointing at me. Beyond them glistened the lights of their city: Tangier. The ship was approaching my first taste of African soil. The last thing on my mind was the return from this paradise, removed from the civilization I had known. I could never have predicted my desperate flight, in a Ferry going in the opposite direction.

I felt left out of Abdullah and Mohammad's conversation, but I figured I'd get back with them at the end of the voyage. My eyes were scanning the rolling hills outside of Tangier when I felt a tug on my sleeve. Muhammad was beaming at me. He motioned me away from the rail to a seat inside the cabin area. He sat down and indicated I do the same; I sat next to him. His eyes expressed regret at not having paid any attention to me earlier.

He was talking, mixing Arabic with French, and stopped himself. "Sorry, I'm mixing everything up. Just wanted to know how you are doing." I sensed he had something to tell me, to warn me about—I wasn't sure.

Finally, he blurted out, "Well, just wanted to tell you that Abdullah regrets that he can't take you to his home after all." I looked over to the opposite rail. Abdullah nodded without joining us. Then he looked away towards his Tangier.

I was puzzled that he didn't come over and tell me himself. I asked Muhammad, "Did he tell you why?" No answer. His eyes were also perusing the lights of the city, the ferry growing closer and closer.

I looked away, not wanting to show him disappointment. I was crushed. I was hoping to know a typical family, to gradually integrate into life in Tangier. Now I felt I had been thrown out in the cold.

I turned away. The houses that were mere specks in the distance, gradually swelled into identifiable structures. I looked again to see if Muhammad was still there, but he had vanished to the other side and was again communicating with Abdullah, who had changed into his djellabah (muslin robe), the pant legs blowing wildly in the wind. I wondered now if they were scheming something and felt a surge of paranoia creeping through me as I saw they were arguing. I wasn't sure what plans they had for me. I thought I was perhaps an idiot to trust people who I didn't know.

The ferry was now inching its way closer and closer to the dock, apparently cleared for our arrival. I assumed it was the point of arrival since a crowd of people awaited behind a white rope, in front of which several workers were making preparations. Next to the mooring targeted for our ferry, stevedores unloading and loading a docked cargo ship were scurrying about.

The humid, salty air settled on me like a comforter, cradling me in my thoughts of this new adventure. Our docking was so subtle; no one could have determined when the ferry stopped moving. The fact everyone was preparing to descend the long ramp was proof enough that we had reached our destination.

I followed the crowd down the ramp; our progress was sluggish due to a group of customs agents who were checking passports at the bottom. But even after the passengers were free to go, something also seemed to be detaining them a few yards beyond the line of customs agents. I noticed a line of boys carrying signs and aggressively gesticulating at the travelers.

My turn came and the agents, in drab khaki uniforms, glanced quickly at my passport and unceremoniously waived me through. Then the mad rush began: my long hair and beard, the classical European tourist look, no doubt, was like flypaper to all the "vagabonds" (as the Arabs described them) in the city. They came up to me, pulled at my backpack and offered anything from cheap hotels to cannabis and hashish. My two Arab friends ran interference by setting up a human shield between the vagabonds and me, maintaining it all the way to the streets of Tangier.

A couple of street vendors were not intimidated as they tried to get through my two self-appointed bodyguards. They tugged at my sleeve and showed me a bag supposedly containing hashish for sale, advertising it in three languages: English, Spanish and French. When they got too close, Abdullah and Muhammad spouted a few words that by their tone, were designed to make the intruders withdraw.

One dark boy, wearing dirty jeans with no shirt and shoes—not more than seven years old—came up to me, and before Abdullah could shoo him away, said in a stream of English, "Hey, wanna soma gooood stuff? Yeah, l'herb (marijuana)."

I wondered if he was disguised as a vagrant selling dope but in reality was working for the police, attempting to lure Europeans into buying illegal drugs, after which a police agent, hiding behind a park bench, would drag the unsuspecting buyer to jail. "Bravo," I thought as I sardonically praised myself for another bout of city paranoia.

Groups of young, clean-cut, European-style dressed slicks dangled car keys before my eyes and pointed to a row of neatly parked cars. It wasn't clear what they were offering. I imagined that many a foreigner had bit the bait and perhaps ended up on the Mediterranean seabed. At any rate, I felt secure sandwiched between my new friends as we strolled by the boisterously bustling docks, where cargo was being unloaded and people were disembarking. Vagabonds, people carrying large boxes and baskets, veiled women, turbaned men and barefoot children all moved to their own rhythm and sounds as a myriad of seagulls flew overhead, adding their own piercing calls to the bedlam. Shirt collars emblazoned with radiant hues and scarves and pants, like Mediterranean flags, reminded me at every step that I was entering an unknown world—that of my Italian ancestry, also deeply imbedded in the Mediterranean culture.

After several minutes of weaving in and out of the collage of people, the path narrowed as we arrived at the end of the dock, flanked by rows of cafes. As we walked by the tables full of locals drinking mint tea, I felt an eerie, uneasy feeling as the glare of a thousand eyes watched my every move.

We strode three abreast down a small alleyway, which disintegrated into bleakness. Cafes smaller and dingier than those at the foot of the docks, with chairs and tables sprawled every which way, were inhabited by a motley group sipping tea and staring. . .and staring...like a herd of cows in the meadow, startled by an unfamiliar sight.

Mohammed, without explanation, announced that we were entering the Ancienne Medina. Then, without warning, Abdullah turned to Mohammed and me and said "A la prochaine," crossed the street and was swept up in the maze of people walking in the opposite direction, the bottoms of his djellabah sweeping the ground behind him.

"There went my lodging," I thought. Looking away from Mohammad, an empty feeling assailed my stomach. "How could he have lied to me, between saying prayers on the train?" I wondered, bewildered.

The last traces of his dark shadow escaped through the shanties lining the streets of the Medina of Tangier. The area, now destitute, had been a center for espionage and black markets, so it was said, a far cry from its present identity.

I turned to Muhammad; he innocently shrugged his shoulders. I wondered what he and Abdullah had been discussing on the boat. Had they been trying to figure out how to rob me? Maybe that had been Abdullah's plan all along—perhaps Muhammad had argued against it—or maybe he would take me to some secluded spot where Abdullah would be waiting to finish the task.

We arrived at an outdoor market lined by the usual dingy cafes. In the middle appeared to be a make-shift bus stop. I turned to Muhammad who was frantically searching the billboards above the small cafes with the bus departure times inscribed in Arabic and in French. It occurred to me then that I had no idea where he was going, as I had never spoke to him about it. I had earlier told him that, after Tangier, I had planned to travel to Casablanca. He told me he was headed for Agadir, but didn't see any buses going in that direction. At one point, he spoke to the ticket vendor at the ticket counter. I could only see a deeply tanned face, a shake of his head and shrugging shoulders. Muhammad returned and said that there were neither buses going to Casablanca nor to Agadir, so we were both stuck in Tangier that night.

"Damn it", he cursed. "I wanted to arrive home this evening. Oh, well," he looked at me smiling, "I guess we're stuck with each other tonight." Then, he frowned.

My reaction was a mixture of a growl and a sigh. I almost preferred being alone. At this point, I frankly could not trust him. To sleep the entire night in the same room with him would be with one eye open. I thought, however, that I'd better stay with him since he could find a cheap hotel and, as a long-haired, bearded foreigner, I would clearly be more vulnerable alone, not to mention a target for vagabonds.

Muhammad said he knew of a cheap hotel and that I should follow him there. He told me that the best place for us would be the "Medina" and pointed to the path we were to take. I asked him what it was and he responded that it was the modest part of the city where we'd rent a cheap room in a hotel already known to him.

We walked side by side in the direction of the Medina. There would be no hurrying now, since we were both resigned to our fate of spending the night in Tangier. He placed his hands in his pockets and, turning to me, demonstrated that I needed to do the same at all times due to the pickpockets. After we had trodden the typical maze of tables and chairs with men drinking tea, the road greatly narrowed, leading us to a barricade no cars could pass. Behind this obstruction, a new culture flew in my face: veiled women and robed men wearing turbans, with bronzed skin and roaming eyes, wandered about, speaking with guttural sounds,.

We followed a road transformed from asphalt to dirt in the direction of masses of people milling about; no one seemed to be in a hurry here. I shouted to myself, "So this is Africa!", as I brushed up against another world laden with small alleys against the backdrop of an Arab night. The stinging, smoky smell of meat filled the air as shish-kabobs were grilled over hot coals in cast iron grills bordering each side of the path.

"This is an Arab country!" I blurted, without raising an eyebrow. Muhammad was too busy turning his head from left to right, like a watchdog anticipating an attack from all sides.

There were beggars everywhere, casting their sorrowful eyes on my pockets and backpack, and especially the waist-bag connected to my belt carrying my passport; each had his own gimmick for separating money from passersby. One turbaned fellow brandished a sad-sack expression, his black eyes mirroring the dark, earthen road; his hand grasped that of his son standing at his side, a boy of no more than seven years with straight, dark hair hanging over his jaded eyes. The father studied the passersby and when one seemed an appropriate target, he would nudge his son in the direction of his prey. The boy would hover next to the target, sizing it up, and then move in for the kill. His method was to step in front of the unsuspecting person and flash the most pitiful look, at the same time twisting his mouth in utmost anguish. All the actors in Hollywood would not be able to touch his expression. He would point to his tattered, soiled djellabah, which hung on him like a discarded bathrobe, shedding fibers like cat hair.

I would have given him everything I had if I had not known that his father was orchestrating the show. I still gave him a dirham, even though I knew I had better hold on to every penny I had; in my pocket, the few coins I needed to save for dinner jingled lifelessly.

The boy moved right in front of me. I stopped in my tracks and eyed Muhammad who shook his head as I listened to the boy. He placed the dirham I had given him in a coin purse, quickly stated "Thank you, yes?" and turned to his father with outreached hands. Using a child to "butter up" suckers like me provoked a twinge of nausea in my empty stomach. I marveled its growling could not be heard above the sounds of the Medina in the heart of Tangier.

After the boy left, Muhammad scolded me: "You should ignore these people; they will pump you dry, and before you know it, you'll be required to sleep in the streets like them."

Disgusted, his voice trailed off as a gruesome sight, a man with half a body, which he had positioned in the corner of a small, gray building, cast a shadow of gloom and despair. I comforted myself thinking that the other half of his body was buried beneath him.

Muhammed, yanking my sleeve away from the man, implored me not to cry for him as he made a huge bundle every day. Long after we passed the man, my shock had failed to subside. Muhammad detecting this, explained rather dryly that one makes a living as one can, and we left it at that. But I could not help but wonder just how long this half-man must "stand" on his stump every day to make enough money to live on.

The entire mosaic of this radically different culture spread before me, hitting me head-on, from the radiant Mediterranean colors to the heavy smell of barbecued meat permeating the air; its heaviness sometimes obstructed my vision and I winced as the smoke streamed from the iron grills. Harsh, guttural sounds blotted out my remembrances of the serene boat trip across the Mediterranean—it already seemed to have taken place ages past. Abruptly engulfed by a new culture, I was, at the same time, impassioned by this new frontier and panicked walking through the Medina, a stranger with a stranger at my side. I reflected on my first exposure to Moroccans in Paris—my coworkers in the Health food store—and Abdullah, the first person I met on the trip. I thought how silly I had been to fully trust someone I didn't know the least bit about.

I thought I'd then better stay on my guard with respect to Muhammad, as I noticed him watching me out of the corner of his eye. I thought he might even be able to unveil my innermost thoughts. I must be a wretched simpleton to him as I must have shown by fully trusting Abdullah. I justified it since he seemed to be a man of God, with all the praying. Then again, I thought that this should be a warning not to trust outwardly pious people as one could never be sure of what went on inside.

Thinking Muhammad probably thought I was an idiot, I wondered if he was waiting for his chance to attack or betray me. Maybe he and Abdullah had scheduled a robbery to take place at some predefined time and place, and that the latter was licking his chops as he waited in the dark, the hood of his djellabah covering his face. My paranoia was clearly launched and in full flight, hovering over my destiny.

Muhammad suggested that we should look for a hotel—I did not respond. He nodded as if to say he understood my distrust. He advised that we check out a small, cheap hotel in the Medina, up the road a little ways. I still gave him no answer.

He said, "Look, you can't judge all Moroccans by Abdullah. Anyway, he's just a kid. Look, after we find a hotel, I can show you around Tangier. We'll find a place to stay and then have some dinner. You can get up the next morning and take your bus to Casablanca."

I suspected that he figured I'd believe anything he said, just like I had believed Abdullah. It also crossed my mind that maybe he counted on me sleeping deeply, allowing him to rob me and then hide in the labyrinth of restaurants and cafes in the Medina. I decided that I'd better go my own way and split up from this smooth-talker before giving him a chance to strike. He was definitely slick; he spoke flawless French eloquently—better than I did—even though I had been living in Paris the last year and a half.

In spite of my thoughts, I followed in the wake of his fast pace, intestines quivering at the thought of sharing a room with him, just to save a few dirhams. I was resigned to doing so, however, as I desperately needed to save money. But I wanted to find out what his intentions were, or at least try. So I hurled a series of questions at my lean acquaintance, hoping to catch him off guard—off balance—so maybe he would make a mistake and disclose himself to me. For instance, I asked him where he grew up, if he had spent a lot of time in Tangier and Paris, did he intend to stay in Paris following his studies or return to Morocco. He responded mainly with a yes or no, or one-line answers. My naiveté disgusted me as I knew he wasn't about to reveal anything even if I were to use physical force—which I would never do.

The innocent excitement I had felt leaving Paris was starting to disintegrate as I woke up to the burden of acquiring the necessities of life. It was at that point in my ruminations that Muhammad pointed to the right and announced that we would arrive at the hotel in a few minutes.

Chapter IX

The Trap

We kept walking, a slender Arab leading a naïve, stocky westerner, basically unschooled in the Moroccan culture, loaded down with a back pack, wearing jeans, with long, black hair and a flowing beard. I could not have been a more obvious hippy tourist. By contrast, Muhammad, his tanned, clean-shaven face fringed with short, dark hair was quite poised as he carried a small, brown leather suitcase.

I continued blasting him with questions, such as, "Is it dangerous to walk in the Medina at night? Is it difficult to change money here? Where does one do it?" His short responses always followed.

Muhammad was careful not to alienate me or to give any reason to suspect him. We passed a group of children yelling out something unintelligible, directed at us. Muhammad nodded. I wondered out loud what the children were saying. Muhammad did not respond.

I trembled, feeling physically weak, not having eaten a solid meal in about twenty-four hours, and wondering if trusting Muhammad was smart. All I wanted to do was put something warm in my belly and curl up in some secure place; but I felt like tumbleweed shifting with the wind.

We passed a couple of outdoor cafes where fish was being cooked, sputtering in a large cast iron frying pan. Muhammad's eyes moistened as though he were viewing a familiar sight, while I thought I was being led into a trap beneath the humid, Mediterranean skies. I thought it better to follow Muhammad, wandering around the Medina; I'd never make it back to the buses.

Probably due to fatigue and hunger, I hallucinated a bit as I saw myself cooking fish with my Dad, in the mountains of northern California. That time seemed so distant now; I felt so lost, without the hubris and intrigue that originally inspired me to flee Paris for the warmer coast of Africa, in pursuit of the supreme consciousness. My human weaknesses were visible for the world to see and I to ridicule.

I was disgusted with myself for submitting to such mundane concerns like fear, fatigue and hunger instead of having faith and concentrating on my search for a universal religion. It was like descending from heaven to feel my human needs—I felt distanced from the spiritual passions that had moved me to leave Paris.

Muhammad led me up a flight of stone steps sprouting tufts of grass and weeds. I visualized him leading me to a group of tombs on the side of a hill, with one properly prepared for me. After passing a few shabby-looking flats at the top of the stairway, we came to a rather modest building with a wooden archway; the structure had been battered by time. The faded, off-white paint served as a backdrop to a dusty green sign, one corner dropping below the other, with several, scribbled Arabic words.

Muhammad, without looking back, strutted through the archway. As I reached the top of the stairway to the entrance, my legs began to buckle with fatigue. I waited outside the door, gasping for breath, my body trembling due to lack of sleep and a proper meal. Hunger gnawed at my insides, a sense of helplessness invaded my body. I feared what was behind the dilapidated walls rising in front of me. I thought to just turn around, simply melt into the shadows and sleep in the streets incognito, but I did not know the streets; danger lurked everywhere, beneath every veil. There I knew I must not linger. Fear and fatigue installed themselves in my inner sanctuary.

I had decided to turn around and retrace my steps down the stone staircase when Mohammad appeared under the archway and motioned me to enter. There was a short, fat, bearded man with a smile missing a few upper teeth. I followed them onto a small patio covered with plants growing out of holes in the bricks. I closed my eyes and held my breath.

"Hey, what's the matter with you?" Muhammad grumbled. "Isn't this place fancy enough for you?"

"No, no, it's okay. How much is it?" He didn't answer as we were being led into another courtyard by a robed, turbaned Moslem with clear brown eyes and a warm Mediterranean smile.

He led us up a small, dusty stairway to the second floor and opened curtains fronting a long, dark hallway. Our guide opened the door to a rather barren room, equipped with a sink on the left and two beds, one along the left wall, the other along the right. The drab, pink wallpaper was peeling and hanging down over the top of a huge window overlooking a sea of roofs below. When the hotel clerk handed the key to us, Muhammad reached first, but I quickly grabbed it and in the same motion, freed myself from my backpack. The clerk asked us to pay an advance fee of fifty dirhams, so we each dug out twenty-five from our pockets and handed them to him.

The hotel attendant looked at Muhammad, then at me, back to Muhammad, and then smiled, his silver teeth flashing in the dark as he closed the door. Muhammad, pensive, walked slowly to the beds, selected the one on the left, placed his leather suitcase on it and sat down, looking at me with red, enraged eyes. I tried to distract his attention from my previous action by thanking him for finding the hotel.

"Without you I probably would have slept in the streets." He didn't respond, just sat there mum on the bed, looking around the room.

I wondered when he was going to either chastise me for taking the key, or himself for rooming with me. We were reluctant roommates in the middle of a strange city.

Suspecting something was about to explode, I decided to take the initiative and, at the same time, establish that no matter what was in store for me, I would not be a pushover.

I blurted out, "Let's get something to eat, like right now." I opened the door and started to leave. The tough, gruff sound of my voice, born and fine-tuned in the subways of Paris, was only an act.

Muhammad silently stood up and followed me out the door. I even tried to decide where we should eat, pointing to an outdoor grill, where pieces of chicken were barbecuing on the charcoal-caked iron grill. Seated around it were several Moroccan men, eating, talking and looking at all that moved in front of them. I had never seen such observant people, comparing them to Parisians sitting in cafes looking nonchalantly at passersby, not paying much attention to others as they sipped their coffee.

I continued to lead the way, and enlivened the pace, trying to show Muhammad that I was unafraid in the streets of Tangier. I still felt uneasy with him following me; he was, after all, in his homeland and I was the foreigner. I dropped back until we were walking beside each other, then I dropped back a bit more, allowing him to be about a step in front of me at all times. I could better watch him—I watched him very closely.

He was not duped and it did not take him long to reproach me for this.

"Look, you don't have to keep me on a leash, like a dog. You don't have to worry about me. I'm not going to stab you in the back and take the key!"

Then he laughed in a controlled way that did not comfort me in the least. I flashed a tight smile in response. I felt that if he could, he would take the key and run back to the hotel. I decided not to give him the chance because he was the one who knew the way back; I would never catch up to him before he had taken my belongings. I did not even know the name of the hotel. As such, we embarked upon a symbiotic relationship: I needed him to take us back to the hotel and he needed me for the key to get back into the room.

I broke the silence—maintaining the initiative—and saying as I pointed to an iron grill, "Hey, that place looks good."

Muhammad finally responded, "These places are all the same. It doesn't matter where we eat, really." Then he added, "I know a great place to eat!" he cried jubilantly.

"Okay, let's go!" I answered, happy to break the negative tone of our interactions.

He led us down a labyrinth of stairs, back to the line of cafes in the middle of the bizarre, dark plaza with a dried-up fountain in the middle. Men in robes, in jeans, in turbans, with hats, bald heads, short hair, beards flying, milled around. We were back in the center of the Medina! The heavy, almost asphyxiating night air fell on us like an invisible blanket. The only light sources emanated from the cafes, and were reflected in the beady, shining black eyes watching me on the plaza. I had heard rumors of Tangier being a center for international crimes: espionage, drugs and the slave trade. I wondered if any of those types were among the seedy characters nursing beers, sitting around the tables.

Muhammad violently yanked my shirt, almost sending me crashing to the dirt floor. He laughed as I regained my balance and pulled me towards one of the grills along the street. It was a shish-kabob stand, a Moroccan-style fast food joint. There were about eight places for patrons to stand at the counter and gobble down oil-drenched chicken and some kind of vegetable. I was so hungry I could have eaten the chicken raw. Muhammad ordered the greasy chicken, an unidentifiable vegetable and bread. In five minutes, he had finished an entire plate and paid the cook/ waiter. He stepped away from the stand wiping his mouth with his handkerchief so I quickly sopped up the grease collecting at the bottom of my plate with a chunk of bread after finishing off a small chicken leg—I needed the energy.

I asked the waiter how much and he responded in broken French, "Two dirhams." I paid him and joined Muhammad, not having taken my eyes off him for a second, even while I was eating. I left the stand in a cloud of grease and joined him, I guessed, already walking back to the hotel.

"How could you eat so fast?" I asked, wanting to encourage conversation.

He responded, without seeming offended, "I never spend much time eating. It's boring and a waste of time!"

He started to walk quickly but I called out I could not keep up so he slowed. I followed his gaze, focused on a small café off to the right. He waited for me to catch up. I was literally dragging my feet; he frowned, staring at them.

"We should have some tea here. You look like you need it!" he observed with a grin, watching the waiter who was approaching from the back of the almost empty café. The carefully wrapped portion of the waiter's golden turban contrasted with a rebellious section flapping in back of him.

Muhammad and the waiter exchanged a few words and then the waiter left, returning a few minutes later with a miniature silver teapot. Steam rose above the table as Muhammad lifted the lid. A tangle of authentic, mint tea leaves spilled out over the top and down the sides of the pot. We waited for the tea leaves to infuse the water, and then Muhammad poured it into small glasses, similar to the ones I had been served in the Paris mosque. They were like miniature stained glass windows of translucent reds and greens, with sun- and moon-shaped figures dancing around the periphery.

Imitating Muhammad, I touched the edge of the glass and sipped the scalding hot, sweetened mint tea. The strong, rich taste suffused my entire body, like a hot toddy on the ski slopes of my native southern Oregon. This magic potion gave me renewed energy, and dissolved the grease sloshing in my stomach.

Muhammad sat contemplating his glass, deeply introspective. I gratefully embraced this pause as a moment to reorganize my thinking. But my thoughts were immediately disturbed by a strange and depressing street scene, notable for its absence of women. I wondered where all the women were? Before I could even fathom and guess, I noticed the streets in front of the café were overflowing with beggars holding their hands out as pedestrians walked by, hardly noticing them. That brought to mind the Parisian philosophy, "Every man for himself." I sobbed internally—very internally, very deeply—for fear Muhammad would interpret an overt demonstration as weakness.

As I sat sipping the tea, and occasionally crunching on the hot, waterlogged tea leaves, a young boy approached me with such an agonized look on his face, I had to give him a dirham. The boy thanked me, pirouetting at the same time, and took off in the opposite direction. About half a block away, I saw an older man, probably his father, grab his arm and take the dirham. I turned away in disgust.

A young man in his twenties, wearing a dirty robe, stood opposite our table on the other side of the street. He was incessantly scratching his head. I asked Muhammad that if the man was a beggar, why he did not approach us. He explained that the poor wretch was probably infested with small black creatures and...before he could finish his sentence, without changing his tone; he asked me if I'd like to take a walk. He indicated that he wanted so show me a little Tangier before heading back to the hotel.

Muhammad paid the waiter and we set off, wading through the night crowd. Fatigue began to set into my bones and the prospect of a short tour of the Medina seemed overwhelming. I was growing accustomed to Muhammad, even though he seemed perpetually distant—in another more joyous world, no doubt, far away from beating the streets with the likes of me.

Several open-air markets where still open for business. We walked down rows and rows of vegetables, fruits and dates and stems with mint leaves piled high on the tables. I bought a pound of dates and some bread and offered some to Muhammad, who met my outstretched, olive-colored hand with his dark, Mediterranean one. Grinning, he took some dates and popped them into his mouth.

It seemed as though in the next breath, I was climbing the familiar stone steps to the hotel. When I unlocked the bedroom door, we took our respective seats that we had claimed earlier. He sat on his bed and I rested my head against the pillow without unclothing myself, looking up at the ceiling. I imagined it would be a very long night as I would not be able to shut my eyes for a second. I still did not know my roommate's intentions—whether or not he planned to take advantage of deep slumber to rob me and then vanish among the shadows of the city.

I was angry at myself for being so paranoid and pessimistic; my confidence in myself and others had all but hit rock bottom.

Chapter X

The Longest Night

I finally understood what my mother and father had been trying to tell me during their visit to Paris three months earlier. I had sent them a letter about two weeks before their visit, sharing my views about a universal religion, and my intention to seek it. I planned to travel through Morocco on my way to Palestine, where I would find what I was looking for and share it with the world. They were convinced I had joined some religious sect and that I planned to journey to the Middle East, from which I may never return.

Believing that I was being manipulated by this "sect" and in danger, a week after receiving my letter, they boarded a plane and were on their way to pay me a surprise visit to Paris. They had traveled from their secure home in Oregon to warn me against such a journey. Dad, having been a Merchant Marine, had traveled to many countries and explored many cultures. He had also discovered the dangers of traveling alone to far-away lands; he was particularly concerned about disease and the instability of the Middle East, especially in Palestine.

As we sat drinking cappuccinos in the Latin Quarter, I had resisted their advice and told them they should have faith in me, that I wouldn't take unnecessary risks. They tried to convince me to return home with them, but I was firm on staying and proceeding with my plans. By the time they returned home, I had convinced them that I would be cautious, but that my voyage to Morocco was necessary.

I thanked my parents for at least planting the seed in my mind to be careful and not to be too trusting of strangers. I tried to remember their advice, but there and then, it was too late: I was sharing a room with someone I knew nothing about. That night was probably the longest I have ever spent in my life. The street was right outside our window, so we could hear all the sounds of the night. It must have been about 11 p.m., on a Tuesday, when the hoards of people began to disperse, but the shuffling of feet outside continued until the early morning hours.

Obscure night visions danced on the wall as I lay watching with my head on my backpack, which was propped up against the window, my emergency escape route. As I watched the shapes and forms of pedestrians walking on the other side of the street, they seemed like the shadows of the cave dwellers projected on the wall in Plato's "Myth of the Cavern." Strange noises accompanied the forms; a woman's voice, a wail like a banshee's that rose above all other sounds. People were singing verses from the Qur'an, yelling and passing vendors sang a similar tune, inviting the residents to buy their goods. I wondered if the people of the Medina slept. It was like a forest at night, when the animals come out from sleeping to hunt.

The humid, restless night brought sweat to my forehead and filled me with apprehension. Human and animal noises pierced the night air in one tormented cry. Rarely were they distinguishable from one another—a baby crying, a dog barking at a night phantom lurking in an abandoned cafe. They blended together like a night storm, pounding the roof of a country chalet. The unknown night dangers seemed to creep into bed with me.

I dozed off, my thoughts taking me far away, again, to another mysterious place—back to the ghetto where I had just taken up residence with Jerome (his name has been changed), back to endless nights and dogs yowling in the middle of the night...

I met Jerome playing pool in a biker bar at the outskirts of Santa Rosa one Friday night. I don't remember what I was doing there; I think someone told me that the music was good and it had a wild west, gritty ambiance. There I was, hanging out at the corner pool table, wondering what I was doing in that rowdy place. The biker mamas yelled as they swirled beer in their hefty mugs, while their tattooed biker friends grunted back as they looked around the room for some imaginary rival. Jerome was probably hanging out at the pool table, like me, for want of something better to do.

He was a wily pool shark, a Black-American biker without a motorcycle (like a beached surfer with no surfboard). He told me he had crashed it one day in the hills outside the city. He was living in a dingy, one-person hotel room downtown. I told him about my rooming house and he laughed at me, saying "You one sad boy!"

Jerome caressed the cue stick as he sent the billiard ball wherever he pleased, banking off the sides of the pool table and hitting the striped ball, which glided smoothly into the pocket. He was a masterful player, in total control. He could do anything he desired while talking, joking, and laughing the jaded laugh of one who has experienced many years guzzling cold beer in smoky rooms.

But there was something special about him, something warm. His boyish face was animated by a long smile stretching from ear to ear, his head crowned by short, frizzy hair. Memorable eyes glistened with humor and hope mixed together, an oasis for the weary perched above a small pudgy nose. I imagined his nostrils, the dark entrances clearly visible, to be tunnels of life, breathing in and exhaling happiness to be alive. He was full of life -almost childlike- submerging the street-smart side of him. As I bounced the ball all over the table, which sometimes landed on the hard wooden floor, Jerome advised me how to approach the game. He expressed himself sensitively, intelligently, like a scientist—I wondered what he was doing in a dingy hole like this.

After he soundly ridiculed my performance with a smile and performed a hat trick, he motioned me to follow him to a table. He spoke to a waitress, a buxom red-head with tattoos on her right arm and wearing a mini-skirt; her bruised, muscular legs testified to the hard life of a biker-bar waitress, her bruises like scars from skirmishes of every day living. Jerome winked at her and she winked back, while serving two sparkling ice-cold beers. Reaching into his pocket, he pulled out a money clip with several 20's and laid one down. The waitress quickly stuffed it in her shirt pocket.

After we both discussed our equally dead-end living conditions, we decided we would both be better off getting away from our living situations and rent an apartment together. He informed me that a landlord was renting a great apartment in the best district and that we'd be better off living "wit the people" than being lonesome "sorry cowboys". He was quite persuasive in a brash sort of way, and of course, quite right!

The next day, I picked him up outside his hotel, which was wedged in between two bars in the part of town inhabited by drunkards and street people. I honked twice, as planned, and he flew out of the sagging, wooden building, clanging the door shut behind him. Slowing his approach, he proudly walked towards my double-parked pick-up truck. He was wearing a brilliantly-colored African dashiki, in hues of peacock feathers. Poking his head through the window, he flashed an almost fatherly smile, saying in a purposeful, low tone, "Son, it's time I showed you the real world."

I let him get away with that one even though it was weird he called me son: I must have been about 21 and he was probably only a year or two ahead of me. I guess he thought he was my elder in life experience. I do admit, on that subject, I was merely a babe in arms.

As we drove to what he referred as the "people's district," I wondered why I trusted him. He could have been leading me into an ambush. After all, this was 1971, and intense racial violence and tension between black and white communities hadn't cooled yet.

Just as I figured out he must be leading me to a Black ghetto, I knew I needed to be there. As a student at San Francisco State, I used to go to a club in Chinatown called the Rickshaw that an African student had recommended for dancing. I remember showing up at midnight by myself, being surrounded by beautiful black ladies—sometimes with dates, sometimes alone, like me—who did not wait for me to ask them to dance. I didn't mind in the least that I was the only non-Black in the place. The black men thought it was cool that I didn't mind being the only white; in fact, after awhile, race didn't seem to matter. I felt welcomed into a culture about which I had dreamed of learning more. I especially enjoyed the music and watching black women sway to the rhythm, as if encouraging me to let myself go in the embrace of the blues, celebrating life in spite of the cruel history they had experienced in the U.S.

This was finally my chance to embrace this culture as my own. After all, we had one common denominator, the fact that Italian and Black Americans were subject to degradation caused by ignorance and racism in the "Promised Land." This linked us together forever; maybe that was why I trusted Jerome, who became my friend for life.

I navigated the car, turning left, then right, as we rode down a labyrinth of streets and passages, finally arriving at the fair grounds. We drove by whitewashed picket fences in communities where the houses seemed to look tidily alike, painted in drab greens and off-whites, surrounded by well-kept lawns and trimmed hedges, each a photocopy of the other.

This neighborhood soon gave way to a confused hodgepodge of streets and front yards long ago overtaken by tangles of weeds, with an occasional flower and spot of lawn struggling up through gaps in the weeds. No picket fences marked their territory. One tangled weed patch lead into another. The houses were run-down and the paint was peeling down the bare boards tacked to the house frames. Brooms, old tires, discarded dolls' heads littered the streets full of children kicking balls, throwing baseballs, and running in front of the car as if it didn't exist. The town folk were lying on the weeds in front of their houses, getting some rays while drinking beer and looking out over the weed tangles to their children playing in the streets. Black heads wearing straw hats peered out the windows as we drove by. The car was now crawling to avoid the kids in full play. A basketball thudded against the car and careened down an alley, chased by a couple of feisty urchins. Someone was yelling behind a garage, I assumed at the kids, but God only knows.

In spite of the mad confusion and trash in the streets, I breathed deeper and deeper, feeling more comfortable and at home as the pick-up progressed. The other district seemed like an eerie graveyard compared to the life in these streets. We drove down a street flanked by loose gravel serving as makeshift sidewalks and Jerome told me to take a right turn into a gravel-laden parking lot in the back of a faded pink apartment complex. I steered around an abandoned car sitting tireless on the ground, its doors and windows stripped and the grille poking out the front. The layers of rust were the only testimony to the existence of paint that had once covered its peeling sides.

We parked at the foot of the stairs leading up what appeared to be two apartments. Jerome broke the silence: "They're waitin' on us. Let's go."

"Who are they?" I asked, wondering who on earth would be waiting for us in a place like this. He didn't respond and waved for me to follow him up the stairs.

At the top of the stairs, we walked down the corridor of what appeared to be a semi-modern building. We passed one apartment and couldn't help but look in. There were covers and newspapers spread all over wooden floors, empty cereal boxes and milk bottles were stashed in the corners.

Jerome was already knocking on the door of the apartment next door. I was relieved that it wasn't the one I'd just seen. As I caught up with him, the door Jerome was pounding opened and a plump, balding man immediately appeared.

He looked us over as if we were merchandise. I knew he must be the landlord. He shook Jerome's hand and then mine; a pack of cigarettes was rolled up in his sleeves.

"Tim", he said unceremoniously. "Frank", I responded, turning to Jerome who nodded.

The man stared at me through his beady eyes, holes on a puffy countenance afflicted with fleshy jowls. He walked over to a young lady seated with a cigarette clamped between her lips and a can of beer held tightly by small, white fingers. She tried to stand, but we simultaneously asked her not to bother. As she sat down, I noticed her left hand remained lifeless, inserted in her front, left pocket.

"This is Tiny and as you know, Jerome, she'll be moving out before her lease is up and I'm helping her find a renter." He stroked her hair as she turned her head away. Then her straight, brown hair moved as she turned in our direction. She looked at me with eyes seemingly focused on nothing; her vacant look sent a helpless, empty feeling through me.

It was a typical, modern apartment, built like a box. There was one bedroom through which you had to go to get to the bathroom in back. The kitchen squatted in a little alcove to the left of the living room and was not separated from it by a door. The outside of the white-enameled stove was covered with greasy black spots, traces of a daily diet of deep-fried food. The kitchen table was juxtaposed to the window, overlooking the corridor leading to the door we had just entered.

After a tour of the apartment, we returned to the kitchen, where the landlord had placed a lease on the table. I could see the scribble which must have been his signature in the corner of the forbidding document.

Jerome asked the landlord how much the rent was and he answered, with a well-rehearsed spiel that he normally would rent the facility for $285, but since he wanted to get over with the never-ending search for renters, we could have it for $250.

Jerome said "That's only $125 each. What do you say? Shall we do it?"

I made a quick calculation: I was making about $500 net a month roofing, but I paid $175 for a college loan that I wanted to pay off. I was paying only $65 a month for the room I was renting. I would probably not have enough money to pay for expenses like food and gas. Plus, I was worried about being pressured to live with someone I really didn't know.

Jerome, flashing an expression of exasperation, asked Tim if we could talk it over. So we left.

Back in the pick-up, he asked me to take him back to the hotel. He wouldn't talk to me. As we left the ghetto and began entering the neighborhood of sterile, white houses again, he explained to me about the girl. Her name was Fanny and she was a former San Francisco prostitute who was attacked by a John or by her pimp—he wasn't sure. One day, she found herself three stories down, on the ground, with a cracked rib and paralyzed arm. Jerome said that to get her out of the big city, her pimp set her up in this Santa Rosa ghetto, where she set out her shingle.

"How did you find all this out, Jerome?" I inquired, my frown probably giving away my total disbelief in his story.

He replied "I know her." So that was that.

About a block away from his hotel, I dropped him off at the liquor store to buy some beer. He tilted his head and poked into the half closed window, warning me "I'll give you 'til tomorrow to make up your mind, then I'm going to have to find somebody else."

Adopting a nonchalant attitude, I flashed a bland smile. He added, "Hey, it'll be fine; you can trust me. We'll have fun and I'll show you the people's world, okay? Call me." He turned and headed to the corner store.

I gassed the truck and headed for the rooming house, where I parked the truck and walked up the steps splitting the well-tended lawn. Opening the front door, I noticed yet again that no one was around. The living room was inhabited by worn, comfortable furniture surrounded by pictures of old mountain cottages. There was a drab cloth covering the end table supporting an old fashioned lamp with a tasseled lampshade—it looked like it came straight out of a cowboy movie. The chairs were in a semi circle methodically placed in front of the TV. The room was a cross between a dollhouse and a tomb. I'd been coming and going for a month and never did see anyone sitting in the living room or pass anyone in the long hallway that connected the living room to my room in the back of the house.

I shuffled down the corridor, opened the door to my room and flopped down on my bed.

The next day I signed the lease with Jerome. The girl had already vacated the premises and the grease spots covering the stove had been wiped clean.

We moved in that night. It took only one load with the pick-up as neither of us had many belongings. After unpacking my things, which consisted of a couple of pairs of workpants, an extra shirt, a guitar and a harmonica, I offered to help Jerome empty his hotel room, nestled in the back of the mangy, old hotel. As I walked into the room, I noticed it had no window. I thought my friend must have experienced many claustrophobic moments; no wonder he wanted out!

He possessed about the same number of things as I did and brought almost everything in a paper sack. Two pairs of pants and two dashikis hung on metal hangers.

By the time we unloaded our gear, it was midnight. We flopped down on the floor, as we had no furniture yet. The place still looked vacant even after we had moved in. Thanks to friends, we eventually accumulated a couple of beds, a beat-up sofa bed and a kitchen table.

In time, we learned to trust each other. He became protective of me and I of him, when he would let me. I remember one day, the temperature was 110 degrees and the sun was beating down on my head as I worked (as a tar and gravel roofer) to feed the tar pot. While my fellow workers were toiling high above, spreading gravel over hot tar, I was given the task of feeding the tar pot parked in front of the seven story building.

The tar pot consisted of a huge metal vat with a heavy lid, used to melt the blocks of tar. My job was to split the tar blocks with an ax, so the pieces could be fed one by one into the ravenous, boiling pot. I would split each tar block with the ax, breaking it two pieces. Then I would open the tar pot lid until it clicked into position; I could let it go and it would stay open by itself. I would then hold a piece of tar gently on the rim of the pot and ease it into the bubbling black soup.

One day, a piece of tar slid from my hands, dropping into the kettle with molten tar heated to more than 250 degrees— it splashed outward. I sensed danger in time to turn my head away from it but could not get my right arm away in time. It felt as if it were on fire, with splotches of steaming black tar clinging to my skin, causing it to sizzle.

A Mexican co-worker drove me in his beat-up pick-up to the hospital, where I received treatment for first- and second-degree burns. My entire arm was bandaged; I couldn't move it very well and when I did, it mercilessly burned—the pain was intense. Jorge, waiting for me in the waiting room, put his arms around me and asked "Todo bien?" (Everything okay?) I guess I nodded. He took me home and left me at the front of the apartment building. Before he drove away, he told me about a tortilla factory nearby—a great place, he said. I nodded and headed up the stairs. He was really a nice person, but all I wanted to do was lie down and hoped the pain would go away.

Jerome returned that night and saw me spread out over the sofa, seemingly sound asleep. I really wasn't; out of the corner of my eye, I spied him tiptoeing to the kitchen to get a bottle of beer and then going to his bedroom. As usual, he closed the door behind him.

I must have cried out in pain during my sleep; I awoke with Jerome standing beside me in the dark asking "What's up, man?" as he turned on the lamp beside the sofa. He frowned as he touched the bandages spotted with blood and the drab yellow antiseptic cream. I told him about the accident. I knew he was sorry but he didn't say anything; he didn't have to. He advised me, "You better eat something. Here, have some beer." He handed me the half-full bottle from which he was drinking. I didn't like beer but it meant contact with him; I needed to bond with him. I felt alone, abandoned, for some reason. I gulped down the foamy liquid and wiped my mouth with the back of my hand.

Jerome made me a hamburger with all the trimmings, loaded with tomatoes, onions, ketchup, mayonnaise and pickles. I felt done in. The pain subsided as I bit into the gigantic sandwich, mayonnaise dripping on the floor. I never knew what he thought about me, but as far as I was concerned, after that night, Jerome was my brother for life. He was my people.

There were also times when I took care of him. When he had no one else, he would let me, then. One sunny, summer day in the ghetto, we were hanging out on the balcony of the apartment complex, sun bathing. He was smoking a joint and playing with his dog, a scraggly German shepherd he called "Joint." He offered me a toke and I refused. I never could smoke the stuff. Maybe my jock days came to mind; I don't know. I just couldn't bring myself to fill my lungs with it.

"Hey!" His loud voice broke the silence of a humdrum day. Taken aback by the volume, I retorted, "I hear you, I'm not deaf."

"Ha, you just a dumb white boy," he said, referring to my lack of drug "social graces." He leaned over to his dog, pretending to talk to him, while he glanced over to me as I dangled my legs out over the side of the balcony.

"Frank boy is just not cool. I'm trying to make him hip, but he won't listen to me, Joint, and me can't do nothing about it! Can we?" He placed his two hands over the snout of the German shepherd and looked directly in his eyes; a forlorn look crossed over his face as he wrinkled his brow and pushed his lips into an exaggerated frown.

"Yes, you can," I responded to his comment. "You can just move out." I was baiting him and he knew it.

Jerome reached over, and grabbed my arm, twisting it behind me. I grabbed his neck and pulled him into the apartment. "What you doing? You're too light for me. I'm too strong for you."

"Oh, yeah?" I screamed as I got him in a headlock, which he quickly escaped. He tripped me and I fell heavily on my chest as he fell on top of me; gasping, I grabbed his head and twisted it to one side, but he put me in a headlock. I lifted myself up on all fours; with him still on top I somersaulted forcing him to release the headlock flipping him over me. We both fell and started belly laughing so loudly that it must have reverberated across the entire ghetto.

"You crazy," he yelped, as he handed me a beer. Before I could refuse, he grabbed it, pulled open the top and chugged it down, handing me a coke with his other hand. We drank together in black and white harmony.

"Hey, you alright," he said, "even though you're not cool. I think you're all right. Let's go to the concert."

I had forgotten some of the local groups were giving a free concert at South Park Elementary School, in the field out back. We lay on the grass as the beautiful, rhythmic melody of soul/jazz engulfed us, melding us with other ghetto dwellers. There were hundreds of people; the entire ghetto had showed up and was singing, clapping hands, drinking and smoking.

Usually Jerome was in the middle of all the jive talking and dancing whenever we were at a concert or at a party. This time, he spread out on his stomach, lying flat on the grass. Something was wrong. I asked him "What's up, man?"

He said in clipped voice, "I'm sick; leave me alone." As he moved his head, he coughed and white fluid flowed from his mouth. I felt sorry for him, puking like that in the hot sun, in the middle of the concert. He just lay there, lifeless.

I dared move closer. After all, he was my buddy, I thought, even if he really didn't consider me as his buddy. Watching him as his head dipped into the fresh vomit, I softly said "Move away from it. Come on, man." We moved a few feet away.

That night, he lay sprawled on his bed, listening to slow jazz. He was feeling better. I walked by his room on the way to the kitchen and he called me over.

"You alright, man. Thanks for watching over me today."

I sat down at the kitchen table and prepared a peanut butter sandwich. The lights of the ghetto flickered on an unusually silent night.

Jerome and I slid into a routine. We would both get up early in the morning; he was a carpenter and I was supposed to be at the factory early, working on an assembly line. At night, we would normally cook dinner separately, except for an occasional hamburger dinner where together, we would feast on double burgers, with all the trimmings.

The first week was uneventful, except for the first morning. I descended the steps and opened the door of my pick-up truck. It was cold and the winds were already kicking up from the ocean air sweeping over Santa Rosa, from west to east. I turned the ignition but the motor wouldn't start—it was dead. It seemed I was receiving no juice from the battery. I got out and opened up the hood. A vacant metal slab, normally supporting the battery, greeted me. Someone had stolen it in the night! Slamming the hood shut, I returned to the apartment. I had been warned but didn't listen.

My boss wasn't happy when I told him I'd be late. I walked to a nearby gas station, paid the attendant with a check for $25, and walked home with the new battery. That night I bought a chain lock and key, and from that moment on, I locked the hood. I was suspicious that the neighbors had committed this injustice, but I had no proof and Jerome warned me that there were five tough boys, about my age, living there with their mother next door, so I decided not to pursue it.

The next week, tragedy struck. Poor Jerome, employed as a carpenter, was working on the roof of a house when he slipped and fell through the roof, crashing through to the living room floor below. Fortunately, he did not receive serious wounds, but his back was severely damaged. He had to quit his carpenter position and started to collect state disability.

To pass the time, he slept during the day and partied at night. Often, he would return late at night with friends, with whom he drank beer and talked all night long. On the way to his bedroom, they would pass mine, which was located in the corner of the living room; it consisted of a bed separated from the living room by a tapestry hanging from the ceiling. They would wake me up as they shuffled their feet along the living room floor until they reached Jerome's room, shutting the door behind them. On weekends, he would invite his friends over and they'd drink beer and listen to music, while sitting on the sofa. I would sometimes join in, but occasionally they would light up joints (marijuana cigarettes) and invite me to participate with them. I always refused, in spite of Jerome's frowns.

I'll never forget one weekend, when he invited all the hippy and bohemian street people to a party at the place. It was a rare gathering of people, including some with faces covered by long hair flowing down over rawhide jackets, and blacks, faces framed by afro hair styles, wearing colorful shirts and tight jeans. People were flailing their arms and legs wildly to the beat of soul music and Latin rock: James Brown, Earth, Wind and Fire, Santana and Gato Barbieri. Every now and again, a joint was passed around. Everyone competed to get his fair share...everyone except me. Jerome nervously laughed as I also refused my portion of puffs on a hash pipe that was shared among the partygoers.

After the last person left, I lay back in my bed behind the curtains in the living room, refusing to acknowledge the reality that the apartment looked like it had been bombarded, ravaged and abandoned to the Geneva Convention to sort out the losses. Bottles, beer cans, cigarette butts, plates and glasses were strewn all over the table and the floor.

The next day when Jerome arose, he stumbled across the living room floor to get to the kitchen, where he fumbled for a pan in which to boil water to make instant coffee. While still lying down, I pulled back the curtain. He scowled at me as he bent over to stir the sugared brew.

That day, we ignored each other—as we did from time to time—and counted the losses in the living room while cleaning up the mess.

That evening as I lay in my bed, Jerome stirred in his bedroom. The bedroom door creaked open and out popped his upper torso, his face shining in the semi-darkness—his smile was always easily detected.

He began what was to be a long monologue: "Hey, man, you know, you ain't cool. I thought you was but you're not. You don't get with the program, you know...let yourself go, be one of the people. I mean, my friends like you and all; that's no problem, but you ain't with the action. You're just too slow. You listen to slow music—like slow jazz instead of real rock or soul music—and you eat slow food, like cheese, instead of a good burger or hotdog. You just slow; I never thought you'd be like that. Sometimes you act like you're cool but you're just trying to fool yo'self cause you ain't. I know you don't like grass, but all you have to do is puff on the joint a little, and my friends would think you are cool. Hey, man, what's wrong with toking on a hash pipe? What is it? You scared?"

I felt insulted and I cut him off. "You don't remember, do you, before we moved into this dump, you agreed that no dope would be used here. After all, I hate the stuff. You said, "Okay, man," but you went ahead and encouraged your friends to puff the stuff like human chimneys, in the dump we call our living room, which is, by the way, none other than my bedroom."

I looked over to Jerome. He just shook his head, looking disgusted. He became silent and I sighed, thinking the long diatribe was over and maybe we had averted another fight—but it tuned out that he'd only just started the roast. "I'm trying to turn you on to the people and sometimes you try to get with the picture. And man, you funny; you dance the honky dance. Looky hear, you might learn something."

I thought, "That's enough. I don't need to hear this senseless talk." I raised my hand to contest; he waved it aside, got up, put on James Brown and began dancing like a crazed beast in the eye of a wild storm.

As he shifted his body from side to side, he laughed and said, "Look, this is how white boys dance. You see? No rhythm and they don't often move their arms and legs. Hey, watch me. I'll show you how to dance."

He swerved and swayed with the music, his body perfectly harmonized with the sweet James Brown melody. His hands curved down and up, in sync with his legs turning in, and caressed every drumbeat. Even his shoulders seem to shake in time with the base guitar, which seemed to echo the power behind the simmering ghetto walls. He moved to the pulsing rhythm, the embodiment of soulful grace flowing from the mean streets of the ghetto. When the tune ended, Jerome turned to me and shrugged his shoulders. I had to clap; it was an incredible exhibition of pure harmony and heart.

He laughed, proud of his performance, and hopeful he had helped to cure me of being "un-cool," loosening my uptight "honky" legs. He jumped to the fridge and took out two beer bottles. Even though I didn't like beer, I drank with him, in silence; it was another solemn bonding session.

As time wore on, I started to integrate better into the ghetto life style—the dancing, the jive talking—minus the drugs. In the middle of a dance crowd Jerome, my mentor, would nod as if approving my performance. I even thought he respected me, in my being square, when it came to drugs. In fact, whenever someone alluded to smoking grass or taking drugs, Jerome would motion them to approach and whisper to them they had to do it outside. I interpreted that as some recognition of me, some respect.

We grew very close; on Fridays and Saturdays, we often went to rock concerts at the Sonoma County Fairgrounds. Afterwards, if we did not have dates, we would return to the apartment and talk about all types of subjects until five in the morning.

I was finally settling into my life there and beginning to like it. Through Jerome, I met dozens of ghetto dwellers: blacks, Latinos, poor whites, mostly working class people. When I drove my pickup through the district, people now recognized me, waved and I waved back.

Our friendship was deep and I thought our bond unbreakable until one windy, Sunday night, on my return from visiting my folks across town. As I walked by the outside porch, I passed the door of the first apartment, as I had a many times before. A girl by the name of Joan lived there. Jerome had introduced me to her a few weeks before. As I climbed the steps to the apartment, he had driven up in a Chevy with a short-haired girl at his side. He called to me and said he wanted me to meet his girlfriend, Joan. I waved, said something inane like I was tired, yelled "Nice to meet you" and continued up the stairs. I knew nothing about her other than she was going out with Jerome. He probably told her all about me, that I wasn't like the others, that I was square and not too cool. Since I had fought Jerome and all his friends, and discouraged them from turning me into a drug addict, why should I care what his girlfriend thought of me? Jerome had even told me one day that because he was cool, he got all the girls, that there was no way that I was going to get a "hip" chick the way I was. I had responded that if I had to be cool and smoke dope to get the girls, I'd pass. His belly laugh was heard across the ghetto and resonated against the abandoned rusty cars in the lot next door.

As I search in vain for my apartment keys, I heard the door of the adjacent apartment open. A voice reluctantly called out, "Hey, do you have a minute?" I walked over and Joan appeared in front of me. Her face was pale as a cloudy ghetto day and her voice, sullen and sad. She was a short Caucasian girl with short, straight dark hair, perfectly cut around her head and hanging down over a drab, white blouse tucked into a short, black skirt. She motioned me to follow her; reclining on the sofa, she stretched her beefy legs out in front of her. I stood facing down at her and thought she was being rather brash, trying to seduce me under Jerome's nose. But that was not her reason for inviting me into her immaculate apartment. She sat me down next to her and offered me a drink. I refused.

"Thanks, Joan, but I should be going soon. I have to get ready for work tomorrow."

"Alright, I'll be brief. Have you heard the latest?" she quizzed. The dazed look on my face must have answered her question.

She continued. "I was looking out the window at the lights of the neighborhood when our apartment complex was suddenly surrounded by police. There were two paddy wagons waiting in the parking lot, five police cars with sirens blaring and about fifteen policemen. Two came to your apartment, one carrying a shotgun, the other with a drawn pistol. Man it was scary!" Joan shuddered.

She sat there in the plastic chair, her eyes combing the hardwood floors, as if she was looking for something under the wooden planks. She shivered nervously and looked up at me, shaking her head. "You haven't figured it out, yet?" she asked. I shook my head, shrugged my shoulders, jutting the palms of my hands outwards as if seeking mercy for my total ignorance, for not having a clue.

"Where's Jerome?" she asked. I said I had no idea.

"Come on, use your imagination! Don't you know what's going on?" I must have looked sheepishly at her, like a school kid being scolded and not understanding why.

"I don't know how to tell you this!" she cried, throwing her head back, and staring fixedly at the cracks in the ceiling above. "Alright, this is worse than I thought it would be. Jerome has been selling lids of marijuana under your nose, and you didn't know, did you?"

"What do you mean, I didn't know? I wouldn't let him or his friends use marijuana in the apartment and he promised not to bring home any. You know that. So obviously, I would never have allowed him to sell that stuff, or even have it in the house. Why should you care?" My voice was raised to a feverish pitch, but it wouldn't have been considered unusual by my jaded neighbors.

My world came crashing down: I was shocked, disappointed. My friend had betrayed me, not respected my wishes, placed me at risk without warning me of the dangers, without giving me a choice.

"You mean the police were trying to bust Jerome?" I squawked.

"Duh, and anything else that moved in your apartment! Didn't you notice strangers started popping up late at night? Jerome would whisk them into the bedroom, closing the door. I was in the living room when this happened and you weren't at home. I knew right away, and I told Jerome that I was aware of what was happening. But he promised to tell you!" she exclaimed, looking at me as if I were a complete ignoramus. Maybe she was right: I was square, ignorant about the ghetto ways, not "with the people," as Jerome would say— but I never betrayed him.

"I trusted him; I thought we were friends. Both our names were on the lease and if the police had found drugs for sale in the room, I would have been considered guilty by association. He didn't even care that he could have destroyed my life if I had been accused of being involved in drug trafficking, something that by nature, I detest even thinking about!" My yelling became shrill, my voice, a crescendo of emotion with every word.

"Stop yelling! I hear you, I hear you, and I understand you're hurt. So what are you going to do about it?" Joan yelled back, exasperated with me.

She sank into the sofa as I slumped, my head drooping down; then I looked up and stared out the window. I could only think of the party we had a few weeks ago, black and white seemingly in perfect harmony. Jerome, wearing his African dashiki, was in the middle of the dance floor, pirouetting and swaying to the beat of ghetto soul, two ladies perfectly synchronized to his every move. One wore a red band on her head, with African beads falling down the strands of her bangs. Her black body shimmered and shook, driving hard against Jerome's thigh. Moving to the middle of the dance floor and mixing with hippies, street people, Latinos, WASPs and Indians, it was pure racial harmony. Somehow, the raw sounds of the base lifted me, guiding my body to the dance floor, where it seemed as if a thousand hands caressed me as I swayed. My head swung from side to side; I was mesmerized by the suffering inherent in the blues. My body moved with every drum beat. I knew Jerome, in spite of the crowd around him, was watching me.

That night, I had become, in his eyes, a worthy roommate. He told me the next day, without hesitation, that I was "Italian-white soul." Well, he ignored the English blood in me, but I wouldn't have thought of breaking the ambiance of the moment by correcting him...

My heart plunged to the depths of my unbelieving soul; my dear, dear friend had betrayed me.

The next night, I returned home from work and opened the door to the dark apartment. As I groped for the light switch my nose burned from cigarette smoke. I scanned the room and noticed the red tip of a lit cigarette suspended in mid air. I turned on the light and Jerome turned to me, seated on the sofa next to my bed.

Words didn't come so I didn't force them. I put a bottle of milk I had bought in the refrigerator and headed for the bathroom to wash my hands. Not a word was spoken while I prepared a salad in the kitchen; Jerome stayed on the sofa, smoking.

The tension mounted. I brutally broke the silence: "You betrayed me. To think I was stupid enough to consider you a friend."

He looked at me, his sullen eyes reflecting anticipation of an imminent scolding.

I continued, "You were selling that junk in this apartment and you knew I did not want either you or your friends to bring anything into my house.

"It's my house, too," he whined. His small voice only emphasized his guilt.

"But you did not abide by our deal, or have you forgotten that you had agreed not to bring anything into this apartment, since you would be risking me as well, and I REFUSE TO TAKE THAT RISK FOR JUNK DRUGS LIKE THAT, DO YOU HEAR ME?" I furiously approached him and my index finger almost stabbed his nose.

He knew not to push me further; he sensed not to fool with me now.

So he waited until I had completed my long, windy diatribe—he was clever. I was about to nod out on the couch when he made his move.

"Look, man, I did not stash the lids in this apartment," he exclaimed. "Look!" He jumped up and opened the window. He climbed up on the windowsill and placed his hands outside under the wooden beams propping up the roof, covered with tar and gravel shingles. He continued, "The stuff was all stashed there, outside the apartment. So you see, you jumped the gun for nothing. If I was busted, the heat would not be on you."

I boiled, and exploded, "What do you take me for, an imbecile? That hiding place is within reach of our window, so all the inhabitants inside would be prosecuted for dealing dope, you dope! And, you didn't care if I got busted or not. You were playing with me when you agreed not to bring any dope in the apartment and when you kicked out your friends who had grass on them. You were lying and for that, I'll never trust you again."

He started to mumble something, but I cut him off, saying "And besides, the police were not looking for beer cans, but fortunately we weren't here or our lives would be over. You know that but you don't care."

He shook his head and looked out the window.

"So where's the rest of the stuff?" I asked impatiently.

"I got rid of it."

"I don't believe you!"

"See for yourself." He motioned to me to get up and feel under the beams.

I refused. "It doesn't matter, I'm leaving this place tonight and I'll inform the landlord tomorrow that I'd like him to take my name off the lease. I'm not spending one more night in the cesspool that you've made for us. We're probably still being watched by the police, you dog."

He sat, bewildered, his brow slightly rising, not knowing what to say.

"I'll tell you what; it's not fair that you be the one to leave when I caused all the trouble. I'll leave right now and I'll move in with Joan next door. She already said it was OK."

"Then do it, and don't show your face to me again!"

An hour later, he moved out. While he was closing the door behind him, he tossed the keys on the table. As I lay half-asleep on the couch, he, in a sincere, almost emotional, voice said, "I'm really sorry. No matter what, you're always my brother."

I did not respond. I whispered to myself, "And you will always be my brother. Take care of yourself, Bro." I turned and faced the wall. Tears flooded my eyes as I listened to his boots, the clumping noise growing fainting and fainter until I heard nothing—nothing in the night, in the callous ghetto...

My head bobbed up and down and streams of sweat tickled my cheek on their way down, over my closed eyes squinting at the corners in a semi-conscious attempt to grasp onto remembrances of Jerome. But I realized it was just a dream as I was jolted out of my reflections by a woman screaming, then a man yelling, and more screams echoing in the Tangier night. In addition to the couple fighting, a dog—picking up on the disturbance—started a low-pitched growling and one by one, the other dogs chimed in. Then the entire community awakened, the high and low pitched yelping of dogs echoing throughout.

After listening to this strange mixture of night sounds, I knew I had officially returned to Tangier. A thin layer of "sleep" still covered my eyes, so I could not make out the people scurrying about beneath my window. My bed lay next to the window, which gave me a view to the street. My eyes were finally able to focus just in time to see someone wearing a djellabah scurry away, chased by a scraggly dog.

I fell in and out of sleep, my head sinking into the left side of the pillow, only to be wakened by a new noise. Finally the city slept; the labyrinth of streets was empty. Mediterranean wind tunnels pushed fragments of fog, which settled over the lonely tables and chairs in the myriad cafes hunkering down for the night. It must have been 3:00 in the morning that the streets were finally quiet. I imagined the vibrations of the day past could be felt in the trembling walls of the buildings lining the streets. I had the sense that, at the same time, the city was anticipating the advent of a new day.

I turned my head to get a glimpse of Muhammad, who appeared to be sleeping; I strained my ears to hear the rhythmic breathing of sleep, but couldn't detect it.

All was finally quiet; I could eat the remaining dates in the small bag without being disturbed. While chewing, I reflected that understanding a different culture is like re-discovering oneself. For instance, just watching Abdullah pray to Allah on the train made me realize how important prayer had always been to me; yet I had never had the nerve to openly pray in front of others, except in a church. I mused that if my faith were strong enough, just like Abdullah, it wouldn't matter where, when or how I prayed.

Muhammad rolled over to face me with open eyes; then he fixed his gaze on the ceiling. Sitting up, he looked blankly across the room. I wanted to again break the ice and start up some kind of communication with him. He seemed so cold and aloof, it seemed it would be impossible to break through the barriers we had built between us. I thought that if I spoke about a subject close to his heart that may lead him to open up—I thought it appropriate to discuss Islam. I had studied its main principles and had learned that about 95% of Moroccans were Moslems.

I looked at him and said, "One thing that I would like to do during my trip is to learn about Islam." He nodded, at least not outwardly rejecting my request.

Hesitating, I stumbled along trying to find my words. "I have found that there are many beautiful aspects of the religion. You know, I am rather ignorant of the fine points of Islam, not to mention I know only a little Arabic."

The last comment fired him up a bit—it must have triggered something in him. "Islam is a beautiful religion. Sometimes when I am desperate and lost, I am comforted to remember that I always have Islam," Muhammad sighed.

I told him I once visited a mosque in Paris. He looked surprised that a westerner would be interested in his religion.

I continued, noting the surprise that flashed in his eyes. "I seemed to be submerged in a totally different atmosphere, a culture that I barely understood but respected, and I am curious about its customs and rituals."

Muhammad explained to me the Moslem culture and the changes that Moslem countries had undergone in the last few years. He ended by saying something that seemed carefully rehearsed, "Unfortunately, Arab nations were constantly warring against each other."

He sat up in bed, propping up his head with his left hand. With his head at a slant and speaking through taut lips, he seemed intent on enlightening me. I wondered if he was complying with an obligation—as a Moslem—to spread the word.

He lamented, "Fewer and fewer Moroccans were practicing Islam, resulting in low turnouts at the mosques".

He went on to explain the unfortunate evolution of Moroccan women, "They were becoming like Westerners, walking the streets dressed in low-cut blouses and short skirts, like prostitutes—and refusing to wear the veil."

Muhammad admitted that he was a traditionalist and wished for the return of a life style comparable to that which reflected an ordered society, as outlined in the *Qur'an*. I was fascinated by his words, his descriptions of his culture, his religion.

As the words flowed from his mouth, my uneasiness and fear began to subside, and I began to understand and feel comfortable with my Arab roommate. I felt warmth in his words, which I believed to be a manifestation of his love for his culture and his religion. This was a far cry from the cold, mean streets of Paris where everyone seemed to be at war with each other.

I could have carried on the conversation all night long; I had gotten my "second wind" and his words acted like an energy pill—the more I listened, the more awake I was. Finally, Muhammad, who had had much more experience riding Moroccan buses, pointed to his watch and said that because we had to get up early, we needed to have a good night's sleep before the long ride tomorrow. I turned off the lamp next to the bed and the room returned to darkness.

I wished Muhammad the best of luck—he returned the wish. Then we exchanged mumbled good nights: "Bonsoir," I murmured as he chanted "As-Salamu alaykum." During the moment of silence—of détente—after our deep conversation, curiosity replaced my earlier apprehension of the dark-skinned man lying across the room. No more words were spoken. Minutes later, his even, deep breathing signaled he was already far away. I was lying back trying to relax my body and mind when there was a sudden burst of machine-gun fire as a battle erupted on the screen of an adjacent movie house. Undisturbed, Muhammad began to emit harsh, rasping snores.

Before I fell into a deep sleep, I could hear a distant rooster crowing, the sound piercing through the thick fog on my first Mediterranean morning.

Chapter XI

A Tail Wind to the South

The beginning of the second phase of my journey stimulated a childlike curiosity, fueled by my ideals and illusions. I was not aware, at the time, that my freedom to come and go as I pleased would be transformed into a tightly controlled life, accompanied by strict rules and order.

The next morning, I was awakened by a thumping behind me. I turned, groggy, towards Muhammad, who was sliding into his overalls. I must have mumbled something unintelligible, to which he blurted a train of words. From what he had said, I gleaned that it was late and he had to take his bus to Agadir. The mist outside the window began to disappear and the outline of the street below came into focus.

Then the quiet was disturbed by a bevy of sirens, followed by chanting, coming through loudspeakers from every direction. To the left, I heard a harsh, but fluid voice speaking rhythmically, chanting a song or giving out information. At first, it seemed like we were under attack, that we were being warned of an air raid through loudspeakers deposited all over the city.

I caught a glimpse of the street below and didn't see any panicked citizens; on the contrary, there was no one there. I looked up at Muhammad who was searching in his suitcase for something. I said, "What's going on? Why the bedlam outside?"

He informed me—smiling incredulously at my ignorance—that those were loudspeakers located in the tall, cylindrical towers or minarets of the mosques, which notified the people that mass was to begin, thereby calling them to prayer. He explained, as he hurriedly closed his suitcase, that they were designed to call people to the first prayer session of the day.

In another breath, he said it was 6 a.m. and he had to grab his bus or it would leave without him and he would be stuck in Tangier until late that evening. He advised that I take the bus with him and then get off in Casablanca as I would have better chances of exploring the culture and Islam in a big city, which was the largest Moroccan city, and then third largest in all of Africa. He suggested that in a large city like "Casa"—as he called Casablanca—I would probably have better luck getting things together, and perhaps even find a job.

I did not relish the idea of spending another night in this God-forsaken place, nor could I picture myself trudging the streets of Tangier with my backpack weighing on my back like a sack of potatoes. I did not want to pay for another hotel room, either.

I offered to at least accompany him to the bus depot. He told me to hurry up, that his folks would be waiting for him and he couldn't miss the bus. As he hurried around the room, packing his toothbrush, his towel, he mumbled a few words. I barely made out that he was only visiting his folks for a few days—the rest I couldn't decipher.

After he splashed water on his face, he grabbed his suitcase and hurried out the door, with me stumbling after him, encumbered by my backpack. During the twenty minutes it took us to walk to the bus depot, I asked him many questions about Moroccan towns, especially the places that would be most appropriate for learning Arabic and more about Islam. He spoke much more freely now, no doubt due to our conversation last night. I almost felt I knew him, that we had bonded, even if for a short period of time.

As we turned the corner, I saw a line of buses in the distance, with a haze of exhaust fumes drifting over the tops of them. As we grew closer, the sputtering, churning noise of the engines became distinctly audible above the buzz of the awakening city.

I noticed on the sign above one of the local cafes the departure times of all buses destined for Agadir were written in white. The first bus was to leave in five minutes. Muhammad turned to me with a forlorn, distant look and asked, "Could you please pay for my bus fare? I just realized I have no money."

I had been expecting that he would make a move to separate me from my money; after all, in spite of my beard and long hair, to him I must either have been a rich American in disguise or just a gullible foreigner that he could easily play for a sucker. Or perhaps, he wanted me to compensate him for finding a cheap place and for protecting me from the vagabonds grabbing at my money belt. Without hesitating, I told him I had seen him try to hide a $100 bill by removing it from his suitcase and placing it in his wallet. He looked innocently into my eyes and informed me that he only had dollars and no dirhams. I tried to replace my disgust with sarcasm and informed him that even in Morocco there were banks that could exchange his $100.

Having brought his little con game to light, we let the subject drift away after he purchased his ticket, without a hitch. I had decided not to go with him. We then found ourselves being shoved and pummeled by people waiting on the loading platform for a bus headed for Agadir. The large letters AGADIR were written in chalk on a board next to the loading zone.

A huge bus roared into the loading zone, the trail of exhaust enveloping the entire platform, so that the bus was momentarily hidden from the passengers. After the door flew open, women holding babies, children and men exited onto the loading platform; most of the latter were wearing robes, with gold, white or black turbans. I had just enough time to thank Muhammad for his advice and wished him luck

He headed for the door as the passengers began crowding in, looked back and said, "Good luck, my friend." He waved and then melted into the crush of people, which swept him inside and to the back of the bus. The passengers were followed by a human chain of workers, the beginning located on the ground. The first person in the chain was a young, white, turbaned adolescent, wearing blue jeans. He grasped the handle of a suitcase and tossed it to a second person positioned close to the side of the bus. That person, in turn, heaved the suitcase upwards, to be snagged by the person situated on top of the bus, who proceeded to wedge it close to the others. After all the suitcases and bags were loaded onto the bus, a rectangular, plastic cover was spread over the top and tied in several places to the metal siding of the bus by long strands of rope.

Once all the baggage was carefully strapped down, the bus flew out of the loading zone as furiously as a desert tempest shot from the highest windswept dunes to the lowest plains below, leaving trails of smoke, some settling on the platform, some rising like a massive black genie over the palm trees planted near the station.

The overhead clock in a café announced 6 a.m. I felt very alone with Muhammad gone. I found my way back to the hotel following unfamiliar streets and alleys. I thought about taking the morning and afternoon to tour Tangier but I was too tired. After opening the door to my room, I dragged myself across the floor and collapsed on the bed. I thought that I might finally get some sleep, but I was almost too tired to sleep. A strange, male voice filled the air with long, guttural sounds that sounded like "Waaaaaaaaaaa...aaaaaaaa" His voice trailed off as he drifted down the street. Later, I was told that the sounds were coming from someone begging for scraps of bread to feed his sheep.

Another voice emitted a shrill, "Reeeeeeee...eeeeeee" Children yelled, dragging sticks across the rough wall of the hotel on the way to school. The sounds reminded me of a distant country town instead of a big city. I felt comforted by the cocks crowing in the distance, as if I was again living among the chickens, as I had on a California farm awhile back. Life here seemed harsh and cruel—one was exposed to all the aggressions, the harsh realities of human nature. Perhaps this was a result of so many spirits sharing the same plot of ground, breathing the same air, over and over again.

I lay in bed, contemplating my next move. It was a rare moment in my life that I had not the slightest idea of what I would do or where I would go. I thought about doing some sightseeing in Tangier, only that didn't interest me: I was not here to be a tourist. I even briefly contemplated returning to Paris—striking out into the unknown seemed a bit overwhelming. But, I seemed to be pushed by some inner force to continue the adventure, in spite of the hazards that now appeared everywhere. I desperately needed to conquer my own fears so that I could accomplish my task; this included communicating with people instead of hiding out in some protected corner of the Moroccan desert. I thought if I returned to Paris, I would return empty, without having found that for which I was searching. I lay back, in deep contemplation as to why I was even there. It was clear that I had not even come close to finding a universal religion. I wondered if what I was looking for was inside me—which would not necessitate a long voyage.

I looked at my watch I had set to Moroccan time last night. It was only 7:30 a.m. Perhaps I should lie on the bed until required to give up the room at the scheduled time of noon.

In spite of my fatigue, as if by some invisible force, I pulled myself out of bed and grabbed my backpack. All I could think about was taking a bus to Casablanca, to thrust myself into the world of the unknown, which could lead to something. At least it would be more revealing than closing myself off in a hotel room in the middle of Tangier.

Weariness still enveloped my body, but a renewed force propelled me out the door, down the stone steps, all the way to the bus depot.

The skinny, mustached cashier was holding a glass of hot, mint tea in one hand. I bought a one-way ticket on the first bus to Casablanca. He handed me my ticket and I asked him when the next bus would depart, and he, not speaking French, pointed to one idling to the right of his counter. I handed my backpack to the attendant and boarded.

I was crammed into an ancient, dusty bus with a rack on top for luggage. The seats were barely big enough to comfortably seat two passengers. To find a seat, I had to nudge my way through a Mediterranean collage of colors and faces, veils and turbans, babies crying and children holding their mothers' hands, their round, moon eyes innocently looking me over, probably wondering who I was. I melted into the seat, gasping for fresh air. All around, men and women were engaged in heated discussions as the bus rumbled through Tangier.

I caught a last glimpse of the Mediterranean Sea on a clear day; the magnificent dark- blue sky overhead made me yearn for the sea of my dreams. As the bus followed the well-paved, wind-swept coastal road, I wondered why I had not simply thrown my sleeping bag on the sand instead of heading to the city and paying for a sultry hotel room. (I was later told that if I had done so, I would probably have been attacked by roving bandits during the night or been cooked by the sun during the day).

My scraggly beard and long hair were supposed to represent the Western world. I had to laugh as I thought that maybe Moroccans lived in a more civilized world than we did: civilization is not synonymous with money and power. I wondered if state-of-the-art technology really did mean perfection. On the contrary, the most mechanized, modern country—like the United States—could not be as perfect as the designs sewn in golden threads on the back of the djellabah worn by the man sitting in front of me. Compared to the richness I imagined his emotional life to be, I had felt emptiness in the "Metropolis of Dreams." Neither Paris—nor any modern city, I thought—could escape from the cold, pseudo-intellectual consciousness infesting the minds of beautiful people. They would forever be caught up in the emptiness of indifference.

I had to find some way for this dream of universal religion to appeal to the man in front of me as well as the man living in a large, modern city. Could one religion someday encompass a range of ideologies and theologies, focusing on the similarities among religions, such as the concepts of universal love, God's love and faith?

Would I find the answer inhaling dust in this bus or on the sands of the desert plains in Morocco? Would it make a difference or was all this the nonsensical thinking one engages in for no other reason than just to kill time? Maybe I should be behind a desk at an 8 to 5 job, stacking and shuffling papers. At the end of the day, I would feel tired and then comment, "Boy, I really worked today." But before I die, let there be meaning to my life! I DECIDED, THEN, TO RISK MY LIFE IN THE DESERT TO FIND MEANING. If it's true that faith is what gives meaning to life, I needed to seek the truth of faith, and not shove it off into some closet to live a life of blind faith, the truth to be reviewed another day...which may never come.

At that stage in my life, I realized I would loath to do anything else but what I was doing, there and then; I wouldn't have traded that dusty, noisy bus ride for anything in the world. I felt I would find answers to my longing for some type of meaning to the life I had lived in younger days, beyond daily eating routines, watching TV, reading comics, going to football games and the movies and sleeping...and more sleeping. I wondered if I had become a consumer of life, in my little, intellectual comfort zone in Paris, or if life was actually consuming me. No, I would not have traded that dusty bus ride for a million dollars.

Robed men and women were everywhere. The barefoot children, tumbling, running, laughing and singing in the streets, waved as the bus streaked by. Their endless frivolity contrasted with the mood of the turbaned males, gritting their teeth as they rode sidesaddle on their donkeys, urging their nervous beasts onward by thumping their sides with their bare ankles. Sometimes the rider would yell "Rrrrrrrrrrrrr," causing the donkey to bolt ahead, its ears flattened to the back of its fury head.

As the bus had finally left Tangier, I quickly forgot my cramped anguish as I concentrated on the barren, Moroccan countryside. Makeshift huts dotting the landscape were often made of dried palm leaves and housed entire families, their donkeys and chickens chattering among the dried leaves.

A tall, dark man wearing a brown and white robe ambled along the road, leading a lanky camel. His face was like shiny leather, having withstood years of the sun's relentless rays. He had the appearance of a Bedouin, of which I had seen pictures, and now I was seeing one in person. That so symbolized why I had come to this new and mysterious world. "I have arrived!" I yelled silently. I thought this was like a picture in the encyclopedia; it was the real thing. The bus jumped, snorted like a bull and rambled on, trailing twenty feet of exhaust fumes.

The driver would sometimes stop and let us out to stretch our legs or relieve ourselves. Some of the passengers, at specific times, would descend the bus and immediately unfold a piece of cardboard or a small rug. After carefully laying it on the ground beside the bus, they would kneel down to pray. Often they would do this as the hot sun beat down on them. I was impressed with their faithfulness to what they believed, their piousness, the way they prostrated themselves, with their foreheads all the way to the ground. I wondered if some day I would become so humble, as to give of myself, as they gave, to their God. Others made the tour of the local food stands. The omnipresent grill, with smoke rising all around, was placed in the middle of the rest stop. Juicy brochettes or shish-kabob sizzled and were devoured with hunks of bread. For dessert, the people would munch on grapes dangling between their fingers, raising them to sun-scorched faces, scarred by years of wars waged against the desert winds blowing in from the Sahara. After about ten minutes had elapsed, the driver would blow the horn, and we would all pile in. Before the last person had entered, the bus would already be moving. There was always a white robed man left slightly behind who would run and leap onto the bottom step, burst through the closing doors, which slammed as the bus accelerated. Thub, thub, thub went the tires, faster and faster, onwards and upwards.

We emerged into the flatlands between Tangier and Casablanca; everything seemed so lifeless under the warm, summer sun. Old men squatted beside the road, with shaggy heads and beady eyes, which fastened, unblinking on the bus charging by them.

Everyone in the bus was constantly maneuvering for shade. An older lady draped a layer of clothes—a shirt and part of a djellabah—over the streaked window for shade against the treacherous rays. She soon fell asleep, fanned by the gentle crosswinds blowing through the cracked windows. Others protected their heads by putting on the hoods of their djellabahs or by throwing towels over them. They were ragged but friendly and "down home" local folks, trying to get somewhere in the heat of day. To them this must have been a routine trip; to me it meant everything in the world.

My head rested heavily against the window, my eyes peered aimlessly, eyelids heavy with sleep. I vaguely remembered people along the road, appearing to be searching for shade; they rested under trees or even in the shadow created by an overturned wooden crate or wagon that may have, at one time, carried vegetables and fruit to the many souks (markets) in the valley. I even saw a pair of feet protruding from the shadow of an uprooted tree.

I thought how wretched the lives of these people must be, wandering about all day looking for shade, lives consumed by the desire to survive. My thoughts were full of compassion for them, but I felt deeply estranged from my own life; I was overwhelmed with the desire to find fulfillment in order to justify my survival. Although I felt compassion, I also felt, rather idealistically, that if a person focused exclusively on material fulfillment and not nourishing the soul, that person would remain hungry. I believed the healing and evolution of the soul is our biggest and most important task.

In proportion to the miles rolling by, distancing me from Tangier, I felt increasingly safe. On the other hand, I was also moving farther and farther away from Paris—which had been my home for the past two years—and still farther from the States, my birthplace. Hills and plains separated me from my past; the more the better, I thought. I would start out like a "tabla raza" (clean slate) on my way to my spiritual destiny. I wondered if I was deserting my family and friends; I didn't have an answer. I just knew I had to break from the past completely for a certain period of time.

This awareness was the culmination of changes which had taken place in my life since I had left the Sorbonne to work in the health food store and restaurant. Before arriving in Morocco, while living in Paris, I had moved four or five times during a three-month period, residing several times in the Latin Quarter. I had become acutely disillusioned with city life: the fight for survival, pollution, tumult, and the coldness, or rather aloofness, of the people. To escape from that cement prison, I rented a room outside of Paris in a town called Villennes-sur-Seine, about forty minutes from Paris by train. I could finally say I had made a complete break with the city lifestyle. My quarters were cramped but I was happily rubbing elbows with the plebeians of my dreams, as I had done working on farms and ranches in northern California, during my youth.

My light shone brightly again on the Maghreb Express, traveling from Paris to the Mediterranean, but the sudden change in climate, lack of sleep and food had started to dull the brightness. However once again, on the way to Casablanca, I felt my spirit well up inside me—it had felt numbed from the pull of worldly desires. The women in the bus inspired my respect and their sweet smiles comforted me, but I felt no physical attraction. My hope was to remove myself from fleshly passions during my spiritual search, to relieve myself of a formidable distraction—or perhaps obstacle—to my spiritual growth. In any case, the women were entirely clothed, with veiled faces, and their eyes expressed an inherent distrust of strangers.

My body felt strangely numb as my spirits rose. I finally felt free to think, to feel, to wander, to share, without any stumbling blocks; unbridled, I was free of the controls stemming from my upbringing and preconceptions—I felt mentally and physically free. I dozed off and dreams again invaded me.

Visions of the past haunted my restless, turbulent spirit: I dreamed that my friends in California came to lead me away; my parents shrouded me in their love and with concerned looks, beckoned me to return home. In a fuzzy image, I saw myself explaining to family and friends that I was on a mission to discover why the Jews and Muslims had been warring for so many years and what religion had to do with all that. And at the forefront, I needed to find a meaning to life, the essence of being and the existence of a supreme being. I needed to know if my faith was true and not just a knee-jerk reaction to childhood indoctrination.

In my dreams, I became aware of having been misunderstood by many people; even the ladies in whom I had confided my innermost desires wanted to change or deprogram me—they wanted to tie me to a life in which I could utter only conformist slogans. In Paris, my intentions to help had often been misconstrued: I remembered an elderly lady I had helped across the street who then suggested that she could help me in bed. My desire to help was thought by some Parisians to be motivated by ulterior, more selfish motives. I had to leave Paris before my idealistic spirit withered away in some desolate bar, along with the rest of the lonely souls inhabiting Paris.

As sweat, mixed with dust and a few grains of sand, poured down my face, tickling my cheek, I partially awoke. Half asleep, I whispered to myself that everyone must search for truth, a meaning to life, in his own way; I was searching for the truth in an odd place, i.e., in a dusty, sun-baked sand forest inhabited by strange people. But there, I felt free to ponder the vicissitudes of life in and around a city, compared to life in the country, where freedom, honesty and love for humanity grew out of the love of self. I wanted to feel self-love—only by linking it with love of the Supreme Being, I thought, could I truly love others. There, peace, guided by the sun's rays, showered down in abundance.

As the bus slowed down due to traffic, people approached it with outstretched hands, begging for money or food. I was so close I could see a melancholy heaviness reflected in the eyes of one old man, munching on a crust of bread, as he squatted over a piece of cardboard which served as his bed.

"Oh, God, am I doing the right thing?" I asked myself, my eyes squinting as the bus surged ahead. "Is this plunge into the unknown a search for truth or a suicidal gesture, due to profound unhappiness?"

I rebutted the latter since I did not consider myself profoundly unhappy, just disillusioned with a superficial life in Paris. I then contemplated the delectable truth that I had purposely refused to plan this trip. I shivered in spite of the 105-degree temperature, anticipating the adventure of stepping into the unknown.

My soul searching continued: I could not decide if I had left Paris for new frontiers in order to find spiritual enlightenment or for another reason—namely that maybe I was slowly losing or transcending my mind, as a result of a steady diet of philosophy and vegetarian food. Maybe my best action would be to get off the bus, grab the one going in the opposite direction and head back to Europe. The monotonous desert sand, carried by the wind, collided with the window next to me and rained down, creating miniature sand dunes at the bottom of the windowpane. I felt my bones clanging, warning me that something bizarre was going to happen as I once again dozed off into a meditative sleep.

I was awakened with a start, from this semi-trance, by loud, boisterous laughter; clouds of cigarette smoke wafted through the air. A group of young, bright-eyed Moroccans were poking each other and talking in their course, guttural language. I enjoyed the liveliness of their presence, which momentarily brought me out of a strong desire to withdraw into myself. Then, I finally noticed what the object of their laughter was—a dark-skinned, mustachioed boy sitting next to me was rolling a joint.

"What? In the middle of the bus?" I asked myself.

82

No one seemed to care, except for the excited youths nervously anticipating the high, like kids smoking cigarettes behind the barn on the farm where I had worked. . .on the other side of the Atlantic. When they had lit the monstrous smoke stick, they offered me a toke. I refused, grinning, to give them the impression that I was cool and did not mind if they did. Yet it did bother me as I did not like marijuana, or any type of drugs.

My neighbor, speaking broken French, introduced himself as Ishmael. He explained to me that he was a factory worker in Casablanca, returning from a three-week vacation in Spain. He wore a broad grin on his face, adding a little touch of whimsy to the corners of his mouth. His eyes glazed and he seemed to withdraw into an unknown place as his French became progressively unintelligible. He did not seem bothered that I was a Westerner. On the contrary, he was proud of his culture, his language, and seemed not at all threatened as he displayed his pride by teaching me a few Arabic words.

"Ana Talib, "he said, pointing to himself as he explained it meant, "I am a student." I repeated it after him.

"Misyen," he said, meaning "Good," which he repeated several times. We both laughed at my feeble, but sincere, attempts to speak his language. Then we would lapse into French. It was like looking at myself in the mirror, talking to someone friendly and open to discussion. I was intrigued by this Semitic language, made up of a variety of rich, with some guttural sounds. As I listened to Ishmael speak to his buddies, their conversation revealed all the language sounds I had heard my coworkers use in the health food restaurant in Paris. The language seemed to blend Arabic, French, and Spanish.

I doted on the language, even though I hardly understood a syllable, and the lively group that had now appointed itself the keeper of my Arabic education. I hoped that one of them would give me a guided tour of Casablanca.

A young Muslim named Ahmed, sitting in back of us, introduced himself. He advised his friend, Ishmael, to go over the greetings among Moslems.

"Ah, yes!" exclaimed Ishmael. "Let's continue the lesson."

"When you greet a Muslim, you say, 'As-Salamu alaykum' and that person will respond, 'Wa alykum As-Salamu,'" he proudly revealed.

I repeated "Sala Walecom"...he smiled and said it was a good beginning. Ishmael proceeded to teach me other words, such as, "Kul," which meant to eat.

The bus zoomed past town after small town, the dust rising and walloping the bright little faces of children playing beside the road. The towns were carved by white, cement walls, forming white boxes; clothes hung everywhere. They were surrounded by women, garments trailing, with shawls wrapped around their faces, wearing veils. They carried large jugs or vases on their heads and appeared in doorways and alleys, only to disappear into their, I imagined, little family hideaways.

My companions were now all fast asleep, mouths agape, dreaming of the world I was about to enter—of perhaps the souks of Rabat and the streets of Casablanca, which appeared to me as a dream world on the mystical horizon. I also longed to be in the country, the open air, in the wide, open fields feeling the clean, crisp morning air caress my face—without smelling the exhaust fumes of Parisian cars.

I thought, "Take me to your wide, open fields, where I could work from sun-up to sun- down; take me down to the seashore, where the waves could wash over my entire body, already numbed by too many struggles in a confusing, calculating, manipulative society. Here, incognito in a new world, I would be free of that. Moreover, no one from my past could find me; I could begin anew."

Even then, I was not quite sure nor was I worried about why I had come, where I would stay, what I would eat, or whom I would meet. But I was free—without the shackles of the past—to bind me to empty obligations, filling my unfulfilled life with superficial desires and fast-food dreams. I was, at last, free! I had given my belongings away and left the polluted city of sometimes polluted minds behind. And now I was at the mercy of mercy: propelled into a frothing whirlpool of the unknown. I fantasized I was in the desert, quite amused by the miles and miles of sand; scorched, and parched, I turned left and right, searching...searching...without the desire to imagine an oasis—not even searching for one—and not wanting to know why.

In a sleepy daze, I stumbled off the bus at a rest stop to look for a toilet. Young children scurried past me onto the bus, carrying metal trays filled with peanuts, soda pop and candy for the passengers. Before I was out of sight, they turned and yelled after me "Mussier, Mussier, c'est bon." In their eyes, even a bearded, unwashed westerner was a rich westerner.

A man indicated where I could find the toilet in back of a café—a hole in the ground next to a pail of water. "The devil with civilization," I thought. "Let me welcome back nature; no more complicated flushing mechanisms and empty toilet paper containers." I embraced everything in its crude, natural form and scorned all modern conveniences of the well-heeled society from whence I had come.

On the way back to the bus, I bought fruit from an old, emaciated Arab, patiently standing behind a table stacked high with dates and grapes; I had to compete with swarms of flies swooping down on the crystallized sugar oozing from the dates. I imagined that the vendors worked the fields during the day and sold their produce at night, to earn just enough for bread and mint tea. Beggars stooped low in their designated corners, their long, bony hands—fingernails revealing traces of soil—resting on the long tables.

I thought, "What else could a man want? Love, a good woman, a kid and a warm day. Show me the way, far from the confines of the subway where people pass by stepping on toes, callously slamming into others before jumping through subway doors at their destination.

Maybe I should have stayed in Paris, settled down, raised a family. But I could not stop myself; I needed to outrun death—the death of ideas, beliefs, sentiments. I was dying. . .dying inside, and reviving as the distance between that other world and me increased. I was alone to deal with the confusion clouding my brain. "Help!" I cried to myself as I slid off into oblivion...I was out.

I was awakened by the bumping of my head against the window—the bus driver had probably made a sharp turn. Looking around, everyone appeared to be slumped over, mouths wide open. I imagined the glee the flies must have felt, finding a moist landing spot and a playground of glistening, white teeth. In my half-awake state, my fantasies intruded like persistent phantoms, as I contemplated the solitude necessary to provide me with a rock-bottom starting point to begin a new life. I knew I needed to literally blast myself out of any routine to avoid my life becoming a photocopy of all the others—a life of existing without living, posturing without feeling, performing without doing, going through the motions

84

without empathy or compassion. I felt so much stronger—maybe I had found something of value in a world that had seemed to be without it.

I wondered why so many things that we do appear to be so meaningful yet are so meaningless? Warmth radiated throughout my invigorated body, as I was finally face to face with the empty life I had lived and I was spiritually nourished, in spite of my weakened state, deprived of nutriments and sleep.

Soon, all the people surrounding me would be dispersed throughout the streets of Casablanca. I imagined I would get off the bus there, look for a cheap hotel and lay down my weary bones. For the first time in my life, I had no real itinerary; I was free to absorb life, enjoy, forget the past, meet people hopefully simpler, kinder, closer to the earth—people who ate couscous, loved nature, slurped mint tea, followed Muhammad and prayed with a humble heart.

Around 7 p.m., the bus entered a densely populated urban area, packed with apartment buildings, offices, cafes, restaurants and people massed together on the streets. Fifty brown faces were glued to their windows, watching the world go by outside, a world of which they would soon be a part. The stoned passengers who had been my Arabic language teachers woke up, startled from their peaceful slumbers by the noises emanating from the center of Casablanca, higher in volume after the bus windows were opened.

Ahmed, rising to his feet, pointed to Ishmael and exclaimed, "Darbida (Casablanca). Wow—you see it? He looked to me and said, "This will be your new home. You like?"

I nodded and he laughed. "Nous arrivons" ("We're arriving"). When the bus stopped, they all wished me well before taking off in all directions (as it turned out, I wouldn't be seeing them again). I was the last one off the bus. A lanky boy handed me my backpack from the top of the bus and I, too, escaped into the Casablanca night.

Although I walked the streets in a half sleep, I did notice the square shape of the buildings. Cars prowled the same vacant alleys I traversed, which invariably led to busy streets. I would have liked to crawl into my cozy bed at my family's residence in Oregon, where I knew I would be safe and free of the young urchins who occasionally followed me, trying to sell me marijuana and cocaine.

A group of young Moroccans, with knowing gleams in their eyes, welcomed me: "Bonjour, bonjour," they chorused, as they passed wearing colorful, rustling robes. Their brown eyes winked at me, as if to say they knew I was from another world. It seemed the streets, the cars, even the mules hauling hay carts all knew I was a foreigner. Everyone seemed to be staring at the strange, bearded youth walking the streets of their city.

"Monsieur, want some hashish?" one young boy asked as he followed me, barefoot, wearing loose, white trousers with no shirt. "Looking for a hotel? I have one—come here," he beseeched me.

I kept looking straight ahead, pretending I didn't understand, following the maze of streets lined with cafes and office buildings, their names inscribed in French and Arabic. I kept on walking on and on, without any particular destination.

Chapter XII

Darbida

Turning a corner on the main street, I came upon a cul-de-sac. I followed a dirt road which led to a well-lit, outdoor café. Before reaching it, a group of black market dealers flung gold watches in my face; they were attached by gold chains dangling from the dealers' fingers, like golden strands of spaghetti. "C'est bon marché, cheap, ça coute rien!" (It's cheap, that costs nothing!) they would say over and over again. Their voices trailed away as I continued onward.

I entered the center of town, complete with tall buildings adorned with fancy lights and reception booths in front. It seemed to be the financial district: there were rows of banks, their fancy, stone facades representing solidity in a world of paper transactions. I imagined they all competed for the customers driving BMW's and other pricey cars. Moroccan girls paraded their new dresses and fancy shoes, just like in Paris, flashing shapely legs and figures. I felt I was an outcast in a movie directed in some western European city, with a cast of thousands. Included on the set were some of the features of modern society: discotheques and fast-talking people, armed with one-liners and empty promises, all searching for the world of glitz and glamour.

Naively disappointed, I thought I had left all that behind in Paris. I approached the town plaza and walked around and around, like a caged lion, looking for an entrance to somewhere. Off to the right, I spotted a cluster of cafes and a book and newspaper stand at the mouth of a small street. Small groups of robed men and veiled women walked purposefully and briskly.

I headed in that direction, as it was getting late and I needed to find a cheap hotel in a folksy, comfortable part of town.

Without noticing when, I had left the smooth downtown pavement and was walking on streets caked with crusty mud. As the night shadows fell on gloomy streets, I checked the map that would direct me to the "Ancienne Medina" (Old City)—also known as the slums— where I was sure to find cheap accommodations.

I walked past a stand with newspapers in French and Arabic for sale; I noticed the vendor was wearing a clean, white djellabah, with pointed, yellow shoes. I asked him, in French, where I could find a cheap hotel; he pointed ahead, and with a grin highlighting the beginnings of a mustache on his upper lip, he repeated "Medina, Medina."

I nodded and continued down the dirt road that became crustier as I proceeded; more and more pot holes tripped me in the increasingly shadowy streets. The narrow, dirt streets resembled the Medina of Tangier: beggars sat in doorways with their hands stretched in supplication to the sky, like baby birds in their nests, stretching to the mother bird bringing food.

After trudging up one street and down another for an hour or so, my feet began to ache. Dry goods, dates, bread, cookies and flowers lined the streets in bins or baskets, spilling out of small cafes. I traversed one extremely narrow street with clothing boutiques selling Muslim shirts, djellabahs, pointed shoes of all colors, and red, blue and green material for seamstresses, designers or anyone making clothes.

I could barely move between the rows of boutiques; a very narrow walkway was provided, often blocked due to the large number of vendors and customers. One man was leaning over a bench on which were two neat rows of pointed shoes. His flailing hands and high-pitched voice indicated his attempt to bargain with the seller, who did not seem ready to give in. The vendor was a robust, balding man wearing a golden turban wrapped around the barest part of his head, arranged so as to form a tail in the back. His red cheeks reflected perhaps his feverish opposition to the price the buyer suggested.

I moved onto another booth where a young woman was closely inspecting material unraveled from a large bolt sitting upright in the boutique. The material was woven with a design of golden thread and red and blue circles and stars, sewn on cream-colored muslin. It was beautiful material I thought she probably wanted for a dress. Its beauty brought the entire Middle-Eastern mystique into play before my eyes, as I imagined a genie rising from a secret lamp and plunging into the folds of the muslin design. After the vendor wound the material back into place, I followed his progress all the way to a back room, where he placed the fabric. I assumed the interested lady had left, but before I could walk on, the vendor spoke to me in Arabic, pointing at the material. I guess since he had seen the admiration in my eyes, he probably approached me thinking I would like to buy some of the material. I shook my head, shrugging my shoulders at the same time, to indicate my lack of understanding; he smiled.

I assumed I was leaving this never-ending souk upon seeing several lines of cars moving in front of me, having waded through bolts of material, clothes, shoes and barbecue pits. I turned right only to find myself back in the hustle and bustle of the financial district, quite a contrast to the market I had just visited. I had to blink my eyes several times in order to adjust their focus to fast cars, plush restaurants and the like.

At the corner of the main street and the alley where the souk was located, young shoeshine boys were bent over businessmen's leather shoes. Watching the shoeshine boys evoked memories of big-city life in the U.S., running to work and taking a breather while sitting on an old wooden chair while a white-hired man with a beard shined my shoes.

As the sun began to set on the city, one peculiar thing struck me: fewer women were on the streets. Soon the only woman on the streets was a flippant, blond tourist with curly hair, looking quite out of place.

The Moroccans that I met in Casablanca were different from the ones in Paris: It seemed that the only ones who would talk to me here wanted to sell me a stolen watch, hashish, or have me throw them a few dirhams.

Just as I decided I could walk no more, I stumbled across the bus station from whence I had begun my trek across Casa. It seemed as though I had been walking in circles. I took a quick survey of the hotels nearby and decided that they were all too expensive. Seeing a beggar in his cardboard box shelter buttressed by the back wall of the station, I walked over to him and asked where I could find cheap lodging. He pointed across the street to the entrance to a rather sinister looking dirt road teeming with beggars, small cafés and open-air shops selling bread, dates and fruit. Policemen wearing drab, gray uniforms were milling around, conversing with the shop owners. The noxious stench of dead fish filled the air.

I continued down the road. The night shadows grew longer on the corners of the streets, adding a sinister touch as the sun set. A strange sensation came over me: I felt I was in a dream, meandering down an enchanted street in a make-believe town in some fantastical story. I snapped out of this semi-unconscious state, noticing the shadows were slowly engulfing the shops and people. As I proceeded down the road, only an occasional drunkard mumbling to himself would emerge from and slide back into the shadows consuming most of the road.

I hadn't run into a single hotel; as my feet moved forward, I finally realized I didn't know where I was going. I was concerned that soon I would be lost in the shadows covering the streets or wander into the confusing labyrinth of dirt roads and narrow alleys. I entertained only one thought—to backtrack out of the increasingly foreboding surroundings.

I made it back to the entrance of the street and crossed over as I headed back to the bus station, the focal point of my visit. My knees began to buckle with fatigue and my eyelids began drooping as I desperately searched for a park, a bench or an abandoned corner where I could lay out my sleeping bag. Holding the map beneath the faint light of a street light high overhead, I noticed that the beach was not too far away, so I headed down Hassan II Street, in the direction indicated on the map. I passed a couple of veiled women sleeping in the corner of small plaza—that was odd to see them on the street at night. I could only assume that the wretched creatures were abandoned or thrown out of their homes. More drunkards passed me stumbling home, I assumed, after the bars closed. Staggering, they eventually toppled to the ground, where they crawled around while their dogs hovered over them, growling menacingly at anyone daring to approach.

As I passed by a nightclub, melodious Arab music mesmerized me; I almost expected to see a belly dancer swaying and twirling in a group of swooning men. For a moment, I felt an irresistible urge to enter the bar, backpack and all. Visions of beautiful Arabian women filled my mind as I imagined their soft, seductive ways, using perfumes and potions distilled in the fertile valley of the Nile. A softer melody drifted out from the bar, pulling me forward—like the magical tune of a pied piper—and my entire body was abandoned to the gentle beat of Eastern drums, making me momentarily forget the throbbing pain in my exhausted legs. I drew closer to the door. Before I parted the velvety, red curtains that separated the gray outside from the passionate reds and purples I imagined were inside, a doorman, wearing a tasseled hat, cast a threatening look in my direction, warning me with words unspoken that I would not be appropriate for the atmosphere of the bar.

Reality jolted my weary body and I receded into the shadows from whence I had come. Arabian dreams metamorphosed back into the desperate search for somewhere to rest my aching, exhausted body...and hide.

I came upon a small plaza wedged between towering apartment buildings; I sat on a cold bench to rest my weary bones. The fantasy and excitement of my first encounter with a foreign culture in a strange land had given way to survival needs—to rest and partake of sustenance. I sagged onto the bench as Maghreb braced itself for a new day. I supposed it to be about 4 or 5 a.m., the time I refer to as the "eye of the storm": even though the city was still silent, it was a waiting silence. My fatigue caused me to hallucinate—I imagined an Arab with large, staring eyes stalking me, a smooth, dark dagger clamped tightly between his teeth. Feeling desperate, I abruptly regained my feet, strapped the backpack on and headed across the street—I maintained the faint hope of finding a place to sleep, even for a few minutes.

The night was calm—waves of fog rolled over me as I drearily plodded on. My focus was on rest, but I also knew that soon I would be swept up in the tumultuous activity of a city waking up. I stepped to almost a military beat in order to keep my legs moving.

When the fog cleared, I found myself sitting on a rusty, pale-green bench at the edge of a small island with shrubs, trees and a dried-up fountain; it was bordered by two streets which eventually converged. The damp coldness of the bench caused by weakened body to shiver uncontrollably.

Next to this green island was a small building, a gray, cube-shaped structure, surrounded by long, sleek station wagons—which appeared to be ambulances—all of which were painted creamy white and red.

Suddenly, my body stiffened as I heard a faint dragging of feet not far in back of me. Through the corner of my eye, I identified a stocky, veiled woman approaching me from about twenty feet away. As I turned my head in her direction, she changed course, veering off to the left, and disappearing into the trees. Then I felt that bizarre, buzzing within me, growing stronger; it felt like the wailing of someone drowning, emitting muffled, underwater shouts and gurgling sounds. Silence returned as I dozed off.

Maghreb began to awaken. The red glow of sunrise heralded the return of earthly pursuits; with the return of the noise of living came the sound of voices calling the people to the first prayer session of the morning. I was reminded of similar voices coming from the many mosques in Tangier, proclaiming the beginning of prayer.

Those magical voices seemed to stir the sleeping population: after they stopped, the streets began to come to life. Because I wasn't quite awake, my view of the men on asses heading the procession to town was a little blurry. I speculated that they were on their way to the many souks. Mule- and horse-drawn carts, often leaning to one side or the other, were weighed down by fruits and vegetables in a variety of vibrant colors. Gaunt, sweaty men in turbans yelled angrily at their beasts. One driver wore a white robe and a rose-colored cloth wrapped around his elongated head, mouth gaping; crouching, he gave the impression that he would spring from the cart at any moment.

The new sun slowly lifted its head above the horizon. Finally awake, I headed down Mohammad V Boulevard, one of "Casa's" main streets; it lead to the center of town and, I hoped, the Ancienne Medina. There I hoped to find the hotel that had eluded me last night—and perhaps friendly smiles, of which there appeared to be a shortage downtown.

In spite of having slept a bit the past night, three days of little rest and proper victuals had worn me down and I winced with every painful step. I finally reached the Ancienne Medina, the somewhat familiar dirt road, which was bustling with masses of people, policemen, and barking dogs. I felt a warm, familiar glow entering this place; this was going to be home to me for now.

A mosaic of blurred faces passed me on both sides. Smoke billowed from the barbecues with sizzling lamb shish kabobs. The ubiquitous colorful mix of clothes—bright greens, deep blues, flashy hues of yellow and gold, and a deep, rich violet—and dark and light shades of silk scarves blowing in the morning sea breeze adorned the townsfolk. Shoes boutiques and people covered the dirt road. Before embarking down the street, I reached around my backpack with my left hand making sure that all the pockets were secure while my right hand tightened the front straps. I then jumped into the crowd of people moving down the dirt road of the Ancienne Medina.

People were walking, talking, selling, pimping, crying, begging, singing and mourning. Vendors yelled, "Brochettes (shish kabobs)!" "Candy, monsieur?" "Monsieur, French," and "Monsieur, monsieur" as I walked by; this greatly annoyed me as I did not want to be so readily identified as a foreigner. I guess that was a sign that I would be targeted by the sellers, connivers, and thieves as they watched this naïve European wander aimlessly into their territory; it was like a *Beggars' Opera*, a bevy of thieves and beggars quarreling in the sultry Northern Africa sunlight.

As I walked through the crowd, hands seemed to touch my entire body and backpack, as people tried to discern if I was friend or foe. Beggars reached for the sky as they pleaded and cajoled through wizened, toothless mouths, promising the world for a dirham

"Such poverty and despair!" I lamented to myself—it was so horrible! A young lady was begging in the corner, her hair so sparse and dry that the sun's rays passed right through the strands. Her eyes beckoned me to her. As I got closer, I could see that one side of her face had totally atrophied: the skin was sagging so severely I could not distinguish her eye. It was like a glob of skin with no distinguishable features. The other side of her face was normal, with one sad, brown eye and a small, shiny nose. Her rusty-brown robe—having born the wear and tear of the ages—hung on her like tattered curtains.

I reached in my pocket and gave her all the change I had. "Such poverty and despair," I thought, again. Were there no hospitals for these people? What a wretched life, to be disfigured and condemned to walk the streets with an abominable scar that turned people away from her as she walked by.

How I loathed inequality! I thought of all the royal families and obscenely rich in the world, most of them—there are, in my estimation, few exceptions— often parasitically sucking resources from the host country and lavishing mansions and jewelry upon themselves. They give nothing but a show of empty glamour, following an empty, long-established tradition which for some people, is justified. I remembered seeing the marriage on TV of a member of a royal family; it seemed that the world lauded this person not necessarily for his or her merits but because that person was lucky (or unlucky) enough to have been born to wealth and position. Sometimes the wealthy did nothing but squander an inheritance on parties for the rich and the famous and travels around the world, their entire baseless life a source of fodder to money-hungry tabloids. Such a travesty! I dreamed that some day the people would rise up and require these scalawags to give up most of their wealth to create jobs and fund hospitals for disadvantaged people. Tears of frustration trickled down my cheeks as I proceeded down the dirt road.

The souk here was distinguished from the one I had experienced downtown, in that in the Ancienne Medina, the market had a boisterous, dynamic atmosphere: the sound of haggling voices competed with the voices of the clothes and food merchants. The latter were busy enticing people walking by to examine the silvery, soft fabrics or taste the succulent medjool dates, to join the others standing before the cash register. Sometimes those vendors would grasp at my clothes to draw my attention to their wares carefully laid out on a table,

"Monsieur, come look at these fine materials," or "Monsieur, you are hungry; eat the moist cactus fruit—it will replenish the body in this hot, Moroccan sun," or "C'est bon, c'est bon, monsieur; viens ici (come here)," they begged as I passed.

A group of elderly women, wizened by the hot sun, sat in a circle beside a clothes stall; their gibbering centered on a basket of silk panties, which they caressed with their wrinkled, sturdy fingers.

As I filed down the rows and rows of tissue, fruit, books, shoes, vegetables and everything imaginable, a young Moroccan flung some jewels in my face while repeating something I could not understand. I had learned to keep on walking, looking straight ahead, pretending not to understand, even when French was spoken.

The barbecues referred to earlier were truly smoke pits, surrounded by hungry crowds with brown faces, devouring crusty morsels of meat hidden inside white buns, drops of grease glistening at the corners of their mouths. "What simplicity!" I thought. This was something I came to see, to experience. This was a far cry from the mass confusion that was my daily diet in Paris. In Morocco, the people appeared to live and work together, constantly brushing up against each other in the alleys and souks. Perhaps this served to reassure each other of their existence, their sense of being, their cultural solidarity.

"C'est bon," I said to myself. "I want to be a part of it...consume it...bathe in silk robes and dance to the undulating Arab music playing everywhere." As if echoing my thoughts, strains of "snake charming" music reached my ears, the symbols and woodwind instruments blending in perfect harmony.

I drifted down the line. Smiling faces were fixed upon what seemed to be millions of items, from ancient pipes to dragon's teeth to luscious Persian rugs, hand woven fabrics of deep blues, rosy reds, creamy sands and a myriad of brass-like incense holders, plates and goblets.

Whenever I approached a stand or boutique, there were always one or two men watching my every move, targeting me with their penetrating Nile eyes. As I stooped over a collection of Persian rugs, I felt a gentle but persistent tap on my shoulder. I turned around to find a tall lad, a gaping smile splashed all over his face, his two front teeth missing. But this time, I heard English spoken:

"Hey Joe," he asked, "what you do?"

I did not answer him as my gaze returned to the rugs. He shifted to the other side of the rugs to position himself directly in front of me.

"Parlez vous français?" he asked.

I responded by turning away and walking away from the rugs. But that did not stop him—he followed me wherever I went. He probably thought that I would succumb to his relentless pressure; from behind, he dared whisper in my ear from time to time: "You look for hotel? You want buy hashish?"

My Moroccan co-workers in Paris had warned me not to talk to "street hustlers," so I pretended not to hear the boy and avoided any eye contact with him. As I wandered the streets, he followed close at my heels. I dreaded that sooner or later I would have to confront him since he had insinuated himself into my solitary world.

I turned left and quickly right into an alley, hoping to ditch my persistent persecutor, to no avail. Finally, as I desperately tried to pick up the pace—only to see him out of the corner of my eye running to catch up—I noticed a red, incandescent sign with the word "HOTEL" on it looming directly ahead of me, at the end of the alley.

I tried to take a diversionary path in order to ditch my pursuer by turning into a narrow alley on the left; it wound around like a snake, opening into a main road. Following it to the right, I hoped to make my way back to the hotel. All of a sudden the red hotel sign appeared directly in front of me again at the intersection of two alleys.

I quickly ducked through the curtains that separated the alley from the inside of the hotel without looking back, hoping that the person following me had not seen me. I entered a gloomy corridor, its musty odor similar to that emitted from a suitcase long closed. Suddenly, I felt a force, like a tail wind, as something or someone dashed by me, but I could not see who or what. I finally reached another curtain and parted it; the light from a lamp revealed two figures talking, one behind a desk, the other standing in front.

I immediately recognized the boy who had been following me. I assumed he was talking to the clerk, who was standing behind an aged desk in want of paint. "So that's it!" I thought. "The opportunist wanted to take the credit for finding the hotel room in exchange for a tip." Paranoia began to take over my mind—I imagined that if he were not paid he would return with his friends and beat me up or otherwise seek his revenge. I pictured myself being violently mugged in a dark alleyway in the Medina as the locals looked the other way, being contemptuous of starry-eyed European tourists with pockets full of money. No one would care; no one would come to my aid.

As the two exchanged words I didn't understand, I meditated on the Medina: everything seemed to be a hodgepodge and smelled of rotten cabbage, spoiled meat, mud holes and beggars caked with excrement—flies swarmed everywhere. Garbage was often strewn over the dirt alleyways clogged with screaming children and people fighting, running and pissing at the corners of buildings. There in the whirlwind of dust and people, there was no present or future, only being and survival—period.

I gritted my teeth and approached. The congenial smile flashed by the clerk was so wide, his silver fillings flashed a metallic welcome.

"He says he is with you, right?" he asked, shrugging his shoulders.

"No, I don't know who he is and what he is doing here!" I retorted indignantly as I glanced sternly at the tall boy.

His eyebrows drooped and he frowned as he realized I was in no mood to pay him. He quickly passed me but not without telling me what he thought of me.

"You rotten pig! I'll get you—I have friends and I know where you are," he chuckled as he threw open the curtains and stormed out.

I turned to the clerk whose smile seemed pasted on his face. I asked him the price for the cheapest single room. He quoted me a price of a few dirhams so I accepted and within minutes, he was leading me up a narrow, brightly-colored green staircase. After the darkness of the entrance, my spirits were buoyed by the change, as we rose upwards towards the heavens.

At the top of the stairs, the clerk led me through yet another set of curtains hanging from two nails. He then opened a small door almost immediately to his right and walked inside. It was a modest chamber with running water, a bed and a large window opening out to a vista of rooftops. I thanked him and he left through the door, the same smile on his face as he wished me a good sleep.

I dropped the backpack from my shoulders and climbed on top of the bed, clothes and all. Soon I fell into a troubled sleep. I awoke a few minutes later, perspiration pouring from my body and soaking my clothes. Peeling them off, I lay lifelessly on the bed for awhile. Then I tossed my shirt and pants over a chair in front of the window, got up, splashed water over my entire body, and sank into the bed, wrapping the sheets around me.

The circumstances were perfect for a deep sleep: I had slept probably one hour in the last twenty-four; it was warm and humid but the room was comfortable; the shrill voices of the vendors had grown faint—but I could not sleep.

I kept thinking about the poor, maimed beggars groveling in the dirt, begging for pennies. I would hate myself if I ever ignored them—living and dying in such squalor—with no one to shed a caring tear. A sharp pain temporarily gripped my stomach, as if to echo that indiscernible, mysterious forces had me in their clutches.

I had long ago rebelled against the Cartesian spirit as a philosophy student at the Sorbonne in Paris. I had felt stifled by structured thinking based on Descartes "Cogito," which is "I think therefore I am" or therefore "I exist."[4] I deemed myself open to whims and fantasies, new sensations which would push out the old ways—the rusty, old principles of the "vieille école" (old school)—replacing them with the philosophies of contemporary thinkers, like Sartre and Nietzsche (the latter, especially, attacked the old moral codes and inherent rigidity of intellectually decadent and dead societies). I felt like a young herring swimming in a sea of predators and if I survived, I would be reborn into the vast sea of the unknown.

I wanted to find truth, combat and conquer my prejudices and find the spirit of God at the same time. I fought to discard illusions of false security, of a planned entrance into a superficial society based on illusions propped up by mind controlling messages propagated by the media. I wanted to transcend the constant bombardment of societal values in order not to compromise myself. I wanted to find peace, true love, true values. A poem I had written in college (San Francisco, 1970) flashed before my mind, by then working in overdrive:

---

4 Descartes, *Principes de la philosophie*, I, 7, p. 79.

Festival of Life

The hopes of all will create love
with tidings of a new world, new life...
The beauty of a single grape leaf
representing purity, green, a succulent morsel.
The lone Dionysus is wandering near
he may be dancing with the sun through the trees
or gossiping with inquisitive pigeons around the bend.
Suddenly, inhabitants of the forest come out to play
everyone dances to the beat of the winded trees
bright colors flash as nature swings
food is passed from paw to hand
birds drink nectar from an earthen cup,
everyone gathers to hear the beat of a faraway song
then silence as if nothing happened.
The wind is quiet, the leaves are still, not a sound.
But if you concentrate on the air
love vibrations are faintly felt,
made by soft steps of the Festival of Life.

This unity and love was to be fought for as one penetrated beyond emptiness in search of infinite fullness, overcoming a tremendous weakness that haunts us all, preventing us from saying and doing what our soul deems right and fair, in spite of the circumstances. To do so would be to call upon the unfathomable strength lying inside each of us, connected to the universal life stream of love, living, dying. Before us lies a vast, unknown land—before us and at the edge of humanity. Leaping into the unknown, we fall into blissful nothingness, infinite intelligence...transcending thought, going beyond the now, flying without a sense of time and space.

I believed I had traveled a long way and suffered, as a result of being in a strange land, in order to find myself—to find an identity in a Moroccan society, through a synthesis of Islam, Christianity, Buddhism, Hinduism, Judaism, yoga, politics, poetry, philosophy and, as a unifying force, meditation.

My heart felt separate from my body and it seemed as though I was searching for it somewhere in the Medina. I heard voices calling me outside. I got up from the bed and in a trance-like state, opened the door and glided down the steps, eyes straight ahead, until I found myself in the alley again.

Consciousness returned as the stench shook me from my most penetrating thoughts. I was back walking among the poor of the Medina, which somehow made me feel

94

purified, almost insulated from the evils of the superficial world on the other side of Casablanca. My search for simplicity had led me to a place where I could feel at one with the people around me, as if we were healing together. I felt aligned with them against the modern world of wasteful consumption and weakened principles, morality and spirituality—a world in which amassing a fortune was the main goal of many.

"Help me! Help me reach out" I cried from within. My emotional state was almost unbearable as the ecstasy of the moment, shared with my brothers and sisters in the slums of the city, made me feel one with them and with the universe—nothing separated us from truth and love, since we really owned nothing to distract us from our search for truth. It's the attachment to things that turns us from the path—the desire to accumulate governs our actions and once we have accumulated, the fanatic need to protect our possessions consumes our lives. But no more; my worldly good was, I truly believed, not to be found in the pockets of my clothes, or deep within the rugged lining of my backpack, but in my heart. With this knowledge, I could move forward in freedom. I would abandon false hopes and superficial glory in favor of living my life as I truly am, without exposing myself—my being—to the influence of outside pressures and indoctrination.

I sought to change my thinking by beginning anew in Morocco; then I would travel across North Africa to Egypt and then to Palestine, where I would end my voyage. There, I would lend a hand in resolving the crises between Moslems and Jews. I believed I could help bring peace to those hostile groups after I purified myself. I believed that I was sent from heaven to lead mankind to a better world. I would only look in people's eyes—beggars and professionals alike—in a compassionate way, neither feeling nor showing favoritism, even to people of my own heritage, my own family. This was to initiate the dawn of a new age of tolerance, love and caring for all people, not just for those close to me.

I truly believed in this role and that I was in a place, surrounded by a sore and bleeding humanity, to save the world from suffering caused by ignorance, intolerance, hatred, xenophobia, racism, gender discrimination, homophobia and selfishness. I believed that we are on this earth to help all people through the purity of our hearts, including those outside of family connections. I believed that I returned to earth, to the soil, to share the humble life and to lead all to peace and love.

The sun shone upon my fragile, pale body, weak from a lack of sunny afternoons due to many a rainy summer day. I felt my eyes aglow with purpose. I knew my nomadic life was helping me to transcend any thought of attachment to material objects—the only attachment I felt was to memories. This contributed toward a stable notion of self in the midst of a strange land. My dreams of love gave me sustenance, which gave me courage to share happiness and sadness with the people around me rather than becoming numb or insulating myself from them. I dreamed of love shared among all people. I rubbed my chest, comforting myself with thoughts of a distant future of kindness and tolerance, food for my heart and soul, even as I felt the hunger and fatigue of my body .

As I walked alone on the dirt road, I gazed at a shiny, white tower (minaret) in the distance. I approached, fascinated by its appearance looming above the dirt alleys, symbolizing the advent of a better world.

My appearance, as I passed by tables overlaid with fresh fruit and dates, no longer brought a glint of anticipation to the eyes of the vendors, perhaps because I was now recognized as more of a Medina dweller than tourist. So I walked the dirt streets freely while hardly a head turned, unlike yesterday, when I had felt that all eyes were upon me, scrutinizing my every move.

The sun mesmerized and penetrated me, blanketing me in its warm life-giving rays. I trudged along, mixing with the locals who blinked at me, chatted, gesticulated, while children darted between men dressed in robes and women, playing hide and seek. It brought to mind fond memories of my playing jackrabbit as a youth, in the wild mustard fields of northern California. I felt happy and free then, as did these children running about, but I could not help thinking that the dirt alleys were far from the green meadows where I was raised.

I walked without fear of the threats made by the Moroccan boy earlier. I noticed a group of young boys, playing cards on a carton serving as a table near a barbecue. In spite of smoke billowing over their heads, they seemed undistracted—they were oblivious to the world. Just before casting my eyes elsewhere, one of the boys looked up and I recognized him as my former persecutor; he turned his head away, feigning un-recognition.

White-bearded men stooped and hobbled, bearing the burden of their years; their pointed beards almost swept the ground, while glassy, brown eyes peered from beneath turbans of interwoven strips of cloth encircling their round, shaved heads.

A water faucet consisted of an iron pipe connected to a base fixture—young mothers patiently waited in line to fill their multi-shaped urns, yelling at their children circling and splashing in the mud puddles, wide, brown eyes reflecting the innocence of their age. I thought that perhaps they would live to replace the beggars on the nearby beach, living in makeshift huts surrounded by dried-up, stinking mussel shells. Their lives consisted of such despicable living conditions and endless wandering through the streets, intermingling with the multitude living in the Ancienne Medina.

I asked one of the vendors who offered me a free date (a large medjool) where I could find the beach. Before he could answer, I pointed to one of the largest, most succulent looking dates, which he wrapped in paper and handed to me. He pointed down the dirt alley.

"You go straight ahead, all the way down, you see waves, that's it," he stuttered and grinned as he closely watched other customers eyeing his fresh products.

I followed the path he had indicated, passing a mélange of produce, clothes, djellabahs and shoes. But my attention was focused on the waves of the Atlantic, in sharp contrast to the dust and stench of the Medina. I craved fresh air, feeling the ocean breeze only faintly in the dirt alleyways.

It seemed as though I had walked for miles when I came upon a clearing at the end of the last long line of buildings separating me, I hoped, from the ocean. I was disappointed since I could see only abandoned fields and more apartments and houses on the other side. I looked beyond but saw no signs and heard no sound of pounding waves of the mighty Atlantic.

I crossed the fields reeking of garbage and wondered at the persistent clumps of grass growing over the rusty sides of abandoned automobiles, gravesites of the unfortunate machines. Not one person had appeared as it was now around noon and the sun beat its unsympathetic rays on the hard earth below, evaporating even the slightest hint of moisture beneath its relentless rays.

Reaching the houses, I noticed a patch of blue-gray peering through a sheet of fog and a faint undulation motion. "Yes," I thought, "I have arrived; I am, for the first time in my life, looking at the Atlantic Ocean."

I came upon cleaner streets and even a sidewalk separating the houses, leading to what I assumed was the beach. As I walked, I almost stepped on a mound of brown flesh, the curly hair infested with black bugs, weaving through the locks of hair. What appeared to be a boy's head slanted forward, with eyes closed, almost hidden by caked-on dirt, and shoulders collapsed over his legs, crossed underneath him in a semi-lotus position. His muslin pants, once a light tan, had turned gray with many days use, perhaps combined with the ravages of salt air and dusty road. He looked as if he was praying—bare shoulders protruded from his yellowish shirt, barely concealing his bony frame.

"Allo, allo." I tried to stir him, to no avail.

The corpse-like body began to slightly, very slightly lean forward. It appeared that he was deeply engrossed in something; I thought to stir him by nudging him with my foot—no reaction. I managed to find a dirham at the bottom of my knapsack and as I set it before him, two middle-aged Moroccans wearing European clothes—polyester pants, stripped shirts and shiny shoes—walked by and looked with pity at the boy collapsed on the pavement.

They stopped, hovered over the pitiful spectacle, then smirked and began to turn and walk away. I interrupted their exit by asking them, in French, if there was anything we could do to help the poor boy. The older man, perhaps in his sixties, with short hair and rose-colored polyester pants nudged the younger man to move on. They turned and began walking in the opposite direction. The younger man turned his head and responded, "Nothing. There's nothing you can do for this young fool who is nothing but a drug addict, the scum of the earth." He frowned and shook his head as he continued walking alongside his friend, whose focus had remained straight ahead, showing no concern for the boy folded over on the sidewalk like a crepe.

I could not understand how could they coldly abandon this youngster. How could they not empathize with his plight? I wondered if there were any social organizations which lent a helping hand to lost drug addicts, or were they allowed to wither and die alone on the cruel streets of Casablanca. I supposed that all cultures had their own ways of dealing with such problems, but I could hardly believe that in such a quasi-modern society, there were no clinics or other organizations able to care for those lost souls.

I felt nauseous as I viewed this hopeless situation; frustration imbedded its unwelcome self in my being. I could not derive any solace from the words of the young man, no comfort that this boy would receive any help. I walked away, disgusted at myself for not having a solution and for walking away, and then at the world for creating this situation. There lay a nine-or ten-year-old kid left to dry up and literally be absorbed into the hard, cement sidewalk. He had probably taken drugs to ease the pain of life, the nothingness, in his world of begging and pestilence in the Ancienne Medina.

The sidewalk led me directly to the beach and a dynamic crashing of angry waves on a gently-sloping sandy turf. The freezing white water washed over my sandals, receding and returning with frothy, voluptuous force. For the first time in hours, I dared to breathe in deeply as I stood there, straining my eyes beyond the horizon to behold an image of the east coast of my origins. The fresh, salt air rejuvenated my sagging lungs and saddened heart.

Dancing over the waves and slapping the water to my feverish, sweat-encrusted face, visions swirled in my brain of scenes of long ago—of fighting in Paris to reconcile my need for the simple country life with the hardened reality of city life. I reflected on what I had felt as I dodged cars, walked across the street, avoided a suspicious group of delinquents. It was like playing in a football game, running downfield after the kickoff: I remembered bodies falling, screams, bellowing grunts, the shock of metal on metal as helmets clashed at full speed—the playing field, at the end, was covered with bodies, sweat and tears. . .I suddenly needed to sit down as these visions ran through my mind. I sat, speechless, looking over the water. The tide was receding, and along with it memories of days of swimming in the Pacific and deep-sea fishing with my father, off the coast of Oregon, Washington and Canada.

But my calling was not to bathe, half-dazed in the Moroccan sun and dream about the past—that pearly white minaret in the Medina was calling for noon prayer. I could feel it, somehow calling me. I rose from my sandy seat and headed back—back to the dirt alleys, to a time warp where I envisioned the populace as nomadic Bedouins roaming the streets of the Ancienne Medina, instead of the vast Sahara.

It did not take long for me to return. The serenity of the beach was a sharp contrast to the noisy confusion of the Medina. I was already feeling the influence of turbulent life in the Medina long before actually physically entering its dirt-caked jurisdiction. The hot stench and cries of the vendors assailed me once again; I was sure they extended to the areas outside of the Medina, as well.

Even after walking what seemed like miles, my legs still felt strong although my back began to ache under the weight of the backpack. It was almost as if my legs were like homing pigeons: they seemed to know a lot more about where I was going than I did. My legs kept on carrying me down the dirt road, taking me to a place of rest before a large, white door.

I followed a group of young boys, their djellabahs swishing behind them, through the door into a short corridor. At the end of it were several rows of shoes. The newcomers pulled off their shoes or flipped off their sandals with the opposite foot. I unlaced my black oxfords and leaving them, followed the group into a wash area comprised of sinks, running water and toilets. I tried to imitate the boys on either side of me, who appeared to be following a method of washing their hands and legs. They looked at me and smiled; they knew I was not a Moslem but they did not seem upset about it. One boy, no more than ten years old, was wearing a white djellabah and a green and white turban—he pointed to his arms as he washed them. I tried copying the procedure. He smiled diplomatically, shaking his head, as other boys looked on, grinning in back of him. Then the boy reached down and offered me his sandals to cover my bare feet.

I put them on and thanked the boy; he motioned me to follow him along a long corridor, at the end of which hung heavy, dark-green curtains. I had no idea, at the time, that on the other side of the curtains awaited an astounding adventure, the most revealing, educational, enlightening and dangerous experience of my existence on earth.

Chapter XIII

Into the Jaws of Freedom

An indescribable feeling that some force was leading me somewhere I was supposed to be in space and time could be identified as intuition. Yet I was feeling something far beyond that and, indeed, it was so profound that such a definition held little meaning.

What waited for me at the other side of the green curtains was perhaps a step in the direction of finding a universal religion that would be the synthesis of my studies of Eastern Religions—specifically Buddhism and Hinduism—and other religions, such as Christianity, Islam and Judaism. I intuited that the other side of the green curtain could lead to clarification and perhaps a solution to crises arising from ignorance of the similarities among all religions of the world. Or, would those curtains open the way to a confrontation between those strongly believing that the universality of religion is inherent to a particular religion—the one described within the covers of the *Qur'an*—and me?

An elderly man with a pearl-white turban and a long, white beard led us the final twenty feet of the corridor which was adorned with multicolored tiles forming an arch above us. As we reached the curtains, I noticed that a group of young boys, about six to twelve years old, were following us. The boy who had lent me the rubber sandals opened the curtains on one side, the old man on the other. The boy then reached for my hand and led me into a huge room filled with adult men and boys of all ages. There I was, at the entrance of the temple of God—the Supreme Consciousness—present in all places of worship in the world. I felt the same warmth rush through my body as I had felt entering any other place of worship.

An inner courtyard was laid out before me, the mosaic tiles gleaming in the sun of a scorching afternoon. I watched the old man limp across the tiles as he approached the men and boys sitting or kneeling on mats made with hay-colored reeds. They would sometimes touch the mats with their foreheads, something I had only seen in movies. Some crouched over their books, which I assumed was the *Qur'an*, while others were sitting with their legs crossed looking straight ahead, perhaps meditating.

There were no chairs or altars with crosses. The large columns in the middle of the vast prayer room were surrounded by Moslems dressed in pure, white robes, as if the saints themselves had come together to spread the word of God at the same time—I just happened to be there.

As we entered the room, the boy led me to the back of the room and motioned me to sit down. We were followed by the initial group of boys that had grown to six or seven in number, and included an adolescent of about fourteen years old. They whispered among themselves and waved to other boys in the room to join them as they followed us.

I sat down, crossing my legs, where the boy directed me to sit. He sat next to me while the other boys fanned out around us, also sitting. A moment of silence followed when the boys appeared to make their initial prayers. I felt safe in this house of God; the air was fresh and spirituality enveloped me. I was relieved to have left the misery, filth, flies, slime and stench of the streets, intensified by the tomatoes discarded by the vegetable vendors, rotting beneath the hot strokes of an African sun.

I must have seemed a rather bizarre sight to them, my pant legs rolled up, wearing a tee-shirt, my long, curly hair flowing over a black-reddish beard. I looked around me, intently searching the crowd of men; the older ones were looking at me with warning eyes. I began to concentrate on prayer, thinking of nothingness, emptiness and meditating. The whispers of the older Moslems grew louder—my chest heaved with apprehension.

I did not understand why all eyes seemed to be on me. Was this not a meeting of enlightened people? And was I not there to be as much enlightened as to enlighten? I felt as a suffering ascetic might; my prophet-like suffering would redeem me, save me from the tortures and callousness of modern city dwelling. I was ready to release—as in Janov's *Primal Scream*—all my passions in order to embrace truth and happiness. I greatly desired that peace would then come about—freedom from the violence around the globe, from the pervasive sadness, like a heavy fog in the hearts and minds of people everywhere.

The search for the universality of spirituality, possibly in the form of a religion acknowledging one supreme being, celebrating the pure spirit instead of politically self-interested leaders bent more on self-enrichment than leading us to a peaceful, loving society. . .this is what I envisioned. World leaders would no longer wage war; there would no longer be the danger of destroying us all in the name of preserving national or religious interests. Was the solution to instill in our leaders the ethical, spiritual values of an enlightened Kantian world society?

I was now kneeling on the mat; I had placed my sandals beside me. Somebody behind me rearranged them for me, sole against sole, so that the bottom of the sandals did not touch the mat. I knelt there, shins touching the mat, my hands clasping the upper part of my knees, while Moslems around me prayed, mumbling words in a tuneful rhythm. Everyone appeared to be robed gods sitting in various positions, crying, like me, for release, for truth—for reasons I could not begin to understand.

When the boys had finished their initial prayers, I was again surrounded by their anxious whispers. Then the shadow of two men clothed in long, black robes loomed over me. Their red cheeks glowed in contrast to their black beards flowing over their robes. One of them stood directly in front of me, about a couple of meters away. He spoke to me in rough French, fluidly rolling his Mediterranean 'r'.

"Qu'est-ce que tu fais ici?" (What are you doing here?) he demanded. "Vous n'êtes pas un musulman; ca c'est notre mosque et les infidels n'appartiennent pas ici." (You are not Muslim. This is our mosque and infidels do not belong here.)

I looked directly into his black, enraged eyes and said, "I have come to do the same thing as you—to pray to the supreme consciousness—and I swear to you in my heart, I have no other desire."

He glared back at me and without comment, sat down, keeping his distance while watching my every move. My words and the sincere look in my intense eyes must have communicated something to the young boys, who now flocked to my side, touching my clothes, my hair and fingering my toes, as if I were an enlightened person or a religious leader. The young boy who had led me into the room then kissed my hand. He motioned the other young boys to move closer to us. We were now surrounded by boys and young adolescents, from six to fifteen years old; some were wearing turbans, and some wore white or gold-colored djellabahs, the adolescents showing slight stubble of a beard on their otherwise smooth, brown cheeks.

The boy turned and said, "You are welcome in this house of God because your intentions appear sincere. We Muslims are encouraged to welcome those interested in our religion with peace and tranquility, not with hate and violence."

As he spoke, a great brouhaha was triggered in the main prayer area. Older practitioners were grouped together, yelling something at the young boys that had formed a circle around me. The elders then attempted to penetrate the circle and were waving their arms in my direction, attempting to grab something. (I was later informed that they wanted to lynch me and drag me far away from the mosque). Then they formed a wedge to try to break the circle. Each time, they were repulsed by the young boys, who pushed the elders back. They finally withdrew uttering screams and harsh sounds I could not understand.

As the elder members of the mosque withdrew to a safe location outside the circle of young Moslems, a young Moroccan adolescent with a thin beard and wearing a spotless white turban, separated from the circle and sat down directly in front of me, reaching for my hands. We joined hands and looked into each other's eyes, perhaps for one or two minutes, without saying a word. In back of him, other boys were shoving the old men away, preventing them from approaching. But the old men remained in the prayer area, lurking in the shadows behind the immense columns, listening, peering out from their hiding places, eyes concealed in shrouds of black robes...waiting.

The adolescent opposite me reached out and grabbed my hand. He had short, black hair and was wearing a gold-colored turban. A slight growth shaded his upper lip. He began asking questions:

"Comment vous appelez-vous?" (What is your name?) he asked as his head bent forward.

I told him and he welcomed me to Islam. He introduced himself and told me his name was Yama. He reassured me that all those around us were friends. He smiled and looked around the circle of young men and boys who tried to interrupt the interrogation by waving their arms, nodding and smiling at us.

After Yama held up his hands for silence, he spoke in Arabic and the crowd grew silent; even the elders in back began to whisper among themselves. The young boys behind me holding onto the flaps of my shirt were quiet. My protector stood with eyes gleaming, reflecting a peaceful countenance in the midst of peace-shattering moments. Silently, I justified my arrival as a search for truth, the search for God, at this place of worship. We were, after all, searching together—so be it that the peace is disturbed from time to time, in conjunction with this all-consuming quest.

The interrogation continued:

"Est-ce que tu crois en Dieu?" (Do you believe in God?)

I responded, "Oui, j'y crois." (Yes, I believe in God.)

"Est-ce que tu crois qu'il n'y a qu'un Dieu?" (Do you believe that there is but one God?)

"Oui."

"Est-ce que tu crois en le Prophète, Mohamet?" (Do you believe in the prophet, Muhammad?)

"Oui," I replied, my voice trembling. I believed in the prophet, as I believed in many other prophets—but I felt it unwise to add that to my response.

"Tu ne parles pas la langue arabe?" (You don't speak Arabic?)

"Non," I replied. A commotion broke out in the back of the Mosque, with angry men shouting.

"Ne vous inquiétez pas; je vais vous protéger. Ils sont vieux et ils ne comprennent pas!" (Don't mind them; they are old, they don't understand. I will protect you.)

I nodded but I feared that the older members of the church would organize resistance within and outside the mosque and try to attack again.

"As-tu jamais prié dans une mosquée avant?" (Have you ever before prayed in a mosque?)

I replied, "Non, mais j'ai étudié les principes fondamentaux à Paris et que j'ai visité une mosquée une foi et que je me suis senti bien spirituellement dedans. Je me suis senti une espèce d'unité avec Dieu, de quelque chose si profonde et de spirituelle surgissant en moi. Enfin, une des raisons pour lesquelles je suis venu au Maroc c'était pour découvrir cette religion et pour étudier l'arabe, et pour rechercher la vérité !" (No, but I studied the main principles in Paris and I visited a mosque there one time and I felt good spiritually while inside. I felt a kind of unity with God, something very profound and spiritual. Finally, one of the reasons I came to Morocco was to discover this religion and to study Arabic, and to search for the truth.)

He held his hands out, saying "La ilaha illa Allah" (There is but one God, Allah) proclaimed my young interrogator. After he requested I repeat after him, I did so.

A loud noise broke out in front of us. I looked up and saw three hooded, bearded men wildly clapping their hands, frowning and pointing at me.

Yama ignored them saying, "Wa Muhammad rasul Allah" (and Muhammad is his prophet). He asked me to repeat after him and I did.

He instructed me to repeat those two phrases again which I did. Then he smiled and welcomed me to Islam again and told me I could stay in the mosque and pray and continue learning about Islam if I so desired.

The boys and adolescents reached out and touched me, shaking my hand. They smiled, nodded and rose from the mats, their white robes flowing after them. I understood they had finished praying and were to leave the mosque. I marveled that everyone was so carefully robed in spotless white or blue robes, even the young boys. I rose with them and prepared to put the rubber sandals on my feet. Yama placed his hand gently on my shoulder, informing me that ordinarily I would be able to stay and pray but he believed it would be safer for me to leave with the other boys and him. I nodded and thanked him for all he had done for me.

As we rose and prepared to leave, older members of the church tried to expedite my exit by charging at the group, shoving the youngsters into me, yelling something horrendously guttural and blood curdling. As the group of boys swelled to about thirty, they again formed a human shield around me and we paraded out of the mosque.

One boy carried my shoes as another opened the huge, white door into the dirt alley. The smell of excrement burned my nostrils; the contrast with the clean, mosque air abruptly awakened me from my spiritual meditations.

Yama held my arm, directing me to walk ahead. He glanced in front and turned his head to look in back. I turned my head at the same time and to my amazement, saw a troupe of about fifty or sixty boys following us. As we looked back, they cheerfully smiled and waved. I faintly discerned a group of old men following them, some trying to approach us with threatening gestures, machine-gunning insults. A group of bearded men with gray hair even tried to run ahead to infiltrate the wall of boys, but they were turned away by the impenetrable wall of young men and boys, acting as a buffer against the hostile presence. They finally resorted to screaming at the boys, some even throwing rocks, before vanishing into the connecting alleys, behind fruit stands or into cafés along the alley.

As we walked, the numbers of followers began to thin. Yama and three other young boys took turns explaining to me the teachings of the *Qur'an*. One boy, with short, golden hair wore a striped black and white djellabah and a dark blue ski hat, his eyes barely visible beneath the hat. He held my hand and hugged me as a sign of solidarity, telling me how lucky I was that Allah had spared me by leading me away from the empty passions and material appetites of the Western world.

Yama, walking on the other side of me, listened and smiled and winked at the young boy, as if conspiring to heal my soul and lead me to the Promised Land. The boy assured me that if I became a Moslem by accepting Islam as the only true faith, I would find true happiness. He recited parables and passages from the *Qur'an* and explained their meanings.

I had many questions but I would reserve them for later. Besides, I felt a growing exhaustion welling up inside me from the intensity of the afternoon, beginning in the mosque and continuing as the procession wound its way through the Medina.

I strained to understand every gesture, every word, recognizable or not, but my brain grew fuzzy and distant as it was more and more difficult to concentrate with the noise of the Medina in the background. The constant cajoling of the fruit vendors impeded my hearing, preventing me from completely focusing on the beautiful words being spoken. Spiritually inspiring words have always been comforting and intriguing to me, whether uttered by Moslems, Hindus, Buddhists, Christians or Jews.

I also was intent on hearing about Islam as the search for a universal religion was my all consuming quest, my "raison d'être," my reason for being in the Medina—the desired outcome of all the sacrifices I had made. Yet I wondered if I was also there in search of warm human contact, openness, an alternative to a society where ulterior motives were accepted as necessary to big city survival.

Twenty minutes must have passed since we had left the mosque. I was reminded that we were moving deeper and deeper into the center of the Ancienne Medina as the ragged poor stared at us with outstretched hands and sad, hungry looks of despair. Women carrying babies, their children hanging onto the windmills of their robes, stopped and stared at the curious spectacle of the bearded white man, surrounded by Moroccans, slogging through the broken, pitted streets.

I occasionally looked up from the intense conversations and noticed the familiar, dirty streets I had walked yesterday...until we entered a street that I did not recognize. The others were leading me to an unknown part of the city. But at this point, it hardly mattered where we went as I trusted my young mentors: if they were in charge of the purification of my soul, I knew that I could rely on them. Indeed, I strongly felt that if I could not trust them, I could trust no one. I almost wished the afternoon would never end—so many spiritual principles were being shared with me that I felt my soul, having been hungry on the continent, was being deeply nourished and I would never be spiritually bereft again.

I could not understand why the old men wanted to chase me from the mosque. I was truly there to be one with them and had endeavored to pray, as they had, to the Supreme Consciousness—I had no ulterior motives. No, it did not matter where I went with my supporters. I had come a long way, had experienced many hardships in the last few days and after the skirmish with the elders, was ready to be embraced by loving arms and words.

I wanted to fully express the "me" I saw in the mirror by delving into myself to reveal and question my strengths and weaknesses. I wanted to grow and live without fear, living my own dreams and not those conforming to expectations of family, friends or society. I wanted to be real and live life with all its realities and mysteries. As my father used to say, "Fact is stranger than fiction." I was living that on that afternoon in Casablanca—as incredible as that experience seemed, it was really happening.

Even though my body and mind were in a weakened state and I was confused by the turmoil in the mosque, the "walking" conversation began to stir up new forces in my heart I hardly knew existed. As we continued through the streets, I felt disoriented, as if I was moving in slow and fast motion at the same time. My skin tingled and my legs almost gave out several times.

As we walked arm in arm, for some inexplicable reason, I heard the music of Ravel's Bolero. We had started out softly walking in rhythm. As the voices of my companions gradually increased in volume, so did the intensity of the symphony playing inside me as our march continued through the slums of the city. Camels in nearby fields ambled onward, ever onward, in unison with the music of Bolero, pounding to a crescendo in my mind.

At this stage, I was close to dream-walking as I fantasized that we were arm-in-arm walking across the desert, hardly aware of the sun beating down on us—insulated from hate, fanaticism and dogma as we crossed miles and miles of sand dunes toward the truth...together, without fear.

The spell of my fantasy was temporarily broken by a tug on my sleeve. As I was meditating, I had not noticed that a Black African had pushed his way through the crowd and was now seeking my attention. He shook my hand as he introduced himself as Camara from Guinea, Africa. He wore sunglasses, accentuating the shiny, black skin stretched over high cheekbones.

"La ilaha illa Allah," (There is but one God, Allah) he recited as he placed his hand on my shoulder. He smiled a genuine smile of welcome. He wore a kind of dark-brown African hat I had seen in the movies. It was rounded at the base, resting on his ears, rising to a horizontal point that extended the length of his head. His long, white, spotless djellabah

104

contrasted with the rich, darkness of his skin and earthiness of the dirt road we were following.

"Eh, mais oui, eh, eh, Allah, Allaaaaahhh!! Allah has brought you here, my brother, to show you truth—the only truth. Ah oui, ah oui, the truth in Islam." Camara spoke with conviction, his intense, reddish-brown eyes fixed straight ahead as his head swiveled left and right.

A young Moroccan who I had not met before with slicked-down, graying hair stepped up and tried to push Camara aside, but Camara held his ground, tilting his head in my direction as he spoke:

"Wait, wait brothers," he said, turning his head towards me. "Listen: I know a group of Islamic missionaries in 'Masjid Nord' (North Mosque), which is like an Islamic monastery full of enlightened, Islamic monks with whom you could live and learn the true religion. You could live with them; the cost would be minimal—only about two or three dirhams a day—and all you do is eat, sleep and pray! Ahh oui, mon frère, you must go there! You can't really learn the truth, the true religion here in the Ancienne Medina. At the Masjid, if they accept you to study with them, you will immediately be treated as a brother. They will help you learn Arabic at the same time."

"Tell me, young man," he continued, speaking to me in a righteous, but gentle way, "What do you think about that?"

I was amazed. His suggestion that I join the mission had not fallen on deaf ears. Camara had somehow touched upon my "raison d'être" for traveling such a long way from home: learning about Islam and the Arabic language. Could this be where I would make my move out of the filth and stench of the Ancienne Medina—away from the noise, mud puddles, loose chicken feathers floating everywhere, clogging up the water drains and causing stagnant water to overflow onto the dirt roads?

Camara continued, "Where do you live, brother?"

I hesitated. Even after the spiritual discourse, I hesitated to trust him. But my intuition assuaged my doubts. I also thought that at that point, I must take chances in order to arrive at some esoteric understanding of myself and our Maker— if there really was a God—or if a higher power didn't exist, nihilism, as the true force that reigned in the world. I thought I must trust and if I were to suffer from this trust placed in strangers, one expected to pay a high price for knowledge, for spiritual enlightenment. For that, I was prepared to sacrifice all, to risk everything. For me, I was convinced it was the only way.

In spite of the magic of the day, I felt trepidation in committing myself further before I had time to digest what had taken place. I did not know there were missionary schools or Islamic monasteries like Masjid Nord, alluded to by Camara. I, however, did not doubt my resistance to brainwashing and believed that I would not allow myself to be indoctrinated into believing something in spite of my liberal upbringing. But I still feared the powerful brainwashing techniques that I had heard about even though I could never see them effectively applied to me. I knew I did not have to continue the conversation with him, that if I did, I risked going beyond the point of no return by perhaps entering a fanatic religious sect which I would not be able to leave of my own free will. But then, I thought, I was assuming it was a sect and that it was fanatic, and I was being a coward for fearing the unknown, doubting my capacity to withstand a propaganda onslaught.

"I live in a hotel not far from the mosque," I replied haltingly. It was done: he knew where I lived. I was no longer an unknown in the Medina. I knew I was exposing myself to potential danger by associating with a dogmatic religious sect, even a group appearing enlightened, guided by God's universal love.

Camara told me he had business to take care of and would catch up to me later as he melted into the souk on both sides of the dirt road.

But even though I did not see him, I felt Camara's presence. I knew he was somewhere in the crowd of vendors lining the dirt road, or perhaps he was watching from inside a café, his frame barely visible behind a shaded window, two eyes following my every move.

I glanced in back of me and noticed that the entourage of the fifty or sixty boys had slowly dissipated until only three remained, the ones standing next to me. They included Yama, my interrogator, another boy with slicked-down hair glistening in the sunlight, and a third draped in dark clothing, with curly, light-brown hair and a smooth, hairless face.

Yama stood in back of the others, his sandals barely visible beneath his long, white djellabah. He approached me, reached out and grasped my shoulder, pulled me towards him and hugged me. Then he told me he must go. After mumbling a few unintelligible words in Arabic, he retreated behind the walls of the Medina.

After Yama left, I felt a deep void in the depths of my stomach, as if I had lost someone very close to me. It was almost as if the cloak of security that had covered and protected me at the mosque was stripped away, leaving me vulnerable to the cruel elements an unpredictable life could bring.

The other two were talking between themselves as the void was partially filled with Camara's re-entry on the scene. All of a sudden, I heard, to my left, "Young man, I was talking to my wife and kids who live near here." I turned my head slightly and the sight of Camera's wide toothy grin took some of my pain away. "She agrees that you can live with us for a few days while I prepare you for entry into the Masjid Nord. Camara trained his eyes on the two boys who appeared as surprised as I did at the offer.

He continued, "I have to leave town for a couple of days on a business trip, but I will return in two or three days." He looked at me without moving his gaze from the boys. Then he turned to them: "Could one of you lodge him until I return to Casa in three days?" he asked. "Upon my return, I will promptly come to take him to the Masjid."

Then the curly-headed Muslim introduced himself as Jahan. He said he would invite me to stay with his family and him. He added I could stay as long as I wanted to, that I could eat and sleep there without paying. He smiled and hugged me. (Although I was a little dizzy with all the hugging as I was not used to doing that with males other than close friends, it felt perfectly natural to express friendship in that way).

So it was settled! Jahan would house me until Camara returned from a voyage. Then he would take me into his home to train me for entry into the monastery. Jahan wrote his address on a piece of paper and handed it to Camara. They both hugged each other and then me.

Camara said "Allahu Akbar!" (God is Great!) before disappearing into the masses patronizing the fruit stands.

Jahan suggested that we pick up my things at the hotel and take them to the apartment he shared with his family. He turned to the boy standing next to him (with the slicked-down, graying black hair) and introduced him as Abou Bakr.

Jahan spoke to me in broken English, "I happy meet you, and I help you Islam, too. You come my house first; my family like you there."

As I led them to the hotel, I could not quite fathom why they were so bubbling with enthusiasm to teach me about their religion. I thought it must truly be an incredible philosophy to have such faithful followers ready to share it with a complete stranger.

As we strolled through the interweaving streets, I thought how different things were compared to the past night when I wandered the streets of Casablanca alone. It was as if my cry in the vast desert had been mysteriously answered.

I was ecstatic to think that I had three friends committed to my religious education. Their sincerity was striking and so refreshing—they were like an oasis in a desert of serpents and desolation. The contrast was enormous.

We had trouble finding the hotel due to the labyrinth of small, narrow paths of the Medina. After wandering for awhile, we arrived at the hotel. I mused at how differently I viewed the hotel sign—when I saw it for the first time I was relieved and could think only of closing myself off in a room and throwing my weary bones on the bed. Now, everything was like a dream world, where I was no longer so alone in my quest for truth; I had three friends, especially the two with me who had been with me at the mosque, with whom an unbreakable bond had been created because of the trouble there.

Within a few minutes, and after paying the hotel owner, we were back on the dirt streets of the Medina. I followed Abou Bakr and Jahan as we set out for my host's apartment in the Medina. The powerful strains of Bolero sounded again in my mind, accompanied by an incessant ringing in my ears, as if in warning.

After what seemed like endless wandering down paths sometimes leading nowhere, sometimes leading into a sea of people, after the last bit of hardened dirt cracked beneath our feet, we stood before a small, weathered door. Jahan turned the key.

We entered a musty hallway that smelled like decaying wood and soggy moss. He closed the door and pointed to a doorway just ahead of us. We continued walking until we found ourselves standing in a completely dark cellar smelling of chalk. He flipped on the light and I found myself facing a blackboard covering the entire wall. The surrounding walls were covered with photos and an assortment of wrinkled papers. Pointless pencils and paper clips were strewn about the room, either on the crude, sagging desk in the far corner of the room, or on the floor in front of us. Jahan helped me remove my backpack, which he carefully placed on a white chair next to the entrance.

Abou Bakr walked over to the left and sat down on a sofa torn in several places, the stuffing spilling out of the holes. Jahan motioned to me to follow him as he crossed the room to the other side, where two chairs were placed a few feet in front of the sofa where Abou Bakr sat. Jahan invited me to sit in one of the chairs next to him. As we turned our chairs to face each other, Jahan's eyes pierced mine with questioning looks, but his mouth remained silent. I broke the silence by expressing my relief to have escaped the stench of the muddy streets infested by bugs and worms of all shapes and sizes. As I spoke French, I noticed a faint frown curl his brow.

He winced and speaking English he said, "Please, not speak French me, as I don't like the French. They had one time dominated Morocco."

Besides, he explained, that he had been studying English at school because he wanted to visit and study in the United States some day. His motives for befriending me were beginning to surface.

I wondered if I would be sleeping in this cage-like room, a classroom of nightmares with bizarre faces on the wall and crumpled up papers pinned here and there. His anxious smile pled with me to take him to America with me. I told Jahan that I would like to learn Arab.

His response was clear: "You'd be better off going to Saudi Arabia and visiting Mecca where Arabic is spoken in its purist form." He offered to take me to the holy city. I thanked him but suspected he would expect me to pay our voyage. Perhaps this was a way he contrived to find out how much money I had, but I was not sure. In any case, it was clear that he wanted to leave Morocco in the worst way.

A gloomy look cloaked the shine in his brown eyes as he prepared to tell me something. He cleared his throat and glanced at me and occasionally back at Abou Bakr.

"I want leave Morocco now—I find my girlfriend with man. I want to kill him. I will kill him if I don't leave. I want get away, escape frustration of see her at school every day with someone else. I am dishonored before friends. Then I return with money in pocket and new wife to show off everyone."

His eyes sparkled, reflecting contentment with his scheme. He looked at me for approval and I nodded. He grinned and without a word, jumped up, opened the door and dashed up the stairs outside the entrance to the room. I glanced back at Abou Bakr who looked back and shrugged his shoulders.

In a few minutes, Jahan returned with a pot of mint tea, overflowing with fresh mint leaves, and a dish of homemade sugar cookies, some with sprinkles of nutmeg on top. I devoured the cookies and slurped the delicious mint tea as Jahan quietly sipped his; he watched me in silent curiosity. Abou Bakr, who had been patiently sitting in back, got up, said something quickly in Arabic to Jahan, opened the door, and with a wave to me, left.

Jahan gently placed his empty glass on the table. His gaze met mine as he watched the last crumbs of sugar cookies fall from my mouth onto the floor. He carefully chose his words as he began to speak English in a low, purposeful voice. In spite of his sometimes abrasive, guttural accent, he spoke with amazing facility, using an extensive, sometimes intellectual, vocabulary, like someone who was well read but had not often practiced speaking the language. I, thus, rarely corrected his English, primarily because I did not want to interrupt his incredibly rich monologues concerning Islam. We discussed the differences between the American and the Arabic cultures for about a half hour until I asked him if he would mind teaching me a few Arabic words.

"Yes," he replied, "you teach me English, I teach you Arabic." Jahan suggested that I first learn to count from one to ten. After a few minutes of guttural ecstasy, I fumbled my way through counting to ten. After that we started speaking English again since Jahan was far more interested in speaking English than teaching me his language.

"So much for the Arabic lesson," I sighed silently.

We continued our conversation which seemed to last for hours. My attention often drifted—while Jahan engaged in long monologues about how much he loved the U.S., my mind visited far away places, like my room in Paris. There, I often contemplated creation or the discovery of a universal religious movement, based on the unity of all religious doctrines—I was riding a wave of idealism at that time, somewhat inspired by the Seine River, relentlessly flowing beneath my window. I dreamed that someday I would help find the key to peace in the Middle East: that the hatred between Jews and Arabs—perpetuated by continuous war, suffering and the endless spilling of blood—would lessen, and eventually be forgotten. I dreamed the Middle East would be a test area for a new ideology based on unity and tolerance, as opposed to segregation and sectarianism. I dreamed that every town and every city in the world would construct a temple alongside local houses of worship, where people of all religious and non-religious backgrounds would come together in peace and love, to worship and freely discuss the common denominator that unites us in one supreme consciousness. People could actually worship with people from all denominations, without losing touch with their own religious and cultural heritage.

How could people hate so much, I wondered, and live so little in the rejuvenating spring of water, which is life? How could one blame parents or grandparents for what they had done? I wondered if it were possible to break the cycle of hate begetting hate all over the world.

This fanatical dream perhaps blinded me to seeing certain realities of life until I had tasted danger's intriguing but poisonous fruit, such as hate itself. Maybe I had tasted it for the first time in the mosque during the heated scolding by the older Moslems. I feared that such an occurrence prophesied times to come. Before I could delve further into that, my thoughts faded with a brisk rapping at the door. Jahan swiftly responded by opening it to behold another adolescent wearing a vertically striped djellabah. As he smiled, silver flashed in his back teeth and his two front teeth bore the yellow tinge of a cigarette smoker. His brown eyes showed no hostility.

Jahan introduced the newcomer as Azedine. I recognized him as one of the boys who had helped defend me in the mosque and who had walked with me in the Medina until he had vanished into the warm air earlier that afternoon.

Jahan and Azedine spoke a few undecipherable words together and then turned towards me. Jahan spoke up and said it would be better if I slept at Azedine's that night. As he spoke, his teeth shone against the backdrop of his clear, brown skin. He explained to me that he had a seriously handicapped brother who roamed the house at night and would surely prevent me from sleeping.

I nodded perfunctorily. Jahan helped me with my backpack. I thanked him for his hospitality and Arabic lesson. He returned the compliment, thanking me for speaking to him in English. Well, it had not been a real exchange as most of the conversation was in English, but I resigned myself to such disappointments as I had not much choice, for the moment, but to submit to the rhythm of my surroundings. As I followed Azedine out the door, Jahan, about to close the door behind us, said instead that he would join us. Soon, we three were traipsing down the familiar dirt roads, on the way to Azedine's house.

Azedine led the way. It was late afternoon and the rays of the sun no longer touched this somber part of the Medina—only the shadows reveled. Every few steps, he would look back at us, and then he would smile. A yellow spot imbedded in the middle of the upper row of teeth made him look like an old sea captain with the moon reflected in his smile.

Other than a few scrawny, stray cats with mangy gray and black fur, darting from time to time across the alley in front us, there was nary a soul. Making no secret of my surprise, Azedine explained to me that the people were taking their Saturday afternoon nap. He spoke good French so we conversed in that language. Jahan would intercede in our conversation, speaking English. At one point, I became confused as to whom I should speak what language: I spoke English to Jahan and French to Azedine. The former pretended to neither understand nor speak French. We stood there laughing since Azedine could not understand a word of English.

We soon arrived at Azedine's door. He knocked and a beautiful, dark-haired girl who I nicknamed "Arabian princess" (who was a Berber and not an Arab) opened the door. Azedine introduced her as Asana. Her sweet, rosy smile transported me to my grandmother's flower patches in the Oregon springtime. Asana's midnight-black hair was swept back into a long ponytail, which hung down over her long white muslin robe. Her eyes symbolized beauty in its most natural form, as in one born in the Himalayas. Such beauty I had seldom witnessed—it pierced the center of my heart. I imagined if she were my wife, I would readily agree that if she so desired, she could wear a veil upon leaving the nest. Such was an indication of a truly blinding, crazy attraction since I normally would abhor such an idea.

She stepped aside and motioned us inside; I was greeted by a swarm of children, girls and boys of all ages, who were laughing and rolling on the well-scrubbed floors. Their joyous cries elevated my mind from the stench and mud of the Medina into a new, lighter world. I was still amazed by the striking contrasts in this strange land, such as the clean air and floors of the mosque compared to the smell of decay and human excrement outside its lavish white walls.

Azedine introduced his father and mother to me as they emerged from an adjacent room and we warmly shook hands. His young brother wrapped his arms and legs around Jahan, who introduced the excited child as Abel. The mother's warm, brown eyes were somewhat overshadowed by two large, front teeth that dominated her large mouth. She wore a colorful scarf with a blouse of shades of violet and gold tucked into a typical muslin skirt. The father's short, graying hair contrasted with his smooth, youthful face; he had a small neck, a thin frame and was wearing a western style, checkered shirt tucked into a pair of faded jeans. This family portrait reminded me of a typical scene in any northern California household on a Saturday afternoon.

The beautiful "Arabian princess" came to me, and in broken French, reintroduced herself. She gently pulled on my sleeve, entreating me to come inside an adjoining room. At the center, there was a round table covered by a flowered tablecloth, around which her family was seated. I was placed in front of the entrance, opposite the father and mother. To the right of me sat three young girls, including Asana. One had short hair and large jowls— her smile revealed a number of silver fillings and when she stood up to leave, her stocky body could barely fit around the others as she squeezed behind them on her way out. In a few moments, she returned with a huge, round silver platter with a steaming mixture of rice and vegetables.

110

Azedine, sitting on my left, informed me that this was the national dish, called couscous. He pointed to his stocky sister and introduced her as Khadidja. I noted that Jahan sat next to him, his attention focused on the hot victuals laid before him—he did not even notice me looking at him. Khadidja served me the delectable mixture; the steam carried a delightful aroma to my nostrils. My relief was great, having been besieged by rancid odors outside in the streets.

Khadidja, pointing to the plate overflowing with small kernels of rice, vegetables and small pieces of lamb, said "Kul, kul (eat,eat) couscous."

I looked around the table and saw no utensils. The father followed my eyes and smiling warmly, said "Here, I will show you!"

He loaded the palm of his right hand with the concoction, and then curling his fingers around it, he carefully kneaded it, after which he opened his hand. In place of the handful of rice and vegetables was a tight, round ball. I smiled looking up into his grinning face; a couple of teeth missing in front did not take away from his warm countenance. I took my eyes off his hand for an instant, to search out Asana's eyes.

Before I could accomplish that, Azedine's father pointed his index finger at me and, as if he was preparing a magic trick, said, "Hey, watch." He placed the thumb of his right hand underneath the ball, and with one upward thrust popped it into his month.

My eyes must have lit up like a young boy's seeing a magic trick for the first time. He let out a "Hah hah!" and the rest of the family joined in.

He motioned me to imitate him; he followed the same steps, filling his palm with the couscous, wrapping his fingers around it, etc. When he produced a neat and clean ball, I opened up my palm and showed a less than perfect, greatly lopsided, messy, rectangular glob of rice. His expression seemed to say, "Not bad." Then he popped his neatly in his mouth.

Buoyed by his response, I decided to go for it, and pop the rectangular object in my mouth. All eyes were on me so I tried to make the best of the show. I carefully placed my right thumb under it, guided my hand to my mouth, and with a single thrust, flipped it toward my mouth. Only my pretty rectangle seemed to disintegrate in a thousand grains of rice before reaching the target. This time, the entire family exploded in laughter, pointing to the grains of rice sticking to my scraggly beard. I imagined what I must have looked like, so I also had to let out a healthy belly laugh. Even Jahan raised his head from his plate, offering a fleeting grin.

After awhile, hunger churning my insides, I started perfecting my style, thus insuring that more crushed steamed wheat entered my mouth than decorated my cheeks and beard. As I was able to eat more couscous, I began to feel the intense sensations subside in my stomach. Khadidja bent over me with another spoonful of this ambrosia.

She asked first, before serving me, "La basse? (Everything okay?) Tu veux encore? (Do you want some more?)" in broken French as her small smile widened, accentuated by two little dimples appearing on her creamy cheeks.

I had to refuse due to an overpowering sensation of fullness, causing my stomach to strain against my belt. After dinner, Jahan took his leave, hurrying out the door after bidding us a quick good night. I was surrounded by children, a couple of young girls about six or seven years old and a ten-year-old boy. They shook my hand and then kissed the hand that touched mine or placed their hands over their hearts as if they were pledging allegiance to the flag. I was touched by the whole scene; tears filled the corners of my eyes.

Azedine called to me as he stood in an archway leading into another room, in front of several hanging strands of beads serving as a colorful curtain. I parted the beads, which made a soft clacking noise as I walked through them, and followed him into a large rectangular room. Benches lined the walls, covered with a richly woven material and brightly colored cushions with golden embroidery.

Azedine pointed to a bench on the other side of the room, inviting me to sit on a cushion there. He sat next to me. He explained that the scenes on the cloth covering the benches were of the countryside in Morocco, and was woven by a member of the family. I saw rolling sand dunes, traversed by a group of camels—a theme repeated throughout—against the backdrop of a brilliant blue sky on a desert afternoon. In one corner of the room was a large, metal tea pot on a large, round, silver platter engraved with designs resembling flowers, extending to the outer edge. The relaxing surroundings made it propitious for an evening snooze; I felt my eyelids slowly drop over my eyes as we sat there in silence.

Azedine and I continued to sit there next to each other, both fatigued from the exciting, full day. A few minutes later, I saw the black, velvety hair of Asana appear through the beaded curtains. She entered the room and spoke a few Arabic words to Azedine, who responded by pointing to the silver teapot in the corner. Its spout curled, pointing towards the ceiling, and inscriptions were engraved on its sides. He leaned over to me and announced that the tea service would begin in a few minutes: he proudly explained that serving and drinking mint tea is an important part of the Moroccan culture.

The cushion deflated a little under my weight. I continued to grow more and more relaxed, nearing slumber. Azedine did not speak so I figured the same sensation had befallen him.

My drowsy state was interrupted by the father entering the room wearing a fez, a cone-shaped hat flat across the top, with a tassel attached. He was laughing as he sat down next to Azedine.

In a moment, the tea service began, with the father receiving the silver platter with the tea kettle filled with water from Azedine, who placed it in front of him. He set the kettle on a heating device which was like a kerosene stove, made specially to fit the tea kettle. While the water was being heated, he trimmed the mint leaves in a pile next to the kettle. After the water was hot enough, he dropped in pellets of what looked like a tea—I noticed the box was labeled "Gun powder." Then, the mint leaves were carefully placed in the water, followed by large pieces of sugar that the father had shaved from a sugar block. Asana brought in what appeared to be a brown, clay plate with several kinds of round cookies resembling shortbread, but in a more robust form than what I was accustomed to being served at my British-American grandmother's tea parties. They were actually delicious sugar cookies, which had a rich, almond taste that blended perfectly with the mint tea.

The end product was an extraordinarily delicious glass of tea served to Azedine and me, after which the father served himself a glass. It seemed that we sat in the living room for hours, chatting and drinking tea. The father told me he was the straw boss in a factory of about twenty workers. He said he loved the Americans, who had maintained a naval base in Morocco after World War II. He recounted that he had worked there for a year and afterwards the Americans gave him an excellent letter of recommendation, which facilitated future employment. He stood up and went to a mantel displaying various items, including a framed document, yellowed with age. It, indeed, was a letter of recommendation written in English and signed and stamped by the Commander-in-Chief of the U.S. Navy. The letter commended the father for his loyal service while working on the U.S. Naval Base in Morocco after World War II.

I congratulated him and he smiled and nodded, his small, brown eyes squinting with pleasure; he shook my hand, holding it for the longest time, as he showered me with a fatherly smile.

After the tea service, the young "princess" cleared off the round silver platter, brushed the cookie crumbs into her hand, grasped the handle of the tea kettle and vanished through the beaded curtain. As the contours of her graceful, tan body slipped away, I noticed two pairs of brown, desert eyes staring at me from behind the beads. I leaned over to Azedine and asked him who was spying on me. He told me that his other two sisters, who were very timid, were watching me. He then frowned, pointed to the curtains and the spying eyes vanished.

Azedine then informed his father that I might convert to Islam. The latter raised his hand, shrugging his shoulders, and without changing his fatherly expression, other than wrinkling his brow a bit, said, "Shooweeya," which means "Little by little." He did not really seem enthusiastic that I embrace his religion. After he left the room to retire for the night, I asked Azedine why his father was not as excited that I join in the practice of Islam as the boys in the mosque had been that afternoon.

He responded, "I need to explain something to you. I am a little tired so I'll talk to you more about it another time. Just remember that we are Berbers and not Arabs. Do you know what that means?"

I replied that I did not know what the word "Berber" meant.

He responded quite eloquently, "Suffice it to say that we were the original inhabitants of Morocco before the Arab Moslems came and converted us, by force, to Islam."

He calmly looked over at me to determine if I had understood. I nodded. He looked into my eyes for almost thirty seconds, probably wondering what I was thinking. He smiled; I think he knew I understood.

We were then approached by two little "bandit" sisters following Asana, who greeted me with dreamy, cheerful brown eyes. One had long, brown hair and was wearing a cute, flowery dress; her cheeks dimpled with her congenial, curious smile. The other was a little older and wore a green and gold-colored bandana around her head, with black, shiny curls spiraling down over the pleats of the bandana across her forehead.

Asana took the initiative: "The girls wanted to say good night to you."

They both bid me goodnight and were quickly whisked away by Asana as they giggled, looking back over their shoulders.

The warmth of the family surrounded and engulfed my being, pushing away the weary, lonely moments recently spent. When I leaned back and rested my back against the wall, Azedine asked me if I was tired. I nodded and he stood up and walked to the opposite wall where he opened a cupboard door containing my backpack on one side, and a drawer full of blankets, pillows and sheets. He asked me if I needed my backpack. I shook my head and waited for him to hand me the covers. Instead, he arranged the covers on the bench next to me and selected a soft cushion that would serve as my pillow. He then entreated me to go to that bed, while he made a similar bed on the opposite wall.

In the dark, I stripped to my shorts and t-shirt, lay down and soon was out. I literally sank into the bench and cushion and into a deep, deep sleep. The mental and physical strain of the day had been almost overwhelming. I was exhausted from the tip of my toes to the ends of my long, black hair.

After all I had seen and done the past few days, and all the suffering and madness that I had experienced, the warmth of the family had restored my confidence in people. I was content that I had found a base from which to begin my work—to realize the goals I had laid out and which were now the "raison d'être" for my existence.

That night I dreamed of my departure from Paris. I stood with Peggy on the loading dock and we peered into each other's eyes. She then shared with me a dream she had had the night before, as she was wrapped around my perspiring body. In her dream, I descended into deep, crystal-clear water. She could see my image while I was submerged. Then she envisioned me pulling myself out of the deep lake. In the clear water, she could see many objects below the surface. The light-brown grains of sand swept brightly-colored Persian rugs and metallic tables. Dark animal skins were draped over my long, black, wavy hair while my head eerily turned left and right, in slow motion. She watched me as I plunged deeper into obscurity, and then she lost me. Finally, she could only see a black tunnel below the surface from which she could only hope that I would emerge. She began making these strange sighing sounds. I awoke and felt her head; it was drenched with perspiration. As I carefully dabbed her forehead, she fell into a deep, silent sleep.

Chapter XIV

Home or Illusion

For the next few days, I was treated like a king by the family. I could also come and go as I pleased. I followed the same daily routine: at about 9:00 every morning, I woke up to the sound of little waterfalls of a sugary drink being poured into awaiting glasses in the kitchen. I arose and would head to the bathroom where I would perform my ablutions. Next, I proceeded to the toilet, which consisted of a hole in the ground and a water faucet next to it. I would perform my duty and then wash with the water flowing from the faucet. There was no toilet paper, but I quickly became accustomed to the new procedures.

Then I would proceed to the kitchen and take a seat at the wooden table where we had supped the first night I had arrived at the house. The father would have already left since he was due to commence work in the wee hours of the morning. The mother was in charge. She, dressed in silks and soft tissues, sat patiently behind an enormous cooking pot and ladled into an individual glass the sugared café au lait with a touch of cinnamon or other spice which I drank while munching on buttered bread. She always greeted me warmly, the corner of her mouth fluttering timidly.

"La bas?" (Everything alright?), she would ask as she poured the drink into another cup.

"La basse," I would answer sleepily as I had not yet fully awakened.

I often thought that that entire scene must have been a dream. Everyone would have gone to school except the mother, later joined by the Arabian princess, always flashing a sweet, silky smile. She would hand me another buttered slice of bread the mother had carved from a large round loaf stored in a red and gold basket with a cone-shaped lid. The mother would then pour me another glass of café au lait, which soothed my insides. After I finished the second slice, the mother and daughter team would offer more. I would hold up my hand to refuse, but they insisted that I eat and drink. These people were as sweet as buttercups blooming on the side of a green hill, waving in the California summer breeze.

I took advantage of the comfort of my surroundings and the serenity of the family to rest and recuperate from my long voyage. I also learned a little Arabic and watched the mother make bread every morning after breakfast. Her shiny, black hair was wrapped in a green cloth tied in the back.

I scrutinized her preparations for making bread: first, she would place a scrubbed wooden board down on the spotless floor. She then poured the powdery, white flour from a gray paper sack onto the board. She added water, working it in with the flour, producing something that looked like gray mud. From another sack, she poured in a dark powder. My wrinkled brow must have indicated my surprise, since she took pains to explain to me that the powder was yeast. She explained to me that it was to help the bread rise, raising her hand above her face to show me the direction the bread would go while baking in the oven.

She proceeded to knead and flatten the dough then continue working with it. After that, she began a long kneading process: she pounded the doughy glob into a pizza-like form, and then folded the edges followed by more kneading, while her head rhythmically bobbed back and forth, back and forth, as perspiration trickled down her soft, olive face. She had a thoughtful, aquiline nose, determined lips and a jaw which was resolutely set. Thin strands of hair touched the upper part of her pursed lips.

She then divided the dough, pounding it into long, firm strips and then kneading the strips separately. They would be shaped, pounded and molded into three neat little pillow-shaped mounds of dough and carefully placed, side by side, on a board dusted with flour. They were then covered with a thin, brown cloth. She would set the board aside for awhile until the bread rose. When the dough had sufficiently puffed up, Asana would gently place the board with the strips of dough on her head and the mother would open the door for her as she set out for the communal ovens located about three minutes from the apartment.

About forty-five minutes later, she would return, the bread board on her head, with two or three plump, rounded loaves of bread, warm and tantalizing; they filled the house with a sweet scent of freshly baked bread.

It was time for lunch. The children—having returned from school—and I would all crouch down or sit in front of the round, wooden table on which a hearty stew of vegetables and sometimes a little meat was placed in a huge pot. Each one of us was given a healthy chunk of warm bread which we put either next to our bowl or in our laps. The mother ladled the stew into a large clay platter in the middle of the table, equidistant from those sitting around the table. We would dip small pieces of warm bread in the stew and spoon up a mixture of vegetables and a little meat on the piece of bread and pop it in our mouths. In leaning over the table to dunk the bread in the communal platter, we touched hands from time to time.

The mother looked on from the same sitting position in which she had made the bread. She hovered over us like a contented hen making sure that her chicks had enough to eat. She continued to slice the bread and then handed the thick slices to waiting hands. Finally, after everyone had finished and had either leaned back against the wall or left the kitchen, the mother felt free to eat, provided there was food left. Sometimes she would just eat the bread that had probably cooled, at the same time insisting that I eat more stew. I reveled in being able to eat with my hands as I had as a California farm worker; my hands dripped with the vegetable and meat sauce, mixed with bread crumbs. I wiped them on the communal napkin handed to me by one of the daughters.

After lunch, I would sit back against the cushion, contentedly and silently burping as I watched the children invent games on the floor of the adjoining room. I had no itinerary for the first two days as I was happy to relax and read and share repasts with the family. After I had recuperated my strength, I began to dream of finding an appropriate time to free myself from this family nest, so I could contemplate what I had been doing on neutral territory, even if that meant walking the alleys and streets of the Medina. I hung around a little while longer, waiting to make my move towards the door. I intuited that they might think me an opportunist or unappreciative of them if I left the house right after lunch, as if to say "Thanks for lunch—ciao!"

After the mother finished eating, wiping her mouth on the communal cloth, she proceeded to clean up with her daughters. I offered to help but their reaction was one of surprise: it was not at all my place to help in any household chores. It was not clear that precluding me from such tasks was because I was a guest or a man. In any case, it was clear that the work in the home was reserved for the females. I did see the boys occasionally help sweep or scrub the floors. However, they were soon waved outside as the job was finished by the mother, assisted by the daughters.

After lunch, the kids went back to school and I was left alone with the princess and her mother in the dining room. The first two days, I would withdraw into the living room where I had slept the night before and read or take naps all afternoon. During those moments of silence, I was left completely alone. I reminisced about my past, in particular, about my life in Paris and California. I also thought about Camara's suggestion that I join the Islamic monastery. I wondered if being totally immersed in Islam would be the best way to understand it, or would it expose me to brainwashing, perhaps from which I would never recover. On the other hand, I have always strongly believed that in order to understand fully a culture—its religion and way of life—one must throw himself fully into the learning process and trust that the strength to fight any evil or overcome any adversity would always be there. I believed that one must even go as far as risking one's life for knowledge and understanding of the truth. I shuddered to even think about that but I knew I had to risk all in order to open the mysterious door to understanding that had been closed to me.

I began to take short walks in the Medina, visiting the nooks and crannies of a slum of which I felt I was somehow a part. The vendors calling out to passersby behind fresh fruit heaped into little hills were no longer abrasive to me. They seemed to sense that I was somehow a local and stopped trying to entice me to spend the tourist money jingling in the pockets of my baggy trousers.

Even the putrid stench of the stagnant pools of water, containing pieces of raw meat and spoiled fruit, did not seem to bother me as much as before. It was all part of living in a warm family neighborhood where families lived rustically but happily. I measured the simplicity of my life compared to what it had been in Paris, and I felt that I had indeed come full circle—back to nature, conforming to my country upbringing. Yet something was missing...perhaps the wide-open spaces at the foot of the rolling northern California hills. I sought such vastness on the Casablanca beach, where I often strolled. There, I would meditate while perched over the vast waters of the mighty Atlantic, its white foam splashing up all the way to my bare toes. I reveled in its frothy wetness and imagined it to be a dynamic arm reaching out as an intermediary between the African and North, Central and South American continents.

After my walks, I would return to the nest refreshed by my independent action and the knowledge that I had also given Azedine's family an opportunity to take a break from my watchful presence. Over time, I developed a great respect and love for this hospitable, generous, warm family that had literally pulled me off the streets and into their world.

One day, I was visited by a group of boys who were friends of Azedine's, some of whom had been present at the mosque during my visit. I recognized a couple young Moroccans, no older than ten, both wearing burgundy-colored djellabahs and carrying knapsacks on their backs. We embraced each other. By now, I had grown accustomed to kissing both cheeks of those I was greeting. I especially felt a warm glow at perceiving the two who had been with me during the makeshift trial at the mosque. The other boys were about the same age and I had never seen them before. They were carrying what appeared to be books and magazines.

The boys I didn't know had obviously come to feast their eyes on Medina's new phenomenon, a bearded, glassy-eyed American interested in Islam. Their hungry looks took in my entire body as if I were an animal in the zoo. Feeling a little uncomfortable, I responded with a blank look.

They huddled together, conversing in Arabic. One of them approached me and began speaking in clear, but broken, French. On behalf of the others and himself, he asked me why I had come to Morocco; they were curious to know why I would leave a city like Paris for the dirt alleyways of the Medina. I fed them my reasons while their curious, brown faces broke out in smiles as they looked at each other, almost in disbelief. They were then invited to sit around the wooden kitchen table and drink mint tea served by the mother, after which they left.

The next day, a couple of young Moslems whom I had met at the mosque knocked on the door. After introducing themselves, they were admitted by the mother after I waved them in. She cast a wary eye over the two as she clearly didn't trust them. The two were about fifteen years old and both wore immaculate white robes and gold-colored turbans, carefully placed over their shaved heads. They had brought with them several French translations of the *Qur'an* and religious commentaries in French and even in English.

I received them in the hallway and asked the mother if we could retire to the living room. She nodded, her worried eyes again raking over the two adolescents. They were apparently sent by the mosque to teach me Arabic and to introduce Islam to my eager eyes and ears. They went over the fist ten letters of the alphabet, which I repeated several times with them. They were fortunately patient and enthusiastic teachers, since my knowledge was limited. From time to time, they would stop the session to diverge from the topic a little by marveling that I had traveled so far to learn their language and religion. One short boy who was a shade darker than the other, and whose face was round and jovial, told me, in French, that I was a rare specimen of the American culture! I was amazed at how well he articulated the French language. Even though I considered myself very rough around the edges as their pupil, they observed that I was very curious about their culture and hence a very fast learner, much to their amazement.

Later that afternoon, and a full four days since I had been installed in the apartment with Azedine's family, I was finally visited by Camara, the black African, who had informed me about the Islamic mission after my visit to the mosque. His mysterious entrance back into my life took me by surprise, and my intuition warned me of impending danger, yet I felt a relentless pulling towards Camara's mosque.

When he called, I was reading in the living room. Camara was ushered in by the mother; he was wearing a brown fur cap, peaked at both ends, resembling a smaller version of a Russian hat.

When he saw me reading, he stopped in the middle of the living room floor and declared, "Allahu Akbar" (God is great). "It looks like this family has taken good care of you. Thanks be to God."

Without waiting for a response, Camara continued, "As promised you, I have returned. I hope you have had time to think about my offer?"

I responded, "I have been learning Arabic and about Islam for the last few days and I think I would like more intensive training."

He stated, "But you must be sure that you desire the life of an Islamic monk. You must be motivated to do that above all other things. You must set up a serious study plan and stick to it. And, when you are within the walls of this monastery, you must first learn to listen carefully to what they are teaching you—don't express doubts as to the knowledge they offer you until you have studied carefully. Are you ready to live an ascetic life without women, only with the holy *Qur'an* for your bed partner?"

"I'm ready," I said, without hesitation.

"Then let's get started. Before entering the monastery, you will need to prove to them that you have learned the main prayers. To do that you need to be surrounded by the *Qur'an* every day. I advise that you grab your belongings and move in with me and my family today. I would be honored to be in charge of your spiritual education until I deliver you to the monastery."

"It'll just take a few minutes and I'll be ready," I stated, looking over to the cupboard that contained my knapsack.

I went to the cupboard, opened it and saw that my knapsack was neatly placed in the corner. I dragged it out. As I was going through my belongings, Camara came up to me; I could feel his breath on my hair.

"By the way, you will have to contribute something for your room and board for about two or three weeks. But we'll talk about that later."

I had no trepidation that a complete stranger had invited me to his home, to sup with his family and him, in order to help me prepare for entrance into an Islamic monastery. There, I would live, learn Arabic and the fundamentals of the Islamic religion. That, I believed, was my destiny and I knew I could trust Camara, even without knowing the least thing about him. But, apart from enduring those formalities in the monastery, an even greater challenge lay ahead of me: after a period of relative comfort, sharing with such a warm and open family, I was about to return to the world of endless soul-searching, endless questions, endless insecurity as I followed the path—or paths— I hoped would lead me to the truth. During that process, I would attempt to free myself from all layers of false identity; the truth of my identity would emerge as I struggled to solve the mysteries imbedded in my soul.

The time had come to say goodbye to the mother and Asana, who stood in the hallway faithfully by her mother's side, waiting for me to leave the living room with Camara. I could also see Azedine, who had just joined his mother and sister. As I reached them, the mother touched my hand, and kissed the hand that had touched mine; Asana and Azedine did the same. They had taken me off the streets of the Medina into their warm abode; I thanked them with all the sincerity that a human being can muster. I was particularly attached to Azedine who had been my "protective angel," beginning at the mosque, during that memorable afternoon not long ago.

He had brought me into his home without knowing anything about me. He had faith that I would respect his family, and that I was not bringing in some awful disease, that my objectives were true. My feelings surged like a storm within me and it was all I could do to contain them. This family and demonstrated by their acts the true meaning of faith and helping others, apart from their incredible hospitality, considered a generalized trait of Mediterranean people.

My eyes moistened as I looked away. The mother spoke to me in Arabic while Azedine translated her words into French. She insisted that I return soon and live with them again. Her eyes were full of apprehension as she grasped my hands and embraced me with a motherly regard. This uneducated woman, who rarely left her home and wore a veil when she shopped in the market, had sensed something—a hidden danger—that I would only understand later. Her eyes warned me but I could not, would not see it.

Camara led me back to the mouth of the labyrinth, the souk in the Medina, which entailed walking down winding alleys, passing rows and rows of fruit, dates, bolts of material and shoes. It took us hours to make our way through since we stopped at nearly every stand to greet the vendors; Camara knew them all by name, and they all knew his name.

One leaned over rows of medjool dates, and said, "La basse, Camara, mon ami," (Everything okay, Camara, my friend), a mixture of French and Arab.

Camara had almost always the same response, "Al hamdu li Ilâhi." (Praise Allah.)

They all stood in front of their booths, lined up along the small dirt paths we followed. The stalls were crudely constructed of unfinished wooden slabs and laden with silk fabrics, clothes of all shapes and sizes, shoes and books. Virtually all the latter related somehow to Islam.

We finally entered a small café and contentedly plopped down on an old rickety bench facing a table covered with a coffee-stained, plastic tablecloth. Camara ordered a glass of hot tea and I a café au lait.

He sighed, and then spoke in a low voice, "Ah, my brother, Allah has shown you his grace. Ah oui, ah oui." He put both hands on my shoulders and continued, "You will learn many beautiful things if you accept Islam and love Allah with all your heart."

I told him that I believed in peace and unity and that a universal religion was needed in the world to unify the people because the world had divided into warring entities, and religious leaders had, unfortunately, often inspired hate, distrust and ultimately destruction instead of love and peace. Camara observed me with his reddish, dark eyes, letting me continue.

I observed, "Countries today have merely retreated inside themselves, into the flames of nationalism and a fervent desire for self-preservation. Isolation also breeds ignorance and war."

"Al hamdu li illâhi," he proudly voiced. "Ah oui, mon frère."

Camara rose to his feet and I followed him out the door. He led me deeper and deeper into the Ancienne Medina. We soon came to a water fountain gushing forth a continuous stream of water which filled the adjoining paths, creating long, muddy puddles of water filled with squashed fruit and decaying meat. The odor of wet feces collecting in still water made the air more pungent. Rotting chicken feet lay everywhere—in the mud puddles, and even on doorsteps. We pulled up our trousers and waded through the slime until we came to a doorway hidden behind an old sheet tacked onto the decaying wooden frame.

The noxious air had made my stomach queasy. Camara draped one end of the sheet over the other and waved me inside the hovel. The smell subsided as he led me up a flight of extremely narrow wooden steps; at the top, we entered a small room filled with tapestries, embroidered images of Mecca, the holy Islamic city, and Kaaba, the center of spiritual activity therein. Silver chalices and teapots lined the walls.

120

Camara invited me into the living room to sit in an easy chair, with stuffing pouring down its sides, until his return. He returned a few minutes later wearing a black djellabah with a white turban. I lapsed into fear, imagining he was a witch doctor from some African tribe, and that all this talk about Islam was merely a facade. Without saying a word, he sat in a metal chair opposite me. I offered him the more comfortable sofa but he refused, telling me that he wished me to be completely at ease. One hand was clenched as it rested in his lap; the other was resting on a metal table that separated us.

He looked at me with sober brown eyes; faint hues of red streaked the whites of his eyes. The intensity of his gaze seemed to express a power from which I wondered if I would ever be able to escape.

"I'm glad that we can finally spend some time together. You have much to learn, you know. But, little by little, you'll see." Camara finished his introductory speech and rose, looking at me intently. Then he turned and brushed aside the curtain serving as a door and vanished behind it.

"First, we are going to eat," Camara hurriedly announced as he poked his head through the curtains. He vanished but not before I observed the image of his head, hatless for the first time in my company. The hair at the top of his head was cut short and formed into minute spirals, typical of his African heritage. Without the hat, his face seemed rounder and his nose rather flat, with pronounced nostrils. His cheeks were round and shiny, enclosing a lively mouth with the hint of a mustache clinging to the upper lip.

A few minutes later, a young black woman slid through the curtain, carrying a large, metal plate. Her hair was hidden beneath a colorful yellow and green scarf. Her long, spindly legs contrasted with a bloated paunch under full breasts, suggesting a new life to be brought into the world. Her face was light and her nose slanted down like an aquiline slide jutting out over voluptuous lips, curved in an expression of motherly love. Columns of steam rose from the platter as she set it in front of me.

Camara followed her into the room and placing his arms around her waist, introduced her: "Voila, my wife," he proudly proclaimed, grinning from ear to ear. Her dark mouth opened into a faint, cautious smile, her long, black fingers resting on the mountainous belly exposing her pregnant condition. In spite of her pregnancy, sleek features were revealed in her thin neck and gaunt cheeks, portraying a mystical elegance. Camara sat down beside me as his wife retreated back through the curtains. He pointed to a set of plastic curtains in the corner leading to the bathroom. I raised the curtains and saw before me a rustic but very clean sink. As at Azedine's house, I did not see any soap so I thoroughly scrubbed my hands, wiped them on the communal towel hanging next to the sink and returned to my chair.

The metal platter was heaped with potatoes, carrots and hunks of meat in a meat sauce. My mouth watered as Camara beckoned me to dig in. We ate by filling our cupped hands with the stew and then stuffing our mouths. His wife joined us, sitting next to Camara. She motioned to a pair of frightened black eyes peeking out from the edge of the curtains. After waiting a few seconds, in popped a small boy with a small, frizzy head and curious, gleaming eyes. His young eyes reflected the turmoil and despair of the ghetto life of the Ancienne Medina.

But as he approached us, his dark-brown eyes began to sparkle, lighting up the entire room. Following him was his sister and older brother. The sister had long, frizzy hair; a tassel above her braid was adorned by a small pink ribbon. The older boy had rebel's eyes; his short, frizzy hair was highlighted with a dark comb planted on the side. He wore jeans and a western style, checkered shirt. His look penetrated me and transformed into a disdainful glare. I could guess that he was probably wondering why I was to be their houseguest.

The children's ages were four (the youngest son) and six or seven (the daughter's age). The older boy was probably about fourteen years old, expressing a mixture of hormones and rebellion. He and his sister carefully surveyed my every move, as if I might turn against them at any moment. Either their ghetto survival instincts were manifesting or perhaps they kept a suspicious distance due to my American nationality.

Camara, with one swish of his arm, waved the children away, who retreated to an adjoining room. He smiled and gestured with his hand to imitate the motion of eating: he held his plate in one hand and pretended to scoop food in his mouth with the other. I looked at him, uncomprehending.

"Eat," he urged. I nodded as my eyes looked at the door through which the children passed. He then waved his hand in front of my face: "Eat; you will have plenty of time to meet and talk with my children."

Only Camara and I ate, at first. His wife was in the adjoining room with the children. Then she entered with the children trailing behind her. They all took their places around the silver platter and the mother served them healthy portions of the food. The mother and children rapidly gobbled down the victuals; there must have been a dozen hands in the stew at all times. After eating, they got up and followed her back through the curtains into the adjoining room. The youngest looked over his shoulder, flashing a kindly, curious smile. His look reflected an infantile passion to learn, to live, without reservation, without motives other than to experience the moment. I thought that was also one of the reasons I had come to Morocco: to recapture the essence of being young and curious; to open up my heart like a child; to breathe the air of tolerance, release the encumbering chains of fear, and return to pure freedom, happiness and wisdom.

Such did the smile of the young boy inspire me.

Camara leaned back in his chair and invited me to finish the stew, which I did without hesitation. He leaned forward and asked me when was the last time I had taken a bath. I told him several days ago in Paris. His eyebrows raised; he told me that if I desired to become a Moslem, cleanliness was a fundamental rule.

I secretly was not sure I wanted to become a Moslem, but I closely listened to Camara. I wanted to trust this man; he seemed honest, straightforward and filled with principles. I thought that I would let myself be pulled into this religion, first with his words and principled generosity. I felt confident that I would never allow myself to become brainwashed to the extent that I would accept Islam as the only true religion. That night I slept on a couch opposite Camara whose body had disappeared in the middle of a soft bed which had closed in around my sleeping friend.

True to his principles, Camara took me to a public bathhouse the next day. But it was not an ordinary bathhouse. It was equipped with a small swimming pool, sauna and an expert masseur who could make anyone relax as he had the physique of a professional wrestler.

Camara gave me the grand tour of the facilities. Then he engaged in a lengthy conversation with the masseur, whose matted hair was held together in the back, emphasizing the large earrings in each ear. Afterwards, Camara led me to a metal door, behind which we stripped down to our under shorts. We gave our clothes to the attendant who later returned them, cleaned, pressed and dried.

He led me through another set of large metal doors; when opened, steam billowed through the entire doorway as we walked into the jaws of the dragon. As hot steam blanketed us, Camara led me deeper into a murky room with drops of condensation running down the walls. I followed him through wooden doors into an adjoining room, stifling hot. Camara instructed me to wait in the middle of this gigantic sauna while he fetched buckets filled with water.

Every few minutes I had to gasp for air in this huge oven. The room was nearly empty except for a lone bather busily scrubbing himself in the corner near the entrance, the soapsuds dripping from his naked body.

Copious beads of perspiration gathered on my forehead. As I waited, breathing became more and more difficult and my body turned into a sweaty river pouring down my chest, back, legs and trickling down between my toes. Camara finally returned and led me by the hand into a different room where we lay down next to a man who was pouring water over hot stones. I felt my body melting beneath a wave of even more stifling heat exploding from the blisteringly hot rocks.

Camara began to scrub himself with a metal sponge. When his skin appeared inflamed, he handed the sponge to me. As I scrubbed, the sponge grated my skin like a carrot. I wondered if this sponge was, in reality, a piece of steel wool, used to scrub pots and pans. I could not hold back a muffled laugh, in spite of the pain experienced from scraping my legs. My eyes began to sizzle as the heat intensified.

After I finished, Camara dumped a bucket of water over my head to rinse off the soap. The warm water was a refreshing contrast to the fiery heat in the air. Camara then left the room with the empty buckets. He returned a few minutes later, followed by the dark, burly masseur, both of them carrying two buckets of water. Camara told me to lie down and in a few moments, the huge hands of the masseur forcefully rubbed my back and legs with the infamous metal sponge. I gritted my teeth and sucked in my breath. After the scrubbing was over, my skin radiated a strawberry hue.

Camara gave me a sponge to wash my vital parts underneath my shorts and handed me a razor. He said that the mosque required that all my hair be cut off for beginning monks. He instructed me to commence with my pubic hairs and said he would help me with the rest.

I was shocked—"Why that?" I asked, shaking my head.

Camara responded, "The monastery required that as part of the cleansing process. The act of cutting off all your hair symbolizes the purification of the body."

Due to the lack of air, I was now near fainting. We must have been in that heat for at least an hour now. My body had been completely drained of all liquids. The razor slid over the entangled jungle of pubic hairs and nicked my skin; blood splashed on the brick floor below. I told Camara that I refused to continue this hazardous and somewhat humiliating experience but he took the razor and insisted on shaving under my arms. I winced as the dull blade of the razor tore the hair from my armpits, but my determination to be accepted by the mosque officials helped me to overcome the pain. After all the shaving had ceased, my twenty-seven-year-old body was beginning to look like a young boy's.

But Camara was not finished yet. He led me to the other side of the vast room where he told me he would teach me how to wash myself, the way Moslems do. He first showed me the eight-step ablution procedure, beginning with the hands and ending with the feet.

"Ok, your turn," Camara sighed, cueing me to repeat the procedure.

He watched as I awkwardly tried to imitate his motions. As I finished the fifth step, which was the washing of my arms, Camara intervened. First he told me that I must start with the right arm, which I had not done, and then I was supposed to wash each arm three times. He asked me to repeat the procedures, which I did. As I repeated the ablution process, my stomach and bowels wrenched, as if they were going to empty simultaneously. I could no longer stand the heat—my guts seemed turned inside out.

We had been in the sauna for about two hours. If this continued, I imagined myself drying up like a prune, all my juices flowing down the drain with the dirty water, in the middle of the sauna. My heart began to pound against my rib cage and I wondered if a person could die in a sauna. But I wanted Camara to know that if this—short of death—was the price to pay to be cleansed, even if it was only symbolic, I was ready to make great sacrifices in the name of enlightenment.

But I could take it no more. Just as I began gasping for air and was inspecting the room for side doors—I could crash through, if need be—Camara told me to rinse my body and then follow him to the locker room. "Thank God!" I mumbled under my breath.

Chapter XV

Life's Blood

As Camara opened the wooden door, my body poured out into the next room. With my vision temporarily obstructed, I groped for my clothes. The room felt cool, compared to the sauna, and the drastic climate change sent shivers through my body as I ran to the bathroom. The insides of my body cried for relief; I felt like a human time bomb, ready to explode with every stride. I finally reached the toilet, a crude hole in the ground, but it did not matter, as my bowels expelled their contents for at least fifteen minutes.

After that, my legs could barely carry me even though I felt considerably lighter. The strength in my arms had almost completely vanished, making the act of dressing myself an almost insurmountable task. As Camara helped me put on my shirt, I had to quickly return to the bathroom to vomit. Afterwards, he led me outside the walls of the bathhouse. I followed him to his apartment, stumbled up the stairs and flopped down on one of the cushions in the living room.

"How do you feel?" Camara asked, as he stooped over me with a concerned look.

"Not so good," I mumbled, my voice slurred.

"Oh, that'll pass," he assured me, handing me a piece of paper and a pencil. "I want you to write down and memorize the first prayer which you must memorize before going to the mosque."

All I wanted to do was sleep, but Camara's intense expression meant business—my lessons were to begin immediately. I admired his dedication, his relentless desire to spread the word of God. I leaned over and took the paper and pencil. My longing to learn Arabic welled up inside me and dominated me in spite of my weakness and constant trips to the bathroom, the familiar hole in the concrete floor. I would wash myself each time using the pail of water next to it.

Relieved, I would return and sit next to Camara, who began by dictating "le sourat"– Al Fatiha," one of the principal prayers recited during prayer sessions at the mosque. I told Camara that I greatly desired to begin, except I was feeling faint. He then opened the window and the pale muslin curtains fluffed as a cool breeze entered the room, carrying the pungent odor of decaying flesh and chicken feathers.

As I wrote the first few words of the prayer, "Bismi-l-lâhi-r-rahmâni-r-rahîm…," (In the name of God, the Merciful, the Compassionate….), the heavy, putrid air streaming through the open window caused me to turn my head toward the source: it was the roof of a lower building that served as a garbage dump for the buildings above. I wryly observed that the equivalent of "garbage service" was offered to anyone who surreptitiously opened a window and ejected a piece of chicken, banana peel, dirty rag or a half-eaten melon to the roof below.

That scene inspired my next trip to the bathroom; I had not yet recuperated from the hot ovens of the public bathhouse. My entire body continued to convulse inside and out; my bowels emptied at the same time I vomited. When I returned to the dining room, which doubled as a study, all I wanted to do was lay down. However, as pale as I was, Camera insisted I continue to learn the prayers.

After memorizing the first two lines of the "Al Fatiha", I sank into the cushions in the middle of the couch after having recited them twenty times. Camara tried several times to inspire me to recite a few more lines, but resigned himself to letting me sleep. Before I could doze off, however, I felt a tugging at my sleeve. When my eyelids opened, I beheld a perfect set of ivory teeth as Camera smiled at me. He asked me to stand up; I loathed the tone of voice he used which made it sound more like a command to "stand at attention." Since his tone also suggested he would not in any way take "no" for an answer, I stood up, begrudgingly.

My knees were wobbling terribly so I held them together which helped keep my wretched body upright. Camara, standing next to me, decided to accelerate the lessons by asking me to repeat all of the "al Fatiha" after him. I succeeded that time in reciting every line.

Camara's rather stoic expression was complemented by tempered words of congratulations—"Louange à Dieu" (Praise God) which seemed to pass for "Félicitations." (Congratulations).

He then led me through a series of body motions I was supposed to religiously follow. He knelt down beside me, his gaze fixed on the floor. Then he got on all fours, touching his forehead to the cold, hard floor. I did the same, imitating Camara's every gesture. He bent backwards until only his knees touched the ground then leaned forward until he touched his forehead to the floor.

I tried to follow the last movement but fatigue took over my ragged body—I began to shake at even the thought of the smallest physical effort. Out of the corner of my eye, I noticed that Camara had stopped and was watching me perform in slow motion. Humiliation reddened my cheeks: to think that I could hardly move my body, it was reduced to such a weakened state. He came up to me and placed his hand on the back of my head as I bent it toward the floor.

"You need to place your forehead squarely on the rug. Don't hesitate to prostrate yourself completely before Allah. It shows that you still hesitate to let yourself go completely on the rug, in total humility and acceptance of God in your heart."

He continued, "Insaallah (God willing), you will feel the faith and you will abandon yourself to the rug and to God."

As I had been so proud during my life, this was an awakening for me that grown men could, without hesitation, prostrate their bodies on the ground before an unseen spirit. I had faith in a supreme force, or God, as most people would call it. Yet I rejected acting out this submissive routine, with my forehead touching the ground.

He finally took pity on me and suggested that I take a nap before supper. As I lay on the couch with my head resting on its arm, Camara placed his hat back on his head and before he made his exit through the curtains, promised to return in about an hour.

As I lay on the couch staring at the ceiling, my conscious mind was disturbed by confusing images of being swept away by a tidal wave, to which I gave no resistance. As I was being carried away, I tried to surface, but dark creatures would stop me each time. My eyes opened and I searched the cracked ceiling for an explanation of my experience in the Islamic world. Camara's words "Purify yourself" kept ringing in my ears like a broken record. "To find truth," Camara would say, "one needs to suffer through hard times." My entire life played out before me as I raced from crack to crack in the ceiling overhead—I found myself speedily arriving nowhere. Such mental exertions lulled me to sleep.

I awoke minutes later to the same cracks, shadowed by the descending sun of a blistering afternoon. I could sleep no more and decided to practice the prayers and the body positions Camara had taught me. I gently placed my forehead on the floor as I prayed,

"La ilaha illa Allah wa Muhammad rasul Allah" (There is only one God, Allah, and Muhammad is his prophet). I recited this over and over again.

I prayed and prayed and as I did so, my entire life poured out from within me: my family, the girls I had known, universities, Paris, the Sorbonne, Brussels, the Common Market, the Belgian family I lived with—a maze of faces, emotions and colors swirled with me upwards like a climax, a synthesis of people and feelings harmoniously intertwined, rushing me toward some object of majestic beauty.

I became lost in a labyrinth of images, as my dreams led me back to Paris where I had lived with the young Parisian girl, Peggy. She was late for work because time was forgotten in warm embraces and passionate palpitations one afternoon in her small studio in the Place de la République. The next day, she lamented that she had lost her apartment because the owner was unhappy and jealous of the happiness we shared suspended in the Parisian sky overlooking Paris. Then my dreams led me to the train bound for Morocco. She held my hand, which extended through the open window as the train began to chug forward, ever so slowly; it was almost as if a lifetime was contained in every chug of its ancient motor. I felt the hot tears flow, saddened at the thought that she had lost her apartment because of me. I cried for forgiveness: "Help me, God. La ilaha illa Allah, la ilaha illa Allah..."

This mini catharsis was comforting and reassured me that I had taken the right path to the truth, that my sins had been forgiven—Allah had forgiven me and I was purified. I finally collapsed on the couch. I must have slept for hours when Camara reappeared that evening. I heard floating on a wave, a voice, interrupting the crashing of the wave—it curled, growing larger, finally breaking on the shore. The serene rhythm of this seascape was suddenly pierced by a shrill voice:

"Frank, wake up! Come on, we've got work to do."

My eyes were barely open as Camara leaned in front of me, his eyes shining from the reflection of the moonbeams filtering through the window.

"Frank, if you want to be a Moslem, you must have an Arab name. For now, conforming to your pure desire and your sincerity, it would be appropriate to have the master's name, so I will call you Muhammad. Repeat, then, after me: Muuuhaaaammad."

"Moohaaamad," I repeated.

"OK, good. Repeat again after me: La ilaha illa Allah, la ilaha illa Allah."

Camara coached me in learning the "Al-Fatiha" by heart that evening. I was proud of myself that I could recite it without using any notes. That night I slept on the couch near Camara's bed.

The next day, my intestines went on strike: I could barely eat without vomiting or defecating. The diarrhea now gushed out, sometimes preventing me from arriving at the hole in the ground on time. In between trips to the toilet, Camara taught me other essential prayers in the *Qur'an*. That evening, I slept like a dead man.

The next morning I felt like my entire body, especially my stomach, had been wrung inside out; unable to eat, I refused all food graciously proffered by Camara's kindly wife. I sat on the couch with the look of a zombie as she regarded me with worried brown eyes. Standing next to me, she ventured to lay her hands on my sagging shoulders as she gently said,

"I know you don't feel well, poor boy, and you didn't get much sleep." I sheepishly turned my head away, embarrassed that she had heard me as I carried on in the bathroom during the night. "But you should try to eat something, even if it is broth, or anything. Tell me, my poor young man, what would you like to eat?"

Her sweet words brought me halfway back to life— a faint glow pulsed through my veins, igniting my greatly weakened body. In spite of feeling so weak and helpless, I managed a smile to comfort her and alleviate her worrying.

As a mother and because the house was full of kids, I thought she might be concerned that I could have brought some contagious disease within the sanctity of her nest.

I said, "Don't worry; all this is merely due to the change of bacteria in the food and water—otherwise, I'm completely healthy." But she looked sincerely concerned for my well being and not worried about some contagion.

I suggested she bring me tea and bread. The steaming cup and plate of Moroccan bread seemed to instantly appear before me by a mysterious shake of a magic wand or by a momentary lapse into a dreamlike stupor. I tried sipping the tea and nibbling on the crust of bread, which stayed down and allowed me to breathe easily the rest of the morning, which was spent studying and memorizing other prayers given to me by Camara.

"I hope you are feeling better, now?" she inquired, as she stood over me. I looked up into the face of this complete stranger; gently smiling, she turned her face toward the door as she prepared to leave me with my studies.

At that moment Camara entered the room saying, "Oh, he'll be alright. He's just purifying his body. 'La ilaha illa Allah'—repeat after me."

His enthusiasm re-instilled a feeling of confidence and purpose in me, which had lagged in proportion to how weak I felt. His energy and unfailing dedication to what he believed in infused my previously reticent being, breathing new air into the stalled sails of my mind. As I rose to shake his hand, I felt my forces returning to my famished body and felt the personal significance of the trite but powerful phrase "It's mind over matter."

This same routine repeated itself for an entire week as I totally immersed myself in Islam and Camara's welcoming family. My official entry into Islam was to take place one evening at the end of that time. Camara informed me that he had invited several friends over for dinner during which there would be a modest ceremony. I asked him what kind of ceremony would take place. He sidestepped the question by advising me that I had better finish memorizing the prayers before our visitors arrived. I glanced at the small book sitting in my lap. I picked it up to review the main prayers but my eyes failed to focus; I needed more rest. My body was limp from fatigue due to constantly fighting nausea, which had ruthlessly invaded me...I needed to sleep.

Camara, who had briefly left the room, reentered through the beaded curtains and sat down beside me. My eyes opened to his persistent, almost desperate look: "Why aren't you studying the prayers?" he demanded, with great urgency in his tone of voice.

Before I could answer, he asked me to recite "al Fatiha" and several other less important prayers. I recited it correctly—the upturned corners of his mouth indicated Camera's satisfaction although he tried to conceal it. He helped me learn the pronunciation for the other prayers but before leaving the room, he shook his head and told me to work even harder memorizing the prayers during the next few hours.

A couple of hours later, Camara poked his head through the curtains and told me to prepare myself for a shopping trip. He led me to a small clothes boutique not far from the house with many djellabahs, hanging on what appeared to be white clothes lines stretched across the front of the boutique. From one of the back rows the vendor emerged, his huge smile accentuated by a long, full, black beard. He approached and heartily shook our hands until I thought mine would disconnect and fall to the ground. Camara took the initiative and analyzed every scrap of material with which a few of the djellabahs were made. He scrutinized the back for spots or flaws and felt the material to determine if the djellabah was appropriate for that night's festivities.

Camara told me that I must wear a djellabah that night if I intended to be a true Muslim. He pulled a blue one off the rack, held it up against me, shook his head and returned it to the rack. He then chose a white- and black-striped djellabah, held it up to me and asked me to try it on over my faded jeans. He flipped the hood over my face and then let out a belly laugh so deep and rich I felt it would fill the dirt holes and beggars' pockets and bring gaiety to the streets of the sullen Medina—it was a perfect fit.

I was directed to pay the vendor who cheerfully took the money, shoving it into his pocket while wishing me luck as a new convert to Islam. I left the djellabah on which made me feel more like a Moslem, more Moroccan, as I pranced about the Medina. I was like a disciple of God, as portrayed in a movie I had seen twenty years ago in the U.S., about the life of Jesus Christ. I looked around and was mesmerized by the sun on Moroccan brown skin, protected by multi-colored djellabahs. With my Mediterranean ideas and my djellabah I was, at least physically, one of them—hidden behind the same curtain, conforming to the ritual of Moslem society. With my shaved head and my djellabah, vendors no longer salivated for a sale as I walked by. In their eyes, I must have been just a local, this time without Western money stuffed in my pockets.

This marked my complete liberation from the daily burden, in my mind, of representing the Western world as I fully embraced the Qur'anic music reverberating constantly off the walls of the Medina—I was of this world. As Camara and I walked back to his apartment, he introduced me to more vendors, who apparently did business with him. He told me that he was a shoe salesman; every week he would travel to Melilla, a town in Morocco governed by Spain, buy inexpensive shoes and return to Casablanca, where he sold them to his network in the Medina. He explained that the vendors so vigorously calling out to passersby were actually working for him and for themselves. I thought to myself that this symbiotic relationship was typical between a supplier and distributor of goods.

We returned to Camera's apartment after half an hour of making the rounds of Camara's merchants. For the next few hours, I helped Camara and his wife prepare the house for the festivities to take place that night. I swept the floor of the living room while his wife cooked in the kitchen and Camara mopped the bathroom floor surrounding the lone hole in the middle of it.

After the apartment was cleaned and the food cooked, we sat down at the kitchen table to drink tea; pouring it provided the only sounds during our fatigued silence. Soon after I had taken my last swallow, the guests arrived. A cast of robed Moslems, a total of about eight, paraded into the recently scrubbed living room—the tea service, equally clean, would be put to use during the ceremonies.

The group was a mixture of young and old, from seventeen years to sixty, more or less. The elders stared at me with deep-set, beady, proud eyes, wearing spotless white djellabahs and milky white turbans. They spoke with soft, purposeful voices, their long, bony fingers cradling copies of the holy *Qur'an*. Their bodies sank into the couch or the cushions placed on the floor. I sat on the head sofa of honor, along with Camara. It went unsaid that we all considered ourselves brothers and humble voyagers on the same path leading, I hoped, to truth. Perhaps that was the sole difference that separated us—I was about to embrace the path that I hoped would lead me to truth, to the cosmic spirit of love, but my brothers believed that they were definitely on the path that would lead them to this spirit, to Allah.

We chanted without pretension, with light, pure hearts, "Allahu Akbar, Allahu Akbar: la ilaha illa Allah, la ilaha illa Allah." The pitch of our voices rose higher and higher until we stopped, red-faced and dry-mouthed, after a deafening, climactic stanza of loud bellowing. A younger singer, his face drawn and dejected, was forced to stop halfway through the last stanza as he had grown hoarse.

I thought to myself that this "indoctrination" process was benign as long as I did not embrace it in its totality, or I should say, tautology. A young, black-bearded man with short hair and cloudy brown eyes had brought a cassette recorder and a box of cassette tapes. Camara said a few undistinguishable words in Arabic and all eyes were trained on me. Then the man with the cassette recorder pushed the button and we were soon listening to a group of Americans being converted to Islam. As the cassette played, one blissful revelation after another was related concerning their search for and final discovery of truth.

Then the Americans chorused, "Muhammad is a swell guy!" and then they all seemed to say, in one way or another, "After an intense period of learning the doctrine, I finally accept Muhammad into my heart; I have become a Moslem."

I thought to myself that I wished one day I could blissfully share such revelations, that I could be so sure that truth was within my grasp.

Camara, who was sitting next to me, nudged me with his elbow. I understood this gesture as my cue to begin my performance. I cleared my throat, took a deep breath, and mumbled to myself "God give me strength" and proceeded to recite a couple of basic prayers without pause and without a single error. The lips of Camara made no attempt to hide his satisfaction as they stretched into a mile-wide grin. The guests patted him on the back to congratulate him for his work.

Chapter XVI

The Walls Echoed

The day's festivities had worn me out. After dinner, I requested that Camara allow me to retire early. As I left the kitchen, he wished me a good night. Parting the strands of beads leading to the living room, I heard Camara say, his voice barely audible, "Peace be with you, brother."

I turned my head far enough so that my eyes could see the fatherly smile wrinkling the outside corners of his eyes. I smiled and without uttering a word, retired to the living room to my long-awaited bed.

A cool wind blew, ruffling the curtains to the tune of some invisible, heavenly organ. I meditated to the Supreme Being, to God, to truth, to love and a light was cast in the room, reflected from the dense fog outside. In spite of the intense moments of the day and my utterly exhausted body, my mind felt rejuvenated, uplifted to a light which had shone through the crusty ceiling of closed mindedness. The path visualized through the opening was not necessarily that of one ideology—Islam—but was a path on which Muhammad guided me. Then, like a spiritual tag team, the guide changed to Jesus, and as I ascended, I was met by Muhammad, who continued leading me up to the steady, warm hand of the Buddha, there to embrace me as I continued my ascent. My hand was then grasped by Moses; with strong arms, he held me before him, becoming the many-faceted, omnipresent spirit of Krishna. Proceeding towards the heavens, I was received by all of the prophets and handed by Krishna to Jesus, Muhammad, Buddha and Moses, who received me with spontaneous joy and humility. With their arms around me, I basked in their love shared by the Supreme Consciousness, who was neither man nor woman, but transcending all things, reigned within and without, melding pure love together into one good, pure force. This energy linked me to the love of all creatures, to the peace deep within me, to the tolerance and understanding that armed me against the threat of ignorance, fear and allegiance to material things. I felt finally free of the confining embrace of the superficial, neon world, where pure, innocent love and passions are inhibited in the name of progress.

The spark of this day ignited some strange fire, which had somehow opened me to a renewed faith, renewed force. With such pure and heart-centered thoughts, all desire of sleep faded. I lay contemplating love—pure love—truly the essence of all things, transcending all knowledge and all manifestations of material wealth; this was a spiritual truism I thought could forever guide me forward. Would I ever look back? But I could not yet consider this as a given, or constant, as the search for truth loomed before me as a specter which would vanish the moment I found it. But this did not seem pessimistic in that life is a search for knowledge...for truth...for God...divided into stages, leading to what is clearly stated in Buddhist scriptures as the moment of becoming one with eternity or the moment of reaching nirvana. For me, I interpreted that as the precious moment that my being would converge with the Supreme Being, when I would become one with it, the universe and beyond. That seeking and becoming one with the universe seemed to be clearly set forth in the Bhagavad Gita, which said "Even as the unwise work selfishly in the bondage of selfish works, let the wise man work unselfishly for the good of all the world."[5]

So it isn't the never ending search that serves as the essence of life, but the gradual progression toward truth by following the path and building inner knowledge. This would serve to remove the tight grasp of ignorance begetting hate and fear of people and things not understood, sometimes leading to prejudice. Those feelings are often born of fear and the insecurities felt upon entrance into a "gray area," into an area where contemplation does not always fill in the gaps of doubt, or simply the gaps in our knowledge. Let faith, but not blind faith, fill in the gaps when doubt arises and inner contemplation somehow isn't enough in the moment; there is no place on the path to knowledge for faith without discernment, the acceptance without knowledge or distinctions.

I lay there contemplating my next move. I wondered if I should continue my search in a more peaceful environment, perhaps with Azedine's family—they would surely welcome me back as I believe they perceived my entrance into the monastery as synonymous with the prey being grasped in the tentacles of a giant octopus. Or I could plunge into the more insecure, clearly more intense, life as a Moslem monk. The second choice would lead to the opening of a Pandora's Box I sought to keep closed or at least to master: the box opened would reveal my innermost fears and insecurities regarding my ability to remain objective and not give in to attempts to indoctrinate me. My body shivered as if touched by an icy wind, warning me of danger; "Turn back, turn back" it seemed to say. . .

I was curious as to how I would react to powerful mind control techniques. I felt like I was volunteering myself to be a guinea pig for my own experiment, in order to test my mental independence from persuasion—it was an adventure I should not hesitate to have. I felt confident in my faith to withstand any attempts to mold my way of thinking. But in spite of the year of philosophy in Paris and my own misgivings, I would find out I was ill equipped to fight against the power exerted over me by my future "brothers" in the Islamic monastery.

These thoughts logically flowed through my mind while drinking coffee the next morning and breakfasting with Camara. He asked me if I was ready to submit my application for membership into the monastery. I turned his question around and managed a circuitous response:

"If you consider me ready, then I also figure I am ready," I finally responded.

He seized the opportunity to build my confidence by announcing I was clearly ready and that at the monastery, I would meet beautiful teachers who wore spotless, white turbans and were much more informed about the *Qur'an*. He added that they would take me under their wing and show me how to become a good Moslem every day. His voice grew somber and severe as he said, "You will find an even more strict discipline than what you have experienced here."

I bit my lip, anticipating the potential severity or even austerity of the milieu in this new world. I had difficulty imagining more discipline than what I had gone through with Camara. I felt that I was the work of art so carefully created by an Islamic Pygmalion and that my benefactor, in charge of my instruction, had faithfully carried out his duties, day and night, almost twenty hours a day without much rest. In the end, just like Eliza in "My Fair

---

[5] The Bhagavad Gita, 3.25.

Lady," I had, according to Camara, risen to the occasion and was showing signs of understanding—it was time to test my knowledge in public.

We withdrew to the living room where his son was playing on the rug. He looked up and smiled momentarily as we entered the room, shortly returning his attention to his toy.

I sat on the sofa opposite the metal tray holding the silver teapot. It seemed that since our sharing of tea after an elaborate tea service, so much had happened even though only a few days had transpired since that evening.

Camara walked over to where I was and sat next to me. He said, "I will miss you, brother! After tomorrow, your education will be out of my hands as you live with enlightened soldiers of Allah. That is good because they are much more knowledgeable and enlightened than myself, and THEY have the faith."

I could not imagine another Moslem having more faith and knowledge than Camara. He had taken me into his home and shared his food, had been responsible for my spiritual awakening unto Islam. He had shown me a way of life far from the sins of Europe and America. He had become my spiritual leader, my guru.

That afternoon, Azedine visited me. As he was ushered into the kitchen where Camara and I were going over the last prayers, he took a step backward. Without engaging in the usual greeting formalities he, appalled at my sickly appearance, cried out "You look terrible! You are pale and your gaunt cheeks reflect your weakness elsewhere. What happened to you?"

I explained what happened in the sauna and that I had fully recuperated, except for regaining my weight, since that "cleansing experience."

"Cleansing experience...do you call becoming pale and scrawny, with a dry, parched mouth and a dead man's lifeless gaze in your half-opened eyes a cleansing experience?"

The creases in his frown matched the creases on the brow of Camara. The latter attempted to reestablish order and minimize Azedine's observations.

"Good evening Azedine, I'm glad to see you," Camara greeted. But Azedine, who still felt responsible for what befell me—perhaps acting as an emissary for his family and upholding the principle of hospitality set forth in the Qur'an—relentlessly pursued his objective. It was clear that he was there to warn Camara not to take this "religions experience" too far, at the risk of incurring danger to me.

Neither he nor his family had hid their distrust of Camara and the monks living in the Islamic mission, and they had shared their strong sentiments in that regard before I left their premises.

Azedine continued, looking at me as a brother would, while totally ignoring Camara: "Please be careful and I advise against your involving yourself with the politics of the mission (he glanced over to Camara who was silently contemplating him). And don't forget, my brother, you are always welcome to return to our home, whenever you so desire. We all love you and miss you and are wondering when you will return."

A silence reigned for the next few seconds, as no one dared to speak. The corners of Azedine's mouth curled up in a half smile as he bid me goodbye and walked out of the kitchen.

Camara, a peeved frown in his face, stated, through clenched teeth, "You have good friends and that is wonderful. But do not let him nor his family get in the way of your spiritual progress, my brother. But if you prefer, you may return to his family or stay with me for awhile. You must know you are free to leave at any time."

Normally having something always to say, this time no immediate response came to me. But Camara remained tentative, unsure of my will to proceed. He needed reassurance.

"Well?" he almost grunted.

I felt compelled to say, "I wish to stay with you, Camara, as you have opened many doors for me. And now I wish to enter the mission where I can continue my education—well on its way, thanks to you. I am prepared to leave for the mission as early as tomorrow."

His shrug portrayed indifference to my acclamations. Perhaps he would have been more relieved if I had desired to return to the family, thereby expunging him of his burden. His look was one of worry, as if he alone was the master of my spiritual awakening.

He left the kitchen, and me with my thoughts. I was contemplating the bizarre expression on Azedine's normally stoic face: a mixture of worry and raw fear had shown in his eyes as he left the kitchen, shaking his head. I wished I could have comforted him by explaining my resilience against all fanatic indoctrination. But he was gone and I wondered if I would see him again before my stay with the Islamic monks. So I could not reassure him that he need not worry. But...I was worried.

Camara returned to the kitchen, which temporarily suspended my contemplation.

He asked, "If you are accepted by the mosque tomorrow, you'll still be required to contribute something towards food and lodging."

I told him that I had about 300 dirhams (about $30). He told me that if I intended to live in the mission longer, I'd need at least 100 more. I then suggested to Camara that we could sell my cassette recorder, the only thing of value I owned, which I had left at Azedine's apartment.

Camara led me to Azedine's door; bits of warped paint fluttered to the ground as my knuckles faintly tapped on the ragged surface. A face appeared behind the door and I recognized it as being the mother's. The door opened to her welcoming, wide grin, making me feel as if I were a long lost child returning home after many years. Her grin smoothed, changing to a frown as she spied Camara standing behind me. She motioned us inside while she called Azedine, who appeared in the doorway of the kitchen; his smile welcomed me like a lost brother, in spite of the fact that I had seen him only a little while ago.

We sat around the kitchen table drinking mint tea, Azedine on one side, Camara on the other. Azedine leaned over and at ear level whispered that his mother was overjoyed that I had come to my senses and was returning home. I must have seemed puzzled as he quickly explained that his mother mothered everyone, and, his eyes shifting to Camara, he expressed his concern that I could be brainwashed by the Islamic monks. He explained that upon seeing my face at the door, his mother was convinced that I had abandoned the idea of staying in the monastery and had returned to stay with their family.

"Azedine," I whispered, "I have come to reclaim my cassette recorder. Tomorrow I will enter the mosque, and if God wills it, I will be accepted. But I need money to pay for my room and board."

He shook his head. "Islam advises that we be hospitable, which means, as a guest of the monastery, you shouldn't have to pay for anything."

He grasped the sleeve of my djellabah and led me into the living room where he extracted my belongings from a closed cupboard sitting at floor level. He carefully placed the machine on the floor in front of me. I took it and placed it in a satchel that I held by a strap over my shoulder.

At that moment, Azedine's mother came into the room, gravely looking at the recorder. "That is expensive. Azedine tell me that you must pay the missionaries, but you should not pay anything to them. Put the machine back!"

My eyes moistened at her concern for me, a perfect stranger to her a month ago. I felt her love, and it re-enforced my resolve to meet the spiritual challenges waiting for me at the mission. I hugged her and told her we must go. As the door closed, her face did not move from the crack in the door; her larger-than-life brown eyes reflected her concern and her creased brow wrinkled her smooth forehead.

On our way back to Camara's house, we stopped at a stand in the Medina selling electronic appliances; we were surrounded by irons, toasters and hot plates. Camera asked the merchant to contact the buyer and seller of used goods and then meet us at Camara's house.

As we entered the apartment, with the cassette recorder under my arm and cassette tapes in my hands, I noticed a stranger sitting on the couch. His jagged smile revealed huge, chipmunk teeth; his eyes were intently fixed on the cassette recorder and the tapes that I placed on the round, wooden table.

He stood up with all the enthusiasm of a mortician upon the delivery of a new cadaver, and shuffled to the table—he hadn't yet cast his hawk-like gaze in my direction. As he fondled the recorder, he launched into a long discourse, underscoring he would give more than it was worth, since I wished to become a Moslem. After his speech had extended over several long minutes, he finally made a punch line offer: "300 dirhams."

The recorder was worth twice that much, but I needed the money in the event I was selected by the mission. The young shyster laid the money out on the table and then made his way to the door. He licked his chops as he descended the stairway, still without venturing to cast his shifty eyes on me. I now had 600 dirhams (about $60), more than a sufficient amount to pay for my food and lodging at the mission.

Camara had to take care of some business in the Medina so he left me on the couch poring over the *Qur'an*. After an hour of meditation and prayer, he returned and we decided to take a walk on the beach. On the way, we met Azedine walking in the opposite direction. He told us that he had worked all day long tending a clothes and material boutique in the Medina. He was pale and his face showed exhaustion.

As I told him about the sale of the recorder, his voice trembled with controlled rage; he warned me that I was being duped. Although he refrained from mentioning any names, there was no mystery as to who he was directing his anger. He reiterated that Moslem hospitality does not hinge on a requirement that guests pay money. His flushed cheeks returned to their normal olive complexion as his rage subsided. Normally not a person to show emotion, he sheepishly glanced toward Camara, then towards me. He started to fidget with his hands, his eyes staring at the ground.

"Come," he calmly requested, "come to my home for dinner. Anyway, you need to retrieve your things and your knapsack." I had forgotten that the knapsack was stowed in the living room. Without waiting for a response, Azedine turned and walked toward the entrance to an alley next to a café. I looked at Camara while he looked at me—we both followed Azedine. We passed a small metal table with a glass of tea held by a man with a full beard, his attention on us.

When we arrived, Azedine's door was shut, but before we could knock, two faces appeared at the door—Azedine's sisters were lined up to greet us with their familiar smiles. They beckoned us to enter, waving towards the warm hearth and a place next to their mother, the emissary of peace for the family. A huge platter of couscous was passed around; the semolina, laced with carrots and other vegetables, was heaped high. After the evening meal, the men shuffled to the living room while the mother and her daughters stayed in the kitchen after giving us a warm, smiling send-off.

Camara and I sat on one side of the room which had served as my bedroom for the last several weeks. A new intensity shone from the eyes of Azedine and his father, directed, in unison, at Camara and myself. I was deeply touched by their attempts to dissuade me from entering the mission. Even in the presence of Camara, they warned me that the Islamic monks would try to brainwash me. Camara remained silent.

The father commenced, "You do not know what their objective is. They are more political than religious. We are concerned that they will take you down the wrong path, from which you shall never return to us, your friends, your family. We are afraid of losing—"

"No, you won't lose me," I retorted. "In fact, the next time you see me, we can go to the mosque and pray together as fellow Moslems." Azedine took over: "But you do not know these people! Myself, I do not trust them. They have a reputation of aggressively recruiting people, indoctrinating them and then sending them out to convert others."

"Azedine," I said, "you are like a brother to me, and I will always be like a member of your family. Nothing will change that!"

Azedine's eyes met those of his father; their heads shook slightly. Silence followed. It was finally broken by Azedine's father.

"If you don't mind, Camara, could Frank stay with us his last night before going to the mosque? We can help him pack his things and then send him to you tomorrow morning." Camara, reluctantly said, "Oh, alright, but he must be at my house no later than 8:30 a.m. for we must prepare him for entrance into the mosque before the afternoon prayer session."

Camara stood and headed for the door. I followed him and as he left without turning his head, I called after that I would see him tomorrow. He raised his hand as he disappeared, heading down one of the dark alleyways of the Medina.

There was no more talk about the mosque that evening. I was escorted to the familiar living room where two beds were neatly made on opposite ends of the room. As I lay my head on the familiar cushion, I fell into a deep sleep, the result of the turmoil the day had brought. My eyes opened when darkness still engulfed the misty, sleeping Medina. Mysterious voices echoed through the narrow streets, calling the sleepy Moslems to the mosque for the Morning Prayer, calling me to a new adventure.

Chapter XVII

The Lion's Claw

By the time I had dressed and prepared my knapsack, Azedine called to me to come to the kitchen for coffee and warm Moroccan bread, recently retrieved from the communal ovens. After he informed me it was 8 a.m., I rose and went to the living room where I had left my knapsack in the corner. Bending down, I wriggled into the straps and then stood up with it carefully positioned behind me. I headed for the door. By then, the entire family had assembled in the hallway; the children, with half-closed eyes, were there to bid me farewell and their parents stood behind them.

After kissing everyone on the cheek, I turned to leave with Azedine close behind. He and his father followed me, their concerned looks piercing my heart as I walked out the door. I turned for one last wave, then headed for Camara's apartment deep within the heart of the Medina.

Azedine called out and I stopped abruptly. He ran to me, and grasping my arm with his right hand, he expressed his profound concern over the sale of the recorder for below its value. He suggested that we stop and talk to a detective friend about the unfair price I received for my cassette recorder. I quickly denounced the idea and informed Azedine that I was perfectly capable of handling my own affairs.

I asked him if he could show me the way to Camara's house as I had lost my sense of direction in the maze of streets and alleyways. He walked with me, his eyes downcast the entire time.

When we had made the very last turn and were headed towards the alleyway leading to Camara's door, I saw the outline of Camara's pointed hat at the door. Joining us, we three took off for the mosque, the entrance to a new world, a new step in my spiritual awakening. Azedine, suppressing his anger, the steam rising with every step, walked in silence on one side of me, Camara on the other. After several minutes of winding along the typical dirt paths, we found ourselves at the entrance to the Medina, where I had stood days earlier.

So much had happened—almost a lifetime—since then. I was now happy to be finally leaving the Medina on a journey that would perhaps never take me back. As much as I loved Azedine's and Camara's families and the people I had met, and I truly appreciated the interest in guiding my spiritual awakening, I was beginning to feel the misery in their lives. It seemed like those living in the Medina were condemned to live in filth, sharing the putrid air with armies of flies swarming on the open sores of old beggars, on streets broken and cracked, filled with stagnant pools of water in which children played with abandon.

We came across a four-lane road with cars hurtling down the thoroughfare, horns honking and brakes screeching, like the cars frantically circling the Arc de Triumph in Paris. . .like flies circling in a darkened room for the last time before dive bombing toward the floor.

I was blasted back in time to Europe, to the hustle and bustle of nervous, espresso-nourished westerners caught up in the whirlwind of fervent living, so busy with the daily pursuit of money that no time remained to contemplate the metaphysical, intangible beauties of life—jolted back to the threshold of the frantic world of things, so far away from the spiritual world in which I was immersed. My head spun and my legs buckled as jet lag, resulting from zapping back and forth between the two worlds, set in.

I noticed that the masses of cars seemed to be going towards a blinking neon jungle of lights. Camara signaled a cab. In a few minutes, we climbed into an old Renault, which jerked us as it "burned rubber," propelling us into the main stream of cars. It impatiently carried us past gas stations, restaurants and hotels, human pit stops in the "rat race" of men, women and vehicles, hurrying to get nowhere fast. People were dressed in European clothes and wore pointed Italian shoes.

The taxi screeched between stops. Camara mumbled a few Arabic words to the driver who remained silent. After about fifteen minutes of meandering through traffic, the cab veered to the right, turned off of the main street and onto a narrow road lined with trees and small houses. It now inched along the street. Drooping palm trees adorned the front yards, untrimmed, dry grass gently swayed back and forth in the dry, desert wind as flies frolicked among the various assortment of dog, cat and rodent droppings.

Old men in robes sat on their porches, their sedentary gazes scanning the street in front of their dilapidated houses, the doorways and windows hung with ragged, stained curtains. Abandoned wagons and tires lay strewn about the tall, dry weeds, their final resting place. Dirt paths wound haphazardly around the hovels, with patches of rocks and unidentifiable debris scattered along the primitive walkways. These paths opened into alleys, intersecting the otherwise unvarying lines of hovels.

The monotony of the latter was also broken by an occasional mosque, painted a faded white. A primitive, round minaret rose over the roof of each one; robed, turbaned men were coming and going, some lovingly carrying a *Qur'an*.

The taxi suddenly stopped at a ten-foot high wall, which seemed to extend forever; our vehicle was totally covered by its shadow. Camara motioned Azedine and I to leave the taxi. I pushed the door open and scrambled out. Straining up on my tiptoes, I struggled unsuccessfully to see over the wall while Camara paid the taxi driver. A creamy white, round building towered over us, seemingly beckoning us inside.

The taxi represented the last connection to the Medina. As it sped away, my decision was finalized—I would let destiny take care of the rest. I followed Camara to an opening in the fortress. I was set on proceeding with this experience, no escape routes remained open. Azedine pulled back a few steps; out of the corner of my eye, I watched him examine the structure with concerned, brown eyes. I could almost hear him growling under his breath, like a cornered animal.

I felt proud that I followed Camara without question, even a little superior to Azedine who lagged behind. I peered through the iron gate which provided a fortress-like entrance to inside the walls. Camara passed through the gate and walked up the steps of the mosque before looking back. Realizing we had not yet entered, he nodded, beckoning me to follow. I mechanically began walking toward him, and suddenly stopped, wondering how I could be so proud of following Camara, without questions, without hesitation. A strange, empty feeling echoed within—I was doing something so out of character for me. But

I tried to comfort myself, without feeling convinced, by repeating silently, "All great religious leaders must start by being good students of the word of God." I looked behind me; Azedine had disappeared.

I pushed open the gate and followed Camara up the stairs. As he waited for me at the top, I stopped, shuddering as the heavy iron doors grated shut. All I could think was that I was surrounded by turbaned, white-robed Islamic monks. The turbans and the robes almost gleamed with cleanliness and purity, seeming much whiter than those worn in the Medina. The pure light glowing through the palm leaves enhanced the warm, clean fragrance filling the air, redolent with a sweet, honeysuckle scent—I was drenched in the spiritual aura of this holy place.

Birds were singing in the palm trees, the branches sweeping down over an enclosed courtyard casting shadows over those in djellabahs, piously strolling over the protected grounds, the Holy *Qur'an* in hand. A profound calmness prevailed in the courtyard lined with trees and bushes, leading me slowly, softly into the silence. I was floating in a world of spiritual ecstasy, where only happiness and growth were acceptable; weakness, avarice and other obstacles to personal enrichment were unacceptable and had no place there.

As I walked, unfettered, around the grounds, eyes acknowledged and heads nodded. I wondered if this was the proverbial calm before the storm—or was this the calm before profound revelation, the calm that leads to higher understanding, union with the supreme consciousness?

Yet a deep foreboding invaded my thoughts as I contemplated that the path was long and arduous. No gifts of promised shortcuts would lead me quicker to my destination: my antenna, only half-raised, had picked up subconscious thoughts warning me to beware of easy situations, of false prophets, of avaricious hosts disguised as enlightened beings. The calm gave way to that infernal buzzing noise, which grew louder and louder within me.

A majestic entrance to a magnificently proud building led us inside the mosque. More walls surrounded me; the extraordinarily high ceiling peaked at the top of the mosque, giving the impression that the entire edifice lead to the heavens.

A loud clanking, like two metal bars banging together, filled the air. I turned my head in time to take in the splendor of a sparkling white robe, a spotless, incandescent white turban, two huge, brown eyes and sparkling teeth revealed in a beatific smile. Camara and the Islamic guru approached each other and then hugged like old friends, like brothers.

As Camara and the guru carried on an emotional, high-speed conversation, I leaned up against the wall and thumbed through my copy of prayers written phonetically, reviewing the "Al Fatiha" and others in the book given to me by a bookstore owner, a friend of Camara's. The conversation ended with the guru turning to me and drawing near, he held his hand out with intense conviction:

"As-Salamu alaykum," he said, his deep voice accentuating the last syllable of "alaykum." His profound calm matched the cool breeze lightly ruffling his robe. I was caught up in a "time warp," where everything seemed to be moving in slow motion.

He silently observed me, his curious eyes wondering what I was doing in his place of worship, but it was not a reproach or a threat. On the contrary, his eyes welcomed me. I could hear Camara breathing heavily next to me, watching my every move, watching over me, making sure that his pupil did not slip up.

The guru introduced himself as Muhammad Rushed. I told him that my name was also Muhammad. His Cheshire cat smile widened. He led me by the arm through tall, wooden doors, inscribed with expressions in Arabic. Camara followed us, his head bent forward inquisitively. Muhammad Rushed led us deeper within the walls of the palace-like mosque. Mats made of reeds were laid out vertically as far as the eye could see; they smelled like baskets, filling the air with a woody, homey fragrance. We left our shoes at the entrance and walked barefoot. Sunlight bathed the large room from all sides; birds flew around the room overhead chirping contentedly, their nests probably located somewhere on the beams crisscrossing above.

Men were praying everywhere, their robes of the richest colors: deepest blues, golds and the whitest of whites. Muhammad Rushed whispered in my ear that it was just a few moments before the Morning Prayer session. Black beards were facing in the same direction, toward the East, toward Mecca, the holy center for the Islamic faith. Some were grouped together at the center of the left wall, their legs crossed in a semi-lotus position as they had done probably a thousand or more times. Their robes were spread out over the floor, like flowers, and their shaved heads and turbans formed the stamen. A pearl white turbaned man, his black beard flowing like a waterfall, was reading from the *Qur'an*, while voices echoed, "Allahu Akbar, Allaaaaah Akbar, la ilaha illa Allah, la ilaha illa Allah."

A roomful of turbans surrounded the reader, whose head was bent reverently, his hands supporting the large book as gently as he would a newborn baby. He respectfully turned its pages, surrounded by contented, mustachioed smiles. Intense vibrations reverberated everywhere, within a calm and meditative atmosphere; passions flowed as they praised the great messenger of Allah, Muhammad.

It seemed so natural to join the group that no one turned around as we searched for places to pray among cross-legged, barefooted men, forming lines in prayerful meditation. Camara's dark profile was noticeable at the end of one of the lines. My eyes followed my mentor as he rose and strolled down the line, joining a small assembly of robed, bearded devotees. I watched him embrace each man and sit down cross-legged among them. I got to my feet and walked toward him. Once I reached him he whispered in my ear that soon the interrogation would begin, and that I must relax and remember the prayers he had taught me. Our feet silently brushed the mats as we hastened to join the group.

I was drawn into and mesmerized by the striking holiness of the place. A tingling sense of belonging resonated within me so I hoped the monks would accept me in their house. My mind suddenly flashed on a televised series I had seen in the States portraying the story of a Buddhist monk who had taken his knowledge to common folk of the United States. During one episode, a pupil shook hands with the master in a monastery high in the mountains of Tibet. As I thought of the program, a cold shiver streaked down my spine, remembering how far away from home I was, and how different this place was from where I was raised. But the peaceful, kindly expression of the master standing in front of me calmed my transient thoughts. He smiled benignly, and began speaking to me in French.

"Soyez le bienvenue, mon frère (Welcome). My name is Hassan and I will be like your spiritual adviser." The tone of his voice strangely resembled that of my friend, Camara.

As the stranger pronounced the name of Allah, his head raised and his eyes flashed toward the ceiling, as if beckoning the inspiration of God. A profound, secure feeling came over me with the thought that I was surrounded by friends, by people who would never harm me, who would help me find the truth, who would bring me to the doorstep of the Supreme Being. A cool afternoon breeze coming through the wooden, double doors gently blew against my back, as if coaxing me to enter the new world.

Hassan sat beside me, then faced me. I turned to face him. He reached for my trembling hands, which calmed as soon as they touched his hands. He asked me why I was at the mission and why I had chosen Islam. Following Camara's advice, and without declaring that I had converted to Islam, I simply explained that I wanted to learn more about the religion. He asked me if I had the money to pay for food and transportation in the event I was chosen to participate in a traveling prayer group. I told him that I had brought with me 400 dirhams (about $40). He nodded which told me the amount was sufficient. I thought to myself that these questions were perhaps asked prematurely.

The master rose and beckoned me to follow him. As I was being led into a corner deep within the mosque, my apprehension slid away. This Jesus Christ-like master led me away from Camara who stayed with the prayer group. I felt his eyes on me as I sat down in front of the master, his legs crossed; he motioned I do the same.

The master's hands were folded patiently in his lap, the tips of his fingers stroking each other, as he questioned me about my journey to Morocco and my intentions for joining the mission. I responded by expressing my desire to search for life, for truth. Following Camara's advice, after responding to the question, I paused, waiting for the master to speak. His deep, brown eyes looked into mine and I thought I saw my own reflection. After a minute had lapsed in complete silence, he smiled:

"Praise the lord; all your questions will be answered. You will learn something new every day and with heeman (faith) you will become free to live the truth, the life of a Moslem."

After glancing at Camara, who was now sitting next to me, then at me, the master placed his right hand on my left shoulder.

He spoke with great assurance and authority, saying "Join us brother, and we will help you see the light; but it will be up to you to actually see it!" With those words, I noticed out of the corner of my eye that Camara silently stood up making his way to the door.

The master's broken French flowed without dissonance, without interruption, taking me down the path of faith, of passion and of knowledge. His determined eyes revealed his deep conviction in his belief of Islam.

Our interview was entirely consistent with Camara's statements that the Islamic monks lived, ate, dressed and spoke like the prophet Muhammad and that how they led their lives would be a perfect model for me to follow. The words and demeanor of this saintly person made me feel secure under his tutelage and assured that my education concerning the principles of Islam would be complete and profound.

In addition, the needed security compensated for the turmoil I had experienced in Paris, surrounded by a materialistic way of life. I was now estranged from the material world, from cerebral manipulations of the media, of television, from clawing people, from cold, impersonal city life. I loved Paris, but in the "City of Love," I was withering for want of love in the coldness of its streets, in the heart of the city, in the "Quartier Latin" where sometimes, dry intellectual discussions suppressed the passions of life. There, the tremendous fervor of intellectualism was forever raining on me drops of conventional wisdom, and at the same time, hailing pessimism. The Sorbonne raged—sometimes crucified itself—on the cross of the Cartesian spirit. To the eternal me, the real me, the never-ending merry-go-round of ideas and the evasion of emotions in the "City of Love" remained an illusion.

Perhaps I did not understand Paris; yet there were strong friendships, shared meals of syrup and crepes and cultural seduction in the rich language. But sometimes the lifestyle of the bourgeoisie seemed too strongly imprinted upon Paris. Perhaps I was naively searching for love and simplicity in the wrong places: I was lost within my raging self and rebelled against the Parisian world since my values did not appear to conform to it—nor would they ever. Such propelled me to search the heavens for that which I failed to find on earth. So I retreated into the seeming security of the mosque; it held the tremendous appeal of Eastern mysticism, brotherhood and enlightenment. But despite my education and focus on the mystical aspects of Eastern religions, I was becoming extremely enmeshed in the practice of Islam and quickly losing control.

My visit to the Islamic mission was only the beginning of an intensive indoctrination process, which was to continue during a voyage with a prayer group in a Moroccan desert. For the time being, I plunged into Islam and was surrounded by all aspects of that religion as I lived, ate and prayed in the mosque. I stayed several weeks at the mission in Casablanca, memorizing all the most important prayers in Arabic. I participated in the prayer sessions five times daily, starting at about 5 or 6 o'clock in the morning, when the director of the mosque would climb the narrow stairs leading to a loft perched high above the central prayer room.

In the loft were five students (monks), including me, all in a deep sleep when the director's shadow would flow over us and the jingle of his keys serve as an alarm. His deep, soft voice announced daily that morning prayer was to commence in a few minutes. I would pull myself out of the blue-lined sleeping bag and then stumble down the stairs leading to a patio outside the mosque. A dirt path led to the back where I would, half asleep, perform the morning ablutions, a systematic washing of my entire body, following the system taught to me by my beloved Camara.

At five o'clock in the morning, the cold water splashed on my body and face awoke me from my most profound reveries. While I bathed, the director, whose voice echoed over the entire neighborhood and probably for miles around, stood in the minaret, inviting everyone to pray by reciting the "Shahada":

"Allah akbar, Allah akbar, Allah akbar, Allah akbar, la ilaha illa Allah, la ilaha illa Allah, wa Muhammad rasul Allah sala. . .assalatu kayrun minan-naun" (God is most great; I testify that there is no God but God. I testify that Muhammad is the messenger of God; come to prayer...praying is better than sleeping).

Because he announced mass, the director was also called the "Al-mu'adhdhin." By the time he had finished reciting the "Shahada," we had filed into the prayer room joining other worshippers, who had braved the freezing morning winds to pray with us, facing in the direction (eastward) of the Ka'ba in Mecca.

After about ten minutes had passed since the initial call to prayer, the Imam, the leader of the prayer service, would welcome those who had come. Then the "Iqama," or the second call to prayer, would be announced, ending in the phrase "Worship has begun."

"Allahu Akbar," the Imam would shout convincingly.

The men and boys would stand next to each other, forming several parallel lines in front of the Imam. The Imam would turn his back to the congregation and face an alcove in the mosque, crowned by an overhead arch. From this recess, he would lead the prayers. At these moments, an intense feeling of equality and brotherhood emanated from the pious group, heads bowed and deeply immersed in prayer.

After several introductory statements by the Imam were made as to the type of prayer to be performed, we would recite the "Takbira," or "Allahu Akbar." The "Rak'a" or liturgical cycle, consisting of the recitation of a prayer accompanied by hand gestures and/or prostration (touching the forehead to the ground) would follow. The first Rak'a is called "Al-Fatiha" (The Opener) and was recited standing up. Then we would repeat another prayer from the *Qur'an*, after which we bowed (ruku), reciting the "Takbira," or "Allahu Akbar." While standing, we next stated "Samia allahou limine hamidouhou. Rabanna laka-l-hadu" (May God hear those who praise Him. Allah, our master, Glory be to thee).

Just prior to the conclusion, we performed several acts of prostration, called the "sujud," while praying. At the end of the prayer session, we recited the salutation of peace, called the "salam" or "taslim," during which we stated "As-Salamu alaykum" (Peace be upon you) twice: the first time with the head turned to the right, the second with the head turned to the left.

Following the Morning Prayer session, most of the monks would slip back to bed or remain in the mosque, cross-legged and half asleep, praying individually. Those moments I dedicated to meditation on the Supreme Consciousness. Because I was still searching for universal ties among religions, I would also secretly meditate on the Bhagavad Gita, the Torah of Moses in the Old Testament or teachings of Jesus Christ in the New Testament and sometimes on Buddhist scriptures or the *Qur'an*. At the same time I was seeking a universal religion, I was considering a synthesis of the teachings of the major religions. I had come to realize that my search would only be enhanced by entering the Islamic monastery—at least for the time being—but I was feeling the pressure to focus my spiritual training, the pressure to conform my search to the here and the now, to the principles of Islam.

Mass was given five times daily, after which I retreated to a far corner of the mosque to continue my studies of the *Qur'an*. Between prayer sessions, the mosque was usually empty except for one soul-searching, starry-eyed, skinny man engaging in metaphysical meditations, sometimes "spacing out" as the songbirds flew overhead to their nests nestled in the beams or the trees towering above the mosque outside. Sometimes the master would come and help me learn the prayers, correcting my pronunciation of Arabic and explaining to me the inner meanings of the text. During those sessions, I felt he was testing me as to whether I was unequivocally accepting, or not, Islam into my heart—he wanted to know my progress toward total conversion.

From time to time, he would point to his heart and say "heeman" (Faith!), to accentuate the importance that I feel Allah in my heart as my faith in Him increased.

My task at the monastery was to learn about Islam and to ask the master and monks questions whenever necessary to clarify the gray areas in my studies. The other monks accomplished various tasks: some helped in the kitchen and others helped teach children in the adjoining Islamic grade school. I would remain in the back of the mosque praying, meditating and sleeping until an interruption of my daily routine.

The master showed me the way to Islam. He taught me how to perform the "Salat" or daily prayer ritual, described on the previous page. According to several "hadiths,"[6] the followers of Muhammad are to perform the Salat five times daily. Each Salat is broken down into "Rak'as" (liturgical cycles or specific prayer methods). The master, according to whether it was "Fajr" (the Morning Prayer), "Isha" (evening prayer) or the other three prayer sessions, taught me the procedure to follow: when to stand, bow (ruku) and when to perform the prostration (sujud), or touching foreheads to the mats. None of the body positions he taught me felt natural, so I tried to inconspicuously change my position every two to five minutes. If I made a mistake by sitting down and placing my hands around my legs instead of on my knees, the master would warn me of the mistake by clicking his tongue until I assumed the appropriate position. I was supposed to sit with my feet underneath my buttocks; but every time I tried to maintain that position for more than a few minutes, a sharp pain shot through my ankles. This body position was maintained during each meal. My appetite was usually sharply reduced due to the pain in my legs and ankles, so I did not eat much. But I always drank the hot mint tea served in small, slim glasses, adorned with small roses, gold and red glitter and flower-like designs.

My nose constantly ran since the mosque was chilly, due to the turbulent crosswinds sweeping through it—they entered through two doors on opposite sides of the massive mosque. My bowels continued to evacuate, forcing me to make frequent trips to the bathroom, after which I was obliged, according to Moslem custom, to perform a complete ablution. My skin was beginning to dry and peel from all the washings.

One morning when I was blowing my nose in the ablution room, a young monk— about twenty years old, his light brown hair tucked inside his turban—came up to me. I remembered seeing him in the prayer room; his singular light skin and blue-gray eyes had set himself apart from the typical dark-brown complexion of the other monks.

"My name is Shean, what's yours?"

"Muhammad," I responded.

"Are you sick?" he asked, a concerned look on his face.

"A little bit, but I'll get over it soon, I'm sure." I replied.

"Come to the kitchen; I have something for you."

I followed him to the kitchen, which consisted of a small refrigerator, sink and a large table, where we sat and drank our coffee with hot milk and ate bread in the mornings. He went to the refrigerator and took out a bottle of orange liquid and poured me a glass. The cool, orange juice slid smoothly down my throat.

Another monk came into the kitchen and sat next to me. His full, black beard flowed over his white djellabah and his long hair was tied in a knot in back of his head.

"So you are Muhammad from Paris; welcome." His warm smile filled the room. "My name is Habib and I am in charge of the Qur'anic school attached to the mosque. I see you

---

[6] A record of the teachings of Muhammad, including customs and sayings.

have met my friend, Shean." He turned to me: "You are lucky to be his friend. He has a lot of heart."

Shean blushed, and came over to the table. Grabbing the knot on back of Ali's head, he said, "Don't listen to him."

Habib laughed.

But his mirth was interrupted by the call to prayer (adhan), the loud, recorded voice of the muezzin (mu'adhdhin), alerting the community by way of a powerful loudspeaker— "ALLAAAAHHHU AKBAR, ALLLAHU AKBAR, ALLAAAAHU AKBAR, LA ILAHA ILLA ALLAH, LA ILAHA ILLA ALLAH."

Shean warned, as he put the bottle of orange juice in the refrigerator and my empty glass in the sink, "We'd better quickly do our ablutions since noon prayer is beginning."

I followed Habib to the ablution room with Shean close behind. We entered the prayer room in back of three lines of worshippers just in time, before the master began the prayers.

That day I was not alone; we recited our prayers next to each other. The huge room was entirely filled with warmth...I belonged.

After the prayer session, I withdrew to my usual place in back of the mosque, where I prayed and meditated. Thereafter, those peaceful, meditative moments were interrupted by Shean, usually on Fridays:

"Frank, 'Kul' (eat)," Shean would command, motioning me to join him and the others in an adjoining room.

Over the next few weeks, Shean and I became close, like brothers. I saw Habib rarely, since he was very busy managing and teaching in the Qur'anic school next door. But whenever I passed him, he would always smile warmly. Whenever I was confused about something, I would try and find Shean in the mosque. But he only came to the mosque once a week, usually on Friday afternoons, since he was employed as a shoe salesman downtown. Friday was Islam's holy day or Sabbath[7]. On that day, we would congregate in the prayer room for a special service called "the assembly" (al-jum'a), which took the place of the noon prayer session.

We ate our meals sitting on yellow mats made of reeds smelling like northern California wheat fields, wicker chairs. . .woody, creamy nostalgia. In the middle of several mats were placed several round loaves of Moroccan bread. We were handed a chunk of the sweet tasting bread; we would break off pieces to be dipped in a communal platter filled with vegetables and beans or couscous, garnished with vegetables, or meat or both. With every meal, we drank several glasses of the ubiquitous hot mint tea, which temporarily energized my emaciated body, slowly deteriorating from a lack of nourishment and exercise.

My physical condition spawned an inner yearning to return to nature, to the natural simplicity of everyday life. After two years in the Parisian jungle, the fast pace and the coldness of city dwellers had worn down my naïve country self, pushing me towards the

---

[7] Some Moslems call Friday the Islamic Sabbath, even though most Moslems do not regard Fridays as a holy day or Sabbath. John Hinnells, editor, *The New Penguin Handbook of Religions*, Penguin Books, 1997, p. 187.

sands of sunny Maghreb. As I had not yet reached those sunny sands and was enclosed within four high walls, living in a cold mosque, my physical condition had not improved.

As we sat eating in silence, I recited to myself the words I had written in Paris before taking the train to Morocco:

It's hell—hell at the bottom of a soul's torment
Trying to make out a meaning
Behind the bureaucracy's false blessing.
Security...weakness
Blessing the sad, but live, warmth of the solidarity I feel.
Expecting nothing,
Living intensely with passions mixed
Triumphs of confidence and indecision...
Yet, the meaning endures.
For once, living for principles
Deeply ingrained by the soft touch of a mother's caress
And Dad's embrace in a life of endless coldness,
Breathing life into a hazy, deceptive, strobe-lighted, dancing,
Flirty, superficial world, where essence is buried
and passions are repressed in the name of progress.

I had mastered the art of ablution, but I had yet to learn how to eat properly, the way Muhammad the prophet ate. The master took charge of my education: he taught me how to eat couscous by rolling the grain in the palm of his hand and then saying "Bismi-l-lahi" (In the name of God), as he popped it into his mouth. With each swallow, he would say "Al hamdu li llâhi" (Praise Allah). He placed some in the palm of my hand and watched me as I did the same. I had become much more proficient since living with the Berber family in the Medina, but my technique was still lacking since my efforts often still produced splotches of rice on my cheek. The next attempt brought laughter from my fellow monks, and even the corners of the master's mouth curled up into a smile—he even giggled.

The facilities on the premises were rather primitive; concrete blocks with holes in the middle served as toilets. Also, there was no toilet paper. I was supposed to use water to clean my body after urinating or defecating. Camara had warned me that if I did not follow the prescribed procedures for washing, my prayers would not be accepted by Allah; and if I failed to follow the correct order of washing techniques during ablutions, I must start all over again. Also, according to Camara, if I passed air during mass, I must abruptly leave the praying area and go to the bathroom and wash myself in order to become pure again. Only after following that procedure could I return and finish praying with the group.

I often wondered if my prayers would be ignored by God if I refused to comply with the last rule. But my conscience nagged me whenever I failed to completely follow the washing and other procedures. Whenever I became "impure" during the service, I would try

146

to re-purify my body and then join the group or start ablutions all over again. In this way, I was becoming more and more attached to the Islamic dogma.

In a part of me, somewhere in my mind and body, was the fear that such attachment would lead to the sickness shared by people of many religions and ideologies: a fanatical belief in and adherence to doctrines—dogmatism through tunnel vision.

The Islamic monks, according to the master, lived the life set forth in the Qur'an. That and the "hadith" (story or tradition) of Muhammad gave us guidelines as to how to live our daily lives. I assumed, then, that our activities were patterned after those guidelines. I was told, however, that the hadith was subject to interpretation, and has been explained in many varying ways. So the way we lived represented the master's interpretation of the hadith.

For the next few days, I was to eat, sleep and pray twenty-four hours a day, as a true Moslem, following as closely as possible the guidelines set forth in the hadith by the prophet Muhammad. The inhabitants of the mosque, at least with regard to their words and gestures during prayer and at other times, were almost a carbon copy of one another. I was almost comfortable in this atmosphere even though I had always rejected blind conformity with standards set forth by any organized religion or political system. A growing sense of belonging and fraternal bonding was generated by the warmth of my relationships with my fellow monks. I amazed myself since I was usually impatient and annoyed with those who conformed to a written or unwritten behavior code of any kind. The behavior standards and other policies of the mission were, in fact, becoming normal to me.

Only later was I to discover the sharp differences between the Masjid Nord, where I was living, and other Moslem parishes. Only later was I to understand why Azedine had warned me about the dangers of living with an apparently harmless group of worshipers whose only goal was to follow Allah.

I became more and more enchanted with my own infatuation for this new lifestyle, which seemed more and more a viable alternative to life in a mechanized, seemingly unspiritual city, like the one from whence I had come. It seemed that my rejection of the urban "dream" was the catalyst for inspiring me to embrace this adventure into Islam.

But a voice inside me reverberated from a deep place, sometimes excruciatingly loud; it seemed to be warning me that something was very wrong. Something whispered within me, "Accepting without questioning, accepting without questioning, accepting without questioning, accepting without questioning...???"

I learned from the master that several friends from the Ancienne Medina had visited me, but were refused entrance. He explained, the corners of his mouth rising in the familiar curl that it would be better for me and my faith to concentrate on praying and reading the Qur'an. I deferred to the master's judgment all issues of my spiritual training—I never questioned him.

The mosque was open to the public on Fridays, the Moslem Sabbath day. During one Friday service, as usual, I lined up next to Shean, who was always glowing with energy, and stood shoulder to shoulder with my fellow monks and people from the outside. As I bowed down, I noticed a familiar profile in the row in front of me and off to the right. As I stood up tall during the next step of the prayer session, he looked at me and smiled. After the prayer session, I motioned him to follow me to my place in the back of the mosque where I usually prayed and learned prayers from the Qur'an.

As we walked to the back of the mosque, I felt a tugging of my djellabah sleeve. I turned to the left and was surprised to see the master walking with us, stride for stride. We stopped and I introduced the master to my friend. He smiled and then said a few words in Arabic to Azedine that I could not understand. But the meaning became clear to me as Azedine said goodbye, holding out his hand, which I clasped in mine—he then started for the huge metal door at the entrance, which was beginning to close. I accompanied him, with the master close on our heels. Azedine whispered to me, as one foot reached the doorway that he had visited the mosque several times, only to be turned away. The guards in front would not even tell him my whereabouts. He left without looking back, sliding through the door before it closed. I turned toward the squared shoulders of the master, a concerned look on his face. I smiled, concealing my anxiety, as I receded to my place in the corner of the mosque. The master did not follow me there.

I was alone to contemplate my meeting with Azedine. I was puzzled by the fact that the master did not want to allow me to communicate with my friends on the outside, and that he did not even tell me when they had visited. However, as I read passages from the *Qur'an*, and my mind absorbed a new prayer, a new glow of faith and love engulfed my body and mind—any doubts as to the master's behavior dissipated in the exuberance of spiritual awakening.

I was often left alone to pray and meditate in the back of the mosque. The master continued to join me from time to time and read the *Qur'an* with me, instructing me on the wisdom of Muhammad. One day, he came to me and knelt next to me as I prayed in the corner; his long, wavy beard represented ancient wisdom to my eyes. He leaned close to me and said that Moslems believed that Jesus Christ was not the son of God, of Allah. He said that Jesus was not crucified but ascended into heaven by the power of Allah. Moslems believed that Jesus was a prophet, that the Christians were misled and that the Jews were wrong by not believing in the Christ. Muhammad continued, his eyes luminous, as he looked directly into mine: "Muhammad was the last prophet who would come to the people before the end of the world; he was sent to bring the last message from Allah to his people."

After every sentence, the master would proclaim, "Muhammad rasul Allah" (Muhammad is the messenger of God). Then, he would ask me if I believed in Muhammad, the prophet. I always responded "Yes, but I am not sure that Muhammad was the last prophet sent by Allah before the end of the world, or that Jesus was not the son of God."

He would respond, "Ca va (That's okay). As your heeman (faith) increases, you will understand more clearly the truth about Muhammad, the prophet, and the will of Allah which is clearly described in the *Qur'an*."

But, I would cringe when I heard the master's response. I had accepted my life within these walls among beautiful people and with this beautiful religion, but I wondered how they could be so sure about the origins of Jesus. How could anyone be so sure? Even though the master's deep, brown eyes reflected deep understanding of the world and profound wisdom; I could not fully accept nor fully understand the anti-Christian and anti-Jewish dogmatism reflected by the words of my dear friends living with me in the Mosque. I wondered if maybe I should pray more as the master advised so Allah might eventually reveal the subtle truths of the universe. I longed for truth, honesty and brotherly love, the true characteristics of life that I had always thought essential, but rarely found. I was deeply confused and imagined myself falling, falling, falling down into a crevice so deep within the earth that my cries would not be heard.

Chapter XVIII

The Bottomless Pit

Before traveling to Morocco, I had secretly commenced an intense search for spiritual identity and eventual unity through the study of Hinduism, Buddhism, Christianity, Judaism, Islam and the Baha'i faiths. Even while in the mosque I was constantly comparing these religions by focusing on their conceptual similarities. In particular, I sought to determine the common denominators among them, such as the concepts of divine revelation, faith, a Supreme Being, similar intermediaries between God and man, similar moral values and prayer and/or meditation techniques. For example, the concentrated, meditative state of mind called "Samadhi"[8] and repetition of a phrase or "mantra" in Hinduism and Buddhism is similar to the concentrated, meditative state of mind in Christianity[9] and Judaism[10]. The Christians and Jews share similar beliefs in certain prophets, notably Abraham, Moses and Jesus, who are also revered by Muslims. The mediation between God and man is achieved through the intervention of the archangel Gabriel. Baha'Allah of the Baha'i movement quotes Muhammad and well-known figures representing other religions (Rajinder Singh, *Guérir par la Méditation*, Ellipse, 2005, p.26).

I believed that no religion by itself contained all the pieces to the puzzle that embodied the truth—that individually, all major religions were merely conduits or paths that could lead to the truth, to the supreme consciousness[11], but should never be confused with truth or the essence of the supreme being: pure truth, pure love. I sought a universal religion that could bring all those pieces together in one ideology, without criticizing, rejecting or forcing people to abandon the other religions.

In spite of my pre-Morocco search for such a common denominator among all religions, it seemed to come naturally that I was now consciously and subconsciously beginning to believe that it was Islam. Perhaps my quest for the universal religion would end here in Morocco without proceeding to Palestine, which was my original plan.

The master was trying to slowly disintegrate the connection I felt to other religions by challenging what I thought to be true about Christianity, Judaism, Hinduism and Buddhism. I wondered if I was becoming a fanatical follower of Islam, which would justify a

---

[8] Justin F. Stone, *The Joy of Meditation-An Introduction to Meditation Techniques*, (New York: Square One Publishers, 2002), p. 8.

[9] Silent meditation referred to in: Sue Monk Kidd, *The Dance of the Dissident Daughter*, (New York: HarperCollins Publishers Inc., 2002), p. 14. See William Bodri, *Samadhi Cultivation in Christianity, Islam and Judaism*, www.meditationexpert.com, p. 1, 20.

[10] William Bodri, *Samadhi Cultivation in Christianity*, supra, p. 1.

[11] This thought is inspired by the Hindu teacher, Sri Ramakrishna (1836-1886), Marcus Braybrooke, *Learn to Pray*, (San Francisco: Chronicle Books, 2001, p. 54).

full-blown criticism of other doctrines, pitting Islam against all others, in a war of doctrine against doctrine.

My studies of philosophy in Paris had given me tools with which I could finally analyze the doctrines I had so easily believed in my youth. My studies were meant to clarify— but sometimes confused—my understanding of the various religious ideologies through rigorous, dialectical analysis of each religious doctrine. In comparison with the sometimes elitist, sometimes stuffy, intellectual atmosphere of the "Fac"[12], the Moslems with whom I worked seemed so simple and earthy.

I so yearned for simplicity in a complicated, cold world removed from values so dear to me, like love, spirituality, giving from the heart without expectation of anything in return. Values seemed to be lost in the whirlwind of life's speed and the media blitz geared toward influencing the public into being knee-jerk consumers—finding solace in things and dreams rather than within a higher power.

Maybe now I had found the true children of God freely loving without conditions, without ulterior motives, without a consumer mentality, only desiring to spread love and tolerance within the world. Even the confines of the rules and rituals that surrounded me now seemed an irrelevant impediment to embracing this religion as true and universal.

There still remained the question, feverishly pounding in my mind, of their interest in me. I wanted to believe that their opening their arms to me was to enlighten me and to share their love for humanity. But nothing could stop me from believing that they had other motives, that maybe they yearned for me to be profoundly converted so that I could spread the word to others—to my family and my friends in another world—for the purpose of gaining converts to the cause.

After each training session, the master would recite "Allahu Akbar," then smiling, arise and drift away to another part of the mosque where my fellow monks were praying and studying, leaving me with my prayers and meditations.

After one week of this "educational process," I reached a point of doctrinal suffocation; I walked along the periphery of the mosque, looking for an opening like a caged animal. Fellow monks passed, smiling, saying "As-Salamu alaykum." I responded, "Walecom Salem," and we proceeded. I saw the master speaking to a young monk, whose smile was lightly highlighted by the slight growth of a mustache above the upper lip, with a similar shadow of whiskers below. I tried to avoid the master's gaze as his eyes were everywhere.

I slipped toward the front of the mosque beyond his view, as I continued my stroll along the wall leading up to the front door which was, as always, sealed. I saw the hand of the groundskeeper appear from the other side, pushing the door slightly open. He did not see me as he walked through the opening and entered a small equipment building juxtaposed to the front door. I approached the opening, and as no one was looking, I slid out the door and poured my doctrinally-overdosed body into the street.

I needed to visit my friends in the Medina where I could relax and reflect on my experiences while living with my brothers in the mosque. Having been deprived of sun for days while living there, my eyes squinted as the hot rays grasped and embraced my frail body with strong fingers. The dry heat penetrated my entire being; my toes tingled, affected

---

[12] Literally means Faculty at the University of Paris and at most other French universities.

by the powerful surge of energy commencing with the top of my head and moving through my entire body.

The suburbs of Casablanca included fields of abandoned dry grass and the occasional house, its adobe-like walls displaying cracks where the sun had reveled in yesteryear. Young girls were carrying earthen jars on their heads, their silk robes swaying in the light breeze wafting over the powdery dust of the lonely streets. The proof of the master's impact on me was immediately felt as I automatically turned my back on the young girls—he had warned me not to look at women—so as to prevent my pure thoughts from being invaded by lust, adultery or raw power.

My conversion to Islam had thus taken root; my behavior began to mechanically respond to the prescribed instructions written in the Qur'an and interpreted by the master and the brothers. I walked for miles without speaking to anyone, with my eyes scanning the sidewalk, so my faith would not be corrupted by influences from the outside...by the sexual desire that could be inspired by a beautiful woman. Only occasionally would I glance at the passersby—but my eyes would look right through them. I protected my pureness with the fierceness of a guard dog.

As I slothfully meandered down the dusty road toward the Medina, my legs began to give out. I was not used to walking with sandals and a robe. I moved in and out of consciousness as I roamed the streets in a dreamlike stupor. I passed a group of smiling, happy-go-lucky children, the heat of their enthusiasm bursting as they played soccer in the streets. Their energetic waves hardly touched me as I was in my own little private world.

Paranoia again gnawing at me as I imagined the people were observing my every move along the way; this enhanced my desire to look straight ahead as I plodded on and on. I finally reached the Ancienne Medina, where I felt the pangs of homecoming, to be experienced alone as I drifted through its streets. The misery of its inhabitants returned to invade my consciousness. The skinny, dirty children lined the streets, scattered among the disfigured beggars; the horrible stench blanketed the streets, the residue baked into the firm, clay surface by the burning sun. I already craved the protective ambiance of the mosque and the brothers—the monks, with calm and refreshing spirits dancing together to the music of the grand creator, Allah.

A couple of weeks in the mosque had taken me into a spiritual paradise, far away from the streets and streets of souks, the barrage of calls from vendors to the passersby, and the stench and poverty. I decided to return to the mission without visiting my friends in the Medina for I feared they might convince me to abandon it.

After a few hours of rows and rows of outdoor markets, trudging over dirt roads and open fields smelling of dried excrement, I arrived at the front door to the mission. I was standing again in front of the white barricade that separated the mission from the outside world. The door creaked and opened to the eyes of a brother, which flashed concern. As he held my hand, he drew me into the mosque. The door clanged shut behind me. The white-robed monk said nothing as he led me by the hand through the closed door to the study of the master. A myriad of crisply spoken Arabic words were audible through the closed door of his study; it abruptly opened.

"Salem Walekum" uttered the master as he waved me inside, closing the door behind me. "Where have you been?" he asked, as he pointed to a rug on which were strewn several pillows where I should sit.

"Mon frère, you must not leave without telling us. I hope you did not look at the women in the streets when you left the mission; they are unveiled and all dressed like Europeans, like European prostitutes. They should be home like any respectable woman. If you look at or talk to them, you will instantly lose the faith, and all the progress that you have made will vanish."

Then the master reached out and clasped my hands in his. "You must remember, my brother, that if you do not purify yourself and accept Allah and his teachings, you may die tomorrow and you will never go to paradise!"

"Ah, paradise!" I whispered to myself. That word reminded me of two nights ago when all the monks had congregated in the dining room to eat dinner. As the food was placed in the middle of the long mat, we all repeated "Bismi-l-lahi" (In the name of God) before starting to eat. The master had been sitting on my right side. I reached into the communal platter for a piece of potato. After having popped it into my mouth, I reached for another. Suddenly, a brown hand was restraining mine from reaching its target; the hand was connected to the master's lanky frame. I turned my head to face him directly. His dark brown eyes reflected his disappointment. Then he spoke:

"Did you say "Bismi-l-lahi" before eating the potato?" and without waiting for a response from me, he continued, "Remember, you must say it before taking each bite, and after you have swallowed each morsel, you must say "Al-hamdu li-illahi" (Praise God). He paused, smiling, his beard stretching along his lower lip, as he looked around the table at the brothers who had stopped eating, their eyes fixed on us. He continued, "You'll understand all that one day when your 'heeman' (faith) has grown and you feel it in your 'huk'" (heart).

I finally understood why the room was filled with mumbling; everyone was blessing each morsel of food, in the name of Allah. At first my naturally rebellious nature, which is opposed to any repetitive rituals, raised its outraged head within me. I silently questioned the necessity of verbally exposing one's faith publicly and openly. As flurries of doubt invaded my thinking, my stomach became jittery and my mind swirled with thoughts questioning the necessity of the senseless rituals to which we were subjected. The guilt I felt harboring these thoughts drew me inward, my mind beset with doubts and insecurity. I remained silent, except for muffled "Bismi-l-ilahi's" and "Al-hamdu li-illahi's" as the master looked on.

I dropped my face to hide my confused eyes and furrowed brow as I thought, "My faith, my faith...would not my faith become a pretext for ignoring unanswered questions? I must continue to seek the truth." Weariness froze my bones and reddened my eyes as I looked around to the occupied lips and mouths, and I felt alone—on one hand rebellious, on the other hand afraid—that I was falling into a bottomless pit of fanaticism.

The next morning, Mowi, the director of the mission, sat across from me as he sopped up melted butter with fluffy chunks of homemade bread. His long, gray beard suggested a lifetime of stories, allegories on the human condition, which he did not hesitate to recount over breakfast. He spoke first in Arabic, and then in French, so I would understand. Mowi, his silver mane gracefully swaying as he moved his head, looked directly at me as he spoke; the other monks attentively listened as they sat around the rectangular mat. Their omnipresent turbans, properly placed on their heads, were inclined toward the speaker and their eyes intently glued to his every move, his every gesture.

He sat back, his left hand still holding a crust of bread, to tell us about his exploits after he fought against the Germans in World War II.

"After the war," he began, his beady eyes sweeping over the attentive listeners, "I traveled to different parts of the world as a mercenary soldier, mainly in Africa. Then I was sent to Asia where I was employed in several bloody skirmishes. I remember one day, I passed by a foxhole that had been mercilessly bombed the day before. As I looked down into the bloody mess, I spied a holy *Qur'an* sitting on a mound of dirt. I sat down right there and then and read the book from cover to cover, sliding down into the foxhole among the massacred bodies when the bombs began to drop. That day, I decided to dedicate my life to Allah, to preserve and spread his word through Islam throughout the world."

Then Mowi looked directly into my eyes and told me that there is a place called "paradise" where all good Moslems would go if they were faithful to Allah and had complied with the laws written in the Holy *Qur'an*. Encouraged by the rapt attention of his listeners, he continued:

"Ah, paradise," he sighed. "Unimaginable riches for those who believe. Ah, oui, you will be entitled to umpteen virgins who are more beautiful than you could ever imagine. Huge, juicy dates hanging from voluptuous trees are just waiting to be plucked and eaten. There will be no suffering in paradise, only the good life, and no work; you are a fool if you try to make earth your paradise. It's the afterlife that counts. The choice is yours: either paradise or endless suffering at the hands of Satan."

He cocked his head back and opened his huge mouth, shining with silver and gold-filled teeth, his gray beard spanning his lower chin as he convulsively laughed. Everyone joined in; I had to laugh, too.

Then I faded out into a dreamlike stupor amid mumbling voices and laughter...fading...fading, and then oblivion. I dreamed that I was entering a large, white room in which rested a row of large mats dotted by turbans. Eyes peered out from under the turbans; a group of turbaned heads turned towards me, their faces identically bearded. Their chestnut-colored eyes looked into mine as they shook their heads.

The next thing I knew, I was walking toward the front of the mosque. Through an open door, I noticed the Imam preparing to lead another prayer session. My eyes swept across the earnest faces raptly watching him, that moved forwards, backwards and sideways as the robed bodies contorted into the various positions that accompanied the afternoon prayer session. I joined the group; my Arabic sang out in harmony with the congregation of brothers and members of the community.

After the Imam had said the final prayers, I decided to take my usual position in back of the mosque and learn more prayers. As I sat in the corner of the mosque, my head bent toward the mats, I decided to recite the prayers I had already learned. Before I could get half-way through the first prayer, someone yanked on the sleeve of my djellabah.

"Come on, take a glass of tea," a soft voice suggested among the echoes of the mosque. I looked up and my gaze lit on a tray with a silver tea kettle and beautifully colored glasses, engraved with richly-colored purple roses and steaming with fresh mint tea. Its sweet fragrance permeated the musty air, attracting our senses like the blissful tunes of a snake charmer. All the brothers gathered and sat down around the tray, next to me. I could not tell if they were sitting around the tray, or around me. The master poured the tea from a silver kettle as the brothers looked on, speaking among themselves in low voices.

Chapter XIX

The Lost Souls

The next day, following the afternoon prayer, I asked the master to explain "Al Fatiha," the Lord's Prayer of the Islamic religion. This question pleased him; his omnipresent smile widened and he turned, his djellabah brushing the floor, motioning me to follow. We headed for a remote corner of the mosque and sat down under a huge window, a corner of which was open, letting in the chirping of birds outside. He sat in a semi-lotus position, waiting for me to speak. I imitated him. Seconds passed and I could not utter a word as I perceived we were the image of the classical teacher-student relationship: the teacher was a wise man, dressed in a robe as befitted a master, playing the role of a great religious leader/teacher; and I, playing the role of a wide-eyed student of God, was impressed by the master's shower of attention on me. Were we just role playing?

I snapped out of this dream-like state as I felt the eyes of the master firmly on me.

"Ca va?" he asked, a concerned look furrowing his brow.

"Yes, fine," I quickly responded, fearing he had divined my innermost thoughts. "I understand most of the words of the "Al Fatiha," the first "sourate" of the *Qur'an*, except the last part which says "Ihdina-s-sirata-l-mustaqim. Sirata-l-ladina an amta alayhim, gayri-l-magdubi alayhim, wa la-d-dallin" (Guide us on the straight path, the path of those whom Thou hast blessed, not of those against whom Thou art wrathful, nor of those who go astray).

"Master," I asked with an air of humility, "who are these lost people?"

The master cleared his throat as he smiled his penetrating smile. "The lost people are those who have offended Allah; the Jews are evil, lost people." Also beware—Christians are also lost people."

My heart pounded warnings as a fanatical smile flashed across his face. He sensed my discomfort, so he blurted out a few words designed to comfort me:

"Hwani (My brother), you will understand someday. Just keep praying and your heeman will increase; only then will you begin to understand the mysteries of Islam." He placed his right hand on my left shoulder and uttered "As-Salamu alaykum," in a low voice as he rose to leave.

"Walecom salem," I responded mechanically, as he left me sitting, more perplexed than ever.

I wished that I could go far away so I could have more free time to think. . .to withdraw from the mission and into myself. I was deeply bothered by the master's teachings, especially what he told me about Jews being lost people. Some of my best friends were Jewish and my parents were Christians; I did not find them evil people. Also I wondered why women never entered the mosque but I thought I'd address that question to the master another time.

That night as I lay in my sleeping bag high in the loft above the praying area of the mosque, and after I had exchanged the usual "As-Salamu alaykum's" with my fellow monks, a myriad questions invaded my mind. I stared at the high ceiling, vaguely discernable by the light shining from a shaded street lamp outside the window.

I asked Yusuf, who was lying next to me, why I never saw any women in the mosque. He sleepily responded that an isolated room was set aside for women who rarely came to pray during the day. I asked him why women could not participate in the main prayer session downstairs.

He responded, "Men need to concentrate on praying without the presence of women to distract them." Yusuf turned over in his sleeping bag, adjusted its sides, and soon fell fast asleep.

I did not sleep well that night.

My body tossed and turned within the confines of the sleeping bag as I dreamt about my Jewish friends in California, especially Mark and Richard, with whom I had spent many happy moments. We had met at the University of California, Davis, where we were students....

One long and lonely night, in spite of the fatigue and chronic blood-shot eyes, I plodded along, drafting a research paper for one of my courses. After I heard the sputtering of a sports car outside my window, someone knocked at the door to the house I shared with two other students.

Richard stood in the doorway with his no-holds-barred smile,

"Happy birthday," he exclaimed. He tugged at my arm, pointing to his car where Art, an Italian-American friend was sitting. Art waved. "You see, you can't refuse. We're taking you to the pizzeria tonight, whether you like it or not."

I looked at Art who nodded. They had come to drag me away from my studies and to celebrate my birthday, which I had totally forgotten. I was drained from hours of continuous study so I was happy to get away from the books.

They took me to a local pub where we ate pizza and drank beer. At the end of the meal, they even sang "Happy Birthday" to me while complete strangers sitting around a long table joined in.

I also recalled another night when another close friend, Mark—also Jewish—and I sat alongside a swimming pool; drinking and reminiscing about the fun we had had that year and our plans for the future.

The recollection of those happy moments lulled me to sleep.

I was awakened early the next morning by a nudge on my shoulder. The gray-bearded director was standing over me.

"Time to pray," he said, with a raspy morning voice. I shuffled down the narrow stairs leading to the main prayer room. I usually dozed during most of the five o'clock a.m. prayer session. After mass, instead of withdrawing to the corner of the room, I returned to the sleeping room to sleep until the 12 o'clock noon prayer session.

After noon prayers, I remained seated, my djellabah spread around me, in the main prayer room while meditating/praying. That morning, I was in a dilemma over whether to accept, or not, the words of the master about the lost people, referred to in the "Al Fatiha."

He had specified that they were labeled "lost people" because they had offended Allah. He had also added something that was confusing to me—that the Jews were evil and therefore lost people. My brain grew numb from conflicting thoughts since my Jewish friends had always been extremely supportive and principled, far from the evildoers described by the master. Also, I was raised in the Episcopalian tradition (the Church of England, the Anglican Church) by my parents, who I loved very much and who I did not consider as evil or lost people.

I wondered what the master meant or what his reason was for telling me those things. I looked out over the abandoned prayer room; the corner where the Imam stood seemed so vacant. My mind cried with frustration, alienation—I felt as if I belonged nowhere. I wondered if the Islam of the master was not universal but, instead, isolated within its dogma and rituals like so many other religions, vying for "bragging rights" to the rank of superior or true religion.

I began to doubt that this was the place of worship that I had venerated so much, that I had believed sacred, and an oasis among the infidels on the outside. I was riding on a storm cloud of disbelief floating high above the mosque, ascending into the blue haze, when the master appeared in front of me, like an apparition. When I looked up, I could barely make out his features; his fine black beard appeared fuzzy around the edges. I closed and reopened my eyes, finally realizing that the apparition was, indeed, the master, who patiently stood before me, the corners of his mouth upturned into a gentle smile.

He sat next to me, his djellabah spread over his legs as mine was. He sat silently for several seconds, looking at some imaginary object in front of him, without moving, like a stone sculpture of a revered leader. Then he turned towards me, without moving the rest of his body. The full force of his being attracted me like a magnet, and I found myself facing him directly. He slowly began to talk:

"Several of the monks are preparing to take a voyage to the south of Morocco, to a desert-like area where they will help Moroccans return to the faith by sharing their knowledge among the people."

He looked at me intently, as though he were seeking something. "Would you care to join them? I think this would be a great chance to be instructed by a learned Imam who is leading the group there, and whose group will be allowed to sleep in the village mosque."

His eyes shone like tiny lamps as he told me how calm and beautiful the small village was we would be visiting. He stated that I could continue learning the ways of Muhammad in a more rustic setting, among the good Moslem country people and the monks with whom I would be living. He added that after the voyage, I would then deeply feel and understand the mysterious beauty of Islam.

My refusal would clearly have disappointed him; I feared that he would take it as a rejection of his hospitality, of his advice, which would compromise our warm relationship. But I clearly did not appreciate being pressured into doing anything, since I had not been pressured up to that moment.

I failed to understand the importance of my participation in the journey to such a faraway place. However, I was curious as to the intentions of the prayer group, traveling from mosque to mosque, village to village, speaking to peasants and entreating them to attend mass at the closest mosque.

The master stood up, without taking his eyes off me; I followed suit. As we were about the same height, we stood at eye level. I told him that I agreed to participate in the study group traveling to southern Morocco, in the pilgrimage to the country sites to worship with the Moroccan peasants. He smiled and told me he would inform the other monks. He turned to go and then sweeping around he stopped, and spoke to me again:

"Prepare your things as you will leave first thing in the morning after morning mass."

"Will I have a chance to say goodbye to Shean? He comes to the mosque on Fridays, usually."

He left me alone in the back of the mosque, alone with my thoughts, without answering my question. My confusion as to what was expected of me gave way to my yearning to return to the country. Even though the mosque in which I was living was located in the suburbs of Casablanca and was a protected, serene bastion of Islam, an endless stream of cars and motorbikes outside its walls was a reminder of the turbulence of city living.

Awhile later, the master returned to the back of the mosque where he knew he would always find me. He explained, with childlike enthusiasm, the importance of this spiritual mission. He pointed to the heavens and spoke:

"Allah is pleased with you. You have honored our God by having learned so much about the only true religion in so little time."

He asked a group of monks praying nearby to join us. As they, one by one, formed a circle around the master and me, he continued, looking at me and holding my hands in his. "We all love you, Muhammad. So we have decided to call you 'Muhammad Abdelaziz, which means 'Muhammad, the dearly beloved one.'"

I believed that they all loved me. They could read in my eyes that I was sincerely searching for the truth...for God...for Allah. I could read in their eyes that they had found the truth and I, a lost lamb, would be welcomed into their fold as an enlightened, and therefore saved, person—saved from the suffering attached to following the dark path that led away from Allah. I was deeply touched by their concern for me, a complete stranger, and for my spiritual fulfillment.

The next morning, I followed my fellow monks down the shadowy staircase to the prayer room below where we said our usual morning prayers. Afterwards, instead of sitting and meditating for awhile, one of my fellow monks, Ali, patted me on the back and beckoned me to follow him.

He led me out of the prayer room and into another room, turned to me and whispered, "Muhammad Abdelaziz, we are called to travel to the south of Morocco today. Go now upstairs and prepare your things. You must bring your sleeping bag."

"Will I have a chance to say goodbye to Shean?" I asked.

He responded, "I'm sorry, but there isn't any time left."

He led me through a labyrinth of rooms with the usual praying mats. I felt a cold loneliness while winding through a narrow corridor, thinking that I may never see Shean again. Then we reached the familiar staircase leading to the overhead loft, which had served as my sleeping quarters for the last week.

Ali went to his corner of the room and began rolling up his sleeping bag. I tended to mine, as well, and placed my towel and other personal effects in a tote bag, which I slung over one arm; I heaved the sleeping bag over the other. Ali was waiting for me at the door. I followed him downstairs to the prayer room. The tapping of our sandals on the sections of bare floor echoed in the empty room.

We arrived at the main gate guarded by an agent of the master. Standing next to him in a full djellabah, wearing his omnipresent brown-peaked hat was Camara. He reached out to shake my hand, saying, "As-Salamu alaykum."

I responded, "Walecom Salem."

He said, with a twinkle in his eye, "I'm to accompany you today, Muhammad Abdelaziz."

Camara nodded to the guard who then placed his hand on the huge knob and turned it; the heavy metal hinges made a grinding noise as the door slowly opened. When it was wide enough, we passed through the opening and proceeded down the sidewalk as the great door clanked shut. I wondered if this was the close of an era and the beginning of a new one...

We walked for miles: through the Casablanca suburbs, dried fields, across bridges, past rows of stone houses until we reached the bus station; I had arrived in Casablanca at this very place only a couple of weeks ago. Ali nudged me to follow him as he walked around the station to a line of buses which, he explained, were municipal buses—Camara followed us. We boarded one of them and found ourselves speeding across Casablanca, passing cars and motorcycles, each blowing their horns but giving way to the municipal monster.

As we approached downtown Casablanca, the streets were lined with stalls and vendors offering potted flowers in a rainbow of colors, juicy dates piled high in bins, and many other items. Huge toothless and toothy grins flashed along the way, and together with long, flowing robes and colorful turbans, formed a mélange of colors, movement and faces.

"Allahu Akbar," I cried as I caught sight of a chauffeur wearing a black turban and dressed in a tuxedo, driving a brand new Mercedes. "A chrome camel—wild!" I thought to myself.

As I gazed out the window of the bus, my thoughts dwelled upon the time I had stayed in Camara's apartment in the Ancienne Medina. In my mind, Camara's youngest daughter was staring at me with huge, round moon eyes; her kinky hair was tied up in two little neat ponytails held together by tiny, red rubber bands. She would recite a phrase or two from the *Qur'an*, repeating them over and over again:

"La ilaha illa Allah" (There is but one God Allah) and "Wa Muhammad rasul Allah" (and Muhammad is his Prophet). She would stop only when she found something else to do, such as mischievously punching her brother standing behind the beaded curtains separating the living room from the hallway; the latter was filled with rows of drying clothes hanging from a crude network of wires and ropes.

Camara's finger gently poked my ribcage, awakening me from my nostalgic reminiscence.

"Oui, je suis très fier de toi (Yes, I am proud of you). Muhammad Abdelaziz is your new name. That is one of the names of the prophets—you should be proud that you have merited such a name. The brothers at the mosque have named you thus because they all

158

love you. My brother, I am so proud of you. You have done us all proud! You have made great progress toward becoming a true Moslem. Oui, Allahu Akbar." For the first time, I noticed that Camara's tongue was visible through a small opening between his yellowing, two front teeth—his wide grin made it more obvious.

Camara continued: "When you return from your trip to the country, you will have come into close contact with Islam and you will become an even better Moslem than me."

I wondered if I could ever become a Moslem let alone a better Moslem than Camara, who was truly a devoted worshipper. I respected Camara because he stood by his principles even though his wife, as he had previously explained to me, would often ridicule him for his rigid, fundamentalist belief in Islam. She had also sometimes complained to me that he not only beat a path to the mosque to pray but beat his children for not attending at least the Friday services; they would hide their little faces and sulk after such treatment. It was difficult for me to conciliate the conflicting elements of Camara's character: the incredible kindness towards me and desire to show me the right path contrasted with the violent punishment of his children. He had a warm heart and sincerely believed that everyone would be happy if they faithfully practiced Islam. I thought how fortunate I was to be an adult; otherwise Camara may have been beating the fear of Allah into me as well.

The bus dropped us off at a local mosque in the center of Casablanca where, as Ali explained, we were to participate in study groups with members of the congregation. During those sessions, we learned and recited important prayers from the *Qur'an* and listened to an Imam, his long, white beard seeming to form puddles on the floor; he lectured on the wisdom of the prophet Muhammad. While praying, I felt secure with Camara on one side and Ali on the other.

After the Imam finished leading the prayers one morning, Ali explained in a whisper that we were going to visit another mosque where we were to pray, learn new prayers and relax for a few days, before setting out for the south of Morocco.

After saying goodbye to our hosts, we gathered up our belongings and headed for the now familiar bus stop. We arrived just as the bus was grinding out of the station— Camara yelled, gesticulating wildly. The bus stopped and the doors opened. As we got on, the doors immediately slammed behind us. While we stood in the aisles, the bus shot ahead, trailing clouds of exhaust and dust along the way.

It took us into a quieter zone fronting the beach on the outskirts of Casablanca, a community of stone buildings. Camara and Ali remained silent throughout the short bus ride.

My thoughts floated over the piles of mussel shells covering the sand, against the backdrop of the raging Atlantic Ocean. The bus rumbled down the highway that connected Casablanca with southern Morocco. The waves pounded onto the sand, with a white, crispy freshness, washing away the blues.

Camara tapped me with the tips of his shiny black fingers as he jumped to his feet.

"We get off here!" he exclaimed, with great insistence.

The bus stopped in front of a huge white building, with the Atlantic Ocean in the background. I squirmed and wriggled between the veiled ladies who clogged the aisles of the bus before scrambling down the steps after Ali and Camara. The door slammed shut and the engine growled even before I had reached the curb; a cloud of exhaust surrounded me, momentarily causing me to choke.

The waves crashed in the distance as Camara led the way down a dirt path leading toward the formidable white minaret rising from the rectangular mosque. I almost had to run to keep up with him, dragging my feet as I went—I had not yet adjusted to the new pointed footwear and my legs were weak and somewhat "asleep" from sitting in a scrunched position for what seemed an eternity. Also, I had lost about fifteen pounds since the start of my journey from Paris about a month ago, and I was feeling weak and drained.

We crossed the road and headed away from the beach. Then suddenly, as we rounded a corner, there was the minaret; the stately mosque with its faded white façade stood directly in front of us, in the middle of a field on the edge of Casablanca. There were no other buildings around—the area was a barren delight! Lonely hearts hungry for truth could easily immerse themselves in the quiet beauty surrounding the lone mosque, overlooking the foaming waves.

Camara was already standing in front of the entrance as Ali and I approached along the dirt path. He took off his shoes and vanished behind the white walls followed by Ali. I did not feel like entering the mosque yet, so I turned around and faced my old friend, the ocean; I had gone through all my adolescent changes on the shores of its raging blue cousin on the other side of the world. Such memories seemed so distant now.

As I stared into the waves, I flashed on my brothers and I taking part in a foot race along the shore of Dillon Beach, at Tamales Bay in northern California; the breakers seemed to applaud our competitive fun. John and I continued to race as Tom stopped to inspect the seagulls and shells near the tide pools. He was the artist, the observer of all things, his eagle eyes inquisitively dissecting every tide pool, every seagull hovering overhead. We, the runners, both wore cut-off jeans, no shirts; with muscles bulging, we both strained to get ahead. We were neck and neck, in a "dead heat," as we raced on until we ran out of breath. Gasping, we tumbled on the sand, laughing, grabbing each other, wrestling on the side of a hill, on the windblown, smooth, hot sand dune. Tom joined us as we rolled down the dune, frolicking while being stung by the dune nettles—but we didn't care. We raced to the waves, plunged in and splashed each other, laughing hysterically. After swimming for awhile, we returned to the dunes to sunbathe and watch the sun sink into the sea, the cool wind caressing our scorched, flaking faces. The waves rippled and the gulls cried "Yah yaaac!" As we lay on the sand looking out toward the moody ocean, small, dried pieces of seaweed, partially imbedded in the sand, danced in the soft breeze, like little shadowy angels.

"Muhammad, are you going to join us?" Camara's black face was accentuated against the pale, white door, his neck stretched around it like a giraffe reaching into a tree.

I entered the mosque after taking my shoes off, placing them next to the main entrance. After we bathed ourselves, we entered the immense prayer room. It was about five times the size of the prayer room back at the mission, with rows of floor-to-ceiling columns.

Camara joined the worshippers in the prayer area of the mosque while Ali led me by the hand to an area in back of the mats set out for praying. It was a square space partitioned off by a white rope in which several sleeping bags and bedding were carefully folded. Ali looked back at me and nodded. We entered the area and were greeted by an

160

elderly man, his face covered with birthmarks. As he smiled, two rows of yellowed teeth were revealed above his scraggly, gray beard but his smile was kindly and welcoming.

As we unpacked our bedding, the expected magical voice wailed high above from the minaret entreating anyone within a mile or two of the minaret and those already present in the mosque to join the Imam in prayer. People began lining up in back of mats neatly laid out in several lines, in front of the religious leader; we joined them.

After we all prayed together, the gray-bearded Imam lectured the polite group. Camara was seated on the opposite side of the speaker, whose voice almost trembled as he pronounced the words "Sobhana rabbiya al Al'ala" (Glory be to my Lord, the highest).

After ten minutes of meditative prayer, I joined a study group of about twenty-five men and boys sitting in a circle, their legs crossed in a semi-lotus position. I recognized four of the participants, fellow monks from the Masjid Nord[13]. I felt comforted and confident in their presence and refreshed by the ocean air breezing through an open window across my face.

During the afternoon prayer, after the Imam had spoken the last words of the mass, I bowed down, my forehead gently touching the floor. Tears filled my eyes as I thought about my newfound freedom and happiness. It seemed as though the more I searched for the light of Allah, the more enlightened I became.

After the prayer session, I sat in back of the mosque praying, meditating and sleeping. After a short nap, I opened my eyes to behold the vastness of this strange mosque. My eyes leapt from column to column, to the arched indentations in the walls where the Imam stood to lead the prayer sessions; above the arches were mosaic designs, colored tile in green and white, and large letters in Arabic spelling the name of Allah.

As I sat there contemplating my surroundings, I noticed two eyes from a long shadow at the other side of the mosque trained on me: Jahan, my old friend from the Medina, waved from the opposite side of the mosque. He rose and walked toward me, carefully passing behind the old, bony men wearing turbans, respecting their privacy while praying. In a few minutes, he was standing next to me—his eyes were cool, faded, and somber, his mood indifferent, removed.

"Glad you could join us, Jahan," my voice rang out; I was delighted to see him.

He immediately placed the index finger of his right hand to his lips, hurriedly stating in English, "You must lower your voice, or they will kick you out of this mosque." He did not look at me as his eyes stared straight ahead toward the stack of *Qur'ans* sitting on a chair in front of the Imam's corner. He was counting a string of beads draped over his hands; he looked worried. His face was a ghostly pale.

"Ca va?" I asked as his head drooped downwards, his eyes focusing on the floor in front of him.

"Ca va" he responded. "I've been fasting for a few days to strengthen my faith so I feel a little weak. I'm glad you've decided to become a Moslem; you will discover many

---

13 I called the Masjid Nord "the mission" since *the leaders* aspired to spread the knowledge of Islam throughout the world *by sending* monks, acting as missionaries, out to speak to *people* in small villages.

beautiful secrets and mysteries as you enter more deeply into the religion." He spoke softly as his voice retreated deeper into his chest.

His brow was creased and his eyes were sad and distant, a pale film covering the sparkle I remembered. He spoke again: "I visited the mosque where you have been staying and the man with the black beard would not let me see you, but he told me you were on the way here so I took the next bus to join you." After a long silence, he continued, "We are your friends and we wish no harm to befall you."

I realized that the person he encountered at the mission was surely the master. But I unfortunately paid no attention to Jahan, who was there to warn me to be careful. All I could remember were the words of Camara who had told me that Jahan was not a true Moslem because he did not pray five times daily, he smoked cigarettes and was of little faith. In addition, I had suspected that Jahan had befriended me only because he desired to live and study in the United States, and was hoping I would help him achieve that goal. I concluded that Jahan had come to pry me away from my search for truth, away from Islam, the true path leading to Allah – he was there for reasons of his own personal gain rather than friendship.

I snapped at him, "Look, Jahan, thanks for coming to see me but I cannot spend much time with you. Besides, I must continue learning Arabic and you only want to speak English with me. From this moment forward, we shall speak only Arabic!"

I figured that if Jahan had come to the mosque only to practice his English with me, he would soon leave the premises if I only spoke Arabic with him. That reasoning did not prevent me from being confused as to why I was treating Jahan so harshly. It was as if some mysterious force was manipulating me. I could not accept the possibility that this prayer group was dangerous and could harm me and that Jahan had come to warn me about it. In any case, I refused to heed him.

I left Jahan sitting perplexed on the mat as I strolled across the mosque to join a study group surrounding a young saintly-looking Moslem clothed in the usual white robe. He was reading from the *Qur'an* when I joined the group. I looked back to where Jahan had been sitting, but he had disappeared. As I listened to the speaker whose emotional voice shook with true conviction, my eyes swept the far corners of the mosque, but saw not a trace of Jahan. I wondered if he had left.

Lunch was served after the noon prayers in a small corner of the mosque sectioned off by a long, white rope for the purpose of dividing those living in the mosque from people there to pray. Our sleeping bags and bedding were stacked in a pile beside the hand-woven mats on which our lunch had been placed. Our meal consisted of a mixture of meat, vegetables and couscous. This miniature feast was brought to us by husky, black-robed women with veils, wearing what appeared to be a tattoo on their foreheads. They had set the silver plates of couscous on the brown mats, flattened due to constant use. They were so mashed that they seemed to be a part of the stone floors.

After we all prayed together, the same bearded Imam who had lectured us earlier hustled people in a circle around the food, according to some preconceived plan. I sat by myself in a far corner of the partitioned area since I preferred to fast that day. Finally, he had everyone seated. He quickly mumbled a few prayers and the monks dug into the feast. They reached into the silver plates and grabbed handfuls of couscous, their bony, brown

162

hands rolling the mixture into mouth-sized balls and then flipping them into their mouths with their thumbs. Stray grains of rice stuck to their mouths.

The Imam, his gray beard hanging well below his chin, motioned me to join the group, waving at me as I lay in my sleeping bag in the far corner, trying not to think of the couscous being served in abundance next to me. He stood up and came over to where I was resting, reached out and lightly touched my arm.

"Kul, kul," (Eat, eat) he cajoled.

"I'm fasting, so I won't eat anything until sundown," I said proudly.

A thin smile crossed his lips, revealing a hint of pearly-white teeth. I knew he would be pleased since the brothers at the other mosque honored those who desired to fast. He told me that fasting was good because it cleaned out the body and that Allah was pleased with those who fasted. Then he returned to the feast.

I was consumed by restlessness as I watched them devour the couscous. In order to continue the fast, to keep myself pure, even though my body registered the pangs of intense hunger, I curled up in my sleeping bag as the brothers continued their muffled, mouth-filled conversations and slurped mint tea.

I must have slept for hours. After being nudged by someone, I removed myself from the warmth of my nylon sleeping bag and heard the shrill cries of the muezzin high atop the minaret, summoning all to prayer. After neatly folding my sleeping bag and placing it beside the others, I noticed a familiar face and body dressed in a white robe standing next to me—it was Jahan.

"Hi. Would you like to pray with me?" he asked in a low voice.

I nodded and we joined the back line of worshippers. We stood side by side as the Imam recited the introductory prayers. We knelt down and stood up together, along with the rest of the congregation. Then we placed our foreheads on the mat as we prayed "Sobhana rabbiya al Al'ala" (Glory be to my Lord, the highest).

After praying together, Jahan took me aside, away from the group of worshippers. He squatted down and beckoned me to do the same. His face was distorted, his normal shiny, brown complexion pale; a small sore appeared at the corner of his thin lips. His piercing eyes told me that something was wrong.

"Muhammad, you know when I entered the section of the mosque where you and the others were camped, they would not let me in to see you. I told them that I was a friend of yours, so reluctantly they let me stay. Since you were sleeping, I sat down next to the group. While they pathetically gorged themselves on the food in the bowls, they offered me nothing, Muhammad, and I had been fasting for three days until my family stopped me because I had lost too much weight. My face was pale and I was always tired and nauseated. I have been fasting and praying for you. Be careful! I am glad you are becoming a Moslem, but there still are many things that you do not understand.

"I'm still not sure, "I whispered, hesitating.

"Well," he replied, "I'm glad you are at least learning about the mystical beauty of Islam, but I wouldn't trust the group you are traveling with. They didn't want me to visit you. I don't know what they are trying to hide or to protect you from, so be cautious!"

163

I had stopped listening to Jahan because I did not share the same apprehension about the mosque and the brothers. In fact, I repeated to myself that I loved and respected them. Anyway, I thought to myself again that Jahan had an agenda as he only wanted a free ride to the United States and that was the only reason why he persisted in seeing me.

Jahan retreated even further. "Anyway, I must go now. I wish you well. Please be careful, my brother." We hugged each other and he walked out of the mosque, his robe trailing after him as he disappeared into the cool summer Casablanca air.

I refused to think about Jahan's comments. After all, I thought to myself as I lay down in my sleeping bag, I was in the company of such beautiful people who would never harm me. They were helping me find the truth, the secret behind the existence of God. My eyes targeted the rustic brown ceiling directly overhead as my thoughts blurred into a thousand memories. I fell asleep, dreaming.

Chapter XX

Flight Across the Arid Plains

The next day we broke camp in the corner of the mosque after the morning prayers. I thought that the next item on the itinerary was to proceed to the south of Morocco by bus. Instead, we unexpectedly returned to the Masjid Nord.

As we entered through the familiar iron doors, we were greeted with open arms by another group of monks who had traveled to another mosque in the outskirts of Casablanca. Happily we all prayed together, holding each other's hands, smiling and declaring "Allahu Akbar." Not the smallest worry invaded the peace in my mind. I was surrounded by God's children; I trusted them all. This intense feeling of brotherly love permeated throughout the entire mission. We supped and then slept, following an entire afternoon of sharing insights on the beauty of Islam.

I was consistently surrounded by a myriad of robes and enthusiastic faces and simple, earthy gestures. When the master or the brothers spoke, they often lifted their hands toward the sky, with palms faced upwards and fingers curled, as if they were trying to grasp inspiration from the heavens. They enlightened the group with talk of the holy brotherhood, of Moslem rituals, prayers and more prayers, vigorously moving during intense prayer sessions, singing together, "La ilaha illa Allah wa Muhammad rasul Allah."

We were one community and I had been accepted as a permanent member. I probably gave everyone the impression that I was credulous, gullible and very trusting. My little, sometimes subtle, questions, such as how could they be so sure that Muhammad was the last prophet sent by God to the earth, went unnoticed and, of course, unanswered, for the moment. During our eventual visit to the south of Morocco, I was supposed to meet with a sage guru-type Moslem who was supposed to answer all my questions. At that time, all my doubts were to be laid to rest, perhaps a "last stand" in the face of the heavy indoctrination I was receiving.

For the next two days, I prepared for the journey to a small village located near Fes; I was told it was in central rather than southern Morocco. I was allowed to visit the Medina one last time to pick up the knapsack and the rest of my belongings, such as my clothes and books, and say good-bye to Azedine's family, who had cared for me during my first days in Casablanca.

I knocked on their door and the mother greeted me with a wide grin, grasping my hand and pulling me inside her home. I told her that I had come to say good-bye and pick up my belongings. She led me to the living room where my few possessions had been stored in a large cupboard. She opened it and handed me the knapsack. Several of the daughters were standing behind her, giggling.

"Don't mind them—they can't get used to your shaved head and think it's funny!"

I laughed and the daughters laughed even harder. The mother asked me if I'd like to stay for dinner so her husband and son could wish me good-bye, as well. I told her that I was in a hurry and thanked her again for offering her hospitality. I picked up my knapsack and headed for the door. With concerned looks on their faces, they let me go. The youngest son, Abel, however, while shaking my hands, clasped his hands around mine and would not let go. I had to literally break away. The mother and daughters wished me luck; they stood outside the open door waving to their prodigal, starry-eyed son and brother.

I returned to the mission in time for the last prayer session. As soon as the iron door creaked open and I sauntered in, I was immediately surrounded by several monks. They barraged me with questions:

"Have you prayed today?"

"Have you prayed four times today?"

"Did you wash yourself before every prayer session?"

"Did you ignore the women in the Medina?"

All I could do was nod. They sighed in relief as they realized that I had not missed a beat as a practicing Moslem. I thought to myself how strange it was to be wrong to have missed a prayer session. "Big deal," I thought! I wondered what everybody was afraid of. . . that I would pick up bad habits?

For the next few days, we discussed and prepared for my journey to southern Morocco. I was to soon savor my first taste of the Moroccan countryside, in the pure air, where I expected to continue my search for God, for the truth in nature, near the soil from whence it came and to which I would eventually go.

We would travel to an unfamiliar part of Morocco and visit people living in a crude, earthy simplicity that would mask reality and a thousand dangers. I did not realize that the most revealing chapter of my African adventure was about to begin.

Shean joined me in the back of the mosque one of the days before I left to explain the itinerary of the trip. After visiting several villages and staying in the local mosques while directing the masses during prayer sessions, we were to arrive in Marrakech about three days after our departure from Casablanca. Wherever we were to visit, the members of each congregation would look to us for leadership during the prayer sessions. Shean proclaimed that the reputation of enlightenment followed the monks from the Masjid Nord, and I should be proud to be part of it. After Marrakech, the two monks accompanying me and I were to take a bus to Fes where we would join forces with a prayer group camped in a small town nearby. The brothers with me would serve as my protectors to assure no problems would arise on the way. At least, that was the official reason given me; I suspected that the two were selected to preserve my faith, to protect me from the evil forces outside the mission and to assure that I followed the principles of the group, notably the prayer procedures.

One day after morning prayers, I packed the rest of my belongings in the sleeping room. After hoisting the knapsack and rolled sleeping bag over my shoulders, I climbed down the stairs to the kitchen to eat breakfast and wait for my ride to the bus station. I was sipping coffee and eating bread with a couple of monks when Shean walked in and sat next to me on a metal stool.

"I'm sorry I missed your last departure; I was busy at the shoe store. I took the afternoon off just to say goodbye before you leave for the country."

As we hugged each other, Ali drove up on a motorcycle and parked it outside the kitchen door. He opened the door half-way, indicating I should get on the back. I grabbed my gear and headed out the door. As we departed, kicking up a cloud of dust, Shean yelled out, "I'll pray for you! Come back soon."

I waved, wishing he could go with us. His brotherly love gave me strength to engage in the adventure.

A small group of motor scooters and motorcycles and their robed Moslem drivers conducted us to the bus station. With blue, white and green robes flying, we cried "Allahu Akbar" and "La ilaha illa Allah," as we swerved around cars and circled around monuments dedicated to King Hassan II.

When we arrived at the station, Ali helped me descend from the motorcycle. He led me to the sidewalk as we approached two monks I had seen from time to time at the mission, but with whom I had never spoken. Ali introduced me to Oman and Izneh, who would be accompanying me to a mosque in central Morocco. I shook their hands, then we turned to enter the station. After waving good-bye to Ali and a troop of kindly brothers that had accompanied us to the bus station, we entered through the glass doors.

Inside the station, we were greeted by the spectacle of more robed men, women in veils and children with candy-stained faces. Exhaust from the adjoining passenger loading zone permeated the air. I could hardly keep up with Oman and Izneh, who were swiftly walking up and down stairs and around sharp corners. After ascending a narrow flight of stairs, we arrived at a prayer area, which could not have measured more than twenty square feet; I had forgotten we were nearing the noon mass. One side overlooked the bus loading area with three buses stacked with suitcases and bags of all shapes and sizes. Bus attendants surrounded the buses below, tying everything together with ropes that formed a web-like net over the assortment of luggage.

We quickly ran through the essential prayers, skinning our knees a little as we executed them. The bus driver blew the horn and gunned the engine, sending more exhaust fumes into the air; our departure was imminent. We ended our prayers hurriedly and scampered down the narrow steps to the loading area. Climbing the steps, we boarded the bus, maneuvering our way past the wall-to-wall people. We found a row of empty seats in the back of the bus and wearily sank into them. As the bus charged out of the terminal, it reminded me of a racehorse freed from the confines of a gate. My companions lay their heads back in preparation for the long voyage. My face was plastered against the streaked window; I retreated into my thoughts as the bus roared out of Casablanca. The motor growled as it pulled the bus through the Medina and then through the middle and upper class districts. The apartments and houses all had gardens surrounded by walls with large doors serving as entrances locked from the inside, protecting the property from intruders.

As the bus rolled by, I wondered why people bought such expensive property if they were to pass the rest of their lives worried about intruders or about losing it. I recalled reading in the *Bhagavad Gita* that only ignorant people are selfishly attached to things and are in bondage of selfish works, that what is important is the wise act, without attachment, and an interest in working for the good of the world, of the universe[14]. I wondered if people

---

14 Bhagavad Gita, Chapter III.

could be detached from possessions, thereby freeing themselves from superficial, selfish worries to do great things, to help the world alleviate ignorance and suffering.

I remembered I had been allowed to have a BB gun in my youth and had shot several birds with it. I buried each bird, after pronouncing a few prayers over each grave. Then I dragged my gun home, placed it in the closet and never shot it again. Later, I contemplated how I had been ridiculously attached to this possession and worried about losing it. Yet it had served as a useless killer of defenseless birds. I learned my lesson, and did not take up arms against animal or insect after that.

The bus must have hit a rut in the road, as my head bumped against the window, awaking me from such deep thoughts. I was relieved that we were finally headed for the country, to an obscure village, to an unfamiliar destination. I was tired of city living, I thought, so onward to the country, to the fresh water and maybe herds of sheep and miles and miles of windswept Moroccan plains—to the vast, dry dunes of the Sahara.

I was absorbing it all hungrily from my little window, fogged by my exhalations of exhilaration at leaving the congested city behind. Many mules passed outside the window, usually with an elderly Moroccan astride, a stick in one hand, the other holding onto the mane. I watched in amusement while bare feet pounded the sides of the stubborn beasts who persisted in stopping every five minutes for tasty tidbits in the dirt or in clumps of dried grass. The bus zoomed on. My feet were cramped and numb; there was not enough space between the seats of Moroccan buses for a long frame like mine—my knees almost touched my chin.

Palm trees and decrepit mud shacks lined the two-lane road. Entire families worked in the fields alongside the road, cutting the hay and tying it into small bundles or digging in the sand for what looked like potatoes or other root vegetables. A longing to settle down spurred me to envision the possibility of letting my roots grow in Morocco: buying a piece of land and starting a family with a Moroccan wife. I would just work the soil, pray, and stumble home—with dirt between my teeth and a piece of straw in my hair—to a happy family after working all day. We would prepare a feast, and after repeating the prayers, eat at a big, round table; afterwards, we would retire contentedly to warm, country beds.

Dreams of country living reminded me once again of the years I had spent in northern California working in the vineyards. I would awaken early on a summer morning and after a breakfast of eggs and bacon, take my hoe to the vineyard and level the soil between the vines, flattening the ridges created by the tractor, making it easier for the grape pickers to do their work.

In the late winter, I would trim the vines so they would yield more grapes during the September harvest. After work, I would place the hoe over my shoulder and drag my feet back to the house, where the mother, father and three daughters served me that good old-fashioned home cooking. After dinner, we all sat around the fire while the mother sang folk songs she had learned on the farm. She was a chicken sexer, by trade, which had something to do with the artificial insemination of chickens in order to create superior eating and laying breeds. She married a chemist. She told me that she once played the guitar and sang at the Purple Onion in San Francisco and was subsequently offered a lucrative contract by a record company. Instead of accepting the offer, she decided to get married, settle down, raise a family, sex chickens and raise roosters (their feathers would be used to tie flies, for sale to stores catering to fishermen). I used to admire her as she

168

expressed no regrets for having made her decision to abandon her career in order to raise a family.

As the bus rumbled on, so did the memories. I yearned to stretch my aching body and wondered if even this bus ride would some day find itself among my memories. The rhythmic drone of the engine and the vibrations of the bus finally lulled me to sleep.

I woke up just in time to see the outskirts of Fes, a traditional center for Islamic culture in Morocco. Palm trees, whose branches rose to the heavens then drooped down to embellish the earth, lined the streets, which were clean and sometimes paved. As the bus approached the center of town, it was increasingly surrounded by people walking in all directions or riding in mule-driven carts. The scene was almost a page out of the history books depicting the Wild West, only the drivers here were robed figures with whips, intent gleams in their eyes. Their wagons were full of vegetables, tomatoes, carrots, mint leaves, gigantic bins of dates or sheep hides and were being driven to the local souks.

Since Fes was considered the cultural as well as intellectual capital of Morocco, it was not surprising to see many students toting books under their arms or sitting on benches and talking as they madly gesticulated. I wondered what life would be like as a student, sitting next to the pretty, dark-skinned Arabian girls.

"Allahu Akbar," I whispered to myself, trying to push the subject out of my mind since I had been carefully instructed not to think about women or I would suffer the consequences: a loss of the purity of spirit.

We were obliged to change buses in Fes. I waited next to the terminal with all the luggage while my two companions searched for another bus that would take us first to Boumalne, where we would take another bus to our final destination.

It did not take long before they returned, pointed to a bus and hurriedly grabbing some of the baggage, guided me to a place in the waiting line. The hour ride to Boumalne was a familiar experience inside the bus, but outside, each small village seemed to be uniquely designed and generally apart from the mainstream.

In an hour, we found ourselves walking through the outskirts of the small town. We washed ourselves in a nearby creek and spread a blanket on some leaves, which crackled as we bowed and began to pray next to the rapids. Oman had been selected to lead and had called us to prayer. His words were only faintly understood over the torrential sound of the water but it did not matter since we all knew them by heart; we simply followed his lips as we repeated the prayers, bowing and lowering our foreheads to the earth.

We were three golden hearts beneath a blue sky, surrounded by trees, our knees crunching the dry leaves. The humidity of the forest brought to my nose the smell of wet logs after a thunderstorm. We mumbled our prayers in rhythm with the creek; its foaming white rapids poured into a pond downstream, the torrential waves transformed into small babbling ripples that spoke to us, imparting the key to the realm of knowledge and opening the door to the mysteries of the universe.

After the prayer session, we walked across the creek to the other side and followed the dirt road which led us to a larger street. Izneh waved his hands wildly at a car traveling in the opposite direction whose driver slammed on the breaks, made a u-turn and drove up alongside us. A rusty sign with an inscription in Arabic on top of the car made it look like a taxi. The driver rolled down the window and Oman spoke to him. After a few undistinguishable words, he signaled us to enter. We piled into the cab, which took us to another bus stop.

We waited for nearly an hour before the bus finally arrived, in the familiar cloud of exhaust fumes. It stopped at the designated place but its doors remained closed. Oman shrugged his shoulders and looked at Izneh who did the same. While a crowd surrounded the bus, we dragged our luggage and sleeping bags near the door, next to a man who appeared to be guarding a pile of plywood. The man's worried, dark eyes shifted to the right and then to the left. A gray-haired old man with crutches stooped to sit on the pile of wood but the man guarding it growled hoarsely, sending the cripple hobbling rapidly away on his crutches.

A woman wearing a black robe approached from the side, her left eye visible over a black veil. When she stopped in front of us, she turned her head revealing eyes seemingly trained on us, but with translucent white spots in place of pupils. She was blind, perhaps the result of a desert sickness. She ran her fingers over our luggage, with the brothers carefully observing her, and walked towards us, holding out her hand; we all dropped coins in her palm. Soon, she drifted away led by a friend, a young barefooted boy with light-brown matchstick legs, almost invisible against the dirt road. He had short, matted brown hair needing washing and was holding a few coins in his other hand. I presumed they were headed for the nearest market where they would find olives, dates, nuts and rounds of bread, a foot in diameter. Then they would perhaps squat somewhere beside the road and nourish their tired, weary bodies. Such a life it would be to beg and sleep in dark corners, behind a mosque—a kind of hand-to-hand combat for survival across the arid, pitiless desert of time. Some were privileged to be able to focus on nourishing the soul while their brothers and sisters struggled to survive. But I wondered how a person's hunger could be satisfied if both the body and soul were not nourished.

The bus driver, after his lunch and short siesta, finally opened the doors to the bus, which was immediately surrounded by people, pressing and maneuvering for a good place in line. All of a sudden, a loud clanking noise and yelling filled the air: two men were engaged in a heated argument. After all the verbal assaults and posturing, the two tore into each other. Fists were flying, accompanied by more screams and the ripping of garments, including their shirts underneath.

As I approached the center of the action, my perception of the fighters became more distinct: both wore turbans and one had a gray beard, the other a black mustache. The former appeared to have the upper hand as he shoved the younger fighter to the ground. The latter momentarily left the scene; I followed as he fled to the other side of the bus and stooped to pick something up. He then quickly returned to the motor side of the bus, and wielding a short metal bar, flung himself into the crowd, looking for his sparring partner.

He was promptly disarmed and thrown to the ground by two robust men, obviously friends of the older man. The young attacker then hid behind the bus, pointing at his enemy, kicking the dirt and screaming insults. His eyes were red with rage and he was frothing at the mouth.

Another bus glided into position behind the first bus. The attacker quickly channeled his energies into fighting with others to board the second bus while his older foe pushed and shoved to enter the first bus. I was so absorbed in this scene that I had forgotten I was also supposed to take one of the buses. I quickly made an about face and joined the other two. When they saw me inching my way through the crowd, they threw their hands up in the air, shaking their heads.

Oman exclaimed, "I thought you had left us! Quick, grab your sleeping bag—we have the rest of your gear—and follow us."

We joined the fray, fighting to find seats on the first bus, finally boarding after making our way to the door and squeezing in. The drivers revved their engines and slowly inched their way through the unhappy crowd that had to wait another hour for the next bus.

We followed one dusty, winding dirt road after another, for what seemed to be an eternity, before finally arriving at our destination. The driver announced our arrival in a low, gruff voice.

Through the fogged window, I could make out a faint line of hills off to the left with an expansive valley stretched out before them, illuminated by the dwindling light of the descending sun. The few shacks to the left and the right of the bus made shadows across the narrow dirt road as the bus inched along, through the middle of this obscure country village. The buildings were all one story high and were made of an adobe-like substance containing dried clay, straw and stones.

When we stopped, the village inhabitants converged from every corner: from behind mud walls children crawled, their mothers slowly dragging the younger ones across the bumpy terrain dotted by a few wayward clumps of grass. All were interested to see what the bus would bring.

It appeared that buses, which emerged from and then disappeared back into a more civilized world, did not visit this tiny village very often. Veiled women stared from behind wooden windows; others stood in back of their gold-turbaned men, distinguished from Casablancans, who mainly wore white turbans. I thought that perhaps the color of turbans signified a particular region. One of my companions told me that the inhabitants of this region were mostly Berbers who spoke several dialects; some spoke Arabic. As the bus sat in the middle of the town, it was surrounded by townsfolk who gazed up at the windows, holding their children in their arms.

Chapter XXI

Mud Huts and Faces

We disembarked from the bus and were immediately handed our luggage, which had been secured on top of the bus. There was something delightfully rustic about this small town. All the shacks looked weather-beaten from constant flogging by the cruel desert winds. I could see as far as possible in all directions, except to the left of the bus; looming in the distance was a group of gigantic, desolate hills. The vast, desert-like valley spread out before us.

A chilly desert wind whipped up the dust around us, forming little whirlwinds, which picked up bits of straw and chicken feathers, displacing them a few feet away. There was virtually no noise in this town.

The people walking along the dirt road next to the bus were ragged, but clean. Horses and mules were pulling wagons while children rolled wooden wheels down a small sand dune. The town was so quiet that cackling chicken could be heard, but not seen; I imagined they came from chicken coops located somewhere behind the shacks. Makeshift clotheslines consisting of heaps of dried bushes were draped by assortments of clothes and rags.

No one came to us to beg. In fact, it seemed like we were completely ignored as we made our way across town. Oman, Izneh and I were wearing typical Moslem clothing, sandals and djellabahs, which also resembled the clothing of the Berbers. I remembered Oman telling me in the bus that Berbers were Moslems but did not regularly attend the mosques, which seemed increasingly empty, especially during mass.

The village was surrounded by grass stubble, like stunted desert growth, and the vast plains, earth, gravel—dryness. What would befall me in this God-forsaken place? The people in this town pretended to ignore us, but I felt every pair of eyes staring intently at every footstep, every gesture—nothing went unnoticed.

The strong desert wind beneath the sea of blue sky coldly slapped my face into consciousness, rousing me from my imaginings. The silence was misleading as a storm was brewing in the air...in the silence...in the emptiness. I felt as if I had lived, learned and died many times as I walked down the dirt road splicing the desolate plains, leading to a flat plain, where I envisioned myself praying, seeking God a thousand years hence.

I sought fulfillment in the barren plains; fertile flowers growing in this arid land would be my point of reference—yellows, blues and reds, representing the hope that still stirred in my heart. Parts of my past came together in one earthly mosaic, as memories drifted in and out, in concert with the desert wind, the conductor of this mental symphony. I chased the bad memories from my mind so I could experience a spiritual rebirth without the past anchoring me to dogmas of distant lands, distant cultures. "Allahu Akbar," I whispered.

I forced my weak, undernourished body to keep up with my companions. They just kept on walking, through the sand and over clumps of grass, onward. . .onward—I was ready to push myself to the far corners of the earth, without hesitation, to find truth. But I wondered if this time I had pushed too far: maybe I'd end up without finding the truth about God, about myself, an anonymous pile of bones with memories drifting in the air above them.

In the midst of this never-ending walk, I began to drag my sandals, wincing as the leather tore into the blisters on the bottom of my feet. I wondered if I would ever get used to wearing sandals; I wondered why I had left Casablanca to endure such pain and doubt. Dark images assailed my mind, of unknown tyrants, rising up from the sand in full armor, wielding their sword at everything that moved, without pity.

I was not feeling as comfortable with my companions in this place as I had within the safe walls of the mission in Casablanca. In fact, I felt less and less comfortable in their presence. This discomfort was triggered during the bus ride, in particular, one time when the bus driver stopped the bus after the first hour of our journey. All the passengers rose to leave the bus in order to stretch their cramped legs. I recalled a fat, veiled mother, with children hanging onto her robe, blocking the aisle: she had stopped in the middle to look for one of her children. Oman yelled out, insulting the woman, who was outraged by the tone of the young man. Oman changed his approach and tried to persuade the woman to move down the aisle so that we could leave the bus with the rest of the passengers. She sat down heavily, frantically looking everywhere for her lost child, at the same time peppering Oman with insults. He ignored her as he followed us down the aisle and exited the bus.

I was disappointed in Oman who had been overly aggressive and very rude to the poor woman. After all, he was a fellow monk, my brother, and one of the "beautiful people" of the mission. I tried to rationalize Oman's behavior as reflecting an over-protectiveness of me or a concern that our time was valuable and the incident with the woman wasted time. The event was sobering in that it showed that Oman was nothing more than human, in spite of his standing at the mission. Also, I was confused because my two companions would not let me carry any of the luggage when we changed busses during our voyage. I was treated like some kind of celebrity, or maybe a prize. "Why all the fuss?" I wondered.

We distanced ourselves from the tiny village, which appeared increasingly mystical the farther away we trudged along the dirt road, skirting the foot of a gigantic hill. My two companions stopped in front of me, engaged in a discussion. I caught up with them and asked if something was wrong. Izneh explained that they were discussing whether to walk the remaining two miles or hitchhike the rest of the way. Then Oman excitedly pointed down the road toward a parked pick-up truck with a camper which appeared to be taking in a couple of people who I remembered from the bus. We ran over. Oman asked, gasping for breath, if we could hop a ride with them and flashed a few dirhams. They agreed to take us to our destination.

The driver pointed to the back of the camper and we climbed aboard over the rails; it was definitely homemade—the walls and roof were built onto the back of the pick-up. In a few minutes, we were all tightly sandwiched between a veiled woman, her sniveling children and a small group of turbaned Moroccans. Oman, who was sitting next to me, winked and explained that he had the same ethnic background as the driver: he was originally from Agadir, a town located in the south of Morocco, where a tribe of Berbers had lived for many generations. He spoke fluent Berber to the driver, who nodded his head as he drove the pick-up down the semi-paved road. I could hardly breathe in back of the vehicle, with so many bodies so tightly interwoven; my torso rested on somebody's legs which occasionally squirmed to remind me to shift my weight elsewhere.

Fortunately it was a short trip; in ten minutes, the camper stopped. Oman and Izneh quickly jumped down, turned around and grabbed their luggage, which had been placed near the opening in back of the vehicle. After extricating myself from the other people, I grabbed my sleeping bag and lowered myself down. I was the last to leave the camper. Oman handed the driver ten dirhams and thanked him for the lift.

There was no doubt that now we were in the arid plains at the foot of the Atlas Mountains—we were surrounded by miles and miles of open space, brown, desert-like country, populated by gray rocks haphazardly strewn about the sand. In front of us, not more than a hundred meters away, lay another village consisting of the typical circle of adobe shacks, grouped together. This time, the ice-cold wind chilled me to the bone until I could stand it no more. I had not brought my jacket or socks and wore only a thin shirt, the djellabah and sandals; my feet were red, swollen and blistered.

The recollection of the words of Camara helped to ease the pain. When I was defecating and vomiting simultaneously after having spent over two hours in the intense heat of the sauna, he explained that the purification of my body and soul would entail great difficulties and take a long time. I could give up anytime, I thought to myself, and return to Paris. But I discarded that option as my journey would be a failure and my growth in the search for truth be stunted. I knew I would deeply regret having given up, especially since I was convinced that I had found the true path to God.

My body was shivering uncontrollably; I hyperventilated to stop the shivering as we slowly walked down the dirt road in the crisp, dry desert air. Oman, who was walking ahead of us, pointed to a small village on the other side of a ravine, built on the slope of a hill—and informed us that was our destination.

On the path leading to the village, we met two Moroccans—sheepherders—wearing the same kind of clothes as the people I had seen in a movie shown in Paris, based on the life of Jesus Christ. Their raggedly robes were draped with shaggy, woolen cloaks and they carried crooked, wooden staffs. Full, black beards seemed to grow out of the dark hoods they both wore. I fantasized that I was in Palestine, where my loyalty to the faith would soon being tested in the same way as Jesus Christ was tested, alone in the desert.

The two young sheepherders pointed in the direction opposite our destination and joined us as we backtracked down the same dirt road. We approached what appeared to be an oasis in the middle of the arid, lifeless hill we were descending. A field of green grass with a herd of grazing sheep lay directly ahead of us, at the bottom of the ravine in which we had been walking in circles for the last hour. As we grew nearer, my eyes focused on a small stream running through the middle of it.

Oman hurried to the edge of the stream and bent down on all fours to wash his face and hands, leaning over the bank. As we drew near, he turned around, his face dripping with the stream's essence, and motioned us to join him.

Staring intently at the sky, he said, "We're going to pray here."

"Ugh!" I thought to myself, as I contemplated bathing in the ice-cold water in the middle of a wind turned ferocious, tearing at my clothes. The intensity of Oman's expression

174

probably meant there would be no debate about his plans. Izneh had already joined him as they amused themselves by splashing water on each other.

"My ears will surely turn to ice cubes and my shivers will rock my entire body if I go into the water," I thought.

Looking at the stream with immeasurable distaste, I decided to join them as they began the prescribed ablutions in the chilly stream. I splashed a few drops of the icy water on my face and looked to see if Oman was watching me. I feared that if I did not perform a complete ablution, he would make me repeat the movements, as I had many times in Casablanca, or perhaps denounce my irreverent behavior to the master upon our return to the city. The cold drops on my face triggered involuntary spasms of shivers rolling up and down my spinal column, shocking my weak and wizened body.

Oman was looking the other way, so I stumbled away from the banks of the creek and joined him, Izneh and the sheepherders, who had formed a line in preparation for the evening prayer session. They spread their motley woolen cloaks on the ground for us to use for our prayers. Oman, as usual, led the session, which was mercifully short; his low voice quickly mumbled the prayers as we rapidly shifted from bowing, to prostrating, to bowing again, until the sequence was completed. He, too, must have been very cold.

Our numbers swelled to five when an older sheepherder joined us as we walked down a semi-paved road bisecting the plains. On one side, there was a low mountain chain; on the other, a continuous expanse of plains, flowing into the luminous, yellow sun, moments before sunset. I was dazed, almost petrified, by my first sight of a setting sun in the two years since I had moved to Paris: over the tall buildings, one could never see even the slightest hint of a setting sun.

As we followed yet another dirt road, the sun, disappearing over the horizon, gave off its final glimmer, signaling the onset of darkness. My Moroccan friends had explained to me this was why the region from Morocco to Algeria was called Maghreb (Al Maghreb), "the land of the setting sun." She loomed before us in all her radiant beauty, sending us her last light beams of the day as we floated down the road—because the darkness had surrounded us with shadows and the impossibility of seeing our feet, we walked down the road like five white-robed ghosts. Not a word was spoken. I transcended the experience as I imagined that we were five infants of God coming to enlighten the people.

As my eyes began to adjust to the dark, I saw the two sheepherders stop in the middle of the road ahead of us. One of them was pointing to the right of the road. My eyes followed his finger and barely made out the faint outline of a group of adobe shacks, their parameters still visible in the dim light remaining. The shacks were defensively huddled together on the far side of a barren stretch of land. An eerie feeling crept into me as the shadows of night closed in, bringing a forlorn emptiness which permeated the lonely night air.

My recently acquired spiritual serenity was rattled, yet with the simple reminder that if I felt alone even in this group of weak humans, the cosmic spirit was with me, within and about—I no longer felt alone. I prayed that my faith not be "blind," that I be reassured that such a spirit, the cosmic Presence that could be labeled God, was more than a figment of my imagination.

I awaited an answer to my questions. But I could never have dreamed of the events and lessons awaiting me in these obscure plains, thousands of miles from my home.

Chapter XXII

Mirage

The two sheepherders we had originally met vigorously shook our hands, their hooded faces bobbing up and down in unison with their actions; then one departed. The older sheepherder stayed with us as we made our way across the field, a gnarled obstacle course of rocky ridges, clumps of dried grass and dark, dried sheep droppings, still visible against the light sand. I felt numb as my legs began to slowly give out. One leg caused me to lose my balance as I fell to one side but my football reflexes still served me—I thrust my hands forward to cushion the blow as I fell to the ground. My right knee landed on a rock and was bleeding a little as I quickly regained my feet. By this time, Oman and Isneh were well ahead of me. They looked back and seeing I was far behind, waited a couple of minutes and then proceeded down the never-ending dirt path leading us to the group of dwellings huddled in the shadows.

The stars were already blinking at us as we appeared at the doorway of a small adobe mosque. Oman pushed on the wooden door, which opened into a small room lit by a kerosene lamp. In the far corner of the mosque was a group of men and boys sitting in a circle around a young man, who sat cross-legged. His djellabah covered his legs and his head was adorned with an almost sparkling white turban wrapped around his small, delicate brown head. A faint dark line above his upper lip hinted at the growth of a mustache. He was explaining something from the *Qur'an* resting in his lap. He nodded, his eyes following us as we entered, weighted down by sleeping bags and luggage. We tried not to disturb the easy flow of the young man's dialogue.

He turned his head to one side then the other, like a swimmer; his head then appeared to sway back and forth on its axis. With a half-smile, he whispered a welcome. Sitting in back of him, his eyes not straying from the golden mat in front of the speaker, was the prophet Muhammad's look-alike, with a long, black beard almost touching the floor and a white djellabah flowing over his knees and onto the floor. His dark cape covered his legs as well as his entire body, except his glistening white turban, like the speaker's; his dark eyes were intense and the ubiquitous black beard unraveled downwards. I secretly called him the "bearded one." In the following days, he rarely ever spoke to me because he either did not or refused to speak French. When our eyes met in passing, on a few rare occasions he touched the outside of his robe near his heart and say, "Souilla," meaning "Little by little," referring to how I was to bring Islam into my soul.

The other worshippers, who were intently watching the speaker, occasionally nodded in unison, repeating "Allahu Akbar," as the young orator mesmerized his listeners with irresistible charm. He often repeated the word "hwanni" (brothers) at the end of his phrases, so I knew he was saying something about peace, love, unity and "Praise Allah," exhorting his listeners to follow the ways of Muhammad, the prophet. The speaker's smile radiated outwards magically, encompassing everyone who came within the realm of its influence. I joined the group, smiling and whispering "Allahu Akbar" along with the others. It was as if I had seen and felt the beauty of all the colors of the rainbow spread over us like a veil of love, binding us forever.

All in the mosque felt the warmth of its welcoming embrace, the light radiating from the kerosene lamp and the smiles on everyone's faces. Here in this modest enclave, I could actually live from day to day according to the Hadith, a roadmap of the life of Muhammad.

His name was Hanify and he was to become my master. He spoke impeccable French, better than mine, even though I had spent two years studying in France before traveling to Morocco.

Hanify continued speaking Arabic, entreating his audience to have "heeman" (faith) in Allah. His voice vibrated with emotion, his phrases ended in a faint whisper. I could understand a few words. To summarize, he pleaded with all listeners to have faith, that only through faith, the secrets of life—of the universe—would be revealed to us.

I was floating on the euphoria permeating the mosque as I humbly sat within its old adobe walls, in the middle of the plains, at the foot of the Atlas Mountains. I fantasized that I had even arrived half-way to heaven. During the silence of the pauses, one could even hear the gurgling of a nearby stream in which we would soon be washing our clothes.

Death and suffering were far removed from us; only love reigned. The grace of Allah seemed to be showing us the way to true happiness. I yearned to purify my body and spirit, inundated with city gloom and pollution for too many years. Here, on the other hand, I shared a place of pure fraternity, prayer and was no longer concerned about what I ate or drank. I only desired to nourish my soul and transcend a daily humdrum, materialistic, egotistical existence, dedicating my life to a higher calling.

Hanify plunged into the final discourse, ending it by saying, "Fa sabbih bi hamdi rabbika wa saghfirhou innahou kâna tawwâba" (Praise then your Lord, and beg his forgiveness for he is very lenient), which I recalled was the last phrase of one of the prayers entitled Sourat-n-nasr. Our eyes met and he came directly to where I was sitting and sat down in front of me. He started speaking Arabic. I rejoiced that he had accepted me as one of them. Oman interrupted Hanify and told him that I could speak and understand French and English perfectly, but my Arabic had not yet become fluent.

"Alors, soyez le bienvenue," cried Hanify as he clasped my hands in his.

As he continued to hold my hands, he explained in perfect French, that my presence had given them a great lift, that my faith had been tested as I had traveled a long distance to be with them in this small, rustic mosque. He went on to say that Allah was the guiding light that would lead me to the truth when I become a true Moslem. He promised me that if I were faithful in every respect to the Islamic doctrine, I would enter paradise with all Moslem brothers and sisters and live in everlasting peace and love.

But the smile faded and his face withdrew into darkness, as if the lights had been dimmed, as he stated, "But be careful—you will be persecuted until the ends of the earth because of apostasy of Islam (renunciation of Islam) and rejection after becoming a Moslem is also punished by death and eternal suffering in Hell."

The eyes that had seemed so kind and understanding became reddened and treacherous. I felt a slow fear spreading through my body as I watched him. Every time my eyes lit upon him, a little voice inside me warned that my fears would be justified! Darkness cast its lonely shadow over my thoughts, which were focused on imminent danger, in spite of the mellow, meditative surroundings.

Oman interrupted us; he reminded me that I had not prayed for the fifth time that day, as required. I must have missed the afternoon prayer as I was focusing on packing my bags and other preparations for the trip, but I could not remember. It surprised me that Oman could keep track of the number of masses I had attended, better than myself. In any case, I decided not to question Oman and I excused myself as I walked toward the prayer area of the mosque. In the meantime, Hanify's words followed me. He had told me that we had all the time in the world to talk and he would teach me all he knew about Islam.

I went through the routine of the evening prayer session by myself in the corner of the mosque. After about forty-five minutes of prayers, I returned to my seat next to Hanify, who was speaking to Oman. Hanify fixed his attention on me and told me to sit closer to him so that he could explain more about the mysteries of Islam. Oman, on the other hand, had watched me do my rakahs[15] and noticed that I had not completed two of the rakahs required during the evening prayer, which consisted of four rakahs. He interrupted our conversation to inform me of my mistake, but I could not see any damage had been done so I continued my conversation with Hanify. I was upset that Oman was quibbling over two rakahs I had failed to complete and I told him so. Besides, I argued that we had already performed the evening prayers (al-isha) and I should only make up one rakah since I was actually making up the sunset prayer session (al-maghrib) which contained only three rakahs. I also thought to myself that Oman was suffocating me with his constant surveillance.

He looked to Hanify for support, whom remained silent, conceding that this dispute was between Oman and me. Then Oman turned to me, his ocean-blue eyes deeply disturbed. He said, "It is true that it is not the prayer in itself that Allah accepted; it was the love in my heart that Allah listened to. But your prayers will not be accepted if you do not follow the rules."

Hanify had been listening without uttering a word. Finally he intervened. "Allahu Akbar. Oman, you are right, but Muhammad," pointing at me, "has a right to question the laws set down by Muhammad. That is why he is with us, sharing our food and drinking tea with us and sharing our sleeping quarters. He is here to learn the ways of Muhammad, the great prophet who brought us the words of Allah."

To diffuse the conflict, before Hanify could finish speaking, I had moved to the back of the mosque and performed the two rakahs. I thought as I prayed that God—Allah—would read my heart and decide whether or not I was faithful to his principles. I was furthermore convinced that a Christian could go to church every Sunday or a Moslem could go through the motions of praying five times daily and still have an evil heart.

After performing the two rakahs, I sat down beside Hanify and told him what I was thinking. Pulling me aside, he placed his hands on my shoulders, assuring me that he welcomed questions and respected my questioning—that Allah did not want followers to blindly accept all that was written in the *Qur'an* without reflecting upon personal values as well as the importance of Islamic laws.

---

[15] A group of gestures and recitations that make up a particular prayer.

Hanify continued, "Now, you are here with us and you can take all the time you want to think about the unity of the world with Islam. Your brothers will help you understand."

I thought to myself that my stay here was to be the final step before total conversion, if that was possible, that many of shady areas of Islam and metaphysics, in general, would come to light here. The fact that I still hungered for answers to my questions and still resisted blindly accepting everything, assuaged my apprehension of being totally converted. I was afraid of all that I had believed to date being usurped, as had been the case while I lived at the mission in Casablanca. There, I had existed in a state of euphoria among people who had accepted me with open arms, as their brother.

I envisioned myself as a young Jesus Christ learning about the Old Testament from the old religious scholars: bearded, in snowy white robe, clutching a staff, hunched over in prayer in a temple of God. Enlightenment, rather than indoctrination, was what I really wanted to experience.

"Come, let us eat," Hanify signaled to me, waving his hand. "Let us break bread together."

The dinner routine followed the same pattern as that of the mission in Casablanca. We ate on hand-woven mats laden with huge bowls of vegetables and meat prepared by a brother in an adjoining room. Rounds of Moroccan bread, richer and thicker than those found in Casablanca, were served. We broke bread in near silence, dipping the pieces in the bowls of food; our hands were oily, dripping with meat fat and crumbs. We ate to the accompaniment of the usual "Bismi-l-lâhi" and "Al hamdu li llâhi" uttered by the contented diners.

After dinner, I was shown where the bathroom was; it consisted of a small hole in a mud floor in an adjoining room. The hole lead to a small canal which was dug in such a way so that urine would run down through it mixing with water and becoming a muddy pool somewhere outside the building. By morning, not a trace of urine and water would remain except for a subtle wetness. Oman instructed me that all ablutions before mass the next day would be performed outside, next to the creek, with water drawn from the creek in a bucket, which I would find at the entrance to the mosque.

After the last prayer was said that evening, and the last hug, everyone prepared for bed. Each person unrolled his sleeping bag and climbed inside, fully clothed. As soon as my head rested on my folded sweater, I fell into deep sleep.

The next thing I knew, someone was pouring words all over me. I opened my eyes to behold Hanify's face hovering directly over mine, telling me to prepare for morning prayer. I rolled to one side, still half asleep and exhausted by the long trip, in total denial that morning had already arrived.

I heard others whispering in the dark shadows and the sound of bedding being folded; as it seemed I would be closely monitored here, especially by Hanify, I could not be late for morning mass. I unzipped the sleeping bag and rolled over on my stomach. From there, I pushed my torso up and placed my knees under me for support. The cold morning desert air brought violent shivers to my thin body.

I finally gritted my teeth and rose to my feet, my body tingling all over with the rush of blood through me. I was without socks and a jacket to insulate my skinny frame from the cold, dank air of the adobe mosque. I rolled up my sleeping bag and placed it with the others in a corner. I looked closely into the shadowed areas of the mosque but didn't see a soul—everyone had already left the mosque to perform their ablutions before mass. I headed for the entrance where I searched for a bucket.

Several buckets where stacked next to the entrance. I took one and left the mosque. As I descended the stone steps to the dirt below, I looked up and saw all the brothers washing themselves along the creek bank and soon joined them.

They all greeted me with smiles tempered under Hanify's watchful regard as they engaged in their morning ablutions. I walked along the rocks of the creek, squeezed through an opening between Oman and Izneh and found myself facing a rapidly flowing creek. I shoved the bucket into the icy creek water, letting the force of the current fill it and then placed it on a rock next to my body. Oman and Izneh finished their ablutions and left me next to the creek. I slowly splashed the water over my body, following the order proscribed by the master in Casablanca. This ritual signified a return to nature and being a nature boy at heart, I was elated. Even the shivers shaking my cold body, intensified by splashes of the frigid water, didn't seem to bother me. As the morning sun arose in the distance, replacing the shadows with light and enveloping me in warmth, I felt as if it were stretching out arms to welcome me. I envisioned a happy existence here where all I had to do was to wash, pray, meditate, eat and commune with nature, and then repeat it all over again five times each day.

I was about half finished when Oman, on his way back to the mosque, warned me that mass would commence in five minutes. I quickly washed the rest of my body, grabbed the bucket and made my way barefoot over the rocks.

I delighted in a flock of wild turkeys (or perhaps geese), ambling by in small groups, creating a moving collage of bobbing heads—back and forth, up and down—black feathers and gold beaks probing the soil with quick thrusts.

"Muhammad, come to pray," cried the cook, Karim, who had just finished washing the dishes in the creek and was walking up the hill towards the mosque. "Look over there; the village Imam has joined the group in the mosque—let's go!"

Suddenly a large balding man poked his head out the door of the mosque; as the Muezzin, he called the people to prayer:

"Allaaaahu Akbar, Allaaaaaaaaaahu Akbar. . ."

I hustled inside and joined the line forming in front of the mosque. After the morning prayer session, I sat down in the back of the mosque with Hanify and asked him a series of pointed questions. He listened patiently.

"Hanify, when I was in Casablanca, one of the brothers living at the mission informed me the *Qur'an* stated women were inferior to men. This I found hard to believe as I have met many brilliant women, in particular, professors and other professionals that I have had in France and in the United States. Also, why aren't women allowed to be seen when they pray in the mosques?"

Hanify was calm as he listened to my questions. When I had finished, he paused to reflect upon them, before answering.

"Muhammad, if I were to respond to your questions in depth, you perhaps would not understand because you need to strengthen your "heeman" (faith) in Allah before you can understand the secrets of the holy *Qur'an*. However, let me partially respond to your question by telling you a story:

"A man and his wife were on vacation and had found a modest hotel in which to stay the night. In the middle of the night, the man got up to go to the bathroom. He was amazed that the room did not include a bathroom and the windows were placed too high for him to be able to urinate out the window. By this time, his wife had awakened; she asked her husband what was the matter. He explained the problem. Finally, he had an idea. He stood on the shoulders of his wife and urinated out the window. When that was successfully accomplished, his wife claimed the need to do the same. So she climbed on the shoulders of her husband and proceeded to urinate on his head. Voila: the difference between man and woman."

When Hanify concluded, I was shocked that such a beautiful person would tell such a chauvinistic and crude story. I had previously imagined Hanify to be a wise man; I wondered how I could be so credulous and unable to be objective as to his true character. I tried to resist the temptation to say anything to Hanify because I was afraid that my anger would show, and our relationship would forever be strained.

I observed the all-wise Hanify, as he awaited my response. He was smiling contentedly as though he was either certain his story had clarified any questions I had about the equality of man and women, or he was baiting me into an angry reaction that he could use against me. He thus might have been testing me. In spite of the warnings going off inside me, my anger got the best of me and I could not prevent my emotional reaction.

"I think that is a very weak way of explaining the superiority of men over women," I blurted it out, in spite of myself.

Hanify was visibly startled that anyone would question his knowledge, his authority; his eyes blinked and his mouth trembled. However, he mastered his emotions and did not express any concern for the harshness of my criticism.

Instead of outwardly showing anger at my brash statement, he stated, carefully choosing his words, "We will all pray for you, Muhammad, that you will eventually accept the truth, the teachings of Muhammad. Ah, my brother," he exclaimed, grabbing my hand and holding it in his, "when your 'heeman' grows stronger, you shall understand."

Even though Hanify had not outwardly shown me malice, I felt a subtle tension building between us thereafter. I thought that I should be careful about what I said and did in his presence...that he could be plotting against me. I felt he probably wanted to punish me for doubting his wisdom, which I assumed had never been questioned by anyone before. Even the Muhammad, the prophet look-alike, seemed to defer to Hanify for all decision making; he appeared to be in charge of all operations.

Unfortunately, I had no clue that Hanify was plotting against me. I was blind to any danger signals, even in Hanify's eyes, which were constantly on me.

Chapter XXIII

Abandoned

I had not yet recuperated from the days of fasting before undertaking the journey—both had taken their toll: I had lost about twenty pounds during an eight-day period and my body was seriously weakened. A positive side effect is that my meditations after the prayer sessions were more intense and focused. But the fasting, coupled with lack of sleep, had weakened my defenses, both physically and mentally. A permanent cold settled into my body, constantly causing my nose to drip and draining the rest of my body. I ached and coughed all the time. My stomach and intestines had still not adjusted from the jolt they received in the Ancienne Medina, particularly with the change in bacteria, causing me to have chronic diarrhea and stomach pains. Even though I was able to ignore this condition mentally, it devastated my already emaciated body. Even though my spirits were high, my seriously weakened constitution began to affect my thinking: thoughts were often fuzzy and distant. This was not a good way to enter into Ramadan, which was to begin on the morrow. During the thirty days of Ramadan, all adults are required to fast from just before sunrise to just after sunset. During the day, they are to think good thoughts, avoid all food and beverages and indecent talk or anger and visit the mosque to pray.

My thoughts kept me awake as I lay in my sleeping bag next to Karim in a room adjoining the mosque. Hanify had shocked my senses into sobriety. I was compelled to reflect upon the spiritual steps I had taken since joining the mission in Casablanca. It was like taking mental inventory of what I had learned there, which had led me to travel to these arid plains, to this place marked for my complete spiritual awakening...to this place where part of me reveled in this mosque while wolves howled outside, looking for scraps of food. I compared myself to them, seeking nourishment, but for my famished soul. I realized how vulnerable I had been upon arriving in Morocco as I walked the streets seeking spiritual truth.

I began to distill the essence of what I had learned during the past few weeks. I chastised myself for my gullibility as I woke up to the realization I had not been transcending spiritually—growing closer to the supreme consciousness, to God—while at the mission but wallowing in a stupor, inhaling the teachings without discernment. I hadn't taken a step back to question the spiritual "food" dished out to me every day.

There, in the mission, the "brain washing," (yes, I dared voice those frightening words, those prohibited words that I had refused to contemplate until now) was more discrete than in this place, deep within the hot, dry Moroccan plains.

I was waking up to what this group of Moslems was trying to do to me. In a way, I thought the brothers meant well: after all, they only wanted me to enter paradise with them. They sincerely believed the only way, after death, to reach that elusive place was to follow ever so closely the teachings of Muhammad. In order for me to become a practicing

Moslem, the "sine qua non" to happiness was to modify the knowledge and personal beliefs I had brought from years of living in the western world.

They wanted me to denounce all non Moslems, in particular Christians and Jews, the "lost" people who refused to believe in the truth: Islam. They wanted me to believe that the Jews were evil because they killed Jesus Christ, who was a prophet but not, according to them, the son of God. They wanted me, for my own good, to recognize Muhammad as the last prophet to visit the earth before the end of the world. They wanted me to believe that women were inferior to men and thus belonged in the home. They wanted me to believe that if a woman were to leave the confines of the home, for one reason or another, she must be veiled and covered from head to toe. They wanted me to believe that the *Qur'an* was written in classical Arabic without any modifications of Allah's words—that the *Qur'an* is a truer source of God's laws than the Bible, which has been interpreted in many different ways in languages other than the one in which it was written.

They wanted me to memorize all the major prayers in the *Qur'an*, notably the "Al Fatiha," the fundamental prayer in Islam, so that when I was to die and the end of the earth was upon us, I would correctly respond to the angel Gabriel's ultimate questions. According to the master, Gabriel would ask me if I believed in one God, and if so, who was his last prophet. In order to be accepted into paradise, I needed, according to the brothers, to respond that there is but one God, Allah, and Muhammad is his messenger.

The next morning, I felt refreshed, as if a cool breeze had blasted my limp sails with a long-awaited wind, renewing ebbing strength. That morning, prayer was even more intense as it provided us with the nourishment needed throughout the day, since neither food nor drink could be consumed from sunrise to sunset. This was according to the strict observance of the month of Ramadan, dedicated to instilling passion in the hearts of Moslems worldwide for the thirsty and hungry. I reveled at the idea that for one month, the focus in my daylight hours would be on prayer and spirituality, providing me with more opportunities to sort out my fate during the meditation after each prayer session. I had no fear that my already emaciated body would further suffer under the desert sun as I observed the discipline of Ramadan.

After afternoon mass and the usual meditation session after the prayers, I looked around and noticed that Oman and I were the only ones in the mosque. The others must have decided to go into town to buy groceries for the Ramadan feast that night or visit the townspeople to convince them to attend mass at the mosque. I got up and left through the front door of the mosque. As I began walking on the dirt path outside, I heard what sounded like quick footsteps behind me. I looked back to see Oman following me. He caught up to me and hugged me.

"Welcome, brother, to Ramadan. By the way, it would be better for you to stay and pray in the mosque."

I told him that I needed some fresh air, that I was going to take a quick walk around and I would probably be back in a few minutes. He withdrew to the door of the mosque; a concerned look darkened his brow.

I took deep breaths, my lungs absorbing the fresh air, and reveled in the sunlight caressing my face with a soft, but firm, stroke. After following the small creek leading to an open field, I spotted a group of women washing clothes upstream. I approached them slowly, not wanting to frighten them, and sat on a rock beside the pool of water where they were occupied, below a small makeshift dam. Stacks of muslin shirts sat on the banks of the creek as the women stood knee-deep in the cold water, vigorously rubbing the shirts together and pounding them on the partially submerged gray rocks, peeking out of the water like the heads of crocodiles. The women's hair was carefully hidden by colorful bandanas. Their eyes followed me as I sauntered downstream, alongside the creek. I tried to focus my mind on the tiny waves slapping the rocks imbedded in the creek; I needed to clear my mind after last night's discussion with Hanify, to capitalize on this moment of distance between the agenda of the followers of Muhammad, the prophet, and me. I wondered if they were truly following his ways as presented in the "Hadith" or if that was their interpretation, their variation on the teachings of Muhammad.

Just ahead of me, an old farmer was trying to coax a mule to cross a narrow part of the creek. He yelled out, "Rrrrrrrrr," rolling his 'r' faster than I had ever heard before. Then a strange feeling came over me as I searched the clear blue sky above the farmer's head; I wondered what I was doing there, feeling lost, disappointed in certain events of the day and the past night, weak, hot, then cold. My insides cried out for sustenance, for water and food, but I ignored the signals, giving way to higher moral ground, in observance of Ramadan. Under the scorching heat, my dry mouth and burning throat testified to the difficulties of maintaining the fast; yet at the same time, I believed I was growing closer to the cosmic being, through sacrifice and discipline. My sincere observance of this Islamic holiday gave me much power and confidence that with Allah, with the force of God, I could do anything—I could make a difference in this world, and I could make a contribution to better the world.

Then, that familiar buzzing echoed in my ear, the warning signal I had heard so clearly in the Medina, after the night I spent sleeping in the streets. Something or someone was telling me to beware as the sound grew louder; I turned around and headed back to the mosque. As I approached the door and saw no one, I entered; still, none of the brothers were in sight. I nodded to Karim, who was arranging the groceries for the evening's events, and went directly to my sleeping bag. Crawling inside, I fell into a deep sleep.

Upon awakening, as I lay listening to the wisdom of the gurgling of the creek outside, I decided to continue the fast even after it was usually broken, after sunset. Not having to face the brothers during the evening Ramadan feast would give me renewed strength. I desperately needed to remove myself as much as possible from their influence, to isolate myself, to be freer to think and to pray. My belief that the answer to the world's problems—and the main reason for my voyage to Morocco—was the creation or recognition of a common religion that would unite people. Now I was not sure so of that, and I was not sure that I had found it. Ramakrishna's words continued to reverberate in my ear, nurturing me and arming me against the barrage of Islamic doctrine. According to him, religions should not be confused with God: they are simply conduits or paths leading to God, and there are many valid paths that lead to the same Supreme Being.[16]

I was confused and isolated. I decided to keep silent as much as possible in order to avoid any more arguments with Hanify. He had certainly spoken to the brothers about my lack of faith and instructed them to avoid me, or their faith in Allah could be compromised. They seldom spoke to me now—I was the black sheep. I also felt paranoid; I was shunned by the brothers...and at their mercy.

---

[16] Marcus Braybrooke, *Learn to Pray*, Ibid., P. 54.

Chapter XXIV

Death Threat

The dream of enlightenment was beginning to fade, along with my hopes of finding the truth, the true religion for mankind.

For the next few weeks, we were scheduled to travel from mosque to mosque, from village to village, facilitating a renewed interest in Islam among the desert people, bringing the word of Muhammad to them. I submissively participated in all prayer sessions, after which I questioned nothing during my discussions with Hanify, who proudly shared with me all the mysteries and beauties of his religion. After our discussions, I ate with my brothers, who remained distant but who began to approach me one by one, almost as if somebody was orchestrating them, advising them to reward me with their attention for my recent more submissive, righteous, unquestioning behavior.

First, Karim, the cook, came to me after I had taken my usual place in the back of the mosque to meditate and recite prayers. He sat opposite me, his quiet voice barely audible:

"Muhammad, I am proud of you. It must be difficult living in a foreign land, speaking a new language. But you have shown us your faith."

Then he moved closer to me, shifting his djellabah to cover his body. He leaned over so that his whiskers were almost touching my left cheek, his voice whispering:

"Muhammad, be careful of Hanify; just listen to him but do not provoke his wrath with your questions. He could harm you. Just smile and listen and learn."

Karim slid away from me, propped his back against the back wall of the mosque and then lowered his head as he opened his *Qur'an*.

Hanify, as usual, would lead the prayer sessions, while the bearded one and the brothers watched, once in awhile interceding with a prayer after being called on by Hanify. Following the prayer sessions, the villagers would ask questions regarding spiritual issues. Hanify or the bearded one answered the individual questions, taking advantage of the occasion to lecture them on the merits of becoming devout Moslems.

We were like traveling missionaries. One day during one of our discussions, Hanify had explained our purpose was to help revive the spirit of Islam in the souls of many lost sheep. He said religious fervor was dying, especially among rural Moslems, who were not frequently attending mass at the mosque.

That evening, we were all invited to dinner at the house of the mayor, in the town where we were staying, who lived a few paces from the mosque. We walked together as a group from the mosque to the mayor's house—I was behind everyone, next to Karim. When we arrived, we left our sandals lined up outside the large, wooden door. We entered a larger, rectangular room where we were carefully seated on benches lining the wall, waiting to be served our dinner. It appeared to be the mayor's living room; we were apparently with all the important male members of the community seated on silk cushions with the images of flowers or veiled women and bearded men woven in bright golds and greens.

Hanify and the bearded one were like a "tag team": first Hanify began reciting passages from the *Qur'an* and then the bearded one intervened, in melodious tones, choosing text deep within the covers of the revered book. They lectured on the beauties of the teachings of Muhammad and the paradise awaiting all faithful followers of the words of Allah. Then, right before we were served, Hanify sang a passage, also from the *Qur'an*.

Afterwards, he smiled, seducing all the listeners into listening to every word, every syllable; he was a master speaker. He began relating a story. I could not understand all the words, except for when he cited America and the word "voyage." Karim, whispering in my ear, explained to me that I was the center of attention as Hanify was dramatizing my voyage from America to Europe, then to Morocco. He passionately told my story, recounting that I had sacrificed everything, even sold all my belongings, to be able to live in the mission and travel with the group. I had done this so that I could become a Moslem, embrace Islam and help fight for the survival of the only true religion.

As Hanify spoke, I looked around to the guests of the mayor, the important townspeople. They were scrutinizing us; as Hanify pointed at me, their eyes shifted to me, perusing me from the turban on top of my shaved head, to my djellabah, down to my bare feet. I felt as if in a cage, to be viewed and discussed. They whispered to each other as I sat there wondering when their attention would be distracted elsewhere. I was an oddity in this little village in the middle of the arid plains; they probably had never seen a European, let alone an American, in this far away place.

In the middle of the living room sat two round, metal tea tables made of copper and silver, bearing inscriptions similar to those I had seen on the table in Azedine's house in the Medina. Near the impeccably polished teapots stood a couple of metal boxes containing freshly cut mint overflowing the shiny confines. Near those metal boxes were a couple of cone-shaped chunks of white sugar. The mayor, the man of the house, was in charge of making the tea. He sat in the middle of the floor surrounded by the tea table, teapot, sugar and the mint. A young man brought him a pot of boiling water which the major carefully took and placed beside the large silver teapot containing pellets of a tea called Chinese Gunpowder. Then he placed the tealeaves into the metal pot and filled it with boiling water; after a few seconds, he chopped bits of sugar, placing them into the pot.

The mayor paused every few minutes, raising his head from time to time to look at Hanify as he recounted a story from the *Qur'an*. He mixed the sugar with the mint tea and then filled several glasses with the steaming green liquid. Then he poured the contents back into the teapot. After about five minutes of pouring and re-pouring, he tasted the tea. Adding a little more sugar, he paused and then filled twenty glasses placed before him by a young man; one at a time, he carefully made sure that each glass contained the same amount of liquid.

The young man and two young girls brought us round trays with the glasses of steaming tea and in a few minutes, we were all sipping the delicious beverage. We partook of the tea very slowly; savoring every last drop; slurping and sipping sounds filled the room.

The tea service lasted about an hour; the mayor repeated the same procedure about three times, until we had all drunk about three glasses. Karim informed me that the tea service custom had been practiced for the last three hundred years in northern Africa.

186

He also told me that much of Moroccan business was conducted around a tea table drinking tea, which could last up to three hours.

I looked up from my empty glass and perceived that all turbans were turned toward Hanify, who was still talking. The bearded one enthusiastically interjected a few words in support of Hanify, but sometimes he stuttered and then became silent. Then he rose to speak again, his head bent forward as his voice projected to every corner of the room. The intensity of his dark eyes caused me to imagine that at any moment, he would jump up on the table, shouting the words of Muhammad, forcing us into spiritual submission. I sat back on the soft cushion and absorbed the moving speech of the bearded one.

After the tea service, a young boy brought a metal basin and set it in front of me. I placed my hands in it and washed them with soap, rinsing as the boy continued to pour water over them from a glass water pitcher.

After the washing of hands, dinner was served, consisting of long, silver platters of steaming hot vegetables, meat and couscous. First, we dipped morsels of bread into the meat gravy as we munched on small chunks of lamb and small, dark olives. The meat course was followed by the hot couscous we ate by rolling it into little balls and popping them into our mouths with the thumb, licking our fingers afterwards.

After everyone had finished eating and all hands were again washed, Hanify said a few prayers before we thanked our hosts and returned to the mosque.

Such was the life we led for the next two weeks, traveling from village to village, sleeping in one mosque after another, eating with members of the community, either in one of their homes, or sometimes the townspeople would bring us our meals as we prayed in the mosque.

"What a life!" I thought to myself as I lay in my sleeping bag, immersed in darkness in the middle of a mosque, somewhere in the forgotten plains. "If only everyone knew how simply, yet happily, one could live. I could spend the rest of my days praying, learning about Islam, talking, eating and thinking good thoughts."

Yet those good thoughts masked a storm that was brewing in the group. It was during my discussions with Hanify that I detected something was bothering him. Even though he encouraged me to ask questions, when I did, his piercing brown eyes looked into mine, incredulous that I could question the only true religion.

For example, I asked him how he could be so sure that the words in the *Qur'an* were the exact words of Allah, of God. It was almost as if I had blasphemed Muhammad. His cold stare seemed to last for hours as it pierced my heart. But his response was restrained; he had probably remembered that he should conduct himself as a religious leader, showing compassion and restraint with lowly infidels, such as myself.

"Muhammad Abdelaziz" he addressed me in a calm, low voice, "Allahu Akbar. Allah has brought us gifts of knowledge and love, and through Muhammad, he shared with us the truth in written form, in the Holy *Qur'an*. You must believe this or you will never be a true Moslem." He placed his hands on the floor, preparing to stand. Before he did, he turned and faced me, bending his turbaned head toward me like a falling tower, and said, "You soon must decide if you want to become a Moslem, or not. We have been very patient with you, but time is going by. One day, you will have to decide if you are with us or against us, and if you embrace Allah as your beloved God. And remember, if you have already become a

Moslem in your heart, and you abandon the religion, you have committed a serious crime and you can be persecuted, even put to death."

He stood and left me sitting in the corner of the mosque, my perfect serenity smashed by his implied threats. He sat down with legs crossed in front of two brothers, their backs turned to me. As he bent his head to speak with them, his eyes searched out mine, to show me that he would only enlighten those believing souls sitting before him. This dashed my last hopes of tranquility and integration into the group—and enhanced the possibility of my revolt.

Chapter XXV

Visit from Shatani

After this last encounter with Hanify, his attitude changed again: all signs indicated that he had given up on me, that he had abandoned me to the devil, to "Shatani." His focus was to preserve and enhance the faith of the brothers, who accepted everything without question. He spent a lot of time with them, explaining the *Qur'an* and praying with them in groups, while his back remained turned as he totally ignored me.

So it appeared that Hanify, all along, was the spiritual, moral leader of the group, as well as the policeman in charge of weeding out bad elements and ostracizing them. In between masses, I was relieved to find out that the brothers still spoke to me. Oman would finish his personal prayers at the end of mass and then seeing me in my usual position in the back of the mosque where I would go to pray, he would walk over to me. I would hear first his soft voice calling my name. Looking up, I would observe him looking into my eyes for the longest time—nor did my eyes stray from his. It seemed as though he was trying to detect whether or not I was a true believer.

He would bend down, and say, "Huk, (heart) will come if you keep praying. It will come, Muhammad Abdelaziz." Then he would leave to join the discussion with Hanify on the other side of the mosque.

Others came to speak with me, trying to cajole me into joining the group, becoming part of the team. One day as I sat in my usual place after early morning mass, praying and sleeping, I heard a soft voice next to me.

"Muhammad..." I thought I was dreaming. The voice repeated, "Muhammad." My eyes opened to the kindly face of Karim, his creamy, green djellabah hanging over his lanky body as he stood before me.

"Listen to me," he said, crouching down to my level, "You should go to Hanify and confess you truly do believe that Muhammad was the last prophet and that you now understand and accept in your heart all Moslem beliefs and values."

In spite of my head drooping with fatigue and limp body, I felt the blood heat up my forehead as the rage at being isolated was released.

I responded with unusual clarity, "Karim, I appreciate your concern, but I think it more appropriate that Hanify come to me first, as he and only he, has decided to totally ignore me for asking him questions, which I feel totally unjustified. What does he want, for me to be a robot or a submissive stooge and to repeat the 'Al Fatiha' when he snaps his fingers, then I shut up until I hear another signal from his pale hands?"

Karim waited a few moments, and then measured his response, "Muhammad, you should make the first move to stop this cold war between you two. Or at least ask for his forgiveness. Believe me, if you don't make a move, it could accelerate and that would be dangerous to you. Be careful!"

"What do you mean 'dangerous,' Karim?" I asked, a tremolo in my normally calm voice.

He left me without responding; he left me to my lonely misery with another warning about my "merciful" master, the one who was to lead me to the promised land of faith and understanding. Before I fell into a semi-sleep, I vowed to wait for Hanify to approach me first, and that I would never meekly succumb to his pressure, wallowing in spineless fear as I cried for forgiveness. Trembling in the cold, the sharp arrow of fear shot through me. I was helpless in a strange land, and to make it worse, I had no idea what I should do.

Before lunch, Oman invited me to join the group and him in their visit to another mosque in a village two miles away. He told me that our goal was to announce the mass at the mosque and to inspire the villagers to attend. I rolled up my sleeping bag, placed my *Qur'an* and special bilingual French-Arab prayer book in my tote bag and joined the others, who were assembled outside the mosque. Karim, whose responsibility it was to pack the mobile kitchen, including all the dishes and gas stove, was the last to join us.

The mosque we were presently occupying was built on the top of a hill, giving us a commanding view of the valley below, dotted with dark green patches. The land there was much greener than the arid plains we had previously walked across; the only plant life had been clumps of dry grass spread unevenly over the harsh, dry terrain. As we traversed the valley, the Imam of the mosque where we were staying was in the lead, with Hanify right behind him. We headed directly toward the green patches; the colors of various fruits and vegetables were more readily distinguishable by my myopic eyes, hiding behind streaked plastic spectacles. The scorching sun mercilessly beat on me as the arid wind kicked up the dust which whirled upwards, covering our mouths with a fine layer.

We passed through a cornfield endowed with tall, green stalks proudly displaying yellow husks clinging to them, holding on until the upcoming harvest. Next, we skirted a large field, a pasture where sheep were busily chewing the grass. Its perimeter was bordered by irrigation trenches full of water. As we walked along, I noticed the back of Hanify's impeccable pearl white turban bobbing up and down, as he climbed over clumps of grass and rocks around the irrigation trenches. The blisters on my feet were so painful, I could not keep up with him, easily climbing ahead of me.

I stumbled on a clump of grass, turning my sandal and tearing the skin from a huge blister behind my big toe. I could not prevent myself from plunging knee-deep into the irrigation ditch. Hanify heard the sound and stopped. For the first time in a week, he faced me, appearing above the ditch.

He coldly asked, "What's wrong with you, Muhammad, can't you keep up with us?" He dug the barb deeper: "Why can't you walk faster? Are you sick?"

I did not answer him, although I wondered why this "beautiful person," this religious leader dressed in a spotless white robe, a God-like being serving as a guide to the lost and weary, had singled me out for special persecution. It was clear he was intent on chastising me for the slightest reason.

I wondered if he had marked me as an evil spirit that must be neutralized, a threat to the increased faith of the brothers, someone who might lead them down a path of rebellion, of infidelity to the only true religion.

190

Was he setting me up for a major fall, or provoking me into an "all out" confrontation he would surely win? Would the ridicule ever stop?

As we walked through the fields, each painful step made me grit my teeth even harder; the skin pulled more and more away from the festering red blisters. Hanify continued to watch me very closely, looking to find fault in my every action. I recalled Camara had told me there would be harsh tests along the path that lead to the truth. I tried to accept the pain as a test, as well as the persecution by Hanify; I thanked Allah for giving me the foresight to help me understand and accept the challenges, as well as the strength to continue. I also asked God—Allah—to forgive those who wished me harm.

We came to another irrigation ditch too deep to wade through, so everyone leaped over it. As I tried to jump over, one of my sandals caught in my djellabah, stalling me in mid air; I fell again into the cold water. Oman reached down and I grabbed his hand as he pulled me out of the ditch. My legs were covered with mud and my djellabah took on a somber black hue, with flecks of mud and small pebbles. Hanify frowned at the pathetic sight and turned away in utter disgust. Perhaps he equated a weak body with weak faith.

I stopped myself from crying out at the top of my lungs. The last thing I wanted to do was to fuel his desire to chastise me further. I did not understand what was happening to me. I had at one time been healthy and extremely strong, but my health had ebbed; my weakened body began to revolt from the strain. The bacteria in the drinking water continued to afflict me with cramps and diarrhea. My weakened condition robbed me of power in my legs and arms—they felt like rubber and I was listless.

After about an hour and a half, we arrived at the mosque at the other side of the valley. It was a flat, stone building without a minaret next to it. We entered the dank, cold building, which echoed with the sound of our footsteps. Small clouds of dust accompanied each footfall as we approached the back end of the building, where we unloaded our sleeping bags and the rest of our gear. My vision was blurred from exhaustion and my feet were numb from rubbing against my plastic sandals. I had no idea of the time or day as I sat on my sleeping bag. The gentle winds of Al Maghrib entered the mosque through the open door, whispered over my body and exited through a rectangular opening in the opposite wall, serving as a window. I rolled over and fell into a deep sleep, in spite of the mud caked on my legs and djellabah.

The next morning before the noon prayer session, Karim invited me to joint Oman and Hanify for a walk to town for the purpose of explaining the purpose of the group to the inhabitants and to convince them to attend noon mass. The mosque was on the outskirts, about a half-mile from the town. I followed the group out the door and walked close to Karim, behind Oman and Hanify. We walked in single file up the dirt path, our djellabahs clean and our turbans in place. My body was still stiff from the night before and my blisters reminded me of their stinging existence. I could barely walk and was unable to keep up with the rest of the group as they passed over the hill; I was alone, edging my way up the path. When I reached the top, the others were crouched down around Hanify, who did not acknowledge my presence as Oman scooted over, allowing me to join the group. Hanify was instructing the others how to conduct themselves in town. He explained that since they were still young monks, with a faith not yet fully developed and minds not yet pure, they would be required to turn their backs when walking by women. I thought this was extremely strange but I was too tired to ask questions, especially since my questions were no longer well received by Hanify. After about five minutes, we entered the village

On one occasion, Hanify knocked on the door of a wooden shack, opened by a woman wearing a headscarf (at that hour, her mate was probably still working in the fields). Oman grabbed my sleeve and tried to gently turn me around so my back would be facing the two conversing. I reluctantly performed what I considered a preposterous act, my body hesitating while partially turned, as I saw Hanify watching me out of the corner of his eye—I felt humiliated and weak. According to Hanify, looking at women at that stage would undo all the training I had undergone up to that point and would compromise my faith. I could not fathom how that could affect my faith, but he was adamant and since he was the master, I tried to follow his directions.

He spoke to the woman, admonishing her to give the message to her husband that he was expected at evening mass. We waited for Hanify to pass us before falling in behind him, like school children waiting in line for the go-ahead from their teacher or like sheep following the shepard. I was uncomfortable with this requirement, and felt that I could maintain my purity even if I was allowed to look at women. I considered myself completely focused on becoming enlightened, drawing closer to God, and therefore was beyond being unduly influenced by them.

After that incident, to punish me for my obstinacy, Hanify restricted me to whatever mosque we were staying in; I was not allowed to participate in the walks to town to talk to the townspeople. Hanify also informed me not to go on walks during the day as the townspeople would think I was a tourist on vacation and not an Islamic monk trying to spread the word of Muhammad (especially since I could not speak Arabic). Upon their return one day, Karim returned with a huge tear in the front of his Djellabah. He told me they had been attacked by ferocious dogs protecting their master's home while he was away working in the fields.

Afternoons, I waited and prayed in the cold, damp mosque. I sat and shivered—my cold grew worse as I was not allowed to go outside. I prayed and prayed and continued to fast as my body grew weaker and weaker. In proportion to the weakening of my body, I began to lose my "edge": I started conforming to all the rules and directions imposed by Hanify, without question. I fasted because he advised me of the goodness of it, especially during Ramadan, and recited the prayers constantly being fed to me.

My daily routine consisted of prayer sessions five times a day, starting at 5:00 in the morning, praying afterwards, followed by a long nap, then mass and more prayers. I also fasted all day long. The others, since they were considered travelers, were not required to fast and usually ate the lunch provided by Karim, as I slept next to them in my sleeping bag. The brothers constantly encouraged me to fast and learn new prayers every day. I imagined myself like a Buddhist monk, living in a monastery high in the mountains of Nepal, totally isolated from the rest of the world. Oman, Isneh or Karim would come to me and ask me how my "heeman" was progressing. I would smile sheepishly, my lips cracking.

Karim usually entered the prayer room after the 6:00 evening service and approached me from behind as I sat on the mat. He would tap me on the shoulder. This was the sign the sun had set and my fast had ended. I would literally stumble to the kitchen, usually a small room next to the prayer area, where he fed me dates and served me coffee and bread, which I ate slowly, staring at the dirt floor. He was tall at six feet and kept his head immaculately shaved; he would often sit in front of me with sympathetic eyes, which appeared to pop out of his delicate, pale face, speckled with chocolate-colored moles. He usually wore a white skullcap, like a halo that was pushed back a little. His eyes were gentle and kind. As I nibbled dates, Karim would return to his kitchen duties, squatting on the packed earth to peel onions and place them into the stew. When he spoke, he spoke slowly, articulating every word. Sometimes he would place his hand over his heart, smiling, his eyes watering in onion glory and religious passion. He once turned to me and said:

"Heeman, Muhammad...with heeman you will gain the world. Since you are the only one fasting now, you have the superior spiritual force now, more than any of us. We are counting on you. Also, you know that life on this earth does not count. We're here to prepare for paradise. On earth, life is hard and here we work and live humbly and pray; but in paradise we shall rejoice."

The ends of his mouth curled into a faint smile, revealing a shiny, silver front tooth; his head was cocked to one side as he stirred something in a green pot. Karim often told me about paradise—about the great food, the giant dates and the beautiful women. Other times, he would tell me about his life in the Medina in Casablanca, before joining the mission. He told me that during that time, he was free to do whatever pleased him, including having as many girlfriends as he pleased. But he was never happy and he had many problems. Now he was the owner of two small grocery stores there in the Old Medina and since he had discovered the true practice of Islam, he explained, he would never sleep with a woman before marriage. At the present time, he told me that he prayed five times daily and was perpetually at peace and always happy; he had finally found happiness in the serene beauty of Islamic worship.

"Now," he advised, "be patient, and keep learning the prayers. Always repeat, 'Allahu Akbar, La ilaha illa Allah' and you will be happy and free of sadness."

The cries of the Muezzin were heard in the distance, calling the village folk to pray. Sometimes faint cries from mosques in adjoining towns hung in the air until the Imam of the village in which we were staying, acting as the Muezzin, called out a prayer to attract locals to mass.

The days ran together like water and the fasting continued. Feeling isolated and confined to the mosque, I began to withdraw within myself, wanting to be left alone to continue my prayers and meditations in back of the mosque. The brothers seemed to lose interest in questioning me as to my progress in learning about Islam. They were probably more concerned with tending to their own spiritual advances and in particular, with pleasing Hanify.

My questions about Islamic doctrine remained unanswered. For fear of more retaliation from Hanify, I asked no more questions of him or of the brothers. I still wondered why they believed that Muhammad was the last prophet to visit the earth before the end of the world. As I sat and prayed in the back of the mosque, I thought about other religions as well, notably Buddhism, Christianity, Judaism, the Baha'i Faith and Hinduism. I thought about progressive Hindus, especially the beloved Mahatma Gandhi, who I secretly believed to have also been sent by Allah to enlighten the world; I felt his purpose was to spread the philosophy of religious tolerance and peace in the world.

I had read about Gandhi's attempts to reform the social structure, in particular, his efforts to eliminate the caste system in India. He believed the most fundamental text of Hindu scriptures setting forth principles for the enlightenment of all mankind was the *Bhagavad Gita*, which includes dialogues between Krishna, the avatar, and the Hindu god, Vishnu. I had read the *Bhagavad Gita* from cover to cover and embraced much of the wisdom within; I believed it to be complementary to the *Bible*, *Torah*, *Qur'an*, and Buddhist scriptures. It was full of love and spiritual wisdom. I clearly remembered Chapter three, featuring a dialogue between Krishna and Arjuna, in which the former had stated, "But great is the man who, free from attachments, and with a mind ruling its powers in harmony, works on the path of Karma Yoga, the path of consecrated action" and "Even as the unwise work selfishly in the bondage of selfish works, let the wise man work unselfishly for the good of all the world."[17] Such, I truly believed, was my calling. At one time, I had wished to be a member of an Ashram formed by Gandhi and had sincerely desired to be his student, his friend. His simplicity, philosophy and his love gave me strength—I needed all I could possibly build for what lay ahead.

One day, after a long meditation session, Hanify came to me in my corner at the back of the mosque. Sitting next to me, he smiled for the first time in two weeks. His face, without a wrinkle and with an expression full of goodwill, indicated he had probably changed his tactics with regard to his indoctrination methods. As he spoke, I played along, my lips forming a bland smile, my eyes directly on his.

"I have not abandoned you, Muhammad, as I have been very busy," he explained unapologetically. "But I see you have been making progress. I hope you are doing well. At any rate, I am free to answer your questions and respond to your observations." A nervous spasm, like a warning signal, jolted my body. Fortunately, it was hidden beneath my djellabah.

I did not respond right away. The first week traveling with the group, I was close to Hanify, who I had considered my guru. But then the period of tension and dissonance between us had ended all that. The past week, he had totally ignored my presence, and because of that, I felt abandoned and pressured to align my thinking with his, or face ostracism from the group and him. He probably could not understand why his persuasive force did not suffice to change me into a "true" Moslem, one who would not question anything: not the prayers, rituals or the *Qur'an*. I felt like a wild horse and Hanify, impatient for my submission to him, was trying to "break" me. I felt resentment towards him. So when he entreated me to ask him questions, I leaped to open wide a "Pandora's box," feeling a surge of energy backing up my desire to jolt his complacency. I also wanted to challenge his treatment of me, without any regard for the consequences, at the risk of my total isolation and who knows what other punishment. I thought the best approach was a show of strength; it was time to go on the offensive. My skeletal body trembled as I contemplated what I was going to say to Hanify, who was batting his eyes, waiting for my response.

I decided to pour oil on the fire and mounted my attack by asking, "Wasn't Gandhi like a prophet as he was also sent by Allah to enlighten the people? Didn't he believe in religions tolerance and the unity of fundamental values in all religions?" Hanify opened his mouth, but the words failed to follow; he just sat there, stone-faced, obviously shocked although he tried not to show it. He immediately turned to the other monks, who had moved closer to listen to our conversation, telling them what I had just said. Hanify, without glancing at me, stood up and walked over to where the bearded one was praying and consulted with him. The latter raised his hand, looked away and continued praying. Hanify, frustrated that the bearded one apparently refused to join in his animosity toward me, stood up and left the mosque.

---

[17] *The Bhagavad Gita*, Translated from Sanskrit by Juan Mascaro, Penguin Books, 1962, p. 17-19.

194

Chapter XXVI

The Outcast

After the latest incident with Hanify, I felt renewed strength that I was able to resist the heavy indoctrination thrust upon me. That week, I totally immersed myself in almost uninterrupted prayer in the corner of the mosque, except for meals in the evening and mass five times a day. I was left alone with my thoughts. I ruminated upon all the religious doctrines I had known. I thought, again, about Gandhi who, being a Hindu, had also studied Christianity and Islam; he had concluded that all three religions were valid because they were based on monotheism, the belief in one God, and thus were basically similar. He had also believed that all three religions were introduced to guide man in his search for eternal life.

I surmised that one thing was certain: I would now be totally ignored by Hanify and the brothers until the end of the journey. But that was not to be! During our travels to several mosques the week after, Oman and Izneh walked beside me, reiterating over and over again that only one true religion existed, namely Islam. They made it a point to inform me that all other religions were heretical and all Christians, Jews, Hindus and Buddhists would eventually go to Hell. One day Hanify, who I had not laid eyes on since our last conversation and who was listening as he followed behind us, interceded with a special condemnation of Hindus; he said they believed cows were like Gods, and they even poured cow urine over themselves to purify their spirits.

Hanify continued, "Allah can't be shaped by any earthly being and Allah's form cannot be rendered tangible, in man's likeness or even as imagined by us."

He also condemned all Christians for elevating Jesus Christ to the level of the Son of God. He said that Jesus was a prophet but was not the Son of God, and thus Christians were wrong by praying to his images in the churches.

My old Christian roots started stirring within me. I wondered how the brothers could be so sure about Islam, that it was the only path to lead mankind out of the misery and into the flourishing gardens of paradise. I believed in one God, but I did not believe that Muhammad was his last prophet sent to earth to save the people. Once more, I remembered the wonderful times shared with Christians, Protestants and Catholics alike, as well as Buddhists and Jews, in the United States and in Europe.

We entered another village, laid out in the same way as the others, with a group of stone houses around a mosque. As we arrived at the mosque, the Muezzin was loudly announcing the afternoon prayer: "AAALLLAAAAAAAHUU, AKBAR!" We quickly entered and took our places in the prayer lines. During the prayer session, I could not stop myself from meditating on my past experiences; a renewed strength warmed my frail, chilled body.

I sat after the prayers, blissfully remembering the impassioned love that filled my secret world, which could not be shared with the brothers. I thought of Plato and his search for wisdom. I prayed in English, French and Arabic, reciting prayers from the *Bible*, the New as well as the Old Testament. I thought of Moses receiving the law (*Torah*) and leading the Jews into the Promised Land (as also told in the *Qur'an*). I remembered the wisdom of the Buddhist Scriptures, the eight-fold path, the four noble truths and the *Bhagavad Gita*. I prayed for the wisdom of the teachings of Gandhi's ashram, his study group. I filled my heart with an amalgam of original prayers which had been locked in my heart for years, sending a warm glow through my body—an ocean of love massaging a much needed strength into the cold corners of my body. I finally began to feel a peace in my troubled soul.

The brothers and Hanify could not hear my prayers, allowing me to follow my heart instead of enslaving my soul to a set doctrine. Although this allowed me to put up some resistance for awhile, the intense indoctrination process started to penetrate my defenses, little by little.

Alone to face this world, the renewed enthusiasm of the brothers and Hanify for assuring my embrace of Islam, their constant involvement in my education and assistance in helping me to pronounce the unfamiliar Arabic during prayer sessions. . .all of this took its toll. My defenses were slowly breaking down. I was not as independent as before, no longer left alone in the corner of the mosque; I was called to participate in study groups with the brothers. I was now in danger of losing everything—my sanity—as time, in conjunction with Hanify and the others, continued to relentlessly chip away at my mental constructs.

Following the afternoon mass, I was no longer allowed to withdraw by myself to the back of the mosque. One afternoon, Hanify tapped me on the shoulder and pointed to a group of monks in back of the mosque. The brothers had been divided into two study groups with three members each. Hanify and the bearded one moved to the front of the mosque and, on this occasion and others, discussed secret things. During these study sessions, each monk recited prayers over and over again as the other members listened and commented. After an hour of doing that, my brain would throb, as it was bloated with prayers—with "La ilaha illa Allah," "Bismi-l-lâhi-r-rahmâni-r-rahîm" and "Al hamdu li Ilâhi," etc.

One afternoon, I felt a strong urge to leave the mosque to air out my mind after the intense prayer drills. Everyone, including Hanify and the bearded one, had snuggled into their sleeping bags for the customary afternoon nap. I restlessly tossed and turned in my bag. In the dark silence, I looked around the aged mosque; the paint was crumbling and caking around the crude openings in the walls that served as windows. Rows of carpets had been carefully laid over the hardened clay floor, upon which the brothers slept contentedly.

Calm reigned over this place of worship, providing me with the possibility of leaving without being detected. I sat up as I slowly unzipped the bag, exposing my spindly, skinny legs and underwear. I thought how those legs were a far cry from the muscular ones I had as a shot-putter and football player in my earlier years. But my smile replaced the frown as I focused on how I had spiritually grown over the past weeks.

I slid on my djellabah and then stood up. No heads turned in my direction as I slipped out the side door. I followed a creek, which led to a steep gorge, divided by the rippling creek. I climbed and climbed until my legs screamed with pain, up the steep cliffs. The branches of the tiny, dried bushes pulled at my djellabah as I continued upward; small indentations in the red rocks were perfectly shaped for my sandals.

With every step, I felt the distance growing between the group and me. With every step, I felt freer, which nourished my desire to leave the group. The higher I climbed, the

196

more I understood what was happening to me. Little by little, I was being brainwashed into submission, total submission to Islam.

In contrast to the cold, dank mosque, outside the air felt fresh and warm. A chill of excitement rolled down my spine as I looked behind me—for the first time in weeks, I was not being followed, either by Oman or surreptitiously by Karim, who perhaps was only pretending to be my friend. Usually when I left the mosque for any reason, even to go to the bathroom if it was located outside, someone was delegated by Hanify to follow me. Every time I passed Hanify on my way to the door, his eyebrows raised, the signal for one, and sometimes two, of the monks to follow me.

The mosques had become prisons. When I was not inside, I was traveling with the group on our way to another "prison." As I wound around the forbidding cliffs of the gorge, I began to wonder why I had agreed to join the group in the first place. The answer came to me quickly as I remembered I had been told by the master that in Morocco, my faith and understanding of Islam would be enhanced.

I also wondered why I had begun to fast even before Ramadan had begun. When I reached the top of the gorge, I sat down contentedly, although my mouth was parched and my stomach churned for want of sustenance. I looked up and noticed a cactus plant in front of me loaded with prickly pears, the fine food of the desert flower; from the sands of the Nile to the Moroccan desert, it had nourished many a lost, famished traveler.

But I was adamant about maintaining the fast. I could only guess that I was fasting for two reasons: one, to purify my body of all the toxins that had accumulated while living in the city and two, to distract myself from the fact that I had been a virtual prisoner of the group since getting on the bus in Casablanca. My internment had continued as I traveled over the hot, arid Moroccan plains, with the group intent on controlling my every gesture, every thought.

As I sat cross-legged in the face of temptation, bent on keeping the fast, I looked into my soul, searching for the elusive free spirit that had originally driven me to come to Morocco. I saw its florescent tail blinking on and off like a strobe light inside me, reminding me that far beneath skin and bones, hidden by a black and white striped djellabah streaked with dirt from the floors of the mosque, it was still alive, curious and dedicated to the search for God, truth, and pure love.

But if I were to leave the group, where would I go? Behind the cactus plant, there was a narrow dirt path which I took, hoping it would lead me back to the creek by a different route than through the gorge. The path zigzagged and then lay parallel to the creek babbling below, an oasis compared to the dusty path I relentlessly followed. After about a half hour, I finally reached the creek, appearing undisturbed by my tribulations, probably unchanged from thousands of years of washing the sands of the hot plains of Morocco. I followed the creek upstream this time, as I headed back to the mosque.

Following the endless turns and watching the frothy water splashing against the sleek, gray desert rocks, my mind danced with the creek, caressing its frothy ripples. I imagined the creek leading me to the doorway of a home and a man entreating me to enter. But the entrance turned into a narrow tunnel through which I tried to pass, to no avail—the light of the lantern hanging over the entrance appeared as far away as when I first started to walk through what seemed like an endless passage...

My trancelike state did not prevent me from trudging onwards until I came to a fork in the creek I had not seen before. I was startled from my dream as I noticed a small windmill between the branches of the creek. I was so absorbed in my thoughts that I had walked right by the mosque.

The windmill was connected to the bank on each side of the divided creek by a wooden platform, which I mounted. A small door to the side of the building was open, so I walked around and peeked in. A pair of crude stone wheels were turning and grinding grains of wheat into flour. Since there was no wind that day, the entire operation was alternatively run by water power, which tripped a lever connected to the stone wheels grinding the wheat.

A white substance coated the inside of the small structure; several full burlap sacks were stacked in the back. I entered through the door and with my hand shaped like a cup, I scooped up some of the powder and tasted it. Sure enough, it was flour and the bags were full of it. Only a small breeze kept the windmill revolving ever so slowly, determined to continue grinding the grain. It looked like a small homemade operation. Not a worker was in sight, but I decided to leave for fear that my intentions would be misconstrued. I was fascinated by the ingenuity of such a little operation in the middle of this creek, in the middle of this arid plain, producing the flour for women to make their bread and other victuals.

After leaving the mill, I continued upstream, away from the mosque, as I did not want to be discovered until my wayward mind had been satisfied. But I imagined that if I returned to the mosque before anyone awoke, my absence would go unnoticed. Hanify, if informed of my temporary escape from his talons, would probably exert more control over my person. So I decided to return to the mosque.

I turned around and headed downstream, following the well-worn dirt path hugging the creek, back over the rocks, which had perhaps occupied the same place for thousands of years of existence. I imagined that the creek split Al Maghrib in two: on one side was the mosque in which lay the sleeping brothers; on the other was the land of the setting sun, the red and gold sunsets bathing the plains in harmony and joy.

It seemed as though the entire world consisted of the desert and the radiant eye of the sun, as golden radiance turned to red, linking all beings in one last warm embrace before its fiery descent.

I spoke to myself in a rasping whisper, "Oh, my; the sun is setting, which means that I have been gone all day!"

I quickened my pace in spite of my aching body's screaming need for replenishment, for water and food. As I reached the door of the mosque, I squatted like a Moroccan in front of it, watching my friend, the sun, set in the distance. As the last light flickered over the horizon, the occasional donkey broke the silence with its rusty-gate cries or a dog barked, perhaps protecting a distant homestead. The serenity of this scene was inevitably broken or interrupted by a face in the doorway—it was Oman's.

"Where have you been? This is not good, this is not good! Come in now; we have been looking for you for hours. You missed Maghrib[18]."

---

[18] Maghrib is the sunset Salat (mass).

Oman repeated his interrogation of me and then stood there, his blue-gray eyes flashing at me, waiting for my response. Shrugging my shoulders, I did not respond. Anger rose to my forehead and warmed it. I was fed up with being constantly under surveillance, constantly followed and treated like a child. I was happy to have escaped their grasp and dogmatic presence for a few hours; I did not care about the consequences. I also felt uncomfortable that Hanify and the brothers were intensely ratcheting up the indoctrination process, suffocating me with the forced prayer groups. Finally, I was relieved that I had found the strength to rebel against the monumental diatribes of Hanify and the others, whose dogmatism threatened to overwhelm me. I thought to myself that I could not stand it any longer.

As I entered the mosque, my hubris turned to mush as I noticed the brothers sitting in a semi-circle, in their post-mass positions, praying and meditating. I knew I was supposed to be where they were—on the carpet, praying just like they were. Their faces sincerely reflected concern and anxiety as they turned towards mine, one by one. I was touched that they should care about me, that they wanted to save what they thought was a wayward soul.

Worry shadowed their faces as their eyes followed Hanify who approached me, his omnipresent smile set in a stern grimace, showing portions of his upper teeth.

"You were not to leave the mosque without asking me, Muhammad. You knew that and you have sinned to have missed Maghrib. Go now to the back of the mosque and prepare for isha[19]."

Ashamed that I had left the mosque without telling anyone, I sheepishly withdrew to its obscure corners without saying a word, where I rested my tired bones. This time Karim did not come to break the fast, to take me to the kitchen where fresh dates, tea and bread would be waiting. My resistance succumbed to intense hunger and thirst, my dry mouth refusing to generate moisture as its roof welded to my equally dry tongue. My insides seemed to turn inside out, mercilessly throbbing with hunger.

After "isha," coldness tainted my relationship with the brothers. Hanify must have instructed them to leave me alone and to focus on their own enlightenment. It was as if he had told them I was an evil influence; they would not even look at me. As we sat around the plate of couscous brought in by the wife of the local Imam, wearing a green veil highlighting dark, Arab eyes, not a pair of the other's eyes met mine—I was an outcast.

An unsettled silence reigned that night, like that maintained by conspirators not wishing to reveal their plans. Hanify had turned the brothers against me. My sleeping bag and backpack were placed by Hanify in the corner of the mosque where I would be surrounded by the brothers, so I could not escape during the night.

Later, I sat on my sleeping bag, not able to find the energy to take my djellabah off. One by one, the brothers passed me, their eyes averted, without wishing me goodnight. Persecuted by Hanify, I could stand it and was used to it. To be ignored by the brothers, that was too much! I felt isolated and helpless, with nowhere to go and no one to talk to.

I was too restless and tired to sleep that night, tossing and turning until a voice penetrated the dark silence, the Muezzin calling us to pray. I pulled myself up, the dankness of night still closed in on us. I lined up with the others and went through the motions; my body and mind was on autopilot. I felt as if I was suspended in air during the entire prayer

---

[19] Isha is the evening Salat which occurs in the dark hours of the night.

session. When the final "salam alay-kum" was spoken, I returned to my sleeping bag and fell into a deep sleep.

That afternoon after "Zuhr," the noon mass, we traveled to another village. This time the distance was seven miles between villages so the townspeople provided us with a mule to carry our supplies. Karim strapped the kitchen supplies to the mule, the pots and pans protruding from the neatly wrapped packages. The rope around the animal's broad, gray neck was firmly pulled by Karim as he lead the mule down the hill; he was followed by Hanify, the bearded one and the rest of the group. Everyone carried his own bedding and personal possessions. I followed behind the others. Oman was stationed behind me a few paces as we descended into a desolate valley, a dust bowl dotted with the familiar gray rocks and dry reddish earth, totally devoid of trees and bushes and overlooked by distant hills.

As the procession continued, I imagined we were some mysterious caravan plodding through the Sahara towards an imaginary destination; that image changed as I fixed my eyes ahead on Karim and his charge and visualized Mary, pregnant with Jesus, and Joseph escaping across the land to Bethlehem, carrying all their supplies on the back of a mule.

About a half an hour into our voyage, the mule refused to budge, uninspired by the pulling of Karim and the prodding and pushing of Izneh and two other brothers from behind. As Karim pulled, extending the snout of the mule outwards until the rope was taught, the mule backed up pulling Karim with him. It then it let out such a loud "hee-haw," the echo reverberated and bounced off the valley walls, returning to greet us as Karim frowned, taking off his turban and fanning himself with it. We laughed as we all crouched down and took a break with the mule. It had won round one. Even Karim reluctantly joined us, bending his head in submission to the obstinate beast, providing comic relief to the otherwise formal procession.

Round two: Karim, through an amazing inspiration, began digging into the packages tied to the mule. I was standing next to him and noticed a thin smile cross his face as he pulled out a scrawny carrot. As we looked on, Karim proceeded to place it in front of the snout of the beast, whose ears immediately flapped with interest; it inched its way forward to meet its cool snack. Only Karim, before the poor mule could clamp its jaws on the tender morsel, moved the carrot a couple of feet ahead, requiring the animal to take a step in the direction of the desired tidbit.

And that was how we proceeded on our journey to the promised land. I walked next to Karim, who was the only brother who would talk to me. On one side of him, he pulled the mule, who was still intent on grasping the carrot carefully held by the cook; I walked on Karim's other side. He continued to explain the wonders of Islam and how much difference it had made to him. I thirsted for his kind words as I traversed the dry plain; I was at least sharing something with Karim while the others were intent on ignoring me. I had become nonexistent to Hanify again; he walked right by me without the slightest acknowledgment of my presence.

As I walked down the endless path next to Karim, I felt a slight tug on my sleeve. I turned around and saw a smiling face I had never seen before. His dark face shadowed the scorching sun in back of him. I stopped as Karim confronted the stranger. The newcomer's face was taut with the dark hue of his skin camouflaging the faint marks on his face.

"My name is Habib, and I joined the group yesterday when you were away. I am from Rabat, and I will be traveling with you and the group until it returns to Casablanca."

My mind was too withdrawn to be terribly open to this new acquaintance. I welcomed him and wished we could speak later; then I continued trying to catch up to Karim who was about twenty yards ahead, with the group still following him. Habib kept up with me as I walked. He offered to teach me a couple of prayers from the *Qur'an*, and I reluctantly agreed. I repeated after him the two prayers, but my heart was not in it. After about a half hour, we caught up to Karim; I had been repeating over and over again the prayers while Habib listened, correcting my pronunciation from time to time.

I finally turned to Habib who had opened his *Qur'an*. I told him I had had enough for the time being and wanted to pray on my own for a while. His brow wrinkled as he pointed to a page he was reading, trying to draw my attention to the words of a new prayer. I turned away and he briskly walked ahead of me.

Karim pointed to the distant line of crude adobe huts and told me our destination was near. As we approached, Habib turned around and asked me how my heeman was and if I finally believed Muhammad was the last prophet. I did not respond to this pushy newcomer. Well, he had been briefed well, had he not?

Our attention was attracted to the huts standing before us; a group of curious, unveiled women, their heads wrapped in multi-colored scarves, greeted us. They approached the caravan and tried to shake our hands but the brothers turned their backs as the outstretched hands grasped air. They acted as if the women did not even exist. I followed their example, the anger burning inside me, my body trembling with disgust. The women finally melted into the collection of shacks and were gone from sight.

We passed a small hay shed; golden strands of straw hung from the wooden slabs forming the exterior of the shack. A few minutes later, we entered a small, dusty mosque. As usual, we stashed our belongings, sleeping bags and kitchen equipment in a corner. Then we bathed ourselves with buckets of water and prepared for Asr, the afternoon prayer session.

Following mass, something else happened to add kindling the fire already burning inside me. A middle-aged woman entered the mosque at the end of the prayer session. At that time, we all typically prayed individually or in small groups of two. The cook had retired to the back of the mosque where he had unwrapped the packages and was washing the dishes. Through the open stone door, I saw the mule contentedly eating the remnants of several carrots clumped under his moist nose. The woman was veiled; two black and white strands of hair fell down over her dark, brown eyes barely visible above the white veil. She cautiously approached the praying brothers, and then she kissed one of the wooden beams supporting the crude, wooden roof. Kneeling before us, she murmured something in a low, unintelligible voice and, as she pointed to the ceiling, bellowed, "Allah, Allaaaaahu."

She began walking around the mosque. I looked up and noticed everyone was ignoring her. The bearded one was sitting up front, continuing his conversation with Hanify who had his back turned to her. Every few minutes, they would recite, "La ilaha illa Allah" while raising their arms to the sky, as the woman made her promenade around the room.

I kept silent, trying not to lose my temper. I felt frustrated because I could not understand what she wanted. Hanify had told me not to speak French or English in front of the townspeople or I would be considered an intruder, so I said nothing. I looked at the poor woman, and then to the brothers. I was in total disbelief at their nonchalance and inactivity. Everyone seemed to be ignoring her, so she left.

Afterwards, I approached the cook who was busy neatly arranging the sleeping bags in the back room. I asked him why the woman had entered the mosque. He told me in a very casual tone that the woman had lost a lamb, a child, or both—he was not sure—and she wanted the group to pray for her. Then I asked him why the brothers had completely ignored her, as if she did not exist. After all, we were here to bring the people back to Islam and help them return to the mosque and pray.

The cook replied, as he continued arranging the sleeping bags, "Because the woman doesn't belong in the mosque. If she does not know how to pray or needs help in that regard, she should ask her husband to teach her, at home."

I wondered if I had heard correctly and if so, if Karim and the brothers and I were on the same planet. The wheels were turning fast in my brain as I sat next to Karim and realized that he and the brothers were so different from me. All I had seen was a desperate woman seeking solace for her pain, and these "men and boys of God," instead of welcoming her in this house of God, shunned her, ignored her very existence.

"This is crazy and I can not take it any longer," I thought to myself as I stood up. Without saying a word to Karim, I headed for the adjoining ablution room. I entered and grabbed a bucket full of water, which had been prepared by Karim for the next mass, and splashed the water on my face and hands. I asked Allah to give me patience and to forgive the brothers who had acted indifferently towards the woman who had entered the mosque. My prayers were interrupted by the soft pitter-patter of footsteps outside the room. Habib stood at the door, his white turban contrasting with his rich, brown skin, his white teeth giving the impression that his face was sandwiched between his mouth and his turban.

"La ilaha illa Allah. Muhammad, what are you doing here in the ablution room? Perhaps you should join the brothers in the mosque and...."

I cut him off, "Why did everyone act so coldly toward the poor woman? She was here to seek our help, to help her pray."

Habib left the room without answering. "Ah," I thought, "no one could give me a solid reason because they knew they were wrong."

The cook then entered the room but he only repeated the same "party line," that the woman did not belong in the mosque. Hanify entered the ablution room where I sat against the wall, staring listlessly at the opposite wall.

He walked towards me until he was standing next to me, his tense arms stiffly at his side. "Excuse me, but the master told me to tell you to refrain from asking more questions." He left as quickly as he had entered, the dust trailing after his slim figure as he passed into the prayer room, leaving me alone.

202

Chapter XXVII

Sabotage: A "Zionist" Plot

As I sat there in the late afternoon silence, my eyes remained focused on the doorway through which Hanify had passed. His pronouncement made it clear to me that the soft-spoken bearded one, who only talked to me about my *heeman*, was behind everything, was even controlling Hanify, who was his eyes and his ears—his stooge.

An angry glare penetrated my thoughts as I imagined Hanify would soon, if he had not already done so, once again emphasize to the group that I was evil and to be avoided, discrediting and isolating me even more.

Later that day the master, the bearded one—as we were grouping together for Maghrib—announced he wanted to send three of the monks to a small village nearby to scout the terrain, the mosque, and inform the townspeople that a Moslem group would soon be visiting. The group would also visit the shacks in the village to try to convince their inhabitants to attend prayer sessions at the mosque where we would be staying.

After mass, as I was sitting in my usual place in back of the mosque, Hanify came to me and in a calm voice, informed me that he and a couple of monks were going to hike to the nearby village, but he preferred that I stay in the mosque since I was fasting and he did not think they would return in time for my supper of dates and bread. I told Hanify that I preferred to go with them. My non-submissive attitude angered him again, and with raised eyebrows, he stomped over to talk with the bearded one who was reading the *Qur'an* in the corner.

I saw the bearded one reluctantly put his hand on the carpet and push himself up to stand next to Hanify. They were soon both in front of me. The bearded one, in his broken French, told me that I must decide what I wanted to do. My eyes glanced at Hanify, who glared at me as I explained I wanted to explore the small village with the small group. The bearded one granted my request; Hanify turned away, his shoulders drooping. He sulked and fumed in silence, withdrawing into the shadows, followed by the master.

Later that evening, with the brothers ignoring me totally, I went into the kitchen to visit Karim, the only person who would still recognize I was alive and breathing. He was scouring the large pots and pans used to cook the vegetables for the couscous. He watched me enter; a faint smile curling the ends of his fine lips, his stalwart mustache immobile as he toiled at removing the remaining food stuck to the sides of a pot. He put it down and reached out his hand to me, his index finger curling, an indication I was to come closer.

As I stepped over to him, he looked over my shoulder, then over his shoulder, and when he was satisfied no one was listening, he whispered, "My friend, remember I warned you about Hanify?"

I nodded, as he continued, "Now you are in danger. Hanify thinks you are controlled by an evil spirit. And, what's worse, he is convinced you are a member of a Jewish or Zionist organization dedicated to sabotaging the mission, infiltrating our traveling Islamic study groups and trying to cause internal problems among their members. He told us so. He told us that that was the real reason he did not want you to go with the group to the village. Beware, Muhammad—he can hurt you!"

The heat of outrage rose like a storm, filling me with an anger that overrode any attempt to whisper.

"That's ridiculous!" Karim placed a finger over his mouth to warn me to lower my voice. In a loud, dry whisper, I sputtered "He's out of his mind! You don't believe that nonsense, do you? Anyway, how can he hurt me?"

Without responding, Karim lowered his eyes, grabbed another pot and tackled the burned remnants of food with a metal scouring pad. That was the sign our conversation had ended.

The next day, against Hanify's wishes, he, Oman, and I set off to visit the nearby town. Hanify was, of course, the spokesman. As we approached the small adobe huts, he called out that we had come to welcome everyone to join us during the prayer sessions in the mosque the following day. Since the men were all in the fields working, we occasionally met a woman or a girl walking on the road ahead of us; Hanify would stop and speak with them. A woman carrying a vase on her head was walking along a dirt path, going in the opposite direction, with one hand placed on the side of the tall vase, the other by her side. Hanify called to her and she stopped and turned, waiting for us to join her. As we drew within about twenty feet of the girl, Oman immediately turned his back to her and motioned me to do the same. As we waited for Hanify to finish the conversation, with our backs turned, ignoring the bearded one's request that I ask no further questions, I asked Oman why we were doing this.

Oman responded in a firm voice, "We should not look at any females or we will lose our heeman, our faith."

As he spoke to me, he did not even turn his head and look me in the eyes, as he had always done. I wondered if it was because he believed that if he did, he would be corrupted by the seeds of the evil force that lingered in me, waiting to be sown in fertile ground. I felt sorry for Oman, a 19-year-old indoctrinated believer, who perhaps thought he was spiritually superior to me as well as the brothers. I remembered back in the mosque that morning, he had cast his suffering eyes towards the heavens as he read portions of the Qur'an. Maybe he had visions of becoming a spiritual leader since he had readily accepted the ascetic lifestyle at such a tender age, living humbly in modest mosques while turning his back on all women.

Now even Oman would not look at me, something he had always done as the self-appointed (or Hanify-appointed) measurer of my heeman. It was clear I had become a marked man. I was isolated, extremely upset and disillusioned with the group, as well as weary—and somewhat fearful of those piercing brown eyes watching my every move. One by one the brothers had shunned me. I was being ignored by those who had once shaken my hand and embraced me with their warm smiles. All that was gone. Even the "wise" bearded one was afraid of corruption and avoided all eye contact with me.

They perhaps all now believed I was the Devil's servant, and for fear of losing their intense spiritual feelings, their heeman in Islam and the prophet, Muhammad, they refused to further associate with me. Upon our return from the village, I approached Izneh to ask him how his day had gone; he turned away from me and began conversing with Oman, standing next to him. They were ignoring me in the same way they had ignored the poor woman who had entered the mosque the other day. They shunned me in the same way they turned away from all women who approached them, their veils and robes trailing behind them, dirty children rolling in the dust at their feet. "La ilaha illa Allah," I whispered to myself. I was convinced—contrary to what Hanify and the brothers thought, in spite of their stony silences and the dark cloud of bitterness hanging over us— that I was also a righteous person doing God's work. I was, again, left alone to take my place among the cobwebs and dust accumulating in the back of the aged mosque. I glanced at the aged adobe walls shedding their crusty mud, sometimes falling to the carpet below; the carpet on which I sat was speckled with adobe powder, shifting as I shifted my body. I felt like the wall.

The others prayed together in small groups, which I was now forbidden to join. I was no longer allowed to accompany the brothers and Hanify to the villages in their quest to encourage the inhabitants to visit the mosque and pray with them. My role had changed to that of the enemy. However, they did use my presence whenever it served their purposes; they point me out to the villagers, warning them that if they did not embrace the religion they were born with, foreigners like me would and they would be left in the streets with "Shatani," the devil.

I was growing weary of fasting and traveling from mosque to mosque, sitting in the corners of the mud-walled mosques next to the neatly piled sleeping bags...isolated from the brothers, insulated from the world. Hanify had sternly warned me never to leave the mosque again and the bearded one submitted to his stern rule.

One afternoon, after Zuhr, everyone left the mosque except for the bearded one who stayed, praying and casting an eye in my direction from time to time. I sat there, my nose running, bone-deep stone cold in my dank prison. An hour passed, then two; silence echoed against the walls, alternating with the muffled snoring of the bearded one. The side door of the mosque consisted of a small opening in the adobe shack through which we crawled to exit the building. I walked over to the opening; the bearded one moved his head to find a more comfortable position against the wall. Soon his groaning snores filled the air. I looked out through the passageway, which unveiled a beautiful, sunny day. Seizing my chance, I crawled out, reassured by the unrelenting magnitude of the loud, sputtering snores. The sun's rays infused my pale skin with their welcome warmth. I walked to the side of the building and sat absorbing the afternoon heat as I closed my eyes to meditate. I envisioned sitting on a warm northern California beach, looking straight into towering, frothing waves crashing to the sands below.

As the imagined waves receded, a muffled pounding caused me to open one eye; the blurred form looked like a veiled woman. My vision began to crystallize and I saw two women, one veiled the other not, dressed in muslin robes, each carrying a load of clothing on their backs. I smiled and they smiled back. Two boys and a girl followed, carrying burlap sacks; they trailed off to the creek with the week's washing.

I crept back to the opening in the mosque, and crawled through, hoping to find the bearded one fast asleep, as I had left him. I lifted my head and found myself staring into his eyes; he sat directly in front of me, his *Qur'an* in his lap, reciting prayers. Without missing a beat and without saying a word, he waved his index finger as if to scold me and then pointed to the back of the mosque, my place.

Chapter XXVIII

The Lynching

For the first time, the mosque was crowded on a Thursday just after sunset and before evening prayer. Going through the motions during the prayer session, I looked around and noticed there were many more townsfolk than usual in the congregation. And even more unusual, after mass, they did not stand up to go home, but stayed; other locals crawled through the opening of the mosque and joined us.

Hanify and the bearded one were positioned in the front, and were conversing with several locals in the front row. A middle-aged man with a golden turban spoke first; raising his voice, he gesticulated wildly. Turning, he looked at me; his brown skin was taut and his closely-shaved beard was the same color as his dark brown eyes. Others spoke that night, some pointing to their *Qur'an*, which they had carried with them, then pointing to the heavens. Others spoke, shrugging their shoulders, as if to say they could not understand. Something was wrong: I expressed my concerns to the brothers, but they just shook their heads.

That night after Karim had served me dates and bread, I informed him that I would definitely break my fast and eat a full meal the next day. His silence confused me; I at least expected some words of encouragement, or anything from my friend.

The next day, the brothers did not go to the village; they stayed in the mosque in their pre-planned study groups. After Zuhr, the noon mass, the bearded one and Hanify were busy going from group to group, giving them advice on the wording of the prayers or on how to pray. I was in my usual place, in the back of the mosque. They sometimes would demonstrate how to articulate prayers themselves, after carefully referring to the omnipresent *Qur'an* opened in front of their crossed legs or tucked carefully under their arms as they stood. Everyone was too occupied to supervise me and thus did not notice me inching towards the opening. When Hanify and the bearded one were occupied reciting parts of the *Qur'an*, I crawled out the door and headed into the hot afternoon sun.

A small stream gurgled and spat as it wound its way around the mosque; I quickly walked downstream along its banks, weaving in and out of the trees to avoid being detected by the brothers who would be sent by Hanify to follow me. This time, however, I walked steadily for twenty minutes and then I turned around. I was completely out of sight of the mosque and no one was following me. If I had had my sleeping bag I would have kept on moving, without returning. I decided to wander alongside the creek for a couple of hours then return to the mosque. That would give me time to contemplate how I was to leave the group and inform Hanify I was no longer obeying anyone. I declared to myself that I was now independent. As I headed back, the sun was at a 45 ° angle, just visible over the tops of the distant clouds. I had stayed away longer than planned and shuddered as I anticipated Hanify's anger. As my paced quickened, I thought to myself, "I don't care what they think and what Hanify says." I felt reassured.

As I got within fifty yards of the mosque, I saw Izneh and Oman scurrying in through the opening. I imagined that the little "puppets" were telling Hanify that the villain had arrived. Several faces peered out the door watching my slow approach. When I arrived, Arabic words filled the air, thundering out the door. When I entered this time, someone was scurrying towards me. It was inevitably the master, wearing the cleanest white robe and turban combination among us. His robe flapped left and right as he hurried to intercept me as I walked toward the back of the mosque. The brothers were grouped together in the ablution room where they were splashing water on themselves in preparation for Maghrib. They stopped like a herd of cows watching an intruder in the pasture, watching my every move. Their eyes followed me as I passed by the room, walking towards my usual place next to the folded bedding and rolled up sleeping bags.

Soon Hanify was upon me; all traces of his ubiquitous, saint-like smile were gone from his face as he grabbed my right shoulder with his left hand and pushed me toward the back of the mosque, away from the brothers. He ordered me to sit down; his eyes flashed at me as I hesitated.

"I am going to relay a message from Haddad (the bearded one). He told me to tell you to keep your mouth shut. He said that you had been obedient and respectful only during the first few days of this trip, but now you have become unruly and disrespectful by insisting on asking questions which serve no other purpose than to reflect your lack of faith and cause the others to doubt theirs."

Hanify continued, his face flushed with anger as the words continued to stream from his mouth: "Furthermore, we warned you not to take walks by yourself and not to look at the villagers, especially the women and girls outside the mosque. You did not heed our warnings. As a result, the entire male population of this village visited us last night in the mosque, complaining that one of us looked at their women. They all identified you as the guilty one."

Habib, approached us, probably to announce the prayer session, but Hanify waved him away—he was livid.

"Also," he went on, his voice rising a decibel as his ears seemed to flatten under his turban, like a cat's before pouncing on its prey, "the townspeople and I am convinced that since you have made great efforts to profoundly disrupt this prayer group and bring unhappiness to this village, you must be a member of a Zionist Jewish organization that sends its spies all over the world. Their purpose is to infiltrate Islamic organizations and disrupt their activities, which are centered around reestablishing the influence of Islam throughout the world, bringing Islam back to the people who have lost their faith. You are lucky to be alive and that we were able to calm the villagers down last night as they wanted to lynch you and drag you out of the mosque. Who knows what the angry crowd would have done to you! You have brought shame and disrespect to our prayer group and we have lost all our credibility with the townspeople, and you are to blame! We are now forced to leave because of you."

He stopped to clear his throat; his usual pale face had flushed to a bright red. Taking a deep breath, he prepared to castigate me further:

"We are soon going to travel to another mosque in another region, so organize your gear and prepare for our departure tomorrow and don't forget what I have told you. Now get up and get back to the mosque." The corners of his mouth quivered with anger as his brown eyes penetrated mine. I stood up and trudged to the back wall of the mosque, reserved for only my weary frame, Hanify following closely behind me. I turned and slowly sat down, my back scraping the wall as my buttocks found the stone floor. My shadow likewise came to rest in the dark gloom. I felt the full force of his icy stare from somewhere within the walls of my prison.

I trembled upon hearing such false accusations. Even though Karim had warned me about Hanify, I was shocked by what he had said...and the gravity of the situation began to sink in. I thought that I must finally awaken and accept the reality that deep in Moslem country, I had been accused of most serious crimes. My heart beat against my rib cage as I contemplated what the consequences could be.

I thought to myself, "So that was what the brouhaha was all about last night in the mosque involving Hanify, the bearded one and the villagers. The heated voices and the concerned looks on everybody's face clearly spelled trouble, but I would never have dreamed that the conflict was over my innocent looking at the local women."

I was astounded that such unjust charges should be directed at me as a result of glances at other human beings, who happened to be women. What did the irate husbands think that I intended to commit a lascivious act against their wives? Even my mind would never have entertained such lowly thoughts. My brain churned as I calmly sat there after Hanify's diatribe. I needed to withdraw and try and understand the non-understandable. Clear thinking was again restored inside my mind, and I remembered that when I viewed the women while I was sitting outside the mosque, I was trying to imagine what kind of lives they lead; I was wondering about their daily routines and their challenges. And now, I was being condemned for my actions although my thoughts had been innocent. It was ridiculous! I felt no regret, and I didn't care if the villagers disapproved—I didn't care if anyone disapproved. This was an insane world—would I submit to it, accept it or fight back?

Now, I understood why everyone had treated me as if I were a ghost after the villagers stormed out of the mosque. Even though I had been visibly upset and had withdrawn into myself in the far corner of the mosque, no one had bothered to explain what had happened. I thought that now everyone was against me, including the peasants in the village; I would need to make haste to prepare my bags, and leave long before the cock crowed. I feared they would publicly lynch me, in their grandiose ignorance. That would probably bring relief as everyone there seemed to be looking for a scapegoat—an enemy—for some mysterious reason. The guiltiest one was Hanify, the master, who had, almost from the beginning, persecuted and chastised me, and was trying to convince everyone I was a Jewish spy. I surmised he had to invent something to justify why his god-like demeanor and phony, angelic smile had failed to bring me to acceptance of Islam. He had failed to recruit me as a devoted Islamic slave to help him fulfill his goal of bringing the wayward Moroccans back to Allah...and what for? Maybe he wanted to exercise complete control over them and achieve total power, perhaps with the ultimate goal of diluting the power of the politicians and the King of Morocco. And this would be IN THE NAME OF ALLAH, IN THE NAME OF GOD?

I was surrounded by ignorance, lies and power-mongering tyrants disguised as saints! I turned away from Hanify who, still sitting in the front of the mosque, continued to stare at me in silence with his dark, piercing eyes. I feared taking the initiative in those lonely, arid plains of Morocco. I bit my lip, and withdrew my thoughts to my lonely corner in the depths of the mosque.

Chapter XXIX

Revelation: Cradled by God

I sat, surrounded by my djellabah, without moving...weak, numb, exhausted. My nose, which had stopped running in the warmth of the summer sun, began to run again in the cold mosque. As the brothers filed in for lunch, my body barely moved, seated in my usual place, looking for any recognition from the monks, in their eyes, in their gestures. Nothing! It was like I was a light fixture—an integral part of the surroundings but not acknowledged.

The feeling of total loneliness and desolation pierced my defenses. I sat as if in a drugged daze, while the minutes passed. Finally, after lunch, the Muezzin announced Asr, the afternoon prayer. I rose and fell into the line of worshippers, my only contact with others during the day. The prayer session consisted of the usual Rak'as (cycle of the Salat), beginning in the standing position, facing the Ka'ba in Mecca. We bent over, placing our hands on our knees. We recited other prayers, made statements, then straightened. Next, we prostrated ourselves, while praying, then assumed sitting, half-lotus, half-kneeling positions, reciting additional prayers.

During the prayer session, my body screamed in agony as I bent forward to touch my forehead to the mat; in spite of the pain, I concentrated on praying. I prayed and prayed, asking for deliverance from this prison...from this nightmare. More prostrations and standing preceded the final "Salam 'alay-kum," pronounced twice, turning the head to the right and then to the left.

But this particular afternoon, something astounding was to happen. Everything was in place for a routine prayer session, to be followed by each worshipper sitting cross-legged or with legs tucked underneath the torso, eyes fixed rigidly ahead as he meditated and recited prayers silently or in whispers.

While I was sitting cross-legged, my arms grasping my knees and balancing my body on my hips, I began to realize my prayers were spoken less and less in Arabic and increasingly in French and English. I found myself praying the Lord's prayer, La Fatiha, and at the same time, repeating the words of the *Bhagavad Gita* as a prayer—notably those regarding detachment from material things, as expressed by Krishna, and shifting ones focus from selfish satisfaction to the good of the world. I recited the beautiful words of Gandhi, deeply soothing me in their expression of peace, love and tolerance. Resonating in my ear were the words of the Buddha voicing the Dhamma (basic truths) in his sermon at Benares. The four noble truths and the eightfold Ariya path, leading to pure wisdom, enlightenment and freedom from slavery to physical desires. My heart followed its own path to the revelation of the Ten Commandments and the *Torah* of Moses, who led the Jews to the Promised Land; then it flowed to Jesus Christ, savior of humanity, carrying and caring for a lost lamb in his arms, his love energizing a hopelessly unspiritual society. And finally, my heart returned to Muhammad, the prophet, with love, delivering the word of God after divine revelation, as did the other aforementioned prophets and spiritually enlightened beings.

And then, a mysterious voice drew my attention deeper, deeper within me, to a river of love, beauty and infinite tolerance.

Breathing heavily, my eyes sealed shut, I concentrated on the love steam and was empty of all distractions; it was the emptiness of space, embracing and becoming the soft clouds, the color of sweet cream. My meditations took me down the golden river—I was aware of a profound sense of the simplicity of life, beauty, faith and hope. I perceived a profound humming noise vibrating within me; "Hummmmm" filled my ears, my being, as Jesus tenderly announced—the draping of a golden blanket over me, protecting my faith from the bitter cold and from Satan's claws. "Ommmm" resonated deep within me as Krishna breathed new life into my hungering soul while Buddha held my hand walking down the eight-fold path. Gandhi's love penetrated all, even the secret biases, prejudices, sickness, wicked thoughts and lies still corrupting my body, sending them forever from my soul, replacing them with the love penetrating me like a laser, coming directly from the heavens and from within me. Muhammad and Moses, embracing each other as one spirit, embracing me within their loving realm, breathed life into my withered body as I opened to the balm of the *Bhagavad Gita*. I focused my strength on the integrity of the world, detaching myself from all physical desires; neither hunger nor thirst, nor pain nor any physical desire disturbed me. I was in harmony with all things. . .with the universe.

The "Hummmmmm" continued, becoming louder, resonating pure love, and even though I was in a deep, trance-like state, I could feel my torso swaying back and forth, totally involuntarily. The "humming" stopped and my body stopped moving. Then "HUMMMMM" reverberated within me again, and my body swayed back and forth, again without any volition on my part; I sat cross-legged as my chest and head moved forward and backward, in rhythmic meditation. Aware of a vast "emptiness," I released. . .released even more, and experienced freedom in my own world, imagining blue skies, scattered sheep visible in the twilight, peacefully sleeping in the green meadows of my mind. Now, I was totally conscious, and to assure myself that I was not dreaming, I "HUMMED" again" and my body swayed back and forth without the slightest effort, without the slightest command from my mind.

I was startled by this power surging through me, but I breathed deeply and soon relaxed into a semi-conscious state, in perfect harmony, while the faces of family and friends phased in and out my conscious mind. I was pure consciousness, searching every corner of my interior terrain, converting any remnants of hate into love. The beautifully rich "OMMMM" returned, transforming into the powerful "HUMMMM," which transitioned naturally into the resonant sound of "LLLLOVVVVVVVE."

As my body vibrated, the words whispered in my ears were part of the stream of universal love— I felt I had discovered something deep within as a result of the last few months of self-searching. Subsequent thoughts flowed like a waterfall from the same place as the mysterious force flowing in and through me. I felt as though I had accessed the wavelength of the supreme consciousness. The secrets of the *Bible*, the *Torah*, the *Bhagavad Gita*, the Upanishads, the Vedas, the *Qur'an*, the Buddhist Scriptures, were somehow unlocked, revealing the truth linking all peoples, races, worlds—even universes.

A synthesis of the spiritual ideas in the above works had revealed the common denominator of one all-encompassing divine intelligence; by meditation on this universal ideology, it appeared that supernatural forces were flowing through me, allowing me to see the past and visualize the future. I also experienced the pure love spirit of this supreme consciousness. A surge of unimaginable power swept through my frail, emaciated body.

Before, I had intellectually imagined a means of communication with the supreme force. What had happened was far from being merely an intellectual experience; the energy pouring through my body had a real physical component—that could never be denied. I had actually felt the warmth of the stream, of the Supreme Consciousness. I experienced the feeling of unconditional love for all races, all religions, without favoring or rejecting anyone, without hate or disdain for others.

I had connected to the love stream during profound meditation, without distraction, while in the shelter of a mosque seemingly thousands of miles from Western civilization, where I had been raised. I felt that by focusing on nothingness, pure love and all knowledge had been naturally revealed to me.

This happened within the context of the protective environment of the mosque and my exploration of Islam, yet the sensation and knowledge that followed opened up worlds extending far beyond one single religion.

I felt a certain truth had been revealed to me—that empty rituals, material things, hate, gossip, cruelty, violence, senseless killings were meaningless, especially since they interfered with my experiencing total release, the feeling of unity with the universe.

It seemed as though I was riding some magic carpet to a land of freedom and happiness, taking me into a new dimension. Even though my body, after many weeks of fasting and walks in the dry plains, was screaming for food and drink, I did not hunger nor thirst because my soul had finally been completely nourished.

Upon returning from this mysterious place, I was perspiring profusely. No longer in a trance, it truly seemed as if I had traveled to a strange, fantastic land, far, far away. Yet I looked around me and saw I was sitting in the same mosque, on the same mat spread over the stone floor, surrounded by brothers praying. Since I had just experienced an ultimate spiritual catharsis, so intense I felt I had become a human volcano of understanding and love; I felt surely the brothers around me would have seen and heard it, that it was too strong to hold inside. Such a profound experience, in which all religions, all faiths were glorified, must have been transparent for all around me to see; the loud humming noise must have disturbed the others during their morning prayers. Yet they continued praying and meditating on all sides of me; I had not been discovered—no one was looking at me.

Fear took over my thoughts as I wondered if I would survive this journey to share this experience. Even if I did, would anyone believe me? Then, a new strength helped me to cast fear aside—I felt I had a power I hadn't had before, that no one could take away.

Again I concentrated and prayed, my body moving back and forth during intense praying, stopping when I ceased praying—I was no longer afraid of this phenomenon. I looked around expecting to see eyes fastened on my strange movements and ears listening to the loud "HUMMING," but saw the brothers still meditating, sitting cross-legged on the carpets, their eyes straight ahead. It was hard to believe they had not witnessed the involuntary movements of my body nor heard the deep "HUMMMMMING" which permeated my being. My body had become a vibrating force; my soul transcended the movement while the intensely-felt energies surged within me. I returned slowly to complete awareness of my surroundings.

Chapter XXX

Off the Ropes

This incredible moment, this explosion of metaphysical power, gave me renewed energy—it left me calm and confident. I looked around to assure myself that no one had witnessed what had happened; the brothers were dispersed throughout the mosque in their post-mass, cross-legged positions while they continued their personal prayers and meditations.

I slept in a sitting position, with legs crossed; my entire body was warm and relaxed for the first time since I had begun to visit the mosques weeks ago. A humming sound resonated through the mosque. After about fifteen minutes of profound rest, my eyes opened and focused on the dusty mat in front of me. Looking around, I noticed some of the brothers were still praying, individually, white robes angled forward, touching the mats, as they mumbled the aged Qur'anic prose. A mule bellowed in the distance.

I heard murmuring in back of me; turning, I saw the bearded one huddled with Hanify and a few of the brothers, who were sitting in front of him as they listened intently. My ears detected that he was instructing them to organize themselves into small groups of two which were to descend on the small village situated at the base of the barren Atlas Mountains.

Soon they crawled through the opening and were gone. I was left alone again, with my thoughts and my prayers. With renewed force and confidence, I vowed to leave this dungeon. My spirit and my health were both suffering and I thought I had learned all I was to learn. No one paid attention to me, except to make sure I was in the back of the mosque where I would bother no one. None of the brothers came to talk to me or help me to learn new prayers. It was time to take some initiative, without fear, without being submissive.

I was determined to leave immediately. I rose to my feet, with bones creaking and muscles contracting. But I was not completely alone. The bearded one sat discreetly in the opposite corner, like a prison guard. As I crawled through the opening, my djellabah caught on something, delaying my escape. I looked back to unhook my robe and saw the bearded walking towards me. I forced my way out the opening, slightly tearing my djellabah; finally outside, the wind gently caressed my face. Karim, who had stayed behind to clean the dishes and arrange the sleeping area, was washing himself outside, next to the opening. He asked me where I was going—I told him I was going for a walk. Then all I could see was his robe twisting through the opening as he vanished inside the mosque.

I supposed he was consulting with the bearded one as to how they would detain me, so I expected one of them to be on my heels in a matter of seconds. Contempt and anger filled me. I surveyed the dirt road descending towards a small creek, and slid down the bank of the creek, riding on my djellabah—sandals and all—without looking behind me.

A cloud of dust floated in the still, dry desert air as Arabic words, spoken shrilly, penetrated the silence. Two of the brothers, Isneh and Habib, were washing clothes in the creek, beating them on the rocks and kneading them in small pools alongside the stream. They splashed powdered soap on the clothes from time to time, sudsing the water which streamed downwards. The soap must gag the fish, I thought.

I approached the two and sat on a large, gray rock at the side of the creek while the water swirled around. Laboriously bent over their work, they did not see me, at first. They looked in my direction, probably having overheard the sound of my sandals on the smooth rocks.

I had a great urge to challenge them about spirituality—about anything; I was ready to battle their dogmatic ways. At the same time, I was determined to remain alongside the creek as long as I wanted to sit on the rock. I would take no further orders to return to the mosque, by anyone; I had had enough. My conviction grew firmer as my eyes followed the bearded one descending the same bank to spy on me. I rose to my feet, slightly wetting my feet and slipped on the rock, falling into a shallow pool between it and the bank. I headed downstream, passing the bearded one without turning my head, without meeting the gaze of his small, beady eyes following me as I headed toward a clump of trees, behind which I intended to relieve myself.

Isneh lifted his head as he continued beating his clothes against the rocks, and asked me where I was going. I told him I wanted to urinate, he told me to hurry up. The bearded one came closer, nodding at the other two, his eyes on me as I vanished behind the trees. I urinated and then returned to my place on the rock. The bearded one had left, probably after having instructed the others to supervise my actions. I wondered if he had reminded them that I was the devil and that I could fool them into allowing me to disappear into the hot plains.

But, all I wanted to do was to watch the water tumble over glistening, slippery rocks peering through the water swirling all around. I wanted to listen to the gurgling sound, and watch the tiny, spinning whirlpools, allowing them to propel me deep within to the place of pure wisdom, as I meditated alongside a small waterfall.

My eyes closed, then opened slightly. The constant slapping of clothes on rock began to fade away as the brothers spread their wet clothes on bare bushes beside the swirling creek. My eyes closed again as I imagined the water tumbling around rocks, rippling and frothing on the other side. At first, I wanted to be the water rushing downstream. After building up more confidence, I decided I wanted to be a rock, anchored to the creek bed, undaunted by the pressures around me; whenever I saw fit, I could just "pull up stakes" and roll down the stream. I could stand up in mid-steam and make the water pound over and around me. I felt so peaceful listening to the subtle chattering of the stream, which I was certain was speaking to me, guiding me, giving me strength. I looked downstream to an enticing new world away from the prison above. Perhaps it was my chance to escape. I would be at peace at last!

My long, drowsy contemplation was interrupted by a heavily accented "Bonjour." I looked up but my eyes did not focus right away on the form in front of me—a part of me was still far away. I saw double as my eyes gazed directly into the sun peering over the shoulder of the mystery person. Oman looked down on me with a gentle smile on his face; his eyes reflected a kindness as if he understood my suffering.

"La basse"? (Okay?) he asked as his head slanted to one side. I was basking in the joy of not being accountable to anyone, and did not want that to change. So I ignored him, looking the other way. He and the brothers, along with Hanify, were only concerned with converting another lost soul.

He continued, unaffected by my attitude: "La basse. Come, Muhammad, to Maghrib, and we will pray together." He stood up and started to walk slowly toward the mosque.

My eyes followed a lone leaf as it glided downstream, floating over the ripples and into a shallow pond where it disappeared. I decided to stand up and follow Oman. I entered the mosque and fell in line with the brothers.

Chapter XXXI

Death Run

I was rolling up my sleeping bag and preparing my gear for departure as I heard Hanify shuffle noisily, in his pointed Arabian shoes, to the other side of the mosque. I reflected upon my meditation yesterday, during which an incredible force had pounded through my veins. I wondered if that had happened for a specific reason, namely, to prepare me for the next and final step—to take initiative with faith, love and understanding and ditch the waves of fear now immobilizing me, wreaking havoc on my nerves. I could hardly move my deteriorating, wasted body. I "hummmmed" and an invisible hand from within brought me to my feet. Blood surged through me, pumping up my frail frame; my heart muscles began to swell and pump blood throughout my body from the depths of my soul. I felt one with God, with the universe within and without. I felt strong and I trembled no more—I feared no more, not even death. Strength galvanized my body. I looked at the brothers who were busily folding their bedding and rolling their sleeping bags as Karim loaded the backpack with cooking utensils, tea kettles, pots and pans and rounds of Moroccan bread.

"Enough is enough!" I cried, loud enough for Karim to turn his head, which he shook from side to side; his eyes did not flash hatred or distrust, but compassion and pity. I nodded at him, and smiled. His response was a confused frown on his pale face.

The moment had come for me to make my move; it was time to inform Hanify I intended to leave the group—now. I walked with confidence past Karim, his wrinkled brow touching the edge of his turban.

I found Hanify, in the middle of rolling the long piece of muslin, which would soon be carefully and tightly wrapped around his head, in the form of a turban. I reached out and tapped him on his arm.

"I can not talk to you now. Can't you see I'm busy?" I smiled within at this petty excuse given by a supposed religious leader.

"You will listen to me now, and then that will be the last time. I'm leaving right now. I've had enough of being treated like a prisoner here and your incessant walking over me like I don't exist. It's over."

I headed back to retrieve my belongings. My eyes caught him shaking his head, his expression frowning and disbelieving. Before I could reach the back of the mosque where I kept my rolled sleeping bag and backpack, he caught up with me, walking at my side.

He raised his voice and without breaking his pace, exclaimed "I've heard enough from you so just go to your place in the back!"

I kept on walking, neither turning my head nor responding.

He kept abreast of me and finally added "You must be kidding! I don't believe you."

215

"Watch me, then!" I retorted.

I did not turn my head as I spied my sleeping bag and backpack waiting for me where I had left them. I picked up the backpack by the straps and reached down and seized the ends of the rope wrapped around the sleeping bag; then I headed for the front of the mosque. As I bolted for the door, the brothers, kneeling over their bedding and folding their clothes stood up but shifted sideways to let me pass. No one would dare block my path as I reached the leather flap covering the opening, the last obstacle to freedom; I pushed the sleeping bag through it followed by the backpack and followed after them.

"Wait!" screamed Hanify, as his torso and head protruded from the opening. "You must stay here as I am responsible for your safety."

I turned my body as my legs continued to distance me from the mosque.

"I am not concerned about your responsibility," I replied. "I refuse to submit further to your despotic rule, and I will leave when I so desire."

Turning back, I proceeded to the semi-paved road, which wound around and passed about a hundred yards within the front of the mosque.

I was walking quickly along the road when I heard Karim call out; I looked back and saw a line of brothers extending from the mosque all the way to the road I was following. Karim was in the lead as he slowly jogged about twenty yards behind me. Then came Oman, Izneh, Habib and two other brothers whose names I did not know. Following them was Hanify and behind him Haddad, the bearded one hobbled, using a walking stick to propel his body forward.

Karim pleaded, "Muhammad, please slow down; I'm going with you. You need me to help you get through this country. Without me, you shall surely perish."

I stopped; Karim was the only one who had truly befriended me and his soft words reminded me I had already forgiven him for shunning me. He certainly had taken great risks to help me, and for a time, he was the only brother who refused to ignore me; I could not ignore him now. He caught up to me and we hugged each other.

"Welcome, Karim, and thanks," I was relieved to have him with me. He nodded and we both started briskly walking down the road, leaving the group with their mouths open. The pause had allowed Hanify and the bearded one to get within speaking distance.

"Wait, Muhammad. Okay, okay—hold on just a second and you can go if that's what you want." Hanify was desperate.

We stopped in the middle of the road. I finally turned around and saw Hanify jogging behind the others, the bearded one hobbling behind him.

Hanify turned to the bearded one, who had completely ignored me as I rampaged in the mosque. Perhaps he was afraid that Satan would grab him if he happened to glance into my Medusa's raging eyes. He and Hanify, pointing at each other aggressively, seemed to be loudly chastising one another as they frantically discussed my impending departure while I scanned the distant, barren hills, an oasis compared to living in the mosque. All progress had stopped, pending the outcome of this conversation. Fear returned and raced through me again as I desperately fought to free myself from the jaws of this draining parasite.

"Muhammad," Hanify said in a placating tone, moving past the group, "you cannot leave the group. If you were to travel through this country, you may be attacked by the villagers, after what happened last night. They could kill you. Also, you do not know how to survive in these dry, arid plains; you would die before you reached the train station, which is far away. We remain responsible for you—it would be in your interests to stay with us until we reach the mission in Casablanca. Then you will be. . .free."

I gritted my teeth as I tried to stay cool. Finally, I growled, "I don't wish to be part of this group any longer. I've got to get out of here! I WILL LEAVE NOW!"

I tried to sound like an enraged beast, but I feared that I sounded more like a frightened child. I was concerned they would hold me by force. I hoped that enough fierceness shot through my voice would deter the brothers from attempting to violently force me to yield to their wishes. I was resolved to challenge them, to hold my ground firmly.

I turned and started walking with solid steps, with Karim next to me.

Not able to ignore the Arabian shoes pounding the pavement behind me, I turned to behold Hanify; his turban had flown off and he was frothing at the mouth. "Alright, Muhammad; you win," Hanify cried desperately. "You tell us what you want to do and we'll follow you. You are the leader now." Hanify looked sheepishly at the bearded one, a few steps behind him, who nodded and looked at me; his beard seemed scraggly and shorter than when I had first met him.

"The choice is yours—either we return to Boumalne, where we will stay for another four or five days, or we take a bus immediately from Boumalne to the train station in another town, where we will take the next train to Casablanca."

It was the first time I had heard Hanify's voice tremble; it almost sounded as if it came from the lowly ranks of human sounds. His tone took me completely by surprise. I stared straight ahead, looking toward the distant horizon.

I turned back. "Hanify," I growled sternly, "I accept on the condition that we leave immediately."

Those were the last words I would speak for the next two days.

Chapter XXXII

The Inquisition Room

I was pleased with myself that after weeks of submissively following Hanify, I had held my ground; I was determined not to let him trick me into staying longer than necessary in this lost corner of the world, a target for all the hatred that ignorance could muster.

It took us one hour to return to town along the same road I had taken alone earlier. As we arrived in Boumalne, it felt as if we were being watched: I was afraid the townspeople in the village we had just left would attack me at the bus station for supposedly betraying Islamic secrets to infidels, to Jews. While Hanify made arrangements for the train transportation to take us back to Casablanca, the rest of us went to the mosque in the center of town.

I sat in my usual place in back of the mosque, next to the sleeping bags. No one came near me except for Oman, who had been accustomed to visiting me before mass to remind me to pray. I completely ignored him and everyone else as I continued to meditate with my back next to the wall and my head inclined toward the mat. I even refused to join the line to pray. No one dared talk to me as, eyes closed, I would point from time to time my obstinate face toward the ceiling in silent meditation and then slowly lower them to their place on the mat.

I must have been sitting there for hours when Hanify came to me and proudly announced that all the arrangements were completed and I should pack, that we would be taking a bus to the train station in fifteen minutes. In spite of my joy upon hearing the news, I had to move slowly as my body creaked and was stiff for having sat in the same position for so long. I grabbed my sleeping bag and gingerly bent down to place my arms through the backpack straps.

The bus met us in front of the mosque and whisked us to the train station, which was exploding with people running in all directions. Children cried after their mothers while lines of tables were occupied with turbaned mint tea drinkers. We remained organized as we walked through the station two-by-two, one pair closely following the other.

We did not have to wait long before boarding our train to Casablanca. Although we sat two to a seat, they were wide enough to allow me to place my sleeping bag next to me, a welcome distance between me and the rest of the world. I leaned my head on the window of the train and watched the plains of yesteryear slip by; all the events of the last few weeks had been engraved permanently in my mind. The desert air entering through a partially opened window gently fluttered at my cheek. I longed for Casablanca on one hand, yet already missed even the dankness permeating the air in the silence of the village mosque, during my meditations after morning prayer.

Hours and hours passed in a blur. Leaning up against the window, my mind suddenly stilled as my spirit rose above me, following the train as it wound it's way toward Darbida. It seemed as though we had just left Boumalne when a loud rustling of bodies standing up and moving woke me from a deep reverie. I recognized the dark streets of Casablanca. The train cruised slowly into its stall at the station; as the brakes of the train brought it to a deafening halt, I looked forward to quickly ridding myself of this group of spiritual jailers.

Walking down the main street searching for a bus to take us to the mission, I realized suddenly I was surrounded by a sea of white: the brothers in their spotless white robes, led by Hanify. I cynically interpreted this maneuver as a rather obvious way of discouraging me from any notions of escaping into the crowds. At that moment, standing at the corner waiting for the light to change, a bizarre synchronicity of actions occurred—as I turned my head to one side, Hanify turned his head towards me. His eyes gleamed as the light changed and he led us across the street to the bus stop on the corner. His expression showed confidence; I knew then he was intent upon my return to the mission, the mosque in Casablanca where he probably would expose me to the master of masters.

I was not surprised he would renege on his promise that upon our arrival, I would be free. I made no attempts to break through the wall of brothers. It felt as if I was being drawn back to Masjid Nord by an irresistible force, mixed with the profound need to face the master in order to test my own newly found spirituality which, I thought, had evolved since I left the mission. I truly believed that this new connection with God would give me strength to resist all the master's powers of persuasion and brainwashing techniques. I did not expect, however, that this would be an ultimate test as well as a fight for my life.

We boarded the municipal bus and despite the crowd, managed to stay together, or I should add that Hanify orchestrated a tight formation, surrounding me as we boarded the bus.

The downtown buildings receded into the past as we approached the outskirts of Casablanca, passing dry fields, some strewn with the garbage flung by passersby, and the occasional wooden house surrounded by the anarchic spread of a high tangle of weeds. Turning the corner, I saw the unforgettable minaret looming before us, behind the huge mosque, surrounded by a high, metallic wall. My weak and trembling body was subdued as we neared the mosque—it seemed as though I had endured the excruciating pain of a lifetime and now there would be an accounting at Masjid Nord, the mission.

We arrived at the "Grande Mosquée" at around noon. The director, Mowi, the master, Hassan, and the resident brothers, the band of white turbans, were off traveling somewhere, but were to arrive later that evening. We all went inside and up the steps, cluttered with the familiar line of sandals waiting outside for worshippers praying inside. The air was calm, as if a ferocious storm had recently blown over.

The director, the master and the resident monks had still not returned when we decided to bed down for the night. I was to sleep alone in the Qur'anic school, a building adjacent to the Grand Mosquée, but within the walls of the sprawling complex, while Hanify and the other travelers slept in the main mosque. It was clear that Hanify had orchestrated everything so that I would feel set apart from the rest. The desert loneliness and the remembrance of the padded cells that had served as my confined quarters in the mosques sifted through my dreams that night. I longed to be with the residents of the mission, with whom I had passed a joyous week before the voyage, learning Arabic and studying prayers in the *Qur'an*.

The master and the director of the mosque had, in fact, sent me to travel with this group in order to be surrounded by the faithful followers of Islam in the country—namely Hanify, and the bearded one. They, I was told, had many conversions to their credit, including an Englishman who, a year ago, after spending time with the two, fervently embraced Islam as the only true religion. I was to meet him later.

The next day, the monks were summoned by the master to discuss what had happened during our trip. I could do nothing to stop the controversy, or rather the scandal, spreading among the various circles in the mosque. I was either condemned as a Jewish spy or defended as an innocent, curious hard-headed westerner looking for the true religion. I could not believe that the mission would consider the validity of the claims that were baseless, but the master and the director were obviously under the persuasive influence of Hanify, who was certainly putting on a "dog and pony show" of the first order.

When the interrogation began, I was certain that the bogus charges would be quickly dropped and ridiculed; but I had not counted on the close relationship between Hanify, the master and the director of the mosque. The inquisition would not go away—it was, moreover, just beginning.

The master and the director set up a kind of inquisitorial panel, which would engage in an investigation and then determine whether the allegations were true. Hanify, of course, was like the prosecutor and, I assumed, would be the self-appointed executioner if I was condemned by the panel. He and the bearded one, along with some of the brothers, viciously denounced me as a traitor and testified to my rebellious, even scandalous, behavior during the voyage. They concluded I was a Jewish spy set on destroying the good relations between the communities and them, in order to stop the advances made in taking Islam to the people and the renewal of interest in Islam. It seemed they were mostly interested in finding some justification for their failure to convert me.

Shean and Ali, my two friends, defended me—especially Shean—who had been very close to me before I left to travel with the prayer group. While a discussion was taking place in the prayer room with the monks, the master and the director, Shean and Ali led me by the hand to a small room next to the mosque for the purpose of interrogating me. The room was Ali's office, where he prepared his lessons and graded papers, etc. The walls were lined with artwork done by students, with an occasional phrase written in Arabic, the yellowed edges testifying to their longevity.

As the door closed behind us, we sat on soft cushions in a circle and reminisced about the times we had enjoyed before I left. Habib served hot mint tea and we spent the rest of the afternoon drinking tea and talking, laughing about the ridiculous allegations against me.

Shean, who had draped his head with a shiny green silk hood, motioned me to come closer—he had something important to tell me: "Hanify condemned you for voicing the name of Gandhi in a village mosque. Muhammad, Ali and I are in favor of peaceful solutions to the world's problems, not like some brothers who are constantly alluding to Jihad[20],

---

[20] Jihad is defined literally "all efforts to achieve a particular goal." Contrary to what most people think, including some brothers of Masjid Nord to whom Shean refers, Jihad does not necessarily mean a

fantasizing that someday we will fight next to each other as we proudly ride our tall, statuesque Arabian horses."

He smiled and continued, saying Hanify and his followers believed it was advocated in the *Qur'an* and by the prophet, Muhammad, that it is the obligation of all true Moslems to force infidels to convert to Islam, even with violence. But the *Qur'an* clearly states that there will be no forcing or imposition of religion on another.

"I don't believe that violence is necessary to achieve political or religious goals," Shean stated.

I interrupted, "I agree. Look at all the accomplishments of Gandhi, including forcing the British to withdraw from India, while practicing nonviolence. He is my role model."

Shean and Ali smiled. Ali brought the hot, colored glass to his lips, sipped his tea and put it down, contentedly. Shean was pensive for a minute and then, pushing aside a part of the hood that was draped over his left eye, said, "For example, we have a history of practicing nonviolence to obtain important political results, even in the face of attacks. A long time ago, the Spanish had seized important portions of the Sahara desert and created an immense colony. That had effectively broken off a part of Moroccan territory traditionally part of this nation. King Feu SM Hassan II, following the spirit of his father, SM Muhammad V, desired to preserve the integrity of his country and reunite the parts annexed by Spain."

He continued, "To do so, the King focused on using peaceful means, engaging in a true dialogue to end the conflict. First, on October 16th, 1975 the International Court of Justice rendered a decision, giving Morocco legal rights to the disputed land. In November 1975, he called all Moroccans to liberate the portions of the Sahara claimed by our country, within the parameters noted in the decision. On November 6th, we all gathered in southern Morocco, all 300,000 of us, armed only with the holy *Qur'an*, our faith and the Moroccan flag. A large group of Moroccans of all ages volunteered to march across the Sahara in order to claim the part unjustly seized by the Spanish government. When we returned, we were treated like heroes, since we had braved a month or two of the cruel desert in order to reclaim territory that belonged to us. Not a drop of blood was spilled as we marched for kilometers and kilometers, without much food and water. I was there, Muhammad—it was incredible!"

As he spoke, tears glistened at the corners of his eyes. Ali just nodded and let Shean do the talking, "That, Muhammad, was called the 'Green March.'" The tears really began to flow as Shean reached out and held my hand. "And you know, Muhammad, Spain left the region in 1976, giving up two-thirds of the colony in the north to Morocco and the other third to Mauritania. So, I understand when you talk about Gandhi and non-violence."

I was fascinated to hear about this great victory of the Moroccan people, especially since it was gained without bloodshed. I asked Shean to tell me more.

"Sure, Muhammad, but first, we need to explain what happened. Several intense meetings took place in the mosque, especially this morning. That was why you slept in the school last night."

---

military struggle. Some pious Muslims believe, as al-Ghazali, that "It's pity that pleases God, not blood and guts...One can be a Jihad warrior without leaving his home" (Roger Caratini, Hocine Raïs, *Presses du Châtelet*, Initiation à l'Islam, 2003, p. 196-197, translated from French by the author).

He assured me that he and Ali had successfully defended me, however, they wanted to hear my version of the story about what happened during the voyage. Ali nodded as he sipped his tea.

I anticipated feeling pain and depression upon recounting the story of the voyage and my experiences with Hanify and the brothers; in addition, I felt a strong aversion towards them. But my friends and benefactors were so sincere, sitting on the soft cushions laid out on the Persian rugs, looking into my eyes with brotherly love and affection. I told them my version of our travels and how I was treated in the village mosques. They both empathized and sided with me; they believed that the overly harsh treatment of me was uncalled for. Our renewed friendship and their compassion for my suffering gave me strength and the confidence that I had followed the right path.

Our conversation had also covered the Hadith of Muhammad and the beautifully simple life set forth by the prophet—a life of tolerance, humility and love. Our little talk moved me so much that it inspired a very mysterious change in me that afternoon: in spite of the voyage and the tempestuous return, I felt closer to Islam and especially Muhammad, the prophet.

Ali excused himself and returned to his teaching duties and Shean had to return to his job downtown. We all hugged and wished each other well, in the name of Allah.

After our discussion, I walked through the passages of the mission on the way to the main prayer area, where the discussion about me had taken place that morning. Not a soul lurked there. I took off my sandals and walked over the mats neatly lined up in several rows, this time, at the front of the mosque. I crossed my legs in a semi-lotus position, watching the birds flying through one door and out the other. Other birds sailed in and out of the small windows overhead, as high as the rafters; perhaps their flight would lead them to heaven some day. I drifted into a light sleep but was awakened when I heard bare feet on the mats.

I opened my eyes and Hassan, the master, was sitting directly in front of me, his long black beard flowing, his warm, dark eyes conveying welcome. He was the master, the original master, who had carefully guided me through the steps to becoming a true Moslem. A brown tinge circled his eyes, contrasting with the dazzling, white turban he had carefully placed on his head.

In broken French, he asked me what had happened during the voyage. I tried to disguise my frown, to no avail. He could see right through my attempts to remain neutral, emotionally in check. Without waiting for a response, he said he was sorry I was disturbed and unhappy. Before we could discuss any of the details, I was relieved to be interrupted by two brothers in robes who sat beside us—that is, until I noticed the intruders were Hanify, the infamous leader of the traveling prayer group, and Oman, his disciple— whose eyes were dutifully fixed on their master.

We were sitting in a circle, with the master in charge; I watched Hanify out of the corner of my eye as he sought for a neutral place on which to focus his eyes. I fixed my gaze on the mats in front of me for fear of engaging the eyes of my opponent. I tired quickly of this game and sought the help of all the celestial powers to help me forgive Hanify, help me look at him...something to break the silence between us, break the ice.

The master, after having heard Hanify's side and the pleadings of Shean and Ali, was convinced we could become brothers again, that he could mediate our differences in order to lead us back on the same path towards the truth. My eyes met Hanify's—the cold sternness had gone; they reflected the soft look of atonement, while I imagined mine reflected a forgiveness I truly felt. He smiled the same welcoming smile that had warmed his face during our first meeting.

The strangest feeling of release and transcendence filled my mind and shook my body, resulting in a burst of tears that fell on the mat below. A bizarre mixture of ecstasy and the feeling of submission to forces far beyond my capacity to resist invaded my very soul.

The next thing that happened was unanticipated, probably influenced by my earlier discussions with Shean and Ali: I involuntarily gave voice to a stream of consciousness; as tears streamed from my eyes, I expressed fervently that I had finally come to believe that Muhammad was the last prophet, that I had been truly converted to Islam and had no further questions regarding the doctrines, nor further doubts as to my allegiance to Allah and teachings of the holy *Qur'an*.

Then we all got up and embraced; Hanify said a few words to the master and left through the side door, followed by his cohort. Hassan hugged me again and praised me for finally becoming a member of Allah's chosen people. I walked to the back of the prayer room and sat in my usual place.

That evening, for the first time in a long while, I was invited to eat dinner with the group, the traveling brothers and Hanify, who had been eating and sleeping together and ignoring me, since arriving in Casablanca. The bearded one was not present. I had been eating dinner and sleeping alone in the school next to the mosque. While we sat on hand-woven mats and dipped pieces of bread in the communal basin filled with chunks of lamb and potatoes marinated in fat, I could not help thinking that I was being compensated for behaving as expected, in robot-like conformation with the rules of Islam as interpreted by this sect, without questioning as I had before. The pieces of lamb were delicious, but a bitter taste remained in my mouth as I ate in silence, wondering if I had reached a stage of total surrender. Had I "sold out" my true being—my individual identity—for a position on the mat next to the brothers, so I could smile, eat, pray and sleep as one of the group?

During the feast, the director of the mosque, Mowi, told us more stories about his life as a mercenary soldier during the wars in Asia. He smiled, his silver teeth flashing; the gray and black hairs of his curly beard waving, an interweaving of the ages, the triumphs and despair. His eyes fixed on mine, he was "witnessing" or explaining how he, another lost soul, had found Islam.

An aura of atonement reigned that evening; I singled out every member of the traveling group that night and asked forgiveness for my behavior during the voyage. Some of them, including the notorious Hanify, offered me gifts such as clean, white turbans, djellabahs and books; they were gifts of appeasement. Hanify, in turn, asked for my forgiveness of him for his harshness towards me and his ill-intentioned accusations of me during the voyage.

The happy glow in the mosque was like the calm before the tempest.

Chapter XXXIII

Agadir

The next morning after morning prayer, Oman tapped me on the shoulder and waved me to the back of the mosque where the master was waiting.

The master announced, as I sat down across from him on the mat, "I want to send you to Agadir for two days with Oman, where you will meet an Englishman who has also lived here as a monk, who has embraced Islam and is even more devout than us. Your ticket was already paid for; just tell us if you want to visit him and when you are prepared to leave."

I thought awhile and then gave him my response: "If it will help me understand Islam, I will do it. I'll be ready tomorrow."

The next morning after morning prayer, Oman and I took the bus to Agadir. Even though we sat next to each other, we did not speak much as there was still tension between us from our previous voyage. I read from a French translation of the *Qur'an* while Oman slept.

We arrived in Agadir after the noon prayer session. Oman led me down a street lined with modern, white apartment buildings. Oman turned into a more modest district, with older buildings scarred by the constant winds from the Atlantic Ocean; there was a plethora of cafes characteristic of the area. He stopped in front of one of these buildings, with the adobe crumbling down the sides.

Oman pressed a series of buttons and the door opened. We walked up a narrow stairway to the fourth or fifth floor. He knocked on a door in the middle of the corridor; it opened, revealing a rather lean, turbaned white man with blue eyes.

"As-Salamu alaykum," he stated, in impeccable Arabic.

Oman smiled, responding, "Wa alykum as-Salamu."

Our host held his hand out and clasped Oman's hand, gently pulling him into the house as I followed. He briefly spoke with Oman, giggling and smiling; they appeared to know each other well.

He reached out his hand to me and in English, said, "Pleased to meet you, Frank. My name is Trevor."

I nodded as I followed the young man to the rooftop area where we would have mint tea. Oman spoke to him first while I sat down on the patio and crossed my legs. Trevor served the tea, with the help of an old female servant. Few words were spoken; Trevor's deep-blue eyes concentrated on the tea service, as his servant poured the hot water into the silver kettle, gripped securely in his hand. His eyes met mine and scrutinized them much as Oman had during our voyage to the arid Moroccan plains.

"I'm glad you could visit me. I see by looking in your eyes you are pure and good and are open to such a beautiful religion."

224

As the others joined me, we drank our tea; Trevor and I talked about the paths that had brought us to Morocco. Oman let us converse as he sat there, sipping his scalding-hot mint tea. Trevor explained to me, in English, that he had arrived in Morocco years before, with a guitar on his back, long hair and a beard. He was an atheist and had lived a nihilistic, rebellious lifestyle without any direction, without any goals—he was lost. He would just sit in the Ancienne Medina and compose, play and sing songs, and travel around. Then he met the master in Casablanca one day at the bus station. The master had smiled and invited him, the lost soul, to visit the mission. After the first visit, he was invited to join and, like me, became an Islamic monk. From then on, he had felt loved and wanted....and that is perhaps the key to why he embraced Islam so whole heartedly.

He had also traveled with a study group to the south of Morocco and afterwards, was hired to teach English in a high school in Agadir, where he still worked. His discourse was extraordinarily articulate and perceptive. Somehow, being an orthodox Moslem, he was still able to pray five times a day, despite his responsibilities at the school. Last year, he had gone to Mecca on a pilgrimage, with a group of fellow teachers.

His voice shook with emotion as he told me about his childhood sweetheart, who he had sent for and who stayed with him for about a month in Agadir. He said that she had begged him to return with her to England, but he said he was too entrenched in the culture, especially in the religion, and did not want to return to his country. Tears glistened in his eyes as he told me she had left him a year ago and had not returned.

Oman interrupted, telling me that we must prepare to take the bus to Rabat, the capital of Morocco, and Trevor was to prepare to go to the mosque for the sunset service (Maghrib).

When we parted, Trevor hugged me and said, "You must be patient and if you are, you will be totally enlightened and accept that Muhammad is the last prophet of God, before the end of the world. If you ever return to Agadir, you are free to stay with me."

We parted, smiling again, before I closed the door. There was something profoundly content and profoundly sad in that smile. I would never meet Trevor again.

We were running late and caught a cab to the bus station. Once in the bus, Oman led the prayers for the sunset service; we bowed our heads and mumbled the prayers together. As the bus drove through the old section of Agadir and then past a row of modern hotels in a more "soigné" district, I could not help but feel loneliness for Trevor; he was, perhaps, forever attached to Agadir, to Islam. Like the rock of Gibraltar, he was fixed, not able to move on, unable to detach from his city or religious affiliation, even to go home.

Oman nudged me with his elbow: "Muhammad, you must get some sleep, since tomorrow you will take a test to determine if you are fit to teach high school in Morocco. The master was able to obtain an interview for you tomorrow, in front of a group representing the minister of education, in Rabat, at 10:30 a.m."

I responded, bewildered, "I don't understand. I don't remember anything about a test!"

"You don't remember one day you asked the master if he could help you find a job? Well, you want to work, don't you?"

"Yes, of course. I just am surprised no one told me about it until now."

"I didn't want to burden you with it until we left Agadir. In fact, the master sent your résumé to the Minister of Education, who has agreed to give you this interview."

"What type of questions will they ask me?" I asked, dreading his response.

"The master has represented that you are a devout Moslem who wants to stay in this country. The Minister of Education favors your candidacy over the others, since you are a Moslem; the others are British and are not Moslems. The members of a committee must determine, first, that you know the main prayers repeated during a Moslem mass. If so, they will certify you to continue the procedure; they will then determine your competence after a review of your file, including your diplomas and courses you have studied. If you pass, the committee will send you a certificate of competence and hopefully a job offer".

I must have looked worried, prompting Oman to add, "But don't worry—you will probably be requested to recite the prayers that you have been reciting every day in the mosque."

We arrived in Rabat about 9 a.m. the next morning. Heading directly to a café, we drank hot tea and ate sugar cookies while I went over the phonetic versions of several prayers, namely the "Al-fatiha," the "Al falaq" and the "N-nasr," the principal prayers in the *Qur'an*.

At about 10:00 a.m., we took a cab, which let us off at the corner of a street in the suburbs. We walked about two blocks to a drab, gray building. Oman explained to me that it was a government building, as we climbed the many steps leading to a revolving door.

We entered and were quickly ushered to a bench in a corridor, in front of large, wooden double doors. Oman looked at me and mouthed "Good luck."

We had not waited long when a man, dressed in a robe and wearing a strange hat I had not seen before—it was like a turban but raised at the forehead and in the back—told us to follow him; we entered a large room. I was told to sit in the middle of the room, facing a group of about eight men dressed in white robes and wearing white turbans. Oman was told to sit in a chair in back of me. It was like being at the zoo at feeding time: my turban, robe and demeanor, most likely, were carefully scrutinized by the members of the committee, who were to determine my destiny.

The same person who had ushered us into the big room sat in the middle and spoke first—he appeared to preside over the session. He welcomed me to Morocco and, more importantly, to Islam and commended me for embracing the only true religion. Then he eased into the questioning by asking me my goals. I explained to him that I wanted to improve my knowledge of Islam; as such, I desired to stay in Morocco and teach English. He seemed satisfied with my response and made a gesture to someone next to him. An older gentleman requested me to recite the Al-Fatiha, which I did slowly and carefully, in Arabic. The members of the jury looked to each other, disbelievingly.

The presiding officer of the committee decided to authenticate my knowledge by asking me to explain, in French, what the first line of the Al-Fatiha meant. I explained the meaning behind the prayer, and the members of the jury looked at each other, again incredulous.

I was told to recite the other two prayers in Arabic and explain their meanings in French. By the time I arrived at the third prayer, I began to tire; thus, I did not dynamically recite the last prayer, "Al falaq," and faltered at explaining its meaning.

After the interview was completed, the presiding officer said a few words in Arabic to me; I nodded, without understanding what he was saying.

After we left the building, I reached over and grabbed Oman's sleeve, asking him his opinion as to my performance. He told me I had succeeded in proving my competency and was considered a Moslem by the group. Oman, his voice trembling with emotion, informed me I had passed the test and a certificate would be sent to me in the mail.

That afternoon, we took the first bus headed to Casablanca, and arrived in the early evening, just in time for evening mass (Isha). Isneh picked us up at the bus station at about 7:30 p.m.; he was waiting outside the door when we descended the steps. We went directly to an upstairs loft in the bus station where we said evening prayers before returning to the mission.

Camara, my first Moslem master, came to visit me the next day, to be a part of the celebration of my recent enlightenment. He came with a full bag of large medjool dates from the Ancienne Medina, which he gave me, as a reward for my entrance into the family of Moslems. I then offered to share the dates with the brothers who now surrounded me with warm glances, coming from eyes that not long ago had condemned and castigated me as a traitor amongst them. The brothers now allowed themselves to look at me, as Satan had been destroyed within me, this destruction of the ultimate evil indicated by my total submission to Islam—I had finally accepted their dogma.

That night we ate together—including Camara—as one happy family.

"La ilaha illa Allah, brother; I knew you could do it!" Camara exclaimed to me in a low voice, as he sat next to me popping rounds of couscous into his mouth.

I wondered what he would have thought of me if I had continued my interrogation on the main precepts of Islam. What if I had not yet been made a "believer" even after the long and arduous trek through the plains of Al Maghrib? As I munched on the last morsel of couscous, I imagined myself being tortured by the group and then thrown out of the mosque onto the cold pavement of the street outside. I wondered if I had accepted Islam because I had no more courage to fight the indoctrination. Had I become like submissive sheep, cowering before a pack of wolves? Had I given up my search to find the truth and settled for comfort over the insecurity of being on the road to discovery? I felt guilty harboring such thoughts as the brothers happily communed after dinner; but still their untempered smiles cast me into the vacuum of doubt and flung me into the bottomless pit of spiritual loneliness; a dark, foreboding cloud hung over me and prevented me from enjoying the evening. Something inside would not release me and I did not know what it was.

Chapter XXXIV

Behind the Four Walls

During the next few days, I prayed, ate and slept as my health and strength were slowly partially restored to my frail body. In proportion to my recovery, I began to understand the underpinnings of the conflicts with Hanify and the brothers.

I began to understand the truth behind their very effective methods used for indoctrinating me; I understood that my unconditional acceptance of all the precepts was due to a highly sophisticated system of brainwashing. I had been encouraged to fast during Ramadan, neither drinking nor eating until nightfall; the others were exempt from fasting. I chose to fast. This practice had left me weak and vulnerable, open to suggestion.

The words "I was victimized" kept echoing off the tall, white walls inside the mosque. I was still followed occasionally, when I left the prayer area and went to the ablutions room. But since my return, the master had more faith in me and did not follow my every move, as he had before.

Even though I outwardly could have been considered the most faithful and most conscientious Moslem in the mission as I learned more and more prayers and Arabic every day, my guts wrenched with inner turmoil. But I loathed the hypocritical smiles on the faces of the brothers, who had totally ignored me just a few days earlier. I felt I believed in the same truth as Shean and Ali—they were sincere in their unconditional love of Muhammad, the prophet, and their belief in tolerance and nonviolent reform. I could easily picture Hanify on a white, Arabian steed, beheading the infidels massing around him with the brothers, his henchmen, following him closely. In spite of the conflicts and indecision, something inside me told me to clear a path elsewhere. I did not know where or how.

It was during one of my frequent meditation sessions that I found enough strength to make a final decision. My free spirit was burdened with adherence to dogmas in which I didn't believe and the ignorance of those surrounding me; all I could see in my future was falling deeper and deeper into a widening hole, engulfing my soul.

I decided to plan my escape from the mosque. The wall was too high to attempt to scale it, and there was always a guard at the impenetrable metal door in front, who had instructions not to allow me to leave under any circumstances. He sat all day long on a stool in front of the locked door, his blue djellabah trailing down over his sandals; his beard was closely shaven, which conformed to his role of "policeman."

One time, I had asked the guard to let me out so I could quickly see my friends in the Medina. He had refused and then called the office of the director who, with the master, came immediately from the former's office. I was interrogated for a long time about my faith in Islam and why I desired to leave.

The master had said, as the director looked on, "You must not leave now, Muhammad, or you could lose your faith in Allah and would be lost. Do you understand?"

"Yes; I shall not want to leave again. I have progressed so much in my faith, I would not want to do anything to jeopardize it, after all the work you have put into my education and your patience with me."

The master smiled and we hugged; I then returned to the back of the mosque, happy to be within the protective walls of this spiritual sanctuary, to be able to discipline myself, following closely the guidelines set forth in the *Qur'an* and the Hadith. However, my need to be independent was overwhelming—I dreamed of walking down the streets of the Medina, breathing the air of freedom without the invisible shackles attached to my hands and feet.

I needed to keep my plans secret because I was afraid the master would interpret my intentions as a rejection of Islam, which he had warned me would oblige him to apply the most severe sanctions. Did that mean even death? Anything could happen behind the high walls of the mission when the main door was closed to the public. So I vowed to tell no one what I was thinking.

I prayed and meditated day and night, nourished by kind memories of freedom of mind and body that I once had experienced—the richness of open human relations without feeling like the sword of Damocles was hanging over my head. I had felt particularly constrained when visiting the villages with the prayer group.

My plan was to be a model monk, to follow all the rules and ask for explanations of the passages in the *Qur'an*, but not ask questions as I had before, nothing that could be interpreted as a lack of faith in Islam. I was careful to always be on time and make sure my prayers and positions assumed during mass were irreproachable. After each mass, I stayed in the mosque, as usual, and prayed, later withdrawing to the back and continuing my studies of Islam. My plan was to gain their total confidence, show them I was a true soldier of Islam. I hoped they would give me more freedom, maybe even allow me to leave the mission alone.

But no occasion to leave the mosque presented itself. When the brothers visited other mosques, I was left in the mission to pray and read the *Qur'an*. I fantasized that someday the master would take me with the others to pray with them in a different mosque in Casablanca, as we had done before we left on the voyage. I dreamed that during the mass, I would be able to excuse myself to go to the toilets, and instead of doing that, I would exit through the front door, quickly descend the steps and enter a waiting taxi. Flooring the accelerator, the driver would "burn rubber" to get me to the Ancienne Medina, where my friends could hide me.

I was becoming more anxious about leaving, my living situation feeling increasingly like a prison. It was turning into an excruciating experience, as every day I had to struggle against total indoctrination, as well as becoming used to life at the mission. I was also afraid I could not survive on the outside; perhaps I would be like the prisoner who becomes so accustomed to life inside the walls that once released, being unable to adapt to normal life, chooses to commit a serious enough crime to be condemned for life.

I was afraid and could not trust anyone. Shean, Ali and the brothers were in the south of Morocco traveling with another prayer group, so I was left alone all day in the mosque. I saw the master during prayer sessions, but he came to me less and less, as he was the teacher replacing Ali and was very busy with his young students in the school next door. Also, I think I had convinced him that I no longer needed to be under his tutelage since I had made such great progress.

I reasoned that the only way to escape was to learn the scheduled times the metal doors were opened and when the guards replaced each other. I carried my *Qur'an* with me as I strolled through the grounds around the mosque. There was a walkway about thirty feet wide between the high outside wall and the mosque, which provided me with terrain for my walks, ending in front of the gate. I always nodded to the guards.

One afternoon, after I made my daily rounds and arrived at the door, I noticed a guard who I had not met before. He smiled at me and I smiled back. I approached. He stuck his hand out and said, "Salem Walekum."

I responded, "Walekum Salem" and continued, "Brother, I haven't seen you before. My name is Muhammad Abdelazis."

"My name is Brahim; this is my first day. I'm replacing one of the guards who is on vacation." He added, somewhat bitterly, "It's nice that some of us can afford that. I haven't taken one for a long time. By the way, where are you from?"

By that question, I gleaned that he had not been warned about me yet, so maybe he would not report our conversation to the master. Anyway, I had to take a chance.

"I'm American, but before I came to Morocco, I had been studying in Paris." His eyes sparkled. Abruptly, his eyebrows rose ever so slightly to warn me that someone was approaching. I changed the conversation.

"I hope you enjoy…" I was interrupted by the master, who grasped my arm and pulled me toward him.

"You seem to be happy here. Have you any questions about the text?" His eyes looked into mine, trying to determine the intention of my conversation with the guard.

"Oh yes, master; I feel I am making progress every day," I replied.

He led me into the prayer room where the director was straightening the mats for the evening mass and was bent over. His head turned to one side and I could see his red, strained face as he said, "Muhammad, perhaps you could help me straighten the mats for evening service."

"Yes, with pleasure." I was relieved to detach myself from the master, for fear he would divine my thoughts. I looked back, but he had left.

After assisting the director, I returned to my walk, circling around the mosque on the path. I passed by the guard who was talking to someone else, so I did not interrupt him.

The same time the next day, I again took a walk on the path leading up to the door. I held my breath as I turned the corner and noted that the same guard was sitting on the stool in front of the door, looking off into space.

I approached cautiously, this time looking in all directions for any sign of the master, who had followed me last night as I walked around the path during my nightly constitutional. As I drew within about ten feet of him, the sound of my footfalls finally attracted his attention. He looked up, his placid expression quickly changing to a wide smile.

To his "Salem Walekum," I responded, "Walekum Salem. I see you're still here preventing the demons from entering and the saints from leaving."

He giggled, "It does seem a little ridiculous for a guard to be at this door. I noticed that when you continued your walk yesterday after our conversation, Hassan was following you."

I do not know what prompted me, but I thought I should make a move; the guard did not appear to be like a "faithful dog" as the others were, and even he had questioned the strict guarding of the door. I still was not sure if he clearly understood that the brothers, notably me, could not leave the building without permission. I was amazed to think that he seemed to read my mind as he looked at me almost sympathetically, with wide, dark eyes, from under his golden turban. I made my move.

"I thought about what you told me yesterday, and I wish that you could go on vacation like the other guards. Here; I have a little money. Please take it since I would rather make you happy than hold it in my pocket. Besides, I don't need it." I was hoping he would believe me since all Americans were considered rich by most of the people I had met, in Europe and in Africa.

He did not say anything; he turned his head as his eyes scanned the door to the mosque in back of me. I interpreted that as an acceptance.

I reached in my pocket and pulled out a fist full of dirhams, in bills, which represented almost all the money I had in my possession. I turned my head enough to see the door to the mosque and the path around it.

"Please take them—I am happy to help."

"Are you sure you don't need the money?"

I reached toward his palm, enveloping it with my hand, as I shook his hand. He casually placed the bills in his pocket.

"Be happy. I should go now."

I left as his eyes scanned the path in back of me. My heart palpitated violently, afraid that the master had witnessed the entire scene. I moved my head just enough to scan the area behind me, only to see the wind gently move the green leaves of the bushes planted next to the mosque and the dust swirling in the air—but no master. I sighed and walked up the stairs and into the mosque, without looking back.

That night I planned the next move: I would ask the guard to let me out so I could take care of some business, in view of returning before the next mass. I had fantasized a thousand times him opening the door just wide enough so I could slide out, closing it behind me. That night, for the last time, I tossed and turned, dreaming about the door opening, me slipping out and my escape to freedom. My heart stopped: the master was standing directly in front of me. He seized me with his strong hands and dragged me back behind the door, which slammed with a deafening, metallic clank. I awoke, completely soaked with sweat, trembling.

I readied myself to act on my plan. I sat in the back of the mosque until everyone had left, leaving me alone. I got up slowly, and walked steadily to the front of the mosque. After confirming that I was the only one within, I opened the side door and slid out onto the path that would lead me to the central door; if the guard cooperated, I would finally be free. As I slowly ambled around the corner, I noted that Brahim was not there. Adam, the guard who had gone on vacation, was back. That meant the substitute guard would not return. Oh, loathsome moment of anguish and torment! I swallowed the low wail that threatened to emerge and quickly returned to the mosque, to take my position in the back. . .defeated. I succumbed to the reality that I would perhaps never escape this ungodly confinement, or die trying.

The days passed, one similar to the next. Still, no sign of Shean, Ali or the brothers. I began to focus more on speaking Arabic, which occupied my time; I would spend my afternoons with the janitor, who I had recently met, and who was glad to share his knowledge of the language.

One afternoon after a lesson with my tutor, I was walking around the mosque as I had done many times, and glanced at the front door, which was slightly ajar. . .but the guard was sitting next to it on the omnipresent stool.

The profile was similar to one I had seen before; he was probably one of the usual guards who would never let me even get close to the door, open or closed. As I neared, the guard turned his head and I immediately recognized my ticket out of my prison. He smiled...I approached.

"Brahim"

"Salem Walekum." He responded.

"Walekum Salem."

Silence; neither he nor I could speak.

I declared, "Well, I thought I would never see you again; what happened?"

"You probably saw Adam had returned, so that was the end of it. But he is sick so I was called in for today to replace him."

I knew this could be my last chance—it was time to act.

"Brahim, my friend, I need to ask you a favor."

He smiled; it was almost obvious that he already anticipated my question.

He nodded, "So, you want to take a turn around the neighborhood?"

I had created an entire story about the necessity to return to the Medina for an hour to take care of important business, but I would return for the next mass, so my presence wouldn't be missed.

"I suppose you'll be back for the next mass." He laughed and with it my hopes plummeted. He knew my plans; there was nothing to add and everything was for naught. I stood, petrified, but pushing myself, I started to recite the lines I had so carefully rehearsed the last time he was doing guard duty. He waved his hand as if to say, "Cut the baloney." Smiling, he did the oddest, most unpredictable thing. He motioned me to pass through the opened door.

My muffled "thank you" was drowned out by his last parting statement of "See you at mass at 5:00."

I started to step through the open door when he violently clanged it shut. The noise scared me and I stepped back a few steps; it was the like the loud clanking of a tomb door. I was doomed.

"You must think I'm an idiot that I would actually believe you would be back. I should tell the master."

I shuddered and started to walk away. As I walked past what I thought was a closed door, I saw a crack of daylight, which meant only one thing. My jittery nerves almost caused my legs to buckle; I returned to the bench where Brahmin sat, grinning at my discomfort.

"Please don't tell the master; he would be very severe with me."

"Oh, for sure he would be! He would probably lock you up in an unused classroom and feed you bread and water until you recanted your sins."

I stood there, dumbfounded, unable to move, unable to speak. My body shook; I thought that my health would not survive another test—I would not survive.

Then an idea came to me and I figured I now had nothing to lose.

"Brahim, look; I have money in my backpack that's locked up in the room next to you. Could you hand it to me? I'll wait for you right here. It will only take you one minute to find it."

He looked at me and grinned, his silver teeth flashing in the bright sun. I thought that a healthy person would not be as affected as I was; but the sun roasted my skin to my bones, leaving little passage for the blood to flow.

"What color is it?" he asked.

"It's dark green. Anyway, you can't miss it; it's in front and it's the only backpack in the room."

"Alright, I'll do it, you're not allowed to go in there, but don't try anything. You wait there. If its not there, I feel sorry for you as I will tell the master you were trying to bribe me. You'll be severely punished. You'll be a walking dead man," Brahim warned.

"Of course it's there; I would not risk the wrath of the master for something so foolish. What can I do? I can't leave here," I responded.

He was not stupid; he suspected something. He must have seen my eyes glance back to the door. He got off the stool and walked toward the door, but for some reason stopped, turned around and headed toward the locked storage room next to the bench. I crouched down, my djellabah covering the ground around me, to show him I would stay put until he returned.

He unlocked the heavy, rusted padlock, hung it on one of the hooks, and entered.

I heard him rummaging through the backpack, probably looking for the money.

I stood up and silently lifted my sandals, walking ever so stealthily toward the door. It was indeed unlocked. The violence of his slamming it must have knocked it back, preventing it from closing. The light showing through gave me a glimpse of freedom. I had no idea if I even had the strength to run at all, my legs ached so. Reaching out, I clasped my hand over the edge of the door, which moved slightly. I opened it wider ever so slowly and slipped through. My djellabah caught on something and I thought wildly that I could take it off and run without it. My body was on the outside but my djellabah was caught on the inside; I reached around and with fingers trembling somehow pried it loose.

I kicked off my sandals and ran and ran, breathing deeply as I forced air into my lungs and closing to my ears to the screams and footsteps behind me.

Chapter XXXV

Run to Blue

The sound of stampeding feet behind me played over and over in my mind as I ran to freedom, even after I could no longer hear the clamor behind me.

My lungs screamed for air, my body craved any kind of liquid. I could have urinated in my hands and drunk it, but I had no time to even do that, as I dodged in and out of alleys and ran through abandoned fields, stepping on broken glass; fortunately, I later discovered I had only sustained small cuts. I imagined I could fly like the buzzard overhead—maybe he was waiting, waiting—and then I imagined I was pure spirit and had no physical body as I flew over the dry turf approaching the sidewalks that would eventually lead me to the inner city of Casablanca.

At one point, I felt the hammering of my heart; forced to continue, I thought I would surely die, that my heart would stop beating and my lungs stop functioning. But at least I would die a free man.

I was paranoid that the master would try to find me while driving one of the automobiles used by the mission, and with the help of the brothers, take me back to the mission, by force. Even though I had gained some weight and my nose had stopped running, I was still very weak from constant diarrhea. Just in case, I stayed in the back alleys and streets as I advanced toward the center of the Medina, towards the family who I hoped would take me in and shield me from the master and the mission. . .and let me be free.

I waded through waist-high dry grass, climbed over hills, across abandoned fields, avoiding the main roads. I sloshed through the mud at the bottom of dried-up canals bordering the fields and roads, only surfacing to cross the main road.

My body was so exhausted it almost didn't register I had entered the Ancienne Medina and was in the center of town. Now I could hide in the crowds of people and the myriad souks lining the dirt streets. I avoided the places where Camara did his shopping and avoided walking by any mosques, for fear of running into him or one of the brothers.

After what seemed more than an eternity, I finally arrived at the familiar door of Azedine's home. My first knock must have been too faint, for no one answered. I finally ended up pounding on the door; one of the daughters answered. The mother was behind her— they both smilingly lead me hobbling into the living room and motioned me to sit down.

I slumped over, exhausted; it seemed as if I had been away for years instead of weeks. My feet were scratched and bloody, but I was too drained to feel pain. The mother instructed her daughter to bring me a cushion for my head. As I rolled over on my side, I felt a faint, warm dribble of something running down my feet and onto the floor. I looked down towards my feet and so a small puddle of blood beneath them. Soon, blissful sleep overtook me.

I awoke; the Morning Prayer was being announced by a myriad of muezzins in the neighborhood, each competing with the others to attract as many attendees as possible. The house was quiet. I stood up, reflexively reached for my djellabah and envisaged doing my ablutions in the bathroom before mass. The pain in my feet was unbearable and I had to sit down. A gauze material was wrapped around them and fastened with some type of tape.

My bones creaked as I made a monumental stretch of my arms; extended as far as they could go, the mother came into the living room. She said in her sweet voice, "Kul," (eat) placing her fingers in her mouth to indicate the food was ready.

Those words and the acute pain in my feet helped to break the spell, and instead of walking to the mosque, I walked to the familiar, round kitchen table, where the familiar glass of hot coffee and milk were waiting for me. I sat down to my breakfast which I devoured rather quickly, especially the homemade bread. The mother ate her bread and drank her coffee in silence, smiling at me with her brown, welcoming eyes. I returned her smile, my eyes telling her that I had returned. She continued to smile; no words were necessary.

The next few days were spent peacefully sleeping, reading, praying and sharing family meals...and healing. The warm, family atmosphere helped me through a period of detoxification or perhaps more like deprogramming, after a month and a half of brainwashing.

My serenity was only interrupted by daily visits by a monk from the mission who asked the mother if he could speak to me. After he left, she would come into the living room and say, "One person came from the mission asking for you. I told them you were not here."

"Thank you, but you can tell them the truth which is I am unavailable to receive visitors; that would be more honest."

She would laugh, knowing full well that a "white lie" in some circumstances is perfectly justified. In any case, I feared retribution by the master, who was using the brothers to get to me, since my escape from the mission could be considered as a rejection of Islam. And, even though it was difficult to imagine that such a saintly person could harm me, he had warned me that under Islamic law, he could persecute me and even kill me for such an offense. In any case, there was enough doubt or even paranoia in my mind that told me to keep away from him and his devotees.

It took about a week for some of my strength to be restored and my feet to be healed. One day, another brother came to the door which was opened by the mother.

Coming into the living room, she announced, "You had another visit from the mission today, and I told him you were not available."

"I wish they would leave me alone," I snapped.

I was still under the heavy influence of the mission and that day, I was particularly weighed down with intense guilt over having abandoned the master and the brothers—especially Shean and Ali—after all they had done to enlighten me. My detoxification period was proving to be more anguished and challenging than I had originally thought.

One morning, I awoke, having dreamt of some of the happy moments I had had at the mission, praying and sharing thoughts with Shean, and laughing. I was convinced I should return immediately to the Masjid Nord and never leave again. The mother and daughters had left the apartment to shop in the open-air market. As I prepared my things in the living room, I realized that I had left my backpack and sleeping bag at the mission, and for that reason I should return. Before leaving the house, I repeatedly walked in circles, through the round kitchen, bedrooms and the living room, like a caged lion. I finally settled for a walk in the park, so I could pray on the park bench without any disturbances. After a long meditation session, my desire to return to the mission still smoldered within me, tempered, however, by the fear that I would still be punished by the master for abandoning him, for abandoning the pure and enlightened path of truth. I feared that behind the high walls of the mission, he was capable of doing anything, and could do what he pleased in that protected sanctuary. After two hours of mental struggling and appeals to the cosmic, universal being, I calmed down and returned to the family.

I was greeted by the mother, who informed me "Another visitor dressed in a spotless white djellabah left you a message; I think it's a telegram."

She handed me the message: it was written by an employee of the Moroccan Ministry of Education. It said I had been accepted as an English instructor in a high school (Ibn Souliman Roudani) in the small town of Taroudant in southern Morocco. I had applied for the job while living in the mission; the master had favored the idea of teaching English in an area where the Moslems were even more devoted, undoubtedly so that the indoctrination process could continue unbridled and with even more intensity.

Azedine and his father tried to convince me to stay in Casablanca, pointing out that the mission had found yet another way to control me. By sending me to a small town, they argued, I would be closely observed and my freedom would be restricted, as it had been when I lived in the mission.

I thanked them for their concern, but if was to stay in Morocco, I needed a job; I was almost completely broke. They countered, saying I could find work in Casablanca; the father, in particular, committed himself to finding me a job. In the meantime, I would be dependent on the family to lodge and feed me.

In spite of their warnings, I prepared for my voyage to the south of Morocco. The telegram laid out the procedures to be followed before the appointment would be rendered official: I was supposed to fill out certain documents subsequently delivered by another brother from the mission, obtain an official translation of my American B.A. degree and identification photos. After obtaining the required translation, filling out the forms and sending the package to the Moroccan Ministry of Education, I had about a week before I was to take the bus to Taroudant.

Chapter XXXVI

Return to the Desert

Over the next few days, my role of "adopted son" intensified; I stayed a little longer than a week in order to spend more time with the family and do some thinking and praying far away from the influence of the master and the mission. We all huddled together around the tea kettle at night after dinner. The mother would prepare the mint tea and vegetable soup; she would slice off large pieces of bread and hand them to the father, the children and myself. As I sat, waiting for everyone to be served, the mother would turn to me and say, "Kul"; everybody would echo, "Kul" and then dig their spoons into the sumptuous soup.

During this period, the father, concerned that I was still under the influence of the master, deemed it appropriate that he play an active part in deprogramming me. Hence, during the meals, as we were surrounded by the love of the family, the father would talk about the evil monks in the Masjid Nord; he said they were teaching and following a distorted view of Islam. He did not hide his contempt for them, viewed their interpretation of Islam as a fanatical aberration. He asked me to tell him the highlights of my trip to the arid plains of Morocco. As I told him how I was confined to the mosque and described the scandal with the villagers, he was so shocked; he dropped his soup spoon, spilling its contents on the table. No one spoke, wondering what had moved the father so deeply.

Then he smiled his toothless smile, shaking his head in disgust. I told him about the job offer down south; he congratulated me but shook his head again. He expressed to me that he was not duped, that the master was trying a new tactic to bring me back under his control in order to continue the indoctrination process. This could not be accomplished unless I was separated from my adopted family in the Medina—the family that loved me. Tears formed in my tired eyes and trickled down my face. We did not talk for the rest of the meal, but the silence spoke for us.

My Moroccan father worked twelve hours a day, six days a week. His $200-a-month earnings fed and housed his wife and children, in spite of the cost of living, which rivaled that of any major European city. He was poor but spiritually rich. He encouraged me to learn about Islam, but never by force. While I was doing so, he offered me food and shelter for as long as I wanted to be a part of his family. He was so very kind!! I remember how outraged he was to find out I had sold my cassette recorder to pay for my voyage. He even offered me money if I needed it; I would always refuse it and offer him money but he would accept nothing from me since I was a guest in his house and a student of Islam. As we sat around the table after dinner, the father would prop his head up with his strong worker's hands, his eyes glistening as he peered at me. He would smile and then drift off into his thoughts, into a world in which no one dared intrude.

For the next few afternoons, I walked along the seashore and sat on the bench and meditated in a nearby park; this gave me ample time to think about my experiences and plan for my next step.

One day there was a faint knock at the door. The mother and I were alone—I was in the salon taking a nap and she was in the kitchen cleaning up. I heard her open the door and a young man's voice spoke up from the other side. I rose and went to the kitchen which was located next to the front door.

"As-Salamu alaykum. My name is Oman and I must speak to Muhammad. It's about the teaching position. . ."

The mother told him I was sleeping but she would take me a message when I awoke.

Oman responded, "Then please tell him that he must start work Thursday—in two days—which means he must take a bus, at the latest, tomorrow night. Here, this is the address and the name of the principal of the school that he must meet upon his arrival."

He gave her the message and left without saying another word. Then the mother closed the door and walked down the hall. As I appeared in the doorway of the kitchen, she withdrew in fright seeing my tall frame in the doorway.

"It's just me, don't be afraid," I told her as she nervously smiled, handing me the note and shaking her head. I took it and walked to my bed in the living room. On the other side of the piece of paper was a message which read, "We miss you, Muhammad."

I immediately dressed and walked to the bus station, where I was informed that a bus would leave Casablanca, destination Taroudant, the following evening at 9:30 p.m. I bought my ticket with the coins I had found in the pocket of my spare pants and then returned to the apartment. Following the instructions in the telegram, I phoned the principal of the high school where I would be teaching and informed him when I would arrive. He said he would pick me up at the bus stop and take me to his house for breakfast.

Since I had left my sleeping bag and backpack at the mission, the family lent me a small piece of luggage, which I packed the next day. Azedine escorted me to the bus station the following evening. We arrived about thirty minutes early and walked to the loading platform where I was to meet the bus. As we circled around a parked bus, I noticed two boys, dressed in impeccable djellabahs and wearing neatly-wrapped turbans, standing on the loading platform. Their backs were to us, so I grabbed Azedine's sleeve and withdrew behind the parked bus.

Azedine said, "I knew this would happen—they are stalking you. You must return immediately to the house and give up this idea. You will never get rid of them. They'll just make trouble for you."

We waited behind the bus for about twenty minutes. In the meantime, my bus had arrived and was parked in the spot provided for it. Azedine walked to the front of the bus and then returned, telling me that the two were still there and a line had formed in front of the door that was not yet open. I told him I wanted to claim my seat.

We walked around to the rear of the bus parked next to the one I was going to take. The two persons dressed in white turned their heads almost simultaneously; they were Oman and Izneh. They smiled and started walking towards me; seeing that I was accompanied by Azedine, they stopped a few feet in front of us.

"As-Salamu alaykum," said Oman.

"Alaykum As-Salamu," I responded, mechanically.

Oman continued, "We are sad that you do not come to see us anymore; we have tried to visit you but you are never available. Here—we have brought your things." Behind Oman was a knapsack with a carefully-rolled sleeping bag inside.

"Thank you, Oman, Izneh," I said as I reached out to take my knapsack with the sleeping bag.

At that moment, Oman grabbed my hand; looking me in the eyes, he said, "Muhammad, when you secretly left the mosque, we were sure that you had abandoned Islam, especially when you never tried to contact us. We love you and we will wait for your return."

The bus driver started the engine, and looked in the overhead mirror noting that everyone waiting in line had boarded the bus.

Azedine interrupted, "You are going to miss the bus!"

I hugged him, Oman and Izneh. "As-Salamu alaykum!" I shouted as I climbed on board. "Give my best to all at the mission, especially Shean and Ali."

They all waved as the bus charged forward, like a race horse out of the gates. Still bidding farewell was such a strange mixture of human beings: Azedine, wearing jeans and a shirt, contrasted with the bright, white appearance of the brothers from the mission.

As I drifted out of my thoughts, I looked behind to find that the lights of Casablanca were but a twinkle behind us as the bus churned along on the endless night ride to the south of Morocco.

The several occasions we came to a stop, I would get out to stretch my legs and confronted the usual roadside commerce: lamb shish kebab grilling on metal skewers, the fat dripping on the hot coals beneath; prickly pears, other fruits and vegetables for sale. The outdoor market was usually situated in front of a bar/café, which was patronized by the passengers.

After an evening break, the call to re-board came; back inside, we resumed our journey through the shadows of night, on the Moroccan plains.

At first, I reveled in the calm of the night, thinking deeply about the warm hearth and home of Azedin's family, a place that I could call home. Full of love and kindness, they had brought me into their nest, a complete stranger, and made me one of them. How they had softened the strictness I had endured at the mission, helping me to adapt to a new life "on the outside."

I reveled like a wolf howling in the moonlight, as the bus barreled ahead. I meditated on the spiritual progress I had made and the infinite strength I could feel from what I had learned through my experiences. I thought especially of traveling with the prayer group through the desolate plains, from mosque to mosque; out of sadness and hardship with them had come a renewed inner power and a renewed closeness to the supreme being (at this point, I still wasn't sure what term to use—in fact, I was not sure of the importance of assigning a name.)

Around 2:00 a.m., I tried to sleep since I was not sure if I would be teaching as soon as I arrived, which was scheduled for 9:00 in the morning. I folded my sweater and placed it in the corner of the window and then lay my head on it, trying to rest as the bus jostled on.

With the faint light of day creeping over the distant, desolate-looking hills, my eyes traced the horizon from the far left to the far right, over miles and miles of arid plains. The strange cry of a desert animal echoed in the distance. My eyes finally closed as my head rested against the cold window.

I must have dozed since the next thing I knew, someone was tapping me on the shoulder. I looked up through the blur and made out the bus driver standing next to me, peering through wide-rimmed glasses, a gold turban on top of his head.

"We have arrived in Taroudant. You need to claim your luggage at the side of the bus."

As I descended the steps, a gray object thumped on the ground ahead of me. I vaguely recognized it as my sleeping bag, which had been thrown to the ground from the top of the bus. The attendant brought my backpack and set it next to me; I lay down with my back propped up against it as the bus tore off down the road. I reached and unzipped the corner pocket and was surprised to find a small pile of dirhams; I smiled, the corners of my mouth slightly cracking as I recollected that the guard at the mission was interrupted in his search for my money by my escape from the high walls of the prison mosque. I took a deep breath as I lay there thinking that even though my flight to freedom happened only ten days before, it seemed like such a long, long time ago.

This was not a typical bus station; it was a street corner. The bus had stopped at the curb of a crude, earthen sidewalk. There I lay, waiting for the principal of the high school to pick me up. A white car, streaked with dust, drove up. As I sat up, a large, pot-bellied man opened the door, got out and came to me.

"Hello. My name is Saïd, and I hope you had a good bus ride."

He held out his plump hand and I shook it, as he pulled me toward the car. His smile was warm, partially hidden by a full mustache; his eyes were icy, beady pebbles, embedded in layers of rosy skin. The hood of his plain, brown muslin djellabah covered his round face and blanketed his body like the robe of a catholic monk.

He drove me first to his house, where we sat in the garden and were served a delicious breakfast by his two daughters. It consisted of hot café au lait and warm bread, which we dipped into dishes containing almond and sesame butter, and others filled to the brim with strawberry jelly.

During breakfast, Saïd explained to me that an American Peace Corps volunteer, who had taught English at the high school, was called back to the States after the school year had started and left them "high and dry." With a classroom full of kids, he told me they were anxious to start right away but we would have to fill out some papers.

He drove me to the school where I filled out a series of documents. The plan was that I would work for a month as an English instructor and if I liked it and they liked me, I could sign a one-year contract. After the paperwork was completed, the principal informed me I would teach three English classes that afternoon. I could barely see through my bloodshot eyes due to the almost sleepless night curled up on a small, hard seat on the "red-eye" bus, where I had been surrounded by black veils, robes and inquisitive brown eyes.

At 1:00 that day, I faced a rather boisterous group of eager students. I was shocked at the lack of discipline and their aggressiveness toward each other and toward me. I asked

240

them what their priority was, to learn spoken or written English, and also what their subjects of interest were. That was a mistake—I opened a "Pandora's box" of arguments. They, at least, had been taught to raise their hands before speaking. But when I would call on one student, all the others interrupted him to give me advice on how I should run the classroom. Then I announced that for that day, we would speak French while we established the ground rules of the class, but starting the next day, we would speak only English during class hours, until the end of the year. Bedlam erupted; several students sat shaking their heads saying they could not speak a word of English and would not understand anything.

They were also surprised to see a robed American, converted to Islam, teaching them English. My first lesson was to translate with them the "Al Fatiha," the principle prayer in the *Qur'an*, from French to English. As soon as I announced that we would do that, the students immediately calmed down. They were impressed that I had taken the trouble to learn their prayers in Arabic, which won their undivided attention.

I wrote the prayer on the board in French, and with one eager student's help, I wrote the Arabic translation under each French word. Then I called on several volunteers to come to the board and translate the French and Arab into English. The first one was a young girl with shiny black hair; her brilliant eyes contrasted with the dull lighting in the room.

"Let's see," she said, pointing to the first words. "'Bismi-l-lahi-r-rahmani-r-rahim' means 'in the name of Allah.'"

"That's pretty good," I commented as she sat down. "Let me just ask you what the word for Allah is in English."

A young man with a closely shaved head and the beginnings of a beard on his thin, pale chin spoke up: "Allah is correct, because there is no other valid word than Allah."

"Okay, that's a good start. But let me just underscore to you that the word for Allah in English is the word 'God.'"

To all the students, I had committed blasphemy. They complained, one after another, that I was imposing my culture on them, and in theirs, only Allah was God—no other was acceptable. I looked at the clock on the wall; an hour had passed. The bell rang and the students left the classroom. I sighed to myself, realizing I had successfully stalled until the end of the class, which would be calmer the next time.

I could only catch my breath before the room filled with younger students. The subject matter was the same and the new group acted in the same aggressive manner as the older students.

After three hours of successive classes, I felt a tingle in my weak legs, which began to buckle with fatigue. My voice had become a rasp as the final bell rang and the students rushed out. I was on empty, physically and emotionally. Fortunately it was Friday, allowing me to recuperate during the weekend from my long bus ride and the stress of teaching that afternoon.

After school let out that evening, the principal drove me to a studio apartment that he owned where I was to live until I could afford to rent a place. It consisted of one big room with Persian rugs, an easy chair and a bathroom. He sat in the chair and took the key off his key ring, which he gave to me. Then, he explained the route I would take every day to the cafeteria where I would have two meals a day, lunch and dinner, seven days a week. He stood up, walked to the door and opened it. Standing in the doorway, he invited me to dinner Sunday night at his house, at which time we would discuss the organization of the courses for the first semester. Then he closed the door behind him and I was alone in my own space for the first time since I had arrived in Morocco.

I took a long walk around the dusty village that evening, past long archways and fields of grazing sheep, more archways and tan adobe homes surrounded by cactus plants teeming with prickly pears. Several students greeted me along the road, their grins wide and teeth sparkling in the sunshine. I returned their smiles as much as I could, considering my lips were cracked and teeth, dust-caked. I was motivated by their enthusiasm, sobered by their dogmatism, especially when the subject of religion was invoked. I felt as if I were boiling as I waded through this hot dust bowl, a way station in the familiar, arid plains, the familiar mountains visible in the distance.

But something was wrong from the start of this adventure. As I continued walking down the dirt road, I was jarred out of my thoughts by the voice of a young man behind me. I stopped and the boy caught up to me.

"My name is Yusuf and I have been instructed by the principal to show you the staff and student cafeteria, where dinner will be served tonight. He will pick you up and take you to your apartment after dinner. Can I help you with anything else?"

"Yes, you could show me where the mosque is," I replied.

"I'm glad you asked me that; that just confirms my opinion that you are a devout Moslem and you will be an extremely valuable asset to our community."

As we walked, the powdery dirt around us blew in our faces; my throat was so dry I could barely swallow. We finally arrived at a long, tan building surrounded by tall palm trees. There were several archways leading up to a huge wooden door in the middle. Yusuf led me into a large prayer area; the prayer session had not yet begun so there were not many men gathered around. We turned left into a side corridor which led us to small rooms filled with worshippers studying their *Qur'an*s and mumbling prayers to themselves. We headed back to the corridor.

"Yusuf, what do men do in this town for recreation? I asked, bluntly. "Are there sports gymnasiums, tennis courts and all?"

Yusuf responded, his eyes showing patience and trust: "Mr. Romano, you will find your life will be complete here. You have your work, then you will pray in the mosque and then you will go home to your family."

A sigh escaped me; I hoped Yusuf had not heard it and was not insulted. He looked at me and smiled, a bit mischievously, "Maybe some day you will meet a good Moroccan woman and settle down. That would be the best thing! Right?"

I avoided the question by asking one of my own. "What are the Moroccan women like?"

"They make good wives and are the best mothers. They are faithful and take good care of the home, and that is where they stay. They only briefly leave the home to go to the market and when they do that, they wear the veil."

As I strolled through town, the brothers' motivation to help me find a job in a small town was becoming all too apparent—I would be stuck here with nothing to do but work, visit the mosque and stay home. With little to distract me, I would be more likely to become an extremely devout orthodox Moslem.

Yusuf led me to the cafeteria for visiting teachers and students who lived in the dormitories. He left me at the entrance and said, "I am sorry you can't come over for dinner; we have guests tonight. You should walk to the Kasbah (fortress)." He pointed in back of me. I thanked him for his help and he left me in front of the ramp, which I followed to get to the cafeteria.

As soon as I entered, I joined the line of students and teachers waiting to be served. I did not recognize anyone waiting in line. After being served lamb stew in a large bowl, I sat down by myself and ate slowly, trying to ignore the biting hunger, causing my insides to ache. More students and faculty arrived, ate and left the cafeteria; I followed a group out the door and down the ramp.

It was Friday night, and I was free to do what I pleased. I walked on the hard, packed earth that served as a sidewalk next to the road. I strolled down large stretches of similarly crafted sidewalks bordering long buildings with archways and palm trees, similar to those at the mosque. I arrived at a high wall which looked like it might be a part of the Kasbah or a castle that had, at one time, protected the city. At the top there were openings for arrows or other objects of defense used against an enemy below. I was at the entrance, a massive, arched door.

I continued my walk. After several miles of trudging along the dusty streets, I arrived at the downtown area and recognized, a block away, the building where my studio apartment was located. I passed through a narrow street lined by cafes typical to the area, with family dwellings above; the sounds of talking, babies crying and plates and silverware being put away reached me through the windows.

I found the door to the façade of the apartment complex and turned the key. Climbing the stairs, I became dizzy and seized the banister with both hands, preventing myself from falling. I pulled myself up and made it to the third floor.

Now I had to hurry for my intestines were aching and I needed to reach a toilet quickly. Turning the key in the lock, I threw off my sandals and dashed to the toilet.

In spite of the convulsions which mercilessly attacked my body in waves, followed by shivering and nausea, I was able to remain seated. After the convulsions subsided following an hour of excruciating intestinal pain, I was finally able to find the strength to stand up and, before flushing, I looked into the toilet bowl and noticed that the dark liquid was streaked with blood. Weak and exhausted from a bout of diarrhea, the moment I lay down my bones on top of my sleeping bag, my soul took me away, away, away, deep into the desert light. . .

Chapter XXXVII

Fly, Fly

I imagined that I could, in the name of simple survival, channel my frustrations and sublimate my urge to criticize into something the community would deem constructive, such as teaching the *Qur'an* in English. But the day would inevitably arrive when I could no longer put up with accepting everything, and I would probably shout to the world my frustration, in spite of the consequences. Then I would be hounded and maybe accused again of sabotage and perhaps railroaded out of town. . .or worse. Maybe I would run as far as I could out into the surrounding plains, beyond the point of no return, and just dry up under the hot sun, beating down mercilessly upon me. My skeletal remains would be coated with bird droppings as my face smiled at the sun twenty-four hours a day, my bones gradually becoming part of the sand. . .meaningless dust. Or I would lie on the cold sand one night, my body convulsively twitching after being sliced open by a saber-wielding Moslem, who would then gallop away on a huge Arabian horse, a shadowy phantom wailing like a banshee as he prayed to Allah and was absorbed into the black, desert night.

I was walking barefoot in the desert, nothing but long stretches of sand dunes and fields of sand spread out before me. As I walked along the ridge of a sand dune, I heard a low growl coming from below. I looked down, without breaking stride, and saw a huge lion following me with his eyes, his head stretched upwards. I turned and ran along the ridge, stopping when I reached the edge of the dune. As I turned to backtrack, the low growl warned me that the lion was waiting. I ran until I reached the opposite edge of the dune and looked down; the lion opened his mouth and let out a roar. I fell backwards and began rolling sideways down the dune, towards the lion with jaws open, waiting...waiting.

I awoke, gasping, perspiration drenching my body. My clothes were soaked and my stomach hurt. I went to the bathroom, poured water into a basin and splashed it on my face, drying it with the towel hanging behind the toilet.

I returned to the living room where my sleeping bag was laid out on the Persian rugs. I lay down on top and went into a semi-consciousness state as I meditated and prayed, prayed for the strength to return to my limp limbs and body, so that I would be prepared for my work and for living in this town.

I rose, sat in the easy chair and ate a few nuts and raisins I had carried in my backpack from Paris. I decided to look for a café that would serve fresh mint tea and once again left the building.

Descending the stairs to the street below, I noted there was a multitude of cafes on both sides of the street. I decided I wanted to find one near the bus stop, recalling the ride in the principal's car and several cafes close to where he had picked me up.

I asked for directions and the people smiled; their friendliness was comforting as I walked to the bus stop. In just a few minutes, I was sitting in a dingy café, looking through windows streaked with dust. The view was partially blocked by the leaves, like fingers, of a small palm tree. Drinking a strong glass of mint tea and feasting on a large sugar cookie, time seemed to stop as I sat looking out at the blue skies, without a worry—the weekend was before me.

I sat, my body numb, and thought. The peace I had been feeling soon gave way to anxiety: I wondered what would become of me if I were to hang around this town where everything I did would be carefully scrutinized by everyone. I wondered how I could blend into the timelessness of this world, sacrificing myself to the dry heat and the hot winds rolling over the plains, evaporating the very blood flowing through my veins.

I could maybe live here, conforming to the rhythm of the town: work, mosque, work, mosque, home, family, mosque, and my work for awhile. But I knew myself—sooner or later, I would not hesitate to voice my disagreement with religious customs, like those requiring women to wear veils and pray in small, obscure places in the mosque, away from the men. There was also the obligation to wear a djellabah while teaching or praying at the mosque. I could, however, envision myself praising the wisdom of Mohammad and, in the same breath, the teachings of Gandhi and Hinduism, Buddhism, Judaism and Christianity. I felt an unbridled urge to expound upon inter-religious principles but the need to muffle it in order to survive in my new world.

I decided that this would be my first and last glass of hot mint tea in this turbulent dust bowl of southern Morocco. I paid the waiter and asked him how much it cost for a ticket to Casablanca; he said 100 dirhams. I pulled out all the money I had in my pockets and counted exactly 175 dirhams. How I was to survive afterwards in Casablanca and how I was to afford a train to Paris later never entered my mind—I had to get out of this town immediately. My old paranoia had returned, reminding me of the dangers of Moroccan towns that at first appeared harmless.

The waiter stood next to me patiently; there was only one other occupied table in the café. I asked him where I could purchase tickets.

"You're talking to the ticket cashier, now," he grinned. I managed a weak smile and remembered when I had arrived in town, the bus driver had come into the café and placed a package behind the bar. I pulled out 100 dirhams and gave them to him.

"When is the next bus to Casablanca?" I asked.

He responded that the next one would leave at 10 p.m. and arrive in Casablanca the next day at 7:00 in the morning. I asked him the time and he said it was 8:15. Then he gave me a small red coupon without any markings on it; I scooped it into my nervous hand and left the café immediately. I inhaled fully, breathing in a mixture of sand and dust, joyfully filling my lungs for the first time with the heavy air of the town. The chains fell from me and I was free—untouchable—as I made my way to Saïd's home.

With the help of a student who I met on the way to my studio, I found the home of the principal, surrounded by the omnipresent palm trees and a beautiful garden, green and full of flowers—an oasis in the dry, dusty streets of the town. I walked up the stairs and knocked on the door, which was answered by one of the daughters; her black hair fell to her shoulders, her eyes shone, evidence of the family's love enveloping her. I heard someone calling my name in back of me, turned around and saw Saïd at the foot of the stairs.

He beckoned me to follow him and after a minute we arrived at the table where we had eaten our breakfast yesterday morning. He smiled and since we had had no time to discuss it earlier, he asked me how the first day went. I finessed or tailored my answer to highlight the positive, commenting that the students had been enthusiastic.

He said, "Well I'm not surprised: they have been waiting for an instructor for one month in the same classroom, at the same time, since the other one had to return to the U.S. Another teacher, who is not an English instructor, would show up and give them books to read. As soon as they would ask questions, he would leave since he could not speak the language. Thank God you are here."

I regretfully said, "That makes it even more difficult to explain to you that I may leave Taroudant."

His wide, toothy, almost Mediterranean smile drooped at the corners, becoming a confused frown.

"You are not happy here—why? You just got here! Give it some time."

For the next hour, he tried to convince me of the attributes of living in the town, that I would soon be signing a year's contract, meet a beautiful woman and marry her, like the Frenchman with one finger missing, also a teacher at the school. In the meantime, he would let me use the studio free of charge and see about paying me a small stipend. Then, he said he had an engagement so I prepared to leave.

"Don't make your decision yet—give it a month," he urged, trying to woo me at the last minute; I did not tell him I had already bought my ticket.

We shook hands. As we walked together towards the front gate, I stopped. Turning to him, I stated, "I will give it more thought, but if you don't see me Monday morning, that will mean I have returned to Casablanca."

His smile drooped down to his white djellabah; without saying a word, he turned away and climbed up the stairs to the house.

My legs felt lighter and without the familiar fatigue pains I had experienced the day before. I seemed to fly to the studio to pick up my backpack and sleeping bag, proceeding to the bus stop.

Fear again overwhelmed me as I briskly walked toward my destination. I wondered if I would be stopped by the henchmen of the principal. I was sure all those passing me frowned and were staring at me, thinking of my treasonable actions, my abandonment of the students, who would once again be without an English teacher.

The small café was open upon my arrival but no bus was parked in the usual place across the street. As I entered, the clock on the wall showed it was 10:05. My body felt empty, my head heavy, as I contemplated the possibility of staying even one more night in the town.

I asked the waiter who was serving coffee to a couple if the 10:00 bus had arrived; he shook his head and my heart soared through my rib cage—perhaps I would not have to spend another night in Taroudant after all!

A short while later, the bus finally arrived. After dropping my sleeping bag and backpack next to the bus, I boarded swiftly, thankful no one had tried to stop or dissuade me. I walked down the unlighted aisle noticing the shadows of turbans falling over the faces of those peacefully sleeping. I found a seat next to the lone woman, her face carefully veiled by a white cloth draped over her protruding breasts covered by a dark-blue robe. Minutes later, we were on our way; I prayed that the bus, charging through Taraudant, would not stop until it reached Casablanca...and that I would continue on to Paris.

I slept the entire way back, even during the rest stops; nothing, not the smoke from the grills cooking shish kabob, could disturb me. I was curled up on the hard seats, with my face buried in a rolled-up sweater I used as a pillow. Yet, although I was totally exhausted and physically asleep, I subliminally flew alongside the bus, experiencing every turn and every sputter of its prehistoric engine.

As the bus entered the dark, somber outskirts of Casablanca, I readied myself for the leap to temporary safety. The bus came to a halt at the usual stop, a screaming maelstrom of transients, children crying and spewing exhaust, joined with the smoke from the many shish kabob grills encircling the bus stop.

Chapter XXXVIII

Fleeing Africa

No one would be expecting me to arrive this Sunday morning; the brothers and the master would certainly be content in thinking I was tucked away in a small village, dutifully paying allegiance to Allah at the local mosque, without any big-city distractions. They were, no doubt, assured I would become an even more devoted Moslem, making pilgrimages to Mecca and visits to the Casablanca mission. Perhaps they thought I would also set out with study groups on voyages to villages in Morocco to help reconvert Moroccans, assuming they had been Moslems at one time but had fallen away from the faith. Someday, according to the plan I supposed they had for me, I would become an influential soldier and participate in Jihad.

I jumped from the bus as soon as the door opened. My body shuddered from a renewed onslaught of paranoiac fears as I traversed the city, heading for the Ancienne Medina. There, I planned to recuperate with my adopted family before escaping across the Mediterranean Sea. As I walked through the familiar streets with the many souks, I wondered if it really was an escape from something or from myself—from my temptations, from my almost complete conversion to Islam—an escape from the fear of "giving in" or "giving up."

As my sandals rhythmically beat the paved sidewalks, I made a decision to return to Europe—I wanted out!!! In time, my sandals began to sink into earthen sidewalks; relieved, I knew I was leaving the paved downtown area and entering the outskirts of the Medina. While I walked, I reached into my pocket and pulled out the remaining dirhams. I had just enough money to take the train to Spain, and then I would have to hitchhike to Paris. I planned the voyage as I made my way to the shelter of my friends, where I needed to find comfort, food and lodging so I could calmly plan my next move.

After what seemed like several hours, but was actually closer to one, I reached the familiar corridor of the Medina, with its decrepit shanties and stinking streets. But the smell was heavenly compared to the dank odors of the country mosques in which I had been imprisoned.

I knocked on the warped but sturdy wooden door. Later on, all I would remember were the excited voices of my adopted brothers and sisters and the mother's smile—I lost consciousness on the kitchen floor.

I must have slept the entire day because when I awoke, complete darkness engulfed the living room. Azedine's familiar snoring sounded from the adjacent sofa. It must have been about four or five o'clock in the morning; the muezzins began serenading the people from the minarets of several surrounding mosques, exhorting them to come to Morning Prayer.

I felt a glow of peace and security but I reminded myself that I must rest and plan my strategy for leaving Africa. The calm was soon replaced by fear, remembering I needed to be careful to avoid the brothers and the master of the mission. Tomorrow was Monday, and the principal would find out I had left Taroudant. He would inform my sponsors at the Majgid Nord.

I was not sure how the master would interpret my leaving the job; he had helped me get hired. I trembled as my fears turned into vivid images: the brothers were holding me down while the master whipped me; then he took out a long knife and slit my throat. . .my life bled out before me, like that of a sacrificial lamb on Eid al-kabir.

My muffled yell was heard by no one: "I want to go home! Just let me go home!"

The faces of the brothers crystallized, one by one, in my mind. They would be under orders from the master to pursue me, now that I would certainly be labeled an infidel, an enemy of the mission. They knew the address of the family or could get it from Camara, their friend and faithful soldier. I feared that the brothers could, under the supposed auspices of Islam, do anything, as commanded by the master; he could convince them that their duty was to persecute those that abandoned Islam, especially those under his tutelage. They would really despise me, especially since they had sponsored my appointment as a high school teacher, which I had abandoned after one day on the job. I felt relieved, then, about leaving Taroudant, but I wondered if I would feel guilty later, especially considering all the efforts made by those at the mission—by the master—to enlighten me, and find me a good job.

I burrowed deeper within the covers, imagining the brothers visiting me, staking out the apartment, or even trying to follow me. I was now certainly an enemy of Islam, a saboteur, someone to be punished. I shuddered as I imagined that the brothers would try to organize a propaganda movement designed to denounce me. Maybe they would try to turn the inhabitants of the Medina against me, who would lynch me, mercilessly cut my throat and throw me into the ocean.

I bolted upright, thinking I should take the next train to Spain...at once! My thoughts were tempered as I envisioned my weakened, emaciated self trying to hitchhike through Spain and France, on my way to Paris. If accosted, I had no energy to defend myself; I would be making myself vulnerable to anyone of malicious intent in the streets. What if I was attacked by a street gang? I would be defenseless—I could hardly even run. I also concluded that I had not recuperated my strength enough to travel, so I decided to stay with the family until my health was restored.

The soft pitter-patter of bare feet sounded in the hallway, on the other side of the curtains. "Please, not now," I thought to myself. Maybe they were coming to get me!

My body twitched uncontrollably as the light flicked on. I glared into the smiling face of the father.

"Ca va?" (How's it going?), he asked.

"Ca va!" I responded with a relieved smile.

He nodded and turned the light off.

I finally fell asleep after temporarily—at least so I could sleep—convincing myself the master had no intention of carrying out his threat.

249

Later on that day, we all gathered in the kitchen for lunch. Everyone was curious as to why I had quit a prestigious teaching job. I told bits of the story to Azedine, who translated what I said into Arabic for the eager, concerned family members. The father and mother immediately understood why I was sent to the country and were both relieved I had decided to return. He told me I could stay at his home and eat and sleep for as long as I desired.

The next day, the father brought a lamb to the house that was put in a large, open closet behind a wooden board. I thought he brought it home as a pet for the kids. They pointed to it, saying "howli." During meals, they would give it pieces of vegetables, which it gobbled up. Sometimes I would sit in front of the opening of the closet and feel the cool nose ever so gently nudge my back. I would turn around to find two big, playful brown eyes gazing at me. I would reach over to the bale of hay in the corner and take out a few strands to feed the mischievous creature.

Even after just one day, for lack of exercise, the lamb gained weight. The morning of the fourth day, while drinking my coffee with the rest of the family, the father made an announcement: "It's Eid al-Kabir today, the day that every head of a Muslim family must sacrifice a lamb or goat to symbolize Allah's request of Abraham to sacrifice his son, Ishmael, and the decision or compromise to accept the offering of an animal in his place."

He looked around the table at the sad eyes of the children; they had grown accustomed to the animal and had treated it as one of the family. I was shocked that this innocent being, almost a member of the family, would be mercilessly sacrificed.

After the table was folded and placed in another room and the floor was carefully cleaned, the board was removed from the opening of the closet and the lamb was led to the middle of the room. The father sharpened a long knife. Azedine helped him gently place the lamb on its back, and the father quickly slit the throat of the lamb. Its legs thrashed while the blood flowed like a geyser from the wound, pooling on the floor below; the father and Azedine bled the creature until its legs stopped flailing—the sacrifice was complete.

The mother, father and daughters prepared the meat, first skinning the lamb, then carefully carving it into steaks and small morsels for the couscous. I marveled that none of the animal was wasted; even the eyes and brain were preserved for some future purpose. Azedine, who was sitting next to me, explained that half of the meat would be consumed by the family and the other half would be given to the poor.

That evening, there was plenty of meat for everyone as we feasted on couscous, with a mixture of vegetables and our dear friend, "howli."

Chapter XXXIX

Something is Pulling Me Back

Even though it would have been safer to stay inside, I eventually needed to immerse myself in the open air, since I had not left the apartment for several days. As I walked down the familiar dirt street, surrounded by vendors shouting at me, trying to coax me to their stand, I decided to visit the seashore. To avoid running into the brothers who could be attending mass at one of several mosques in the Medina, I walked around the central part of the Ancienne Medina, until I arrived at the beach; the waves seemed to be undulating and reveling in celebration of my newfound freedom. No sooner had I sat down on the soft sand than I began to relax; I looked out over the blue Atlantic, my eyes following the seagulls flying low over the surface, as I transcended into blissful meditation. I meditated on the beach for hours, allowing the rhythmic breaking of the waves to rock me into a sphere of peaceful thought; I traversed the Mediterranean in my mind, on my way back to Paris.

That evening, after the family and I had partaken once again of the lamb couscous feast, I decided to confide in the father and Azedine in the living room. At first, I did not want to share my plans with anyone—I wanted to take the train and then the ferry to Spain and hitchhike to Paris; I would write a letter to the family afterwards. But I trusted them; I told them I wanted to return to Paris. The father uttered "In charla" meaning "Allah permitting." Without hesitating, he reiterated his invitation to stay with his family as long as I needed, while I prepared for my journey to Paris.

I decided against hitchhiking to Paris after arriving in Spain—I could not imagine surviving the vicissitudes of the precarious route, my physical stamina having been reduced to being able to walk a few paces and then having to sit for awhile. Not having enough money, I wrote a letter to my parents, asking them to help me pay for my voyage back to Paris.

For the next two weeks, I wandered around Casablanca. My only contact with the family was during the evening meal. I spent the rest of the time meditating and mentally preparing myself for the readjustment to the western life style awaiting me in Paris. Each day, before I left the house for my usual place on the sand dune overlooking the ocean or my seat on the wooden bench in the wooded park, I dressed in my stripped djellabah, pulling the hood over my head in order to camouflage my face. I walked the streets facing the ground, hoping that I would not be recognized by the brothers.

When I arrived in the evenings, the mother would tell me that a young man had come to visit me but would not leave his name. She told him I had returned to Europe, to throw his scent off my trail, but strangely, he kept coming back every day, day after day. For some reason, the master knew I had not yet left Morocco.

One day, I was walking around a small plaza when I noticed a bus stopped on the street. I was curious so I asked the bus driver his destination; he told me he was taking the passengers to Rabat. He smiled and said it only cost twenty dirhams, round trip. Without thinking, I paid him the money and took my seat at the back of the bus.

The trip to Rabat took about an hour. The bus was inching its way through a souk when I noticed, about six seats ahead of me, a hooded man giving me a sidelong stare. When I glanced in his direction, he looked away. The bus stopped in the middle of the souk to let us off. I descended the stairs and asked the driver when he would return to pick us up. He said a bus stopped there every hour. I thanked him and walked a few paces towards a rug vendor, whose eyes lit up as I approached his stand.

A bizarre feeling came over me, that someone was watching every move. I casually turned to the right and saw the same hooded man I had seen on the bus behind me, turning to look at flowers in another stand. I faced the vendor, who had already begun his sales pitch, a series of words issuing a rapid-fire delivery of Arabic I could not understand. I moved around to the other side of the stand, pretending I was interested in a particular rug, nodding as the unintelligible drivel continued to flow from his mouth. The hooded man had gone. I walked toward the flower stand, with the rug vendor tugging on the sleeve of my djellabah, trying to turn my attention back to rugs. I looked to the left and to the right, down a row of stands selling anything from radios to fresh dates—he was not there.

I turned and followed the souk down the street until I came to a busy boulevard; cars and mule-drawn wagons were competing with each other in the slow traffic, encumbered by a long light a few rows of cars ahead.

I followed a line of young men and girls as they walked down a path toward a series of huge cement buildings, which reminded me of the University of Paris. The inscription on a wall in front of me was in Arabic so I asked one of the long-haired boys what it meant. He said, in almost perfect French, that I was standing in front of the University of Rabat. His radiant, white smile contrasted with his shiny, brown skin. The corners of his mouth curled up, his demeanor showing enthusiasm. The energy and eagerness of youth, I thought to myself; I wished I could get that back.

He asked, "Where are you from? You speak French with an accent."

"I'm from Paris and I am temporarily residing in Casablanca. Are you a student here?"

"Yes, I'm studying philosophy. This is the Faculty of Letters and Sciences."

I told him I had been studying philosophy at the Sorbonne in Paris when I decided to travel through Morocco.

He said, "Wow! I would like to talk more with you. I can't now; I have a class and I am busy all day. Look, my name is Muhammad Barakat. I'd like to invite you for dinner with my friends. Could you meet me in front of the school at about 5:30 p.m. and I will take you there on my motorcycle?"

"Okay," I said, not thinking about the bus back to Casablanca. "I'll be there."

He smiled, turned and started running in the direction of the big buildings where he soon was lost in the mélange of students. I visited the university, notably the registrar's office. I thought if I changed my mind and stayed in Morocco, maybe I would try to register as a student, in order to change my tourist visa to a student visa.

In the registrar's office, I explained to an attractive, dark-skinned woman wearing a partial veil that I wanted to register at the school; I asked her if the courses were in Arabic or

252

French. She explained that I could take most of the classes in French, but I would be obliged to take some in Arabic. She gave me registration documents, which I put in my book bag, before leaving the building. I walked towards a building that looked like a bar and cafeteria and noticed a man sitting at the counter, wearing the same type of gray hood as the man on the bus. As I approached, he lay down some change and left.

I walked out of the bar, closing the door behind me. When I got outside, I only glimpsed the side of his djellabah as he swept through a narrow passageway between two buildings; I followed him.

"I love it—the pursued becoming the pursuer!" I mumbled under my breath upon reaching the corridor and walking inside; but it was dark and I could not see a thing except shadowy forms at the end of it. Just as I turned around to leave I heard a noise like footsteps sliding on pavement moving towards me; frantically pulling my Djellabah over my knees I ran quickly to the entrance, slamming several times into the sides of the two buildings. Lurching out and falling onto the sidewalk. I rolled over, regained my feet and took off, running up the hill, away from the university. I kept running for what seemed like a long time, before stopping. I was high up, on a hill in a residential area, overlooking Rabat.

I found a small park and sat down to rest. The houses were all modern, made from stone, and had huge picture windows facing out, overlooking Rabat. These homes were a far cry from the modest apartments in the Ancienne Medina. I looked at my watch; it was 12:30. I thought it would be a long, boring wait until I was supposed to meet the student and his friends, and hoped I had gotten rid of the hooded man following me.

Deciding five hours was too long to wait, I descended from my perch overlooking Rabat to the street below. It wound around for awhile until coming to a group of cafes bordering another souk; there were rows and rows of nuts, dates, vegetables and fruits. Sitting down at a table away from the window, I ordered a café au lait. I could have waited there in obscurity for five hours, but I was nervous; after finishing the coffee, I paid the waiter and left. I followed the narrow streets in back of the café, winding around small, white, stone houses with extraordinary-looking parapets, painted blue. I was alone on the narrow streets—it seemed as if I was walking through a ghost town. I was alone. . .or so I thought.

As I climbed rows of uneven stone steps, I followed an old lady carrying freshly-baked bread on her head. After walking straight up for several minutes, I stopped for a breather and looked down at the souk in front the café I had just visited. Standing on the other side of the souk, with his elbow bracing himself against a fruit stand, was the hooded man—and this time, he did not turn his head away. I could not believe he had found me and followed me as I climbed upwards. In a rage, I descended the steps, running—sometimes tripping—over my djellabah. This time, I was going to pull the hood off and accost my stalker. I reached the souk; my eyes scanned all the fruit stands in front of me, but the hooded phantom was nowhere to be seen.

I was frustrated, hot and started trembling. "Will they ever leave me alone?" I cried, desperately looking through the crowd of shoppers perusing the goods. No one seemed to notice; they went on examining the goods and talking to the vendors, as if I did not exist. . .as if I were dead, a walking ghost. I returned to the same café, resigned to nursing a glass of mint tea until it was time to join my newly-made friend.

At 5:00, after several hours of vegetating or relaxing on the barstool, I got up to leave. At this point, I knew I would be followed so it did not matter what I did or how fast I went; "the hood" would be there.

The waiter gave me instructions to the University and I left, the door clanging shut—I was outside, as was the stalker. He was somewhere, behind a fruit stand or perhaps a wall. The street leading to the university was crowded with people, which was preferable to being alone, as I had been after climbing the windy, stone steps to the homes with the blue parapets. I arrived a few minutes later and found a group of young men with books and papers under their arms surrounding my friend.

Muhammad Barakat recognized me as I approached, in my striped djellabah; he beckoned me to join them. After introducing me to everyone, the group dispersed. I was to ride on the back of his motorcycle, parked next to us, and the others would follow on theirs.

We arrived a few minutes later at a modern dormitory for students. It was an uninteresting, rectangular building of about five stories painted in the drabbest possible light pink; Muhammad lived on the ground floor. That night, we had a mixture of couscous, garbanzo beans and vegetables; there was no meat but it was delicious. After dinner, we went into the living room; Muhammad played Arabic dance music as we talked and sat around a circular table.

We discussed various philosophers, in particular Plato, Aristotle and Nietzsche. Because we had all studied philosophy, we shared ideas about specific books, like Plato's *Republic* and *Beyond Good and Evil*, by Nietzsche. We discussed the symbolism behind the myth of the cavern of Plato and different ideas pertaining to other classics and Nietzsche—who was, as well as Plato—an eternal iconoclast and rebellious philosopher.

Then Muhammad stuffed hashish in a huge water pipe and he and his friends took turns puffing and coughing—they passed it to me. I declined as I didn't smoke the stuff. That made me nervous: I was always worried about being caught with people who were drug users and being judged an accomplice even if I had nothing to do with the activity. They were friendly and did not pressure me to smoke with them.

At one point, Muhammad, a red glow on his cheeks, turned to me and said, "You remind me of the orthodox Moslems who refuse to drink and smoke hashish. That's okay—tell us about yourself."

I told them about my travels with an orthodox Islamic group. They suddenly grew very attentive, assessing every word. Feeling comfortable to express myself freely for the first time in a long time, I discussed the pressure put on me by the master to conform to the *Qur'an*.

No one interrupted me so I interpreted that as giving me the green light to express myself as I pleased...I was wrong.

I continued, "I believe rigid interpretation of the *Qur'an* is wrong; in any case, I don't know if it was inspired by God."

Mohammed immediately interrupted me. "Be careful...the holy *Qur'an*, of course, is the word of...Allah, and you need to study it closer to understand it." The others nodded.

I thought to myself that even this group of young philosophers, when it came to discussing Islam and the *Qur'an*, were not open to any criticism of them or even an interpretation different from that of the orthodox Muslims with whom I had lived for a couple of months.

All I could think about was returning to where I could talk about anything, where I could critique anything and impose my own interpretation of sacred texts—where there would be open minds. I learned that even among young, liberal Moroccans, Islam was a delicate subject.

For the rest of the evening, I avoided any discussion of religion. As the night wore on and the young boys began yawning. I told Muhammad, who was sitting across the table, that I needed to return to the bus stop and wait for the bus that would take me back to Casablanca.

Muhammad flashed his kindly smile and said, "Since I am a Moslem, you can stay here as long as you desire; my home is your home."

The others, one by one, left on their motorcycles or scooters, after bidding me goodbye. Their vehicles sputtered down the road until they could no longer be heard.

The next day, I awoke to an empty house. I stumbled through the living room where the water pipe lay, the stench of hashish filling my nostrils as I walked by. Muhammad had probably left early for class, and not wanting to disturb me, let me sleep.

On the kitchen table was a note stating the following: "Muhammad Abdelaziz, help yourself to whatever there is in the fridge. Turn out the lights before leaving. Hope I'll see you tonight." It was signed, Muhammad B.

Such hospitality was so characteristic of these beautiful Moroccan people. But I could only think of one thing, and that was getting out of the house, returning to Casablanca and then traveling on to Paris, where I would be free to do and say what I pleased. I was beginning to feel anxious at the stifling power that certain interpretations of Islam wielded in this country.

I was also afraid of being in the house if the police raided it and found illegal drugs; I would probably be thrown in jail for a long period of time. Besides, I had no way of contacting the family as they had no phone. They were probably already worried sick that something had happened to me. I pulled my djellabah over me and walked to the front door; opening it, I viewed rows of student dormitories in front, to the right and to the left, across from a yard.

I closed the door behind me, walked over the dry lawn of the dormitory building and across the busy street. A group of students appeared to be waiting for a bus on the other side of the crossroad. I joined them and asked a young girl where I could catch a bus that would take me to Casablanca. She told me to take the same one she was, which would go directly downtown.

I sat next to her after we boarded. She stood up at the next stop and smiling, descended the steps. The bus took us directly to the station where a bus bound for Casablanca was waiting. I showed my round trip ticket to the driver and climbed up the stairs to claim my seat at the back of the bus.

This time, I studied the face of every person that boarded. The hooded stalker was not among the passengers and before any others could enter, the driver closed the door as the bus lurched forward. While we were shuttled back to Casablanca, I wondered about my sanity: maybe I had imagined the hooded stalker; perhaps he only existed in my intensely anxious mind, along with feelings of guilt for having abandoned the mission, the master and the brothers.

It had been almost three months since I left Paris for Morocco. It had been exactly three years since I left the country where I was born and raised. "I must go home, I must go home—it's been too long!" I kept repeating over and over again.

Upon my return to Casablanca, I went straight to Azedine's house. It was about 2:00 in the afternoon and the mother would possibly be alone in the house. I knocked and as she opened the door, she let out a strange weeping scream, pulling me inside. She held my hand, asking me what had happened in broken French, telling me everyone had been worried I had been taken away by the brothers at the mission or that "bad people harm you."

She said, "My husband be relieved; oh, he'll be relieved. Oh, my God, oh, my God!. Please sit down and drink some tea. Are you hungry?" She motioned me to sit down with her gentle hands. All this attention was so nice; I guess I really had a home there, after all. I apologized for having left, but I had had no way of calling them.

"Don't worry about—the thing is you here. I serve you tea now."

When Azedine and the father returned, they were full of emotion upon seeing me sitting in my usual place at the table. They came into the living room and, for the first time, hugged me at the same time or simultaneously. When we separated, their red eyes proved that they had really worried.

Although he was glad to see me, Azedine was also very angry, his red eyes flashed wrath more than any other emotion. "Muhammad, you worried my entire family, especially my mom and dad. They were sure you had been harmed by the members of the mosque-you were being punished and we would never see you again. I regretted that I ever brought you into this family. Anyway, we have fulfilled our obligation of hospitality." By those words he seemed to imply that I should be leaving soon.

The father, however, expressed himself differently. "Muhammad, you are safe and that's all that matters. You should stay in the apartment until you take your train; it is too dangerous otherwise. I know these people and they can do wicked things—they can harm you."

The father's words helped me restore confidence in my sanity and belief I was not making up an imaginary stalker, that I had really been followed. The reality of my vulnerability here in this foreign country, without my strength and without money to leave, began to sink in and as it did; my heart sank to the bottom of a quagmire of loneliness and despair, often my only companions. The agony of such moments subsided when I reflected upon the connection I had made with the true cosmic spirit, in that dark, dank mosque in the middle of the arid plains of Morocco. And, feelings of abandonment, emptiness and melancholic sentiments slid into abeyance as I reconnected with the family. I felt the warmth of belonging after dinner that evening, as I recounted my little trip to Rabat, to satisfy the curiosity of the family. I told them that the night before, after having dinner and engaging in spirited conversation, it had been late and I was invited to stay there by my new friend, Muhammad Barakat. I could not contact them because there was no phone in the house. They seemed to understand and did not hold it against me. The children lined up to shake my hand before going to bed.

Chapter XXXX

Paranoia or Danger

Every day seemed like a lifetime as I waited for the money to arrive. I needed it since after my trip to Rabat, I did not even have enough to cross the Mediterranean into Spain; if the money did not come, I would be stuck in Morocco.

I tried staying in the apartment, never leaving. But after three days, I was growing extremely restless; I needed to get out, even if just for an hour or two. I decided I would leave the house during the most unlikely time for a visit—at high noon—since the brothers would be occupied with the noon prayer session, followed by lunch with the master.

The next afternoon, I carried out my plan. As I opened the door, the mother held onto the sleeve of my djellabah, warning me not to leave. I told her not to worry; I would be gone only during the prayer session and lunchtime, after which I would return. Although she was not convinced, she let go of my sleeve. I waved goodbye but she did not respond.

I made my way to the familiar park where I sat on one of the benches overlooking the wooded area teeming with magnificent, expansive trees, greening lusciously. I eased into waves of dreams and meditations on yesteryear as birds were singing overhead. Sometimes the leaves would crackle on the pavement next to me. My body would stiffen and my mind would send messages of warning; I envisioned a sharp blade cleanly slitting my throat as I sat there with my life spewing out of me, my silent screams fading, my body slowly becoming limp, lifeless...I would jerk my head in the direction of the noise only to catch a glimpse of dry leaves drifting to the ground, unhinged by the wind.

Finally, the money arrived. The mother handed me a letter one afternoon, after the postman had delivered it, while declaring something unintelligible in Arabic. Seeing the check inside, I rushed to a local bank where I cashed it.

Azedine went with me to the train station to buy my train ticket from Casablanca and book passage on the ferry from Casablanca to Algeciras; then, I would take the train from Algeciras to Paris. He agreed I should leave as soon as possible, at a time that would be the safest. We decided I should take the train at 6:00 a.m. the next day, since the brothers would be occupied with the morning prayer session.

That afternoon I announced to my host family I would be leaving the following morning. I offered to pay the father to cover some of my expenses over the last few days. He looked at me and frowned, as if I had just insulted him. I hugged him and thanked him—I loved him dearly.

I then conspired with the youngest son, six-year-old Abdel, to help me pick out the best and the biggest cake we could find. I figured the father could not refuse a gift in the form of that night's dessert. The youngster excitedly led me down a narrow street lined with the usual merchants yelling to all passersby, trying for the last time that evening to entice them into buying something...anything. I followed the young, curly-headed boy, who ran ahead until he was almost out of sight, beyond the rows of stalls. He would stop and peer at me with those innocently mischievous, cake-starved eyes. It was evident that he could not wait to bite into one of those sweet, soft Berber or Arab cakes, covered with a creamy, white sugar icing.

After Abdel and I left the cake with the mother, I told him that I had to take care of some business. I had decided to change my appearance as much as possible in order to avoid being detected at the train stations by the brothers, assuming any of them were there. I walked briskly to the barbershop where I had the barber shave off my beard which I had maintained, following the mission rules, once I began living there. My beard had been long and full, covering my neck. Without it, my boyish face emerged once again, a face the master and the brothers had only seen when I entered the mission.

That night was party time; after dinner we sat around the mother in the familiar circle in the living room, while she poured the steaming hot tea into rainbow-colored glasses and served us pieces of cake. Abdel told me he regretted that I was leaving because I was now part of their family. I was touched by his sincerity and reached out to embrace his tiny, curly head.

We all hugged each other before going to bed. They all thanked me for the cake I had bought for them. The children lined up for the last goodnight kiss, their little mouths decorated with crumbs and flakes of icing.

That night I could not sleep, as I did not want to miss the departure of the train. Also, I was worried that the brothers would try to stop me from leaving Casablanca since I knew many of their secrets. The master had intimated that he had been cultivating me to eventually descend on the United States as a converted Moslem, in order to spread the word of Islam and convert other Americans to the true faith. Several scenarios invaded my mind: perhaps the master would find some way to get me thrown in prison where the brothers would exercise their influence; finding some way to infiltrate the prison, they would continue the indoctrination of my restless, captive soul; or, since they now considered me their enemy, perhaps they would feel justified in executing me. My mind inundated me with death scenes, over and over again, until sweat poured down from my hairline onto my undershirt.

I was finally about to doze off a little when the familiar voices rained down upon the Ancienne Medina, calling the people to Morning Prayer. It was probably about 5:00 in the morning so I got up and headed for the bathroom. I positioned myself over the hole in the ground and urinated, cleaning myself with water from a large, gray pail next to the hole. This would probably be the last time I would go through this ritual instead of using toilet paper. Then, I thoroughly washed myself.

As I shuffled back to my place on the couch, Azedine stirred, rustling some papers, and mumbled, "Are you ready to go?" in a sleepy, listless voice.

"Just about," I replied mechanically, looking over to my friend whose eyes were looking into mine. I added, sincerely trying to free him from feeling obliged to take me to the station, "I could go alone; I don't think there will be a problem".

He responded without hesitating, as if what he said had been rehearsed, "I must go. You can never underestimate them—they seem to be everywhere. I need to protect you."

His answer was not reassuring. A faint tremble slid down my spinal cord and settled in my stomach. I remembered Hanify's threat against those that abandoned the path of truth that abandoned Islam and wondered if I should ever see my beloved Europe and my homeland again.

All I had to do was to put my books and papers into my backpack which had already been packed the night before. My fingers were not responding as it seemed to take ages to fold the striped robe and place it in the side pocket. I would wear the jeans and blue shirt I had worn on my voyage to Morocco. I looked in the mirror; without my beard and djellabah, I would appear to be a young European student returning to Europe from a vacation in Morocco. My "disguise" was complete—my appearance had totally changed. I even wore tennis shoes instead of the sandals. I avoided focusing on my red, tired eyes, glimpsing them quickly before turning away from the mirror.

Azedine was up and fumbling for his clothes. In a few minutes we were ready.

He had either volunteered or was chosen by his father to ensure my safe passage to the train station. As we waded through the morning street sewage, the calm and gentle breeze made me flinch; I wondered if this was the calm before a storm, or if the storm had passed. Every shadow in every doorway, in every alley entrance along the way, represented danger, mystical deviance, savage revenge by a dark, hooded demon, acting "in the name of God." We walked abreast down the deserted alleys of the Ancienne Medina, the Old City—not a word was spoken.

After about thirty minutes, the gloomy, grayish shape of the train station appeared ahead. I stopped and adjusted the backpack resting on my shoulders. Azedine reached out and touched my chest with the palm of his hands to detain me while he looked all around—we continued.

The station was almost vacant. A few hooded Moroccans in full, dark-brown djellabahs were loitering in the terminal, leaning up against the dismal cement walls encircling a large platform with several empty benches and a closet-sized food stand. An overhead massive, rusty clock reminded us the train would arrive in twenty minutes. Each minute was like an hour; I desperately wanted to terminate my adventure into the spiritual unknown that had taken me from the streets of Casablanca to the dry plains of central and southern Morocco. More and more people appeared, converging from the unlit corners of the train station.

My dream of unifying all people and their myriad ideologies into one faith had been temporarily shattered; but I was not disappointed as I had found the true spirit, the cosmic force in the arid plains of this mysterious country. It seemed that I had come such a long way to find this unifying spirit of love already existing within and outside of me. It was clear that the framework in which this search had taken place, in particular while residing in the mosque and traveling with the brothers, living according to the Hadith and the Qur'an, had enhanced my spiritual awakening. Of this I was absolutely certain, in spite of my differences with some of the teachings of the spiritual leaders living within the walls of the Masjid Nord.

Even with these calming thoughts, my fear of retribution by the brothers I had loved so dearly was predominant.

Azedine and I leaned against a wall adjacent to the railroad tracks. A rumbling noise echoed in the distance. It grew louder, closer. Then the screeching of metal on metal invaded the silence as the ugly, but welcome, charcoal-colored engine broke through the shadows. The rapid approach of the train finally ebbed to a stop next to the platform where I was standing.

Before boarding, I excitedly bade farewell to my friend: "Au revoir, bonne chance Azedine, et merci pour m'avoir conduit jusqu'à la gare" (Good bye, good luck, Azedine, and thank you for accompanying me to the train station). We hugged, and the overwhelmed Azedine, without saying anything, turned and walked away, his receding body gradually dissolving into the unwashed cobblestones of the Medina. Everything was happening too fast for me to lament our parting—that would come later.

Chapter XXXXI

Never to Leave

I dragged my backpack and sleeping bag up the stairs and opened the door leading to the separate cabins. None were completely empty so I joined two Moroccans, who were chatting rapidly as I entered the cabin. I greeted them with the typical "Bonjour" which was echoed, in kind. One had a light complexion and sandy hair, the other had dark hair and eyes. They briefly stopped their conversation, watching me as I placed my backpack and sleeping bag on the rack overhead and took my seat.

I stared straight ahead impatiently, waiting for the departure of the train, the first step in my detachment from the umbilical cord to the mission. The two continued their conversation, gesticulating wildly. I tried to relax and rest, taking my trip one step at a time, but I kept visualizing the second step of the voyage: entering the ferry that would take me back through the gates of Europe, away from the Medina and the plains and deserts of Morocco—away from the torture, captivity, fanaticism, customs agents. . .away, far away. . .

I sat there, restless, my old, familiar nemesis ravaging my tranquility. . .paranoia. I needed to confide in someone; I needed to talk to someone, but I couldn't trust anyone. So, as the train finally began to rumble forward, I kept silent, falling into an unsettled sleep somewhere between Casablanca and Tangier.

Then screeeeeeeechh—the train halted. I awoke with a neurotic jerk of the head; the two Moroccans were leaning over me, laughing.

"Que se passe-t-il?" (What's going on?), I blurted out, my eyes half closed, providing, no doubt, my cabin buddies with more entertainment.

One of them responded, "Rien; le train s'arrête pendant un petit instant. Alors, vous êtes français? (Nothing; the train is stopping for an instant. So, you are French?)

I told them I was an American and they both smiled. They told me they were going to Europe to find work. The sandy-haired Moroccan, with a scar that ran down his entire left cheek, had a job waiting for him in Germany, where he resided. His name was Kibran; he wore a red shirt, a contrast with his black slacks. Kibran told me he had been visiting his wife and eight kids in Morocco. He explained he had been forced to leave his country in order to find work to feed his family. His sad eyes drooped a little as he told me he could only visit his family for one month annually. Next year, when he returned to Africa, he expected a ninth child to greet him, along with his wife and other children.

The other Moroccan looked more indigenous; his dark, chocolate hair hung over black eyes. He was wearing a gray and brown djellabah, which gave his dusky skin an even darker hue. He introduced himself as Aymeric. He had friends in Paris where he had worked before. His red, glistening eyes sometimes seemed to reflect a madness I had seen in the eyes of some Moroccans who had taken to drink or drugs. But he also had the look of a fighter, someone who was not submissive, but took initiative.

Now it was my turn to talk about myself. In spite of my urge to speak of my adventures in Morocco, I only told them I was a philosophy student in Paris—I hesitated to tell them more. My fear prevented me from confiding in strangers, even though I felt sure they would not have harmed me.

I was relieved of my predicament by the conductor calling out that we were approaching Tangier and everyone was to show his papers to the agents.

"The hell is starting," I mumbled to myself, concerned that a technicality or problem with my passport, the photo, or the visa would prevent me from passing onto the ferry, to freedom.

Our immigration papers and passports were meticulously checked by a nervous, mustachioed police agent; we all passed inspection. I exhaled and readied myself for the descent from the train into Tangier, the gateway to the Straits of Gibraltar.

Before the train halted, we were joined by another Moroccan who had been resting in another cabin. His name was Salim and he was on his way to Spain for a vacation. He had started talking about his plans to roam the beaches when the train screeched again, slamming us into our seats. Before I could collect my thoughts, we were climbing down the narrow steps, lugging our belongings to the platform below which we would follow to the ferryboat.

The four of us stuck together as we shuffled along the platform following the signs to the ferry, amidst massive confusion. I had experienced this same kind of chaos on my trip to Morocco, but then I had been stronger, not drained as I was now. I almost preferred closing my eyes as I followed the others, my weak, spindly legs sluggishly carrying me along in an effort to keep up the pace.

I contemplated leaving the group so I could get my thoughts in focus; besides, my bizarre state of mind would not let me trust anyone. But I thought that if I were hassled by a few of the brothers, who could be following me, or if any policemen sent by them bothered me, maybe my new friends would help. At least, they could serve as witnesses to anything that might happen—and I was expecting anything. It was not possible to think calmly; since my trip to Rabat, I was convinced I was being followed by the master's henchman who would harm me if the occasion presented itself. This was only conjecture, but conjecture was making me crazy with doubt and suspicion—the violent emotions of insecurity I was experiencing I never would have dreamed could exist within me.

We kept following the signs announcing Algeciras, Spain, our ferry's destination. The conductor had warned us, when he was not screaming, that we could not take any Moroccan money outside of Morocco, so we sold all our dirhams at the exchange office en route to the ferry, for French, Spanish and German money. After a labyrinth of turns, signs and more turns, a huge, white hull rose above the fog, in the distance. I hurried to catch up with Kibran who was fearlessly leading the group, and asked him if the hull was that of the ferry which would take us to Spain.

"Obviously," he replied. His smile gave me great confidence in him.

Even from afar, I could see a long line of people waiting to board the ship. I could barely make out that about halfway up the ramp leading to the huge vessel, was a desk where the border guards were probably stationed to check everyone's passport and immigration documents.

"This is it," I whispered to myself. "I must relax, take a deep breath, take one step at a time. If the border guards refuse to let me pass, I will jump in the water and swim ashore—and hide in Tangier until I find a different way to cross the Mediterranean. If the Moroccan officials let me board the vessel, I will be free, at last."

I was encumbering my mind with fear and doubts, yet I did not really know why they would refuse passage, unless the master had filed a complaint and the police had my name on a list, more specifically, on an emigration roster.

The boarding line was excruciatingly long. One by one, the passengers were checked; once in awhile, someone would be set aside from the line and another official would be placed in charge of interrogating the person. I wondered on what grounds the government could stop people from exiting the country after a "vacation" in Morocco.

We inched our way to the top of the ramp. In the meantime, the skies had clouded over and rain looked imminent. Even the climate contributed to an ominous haze around me, and would perhaps make the guards look negatively on my passage home. My raw nerves shook my entire body as I contemplated that the Moroccan government could detain me for having abandoned my post as English instructor in Taraudant.

Finally, our turn came: Aymeric was first, Kibran second, I was next and Salim was last. The officials, including the Moroccan police, customs and other agents—the judges who would decide whether I could escape to freedom or not—sat directly in front of me, dressed in their formidable brown and gray uniforms. It seemed as though they took hours to check us over. First, they asked for our passports and studied every page; then, they scrutinized our tickets and visas. Lastly, they dissected our luggage, opening all the boxes, suitcases and backpacks, strewing their contents over the entrance to the mighty ship—nothing went through without a thorough check.

My heart thumped once or twice, extra strong, as Hannah and Kibran were waved through; they had escaped closer inspection. Then it was my turn. A short, pudgy official with a mustache reached out his hand for my papers; I handed them over. My passport and immigration papers were also ready. The customs agent scoured the pages of my passport, and all the other agents also had an opportunity to peruse my papers, even if only for a few seconds; all the while, they were looking for discrepancies or suspicious expressions on my face.

The agent first returned my passport, then the jumbled mess of personal papers, visas, etc. He looked directly in my eyes for the last litmus test and then.....waved me on. I climbed the ramp to freedom, almost collapsing with excitement. Looking back down the ramp towards the desk with the customs officers, I noticed Salim was frantically rifling through his backpack. The customs officer began impatiently tapping his fingers on the desk.

I turned and kept walking, entering the passenger section of the boat. I decided to break from the group as I lugged my backpack down the white hallway, which opened out into the passenger seating area on the deck. I set my backpack on a small table wedged in a corner. Hunger wrenched my insides but I refused to eat a cheese sandwich packed by the mother until the boat began to move toward Europe, toward freedom...away from the hungry jaws and the vicious claws of the mission...away from the master. I was safe, for the moment, at least. Hunger consumed me so, without waiting for the boat to move, I sat down next to my backpack and ate the sandwich, with relish.

No longer blinded by hunger, I looked around the room; sitting around small, round tables was a mixture of Arab, Spanish and French tourists. Only a couple of Moroccans wore their long robes, intent on showing their devotion to their culture. I sighed with relief that I could wear what I wanted to, say what I pleased, even criticize certain interpretations of Islam, if I so desired. However, my sanity still battled with the rasping pain of fear as I looked for the hooded demon.

Contrary to when I traveled across the Mediterranean towards Morocco, I did not leave the cabin area, even to watch the approach of the European continent—my fears had led me to believe a brother would be waiting at the rail to throw my emaciated body overboard.

The ferry took about three hours to cross the tiny stretch of water separating Africa from Europe, separating the continent from the savage, desert winds. While sitting in the corner, my mind drifted into the sea of hope; its cleansing winds swept the cabin area, flushing out my dry, dust-filled glands. That serene moment was abruptly interrupted by the voice of the captain over the loudspeaker, announcing in French, Arabic and Spanish that we were only one kilometer off the coast of Spain.

As I contemplated a mad dash to the trains, and felt myself leaning toward the reality that a group is stronger than an individual, I decided to seek out my friends before the boat docked. I grabbed my possessions and opened the cabin door to the wind gusting across the deck. I found them on the other side of the boat. Kibran was leaning on the rail, talking to a French couple standing next to him, when he looked on his other side and saw me standing there. His dark eyes flashing a mixture of concern and indignation, he informed me that Salim had been refused access to the boat because his papers were not in order. The last thing he had seen was Salim being led away, his wrists handcuffed behind him. Kibran did not know what had happened to him. My legs trembled as we passed moored fishing boats, a sign we were approaching the Iberian Peninsula.

After the boat docked, we followed the crowd down the narrow steps of a stairway to a huge dock below. Half-way down the ramp a table was set up with two uniformed Spanish officials behind it, quickly checking immigration papers. I flashed my American passport and was waived on without breaking stride. The others were also quickly waived through.

Once we had arrived at the foot of the ramp, we did not have much time to fathom all the confusion, with the forklifts scurrying about, weaving through and around people, as they loaded and unloaded cargo. We boarded a bus parked right in front of us, ready to take us to the train station. Once inside, we huddled close together. Backpacks and suitcases served as seats for some; people clung to each other as the bus rumbled toward the train station. It veered to the left and to the right before coming to a full stop. As we disembarked, a Spanish official checked our papers and train tickets; everything was in order. I breathed a sigh of relief.

As Aymeric and I were watching the approach of another dusty old train, we were joined on the quay by Kibran. I walked ahead of the two—this time, I decided I really wanted to be alone. But the two followed me as I found a cabin midway down the aisle of the train and slid into a seat. They each sat on either side of me. As the train swiftly transported us to the next stop, my eyes began to close; I drifted back to the plains of Morocco...to the smiles, the yellow, tea-stained teeth, the sun, the brilliant reds and greens of the souks, the large, succulent dates, the wind-chapped faces and the mysterious voices announcing mass at 5:00 in the morning—these images were burned deep into my heart.

Kibran was shaking me—my vision was blurry and I barely made out his dark shadow in front of me. "What's happened? Is the train under attack?" I shouted as I abruptly rose, hitting Kibran squarely in the forehead with mine.

"It's alright, just relax," he said calmly. "Get up. We're in Madrid!"

This was the required change of trains before arriving at the French border. I staggered up after our collision; Kibran helped me with my backpack as the train glided into the station.

In a few minutes, we again poured into a gigantic train station swarming with flies and sweat-bathed faces and bodies in the suffocating, humid breezes. Loudspeakers blared in Spanish. I walked in a daze as Kibran led me by the hand to the subway that would take us to another train station.

After several turns and the clanking shut of the Madrid subway door, we rode the few minutes it took to arrived at the next train station. Half asleep, everything was a blur as Kibran continued to lead me by the hand all the way into another train.

Finally registering awareness of my surroundings, I found myself looking out the window to the Spanish countryside, on our way to the French border. The train forged ahead and the landscape became greener, the trees higher and denser. With each passing minute of our approach to France, I felt safer, as if I was about to enter my homeland. But my eyes kept a constant vigil over the backpack, the passengers walking up and down the corridors outside the cabin and my two friends, who were fast asleep, their mouths gaping.

My body cringed; I burrowed down into the seat as I prepared for another onslaught of fear...paranoiac fear—fear of my neighbors, of the conductor, even the wind caressing my hot face. I turned my head away from the aisle and buried it into the torn seat.

Soon I could no longer close my eyes to the green and ever greener fields, to the rolling hills entreating my spirit to emerge from its protective shell and join the free world, as we grew nearer to the French border. As the train chugged closer, a French officer asked to see our passports. After flashing mine, I stared out the window in anticipation; Paris was for my eyes only—Paris, the jealous lady, only awaited me. But first, La France!!

I hoped we would pass through the border towns on our way to northern France, without changing trains. Helas, but no! The train slowed to a crawl entering a tiny border town. I could not identify its nationality but I smelled the familiar French croissants as the train halted in front of a bakery. We had to leave the train and, once again, wait in line to get our papers checked before re-boarding and continuing on to Paris. This would be the last check stop, followed by a train change.

As my turn came, I handed my passport to the French official who carefully regarded it; I whispered to myself, "Let me in, please; I am tired and dispirited and I need the free walls of Paris!"

He asked me if I were a student in Paris—I nodded my head. The visa attached to the passport was for last year; I needed to renew it upon my arrival. He hesitated a moment as he regarded the photograph on my identification card. Maybe the customs officer would refuse my visa as being outdated; maybe the picture did not resemble my gaunt face as I had lost many kilos in the deserts of Morocco. He looked up, searching my eyes, returned my papers and waved me on—I was elated!

This time, I found a cabin all to myself, on the super-clean Paris Express Train. I threw my backpack on the floor, slumped into the cushioned seat and waited impatiently for the train to depart.

"Why doesn't the train depart? Now, what's the hold up?" I voiced out loud. I did not care anymore—I wanted to go home. My adoptive home was Paris; I wanted to be hurled from the border of France to the frontier of a free Paris, where I could hop from café to café, do cartwheels, yell at the top of my lungs, even criticize the President of the Republic, if I wanted. Fortunately, I was still in the cabin, alone.

Instead of feeling the usual grinding of the train as it moved foreword, the train remained wretchedly moored to the tracks as a group of officials boarded. Maybe they thought I looked suspicious. I envisioned the brothers from the mission walking toward the cabin, thrusting the door open and entering, pelting me with accusing words and handcuffing me. I stared out the window, hoping to conceal my face from the passengers or officials peering into the cabin—they must not see the terror in my bloodshot eyes. I sat trembling; my body actually shook with anxiety.

"Please train, move it—now!" I screamed inside my mind.

The screaming turned into wailing, and then shrieks as the train plunged forward. I stood up to release pent up emotions, like a safety valve on a combustive machine. Grasping at the window above, I opened it. Standing on the seat, I thrust my head out the window and gasped for air, more and more air as my lungs expanded, released, expanded and released, while the train flew toward Paris. . .closer, closer. . .

All of a sudden, the door of the cabin flew open and Kibran stuck his head in, smiling that toothy grin which reminded me of the grill of an old Ford Sedan I owned in California. This time, he was a welcome sight. Aymeric followed, lugging his bags. They both flopped down on the seats and shut the door.

Back together as one happy family, Aymeric muttered something and we all laughed. he had bought a bottle of wine; Kibran reached in his backpack and pulled out a plastic bag full of couscous, green peppers, olives and bread. He dumped everything on a paper sack spread out over the table that separated us. He handed out plastic cups and poured us each some wine. Aymeric pointed to the mountainous mess on the table and announced, in his finest Moroccan accent, "Kul."

We toasted Paris, our hopes, our dreams and our loves. Each of us tore off a morsel of bread and dipped it into the couscous, just as I had done so many times with my "family" and the brothers at the mission. But that was far away from me now as the train sped through each French town, with their distinctive stone fences and vibrantly colored flowers. I felt closer to freedom and deliciously farther away from danger as the train proceeded to the threshold of my dreams. It did not slow down until we reached the outskirts of Paris where I reveled in an intensely-felt emotion of warmth and relief, stronger than perhaps I had ever experienced. Yet the torment of fear that had haunted me still burned within, clawing its way to my weary, hungry soul—I imagined an attack of a "hit man" from the depths of Morocco. As the familiar white houses surrounded by cozy green gardens rolled by, my body heaved with ecstatic waves of joy; I was passing through the Parisian suburbs.

* * *

On seeing and feeling Paris, its streets reaching out to comfort me like a welcoming parent or old friend, it was as if I had been far away, for such a long, long time. Distance was actually meaningless as I felt I had truly been in another world. But my thoughts were uneasy: I would no longer dream a man's untroubled dream or sleep a man's untroubled sleep. I had come face to face with something for which I had prepared for years, yet was totally unprepared for the outcome—I had become a marked man. Yet I felt the hope that some day my fear, the ubiquitous evil, would change. . .would eventually be transformed by true faith, love, understanding and acceptance of my experiences and those who had played a role in them. During meditative walks, as buildings passed in a blur, warm vibrations would eventually fill my heart, casting fear back to the dark recesses of somber memories.

I walked around Paris feeling as if I was newly born—all things I had valued before had no meaning to me. It felt as if I had been roaming the arid plains of Morocco for decades. While there, something had arisen from deep within, something I had never imagined possible. Indescribably simple, unfathomably deep, it had—and has—the power to send fear to the gallows of antiquated thinking, grinding away the final impediments to total release into the ever-expanding freedom of love. It encompasses hope and truth, going beyond lies and the perversion of love.

Reflecting on a lifetime of spiritual yearning, I wondered at my willingness to give up all in order to experience a deeper connection with Supreme Consciousness. In an isolated mosque in the heart of the arid Moroccan plains, I received a powerful dose of Universal energy which suffused every part of my being, vibrating with the unfathomable love I knew to be at my core.

My constant companion has now become an energy force propelling love, like a laser, directly into my heart. This light force encompasses the universe I can no longer ignore. In the past, I have suffered upon seeing a homeless person or thinking of senseless killings, ignorance, poverty, starvation and death. Even as I live in the inner city, I refuse to be indifferent in order to protect a fragile sensibility. Now surging through me are not just charitable sympathies but bright, God-inspired solutions.

I have since questioned myself and have been questioned by others as to whether I have simply fallen prey to the classic Messiah complex experienced by others at some point in their lives. Such doubts have given way to understanding that the truth was already imbedded within my heart, that I have simply become a conduit for the love and peace that is the truth of my being...the truth of us all.

My heart has opened to absorbing the violence and ignorance of our time, transforming them into knowledge and love of inconceivable or infinite magnitude. Ever present in my mind and heart, along with what has been expressed, is the word "FORGIVENESS." The need for forgiveness gave and still gives me the strength to make an accounting of all my relationships—with humans and other beings—and to take measures to repair any injury. From this accounting comes the wisdom and motivation to relieve my burdened soul of the profound ignorance begetting fearfulness, hateful prejudice, selfishness and lack of faith.

Though I loved my father dearly, I needed to forgive him for over-zealously disciplining me during my youth. I knew I needed to release the hatred and tension I had

267

carried within me for years and replace it with understanding of the pressures my father had been under at the time. In so doing, the final barriers between my father and I dissipated long before he passed on, clearing the way for the warm, unconditional love I have for him to this day. Strangely, opening up to love with my father helped me to release the problems I was experiencing in other relationships, in a kind of domino effect.

The thorough assessment of my life led me to seek forgiveness from those I had transgressed and to face my ignorance, failures, weaknesses, prejudices and lack of faith. I was thus able to transcend many obstacles on the path of Cosmic Truth, no doubt helping to purify my being and prepare me to share this greater strength in spirituality with others, before my final days...before total, ecstatic union with the Supreme Being.

No, this was not a messiah or Jesus complex, nor did this become a typical spiritual "thing" or "trip" to be unceremoniously dropped upon launching into the next "thing" or "trip." In fact, the truth of this experience has manifested in different ways, notably in subsequent intense meditations during which this unfathomable love force has helped people to heal themselves.

One such experience happened when I was visiting a friend and his family in California. As I was talking with the couple over dinner, they announced to me that I would not be able to visit with their daughter that night because she had been bedridden for one month with a high fever, sometimes reaching 105 degrees. The doctors did not know the cause. I mentioned to the mother that meditative spiritual healing could help and she was open to my suggestion.

That night as I sat on my bed in the guest bedroom, peering through the screen to the darkening shadows in the distance, it seemed as though the stars were aligned with us as my body vibrated with love in connection with the parents, who were praying upstairs next to their daughter's bedroom. I was strangely sure that something had happened that night. The love in that house was so intense that seemingly with little effort, aligned with Supreme Love, we had eased the deadly fever with spiritual "medication."

Nothing was said the next day and as I was riding on a Greyhound bus to visit my mother in Oregon, I continued meditating and praying while visualizing the daughter. During the visit with my mother, I continued meditating for several days, but something told me the daughter was better as I visualized her smiling face. I called the family and the phone was answered by a bright young voice I did not recognize—it was the daughter. I then spoke to her mother who informed me that early in the morning following the night we had engaged in meditative healing, the fever had broken and was a distant memory. The love force had truly flowed through us, from the Divine Source emanating from within and around us.

Over the years, I have lived with Jews, Muslims, Christians, Hindus, Buddhists, atheists, agnostics and others, sharing their happiness, sadness and passion for truth. I have been privileged to finally reach the Holy Land, my original goal before setting out for Morocco so long ago. In Israel and Palestine, I have learned and shared my knowledge by assisting in the organization of interfaith events with Jewish and Muslim friends in Hakuk, a Kibbutz in northern Israel, located near the Sea of Galilee. I hope someday this will help inspire a lasting peace, an ongoing festival of unconditional love. Our hearts have always known the truth of peace and true compassion and will ultimately join together in living the path of love.

I was also blessed to have participated as a speaker during those interfaith dialogues. The participants delegated me to later share the results with some Palestinians who had been invited to attend, but were unable to because they were not allowed to enter Israel. I was to travel there alone because Israeli Jews and Muslims feared they would encounter problems there as both groups held Israeli passports: the Israeli Muslims believed they would be treated like traitors and the Israeli Jews believed they would not be able to return to Israel alive.

I traveled alone to Jerusalem by bus where I took a taxi to Palestine. Within thirty minutes, I entered Ramallah, the capital of Palestine. Because I carried an American passport, I was supposedly in less danger than others. Some of the participants in the dialogues had warned me not to go to Ramallah as Americans are considered Israeli allies and I could be accused of espionage. After intense meditation and prayer, I knew that I would be safe and that I must go in person to share with Palestinian friends the profound unity experienced during that day in Hakuk. In fact, being so clear that I was on a divine mission to Ramallah to spread the word, I knew in my heart that I had no reason to fear, that I would not be in danger as my time had not yet come—somehow I was sure of that.

I thus walked the streets of Ramallah alone, talking to people during the day when my Palestinian friends were working, and then meeting them for dinner at night to share what I had learned. The magical Moroccan glow permeated my being. Never did I feel danger there and, on the contrary, I was welcomed by many peace-loving Palestinians curious as to who the lone foreigner was walking the streets. They did not shun me and were willing to talk to me about the common denominators uniting Islam, Judaism and Christianity. The love force was in me and I did not fear.

I have been intensely energized by several subsequent trips to the Holy Land. I learned that our hearts and minds must never be complacent regarding the suffering of others and that we have more strength than we realize to channel our compassion into action. Such is the cosmic "will" within us. Such is our calling, as the profoundly and fundamentally good people that we are.

My faith in the true meaning and practice of love and respect for the truth have been profoundly bolstered. I discovered that the winds sweeping across the hot, barren plains of Morocco held inner secrets that were revealed to this lonely traveler, bringing him the sweet promise of a new age of peace and happiness. I experienced a confirmation of the importance of remaining loyal to principles supporting the truth of our being, our oneness with the Supreme Being, instead of selling out to the temptations of material gain and meaningless goals that compromise one's soul.

Something happened to me in the arid plains of Morocco. In a sense, I was crucified, died to the person I had been and was reborn; perhaps I left the old part of me there, buried in the desert sands. Did I receive the gift of healing meditation for all time? Will the unity I felt with everything and everyone endure? What I experienced in Morocco was the turning point in a life which has become steeped in meaning and purpose—the deep feeling of Universal Oneness I felt there has grown within me, anchoring me firmly in the knowledge of oneness with my Creator and all life.

Sometimes, when I am so calm the depth of my soul touches my heart, I can still feel the cool evening wind that gently rippled the grass in the crusty soil of the barren plains; it softly beckons to me. Something calls to me, beyond the ripples of the creek before me, pulling me to another dimension, where I immerse myself in ancient wisdom teachings. It waits for me, calls to me; it is out there, yet buried deep within my heart. I am drawn back to the plains shadowed by the Atlas Mountains. Yet I wonder if I ever left.

Frank Romano

Frank Romano earned a PhD at University of Paris I, Panthéon Sorbonne, and a JD at Golden Gate University, Faculty of Law, San Francisco. He is a Maître de conferences (assistant tenured professor) at the University of Paris X in the Anglo-American Literature and Civilization Department and a member of the California and Marseille Bars. At present, he teaches and practices law in France and in the United States. The author actively organizes and participates in interfaith events involving Jews, Moslems and Christians in Israel and Palestine. He is also an active member of a multi-faith group in Paris dedicated to peace in the Middle East. Mr. Romano has authored a book entitled *Globalization of Antitrust Policies* (Mondialisation des politiques de concurrence), published by L'Harmattan in French and has published many articles in Europe and in the United States where he is often invited to speak at conferences. He can be reached at: frankfro@aol.com.

www.worldaudience.org

Printed in the United States
121514LV00003B/3-60/A